FOLLOW THE STORY

*How to Write
Successful
Nonfiction*

JAMES B. STEWART

A TOUCHSTONE BOOK
PUBLISHED BY SIMON & SCHUSTER

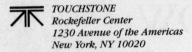
TOUCHSTONE
Rockefeller Center
1230 Avenue of the Americas
New York, NY 10020

10 9 8 7 6 5 4 3 2 1

Library of Congress Cataloging-in-Publication Data
is available.
ISBN 0-684-85067-2

To my students

CONTENTS

INTRODUCTION

I CAME TO WRITING rather late in life. As a child, I loved nothing more than to read. In this I was encouraged by my parents, at least up to a point. My sister and I were taken to the musty, turreted old public library. We rode our bikes or walked to the traveling bookmobile, returning with arms, or bike baskets, full of books. I devoured the small libraries lodged in our elementary school rooms, reading some books—*The Pink Motel, Thunderbolt House,* and *Stories of the Great Operas* stick in my mind— three or four times. To circumvent the lights-out bedtime policy enforced by my parents, I kept a magnetized flashlight affixed to my bed frame so I could continue reading. But in a book titled, as far as I can recall, *Blitz the Wonder Horse,* Blitz's mother was killed, and I burst into tears long after the lights should have been extinguished. My mother rushed to see what was wrong, catching me sobbing over open book and flashlight.

I am often asked, usually by hopeful parents, whether I liked to write as a child. The answer is no. I wrote and delivered a short-lived neighborhood newspaper, but I was more interested in the miniature printing press than in the written content. Nobody ever suggested to me that writing might be enjoyable. I associated writing with the endless sentence diagrams used to drill into our minds the rules of English grammar, and with tortured efforts to write iambic pentameter or haiku. Nobody in my age group was encouraged to "express" themselves as young-sters, let alone view writing as some kind of self-therapy. I be-came interested in journalism in college, where I worked on and eventually edited my college newspaper. But there we thought of ourselves as first and foremost investigative reporters, not writ-ers. Writers were part of a bohemian crowd that hung out in the offices of the literary magazine.

Even now, I'm not convinced that many professional writers "like" to write in the sense that they find writing to be fun—something that, in and of itself, yields pleasure. It may be ab-sorbing, satisfying, even exhilarating, but it is hard work. Joan Didion wrote a memorable essay in *The White Album* describing the pain and descent into near madness that seemed inevitably to accompany her own writing. I have known many colleagues, some of them terrific writers, who seemed all but paralyzed by anxiety before beginning a story. The proverbial writer's block afflicted many of my former colleagues at *The Wall Street Journal* at one time or another. I myself tend to think of writing as much like taking an exam—the experience is deeply absorbing, my concentration is intensely focused, time seems suspended yet suddenly hours have elapsed. At the end of a day of writing, I feel drained. The point is that I don't believe anyone has to innately love the process of writing to be a good writer, and to find it an immensely satisfying pursuit.

For there is enormous pleasure to be derived from writing. In my own work, I find a moment comes when I realize that I have gathered a critical mass of information—enough to ensure that I have the raw material for a good story. At that juncture a great deal of anxiety lifts, and I begin to savor the prospect of organizing the material into written form. For I believe the great-est cause of writer's block, not to mention stage fright, is the fear that one has nothing to say—not that one doesn't know how to say it. Inspiration often comes at odd times—while I'm show-ering, or jogging, or riding the subway. It is a pleasant and stimu-lating experience. And once a first draft is on paper, or in the computer, and the physical task of processing so many words is done, I find there is enormous pleasure in experimenting, in moving things around, in rewriting for particular effect, in fine-tuning one's work. As this book should make clear, much of a writer's work takes place entirely within the mind, not while he or she is sitting at a keyboard. In that sense, writing is an activity that informs nearly every aspect of life. It is a way of thinking, a way of looking at the world, and a way of processing information that not only contributes to stories, articles, and books but also enhances one's appreciation of life.

Very few people are, in my experience, natural writers. Taking the young Mozart as my model, in my youth I assumed genius was something bestowed by God, and so I dabbled in everything from art to music to athletics, hoping that sooner or later genius would manifest itself. Naturally, I was disappointed. Some people may be more gifted than others, but excellence in writing, as in any art form or craft, involves discipline and practice. I have known writers who, early in their careers, demonstrated almost no natural talent. Yet with enough enthusiasm and determination, and years of effort, they have developed into good, even successful, writers. They have usually done so, I should add, with remarkably little guidance.

As for me, I have had the benefit of some fantastic editors: Alice Mayhew at Simon & Schuster, Norman Pearlstine at *The Wall Street Journal,* Tina Brown and John Bennett at *The New Yorker,* Jane Amsterdam at *American Lawyer* and later at *The New Yorker,* Steven Brill at *American Lawyer,* Jane Berentson at *American Lawyer* and *The Wall Street Journal,* and Steve Swartz at *The Wall Street Journal* and *SmartMoney* magazine. Most of what I have learned about writing I have absorbed from them and synthesized into the approach that I use in my own work. As I will make clear at greater length, every writer, no matter how accomplished, needs and can benefit from a good editor. I was lucky to have good editors, and I sought them out. For I wanted to learn how to write better, yet had found that traditional approaches to teaching writing hadn't worked for me.

This book had its genesis during my tenure as Page One editor of *The Wall Street Journal.* The *Journal's* front page is an institution in American journalism, and it was the main reason I applied for a job as a reporter at the paper in 1982. When I had started working at *American Lawyer* several years earlier, then-editor Steven Brill pointed to the *Journal's* front-page stories as models, and he paid for subscriptions to the *Journal* so we had copies on our desks every morning. Under the *Journal's* legendary editor Barney Kilgore, three columns of the paper's front page were devoted to lengthy feature stories, which explored subjects in depth, with style, and often, especially in the middle-column stories, with wit. The front page allowed *Journal* reporters to expand the range of both their reporting and their writing to an astounding degree; that, in turn, enhanced the quality of their news stories. And *Journal* readers encountered subjects that went far beyond what might otherwise be expected from a business newspaper.

When I applied for a job at the *Journal*, I mailed in my résumé and several feature articles I'd written for *American Lawyer.* I knew no one at the *Journal*; I had no contacts; no one had recommended me. In due course I received a call from the editor in charge of hiring, inviting me for an interview. The interview went well, but I heard nothing until I was finally hired, nine months later, by the new managing editor, Norm Pearlstine. From the beginning, I loved writing front-page stories. I could hardly believe my good fortune when Pearlstine moved me directly from staff reporter to Page One editor in 1988.

I inherited a staff of editors who worked exclusively on feature stories for the front page. They were famous for their ability to improve stories; indeed, they were perhaps too talented for some reporters, who relied on them to all but write their stories rather than learn how to write themselves. Certainly the most worrisome revelation I experienced when I moved from reporting to editing was how uneven was much of the material turned in for publication. On the other hand, aspiring writers might very well be encouraged to know that even some very successful, experienced journalists are not very good writers. The conventional wisdom is that it is information gathering that distinguishes the best journalists, and that writing can always be left to editors. But such an attitude, in my view, does a disservice to both editors and writers. As I hope this book makes clear, the approach to writing a story informs the reporting process, just as the reporting helps dictate the form of a story.

As I and my staff worked to improve what was turned in to us, I came to realize that we were spending far too much time performing triage on poorly written copy, rather than elevating good stories to the highest possible level. Although story ideas were submitted to us for approval, we rarely had further contact with a writer until a story was turned in. We were getting involved too late in the process.

My solution was to develop a series of lectures on writing that I could deliver to the *Journal*'s reporting staff both in New York and at the paper's many bureaus, which I tried to visit at least once a year. I have no doubt that my effort met with mixed reactions, but at least some reporters responded with enthusiasm. More important, this undertaking forced me to think through the writing process with a discipline I'd never before brought to the task. Not only did I begin to perceive a noticeable improvement in the work of some reporters, but I found that my own writing benefited as I tried to hold myself to the same standards I was asking others to meet.

Much as I loved *The Wall Street Journal* and editing the front page, I left the paper at the end of 1992 to concentrate on my own writing, both books and feature articles. The next year I began teaching a feature-writing course at the Columbia Journalism School, where I was able to refine and expand upon the material I had developed for my lectures as front-page editor. As the course evolved over the years, I have often thought I would like to set down my thoughts in an organized written form; this book is the result.

In it I have tried to distill what I have learned from others and from nearly twenty years of my own experience as a reporter and writer. I don't mean to suggest that I have all the answers, or that I have mastered the art of writing, or that I consider myself a great writer. I am often awed by the work of others and wonder how they accomplish it. I don't purport to be an expert on literature or creative writing. But I have given the subject of nonfiction writing considerable thought; I have used what I have learned in my own work; I have tested my approach in the classroom and in the newsroom; and—maybe most important—I am sufficiently foolhardy to put it in writing.

I have organized this book as I do my class, which is to follow a story from its inception to publication, beginning with the thought patterns that spawn ideas and continuing through the making of proposals, the reporting, the writing, and the editing. While I refer to the work of others, the primary examples come from my own work. In many cases I have reviewed the original source materials for stories, notes and other references, earlier drafts, and editorial comments, in order to recreate the thinking and editing that went into my published stories. Whenever possible I use this material to show, in concrete terms, how stories are conceived and executed. Only at the end of the book will you find the finished works, and I hope you will read them with fresh insights and appreciation of the often time-consuming and laborious efforts of many besides myself.

Over years of working with reporters and students, I have come to recognize that I alone cannot turn someone into a writer. I cannot supply the curiosity, the enthusiasm, and the determination necessary to succeed as a writer. But if those elements are present, I believe I can guarantee a measure of success. I can at least alleviate the stress and dispel much of the mystery. And perhaps I can impart some of the joy that makes writing stories one of life's most satisfying endeavors.

1
CURIOSITY

We seem to be living in an age of know-it-alls: talk show hosts and guests, expert witnesses, pundits, gurus on every conceivable subject. The information age is exhausting. It is also dull, like a dinner party guest who never stops talking. In my view, this climate is anathema to good writing, which is rooted not in knowledge, but in curiosity.

This may seem paradoxical, since one of the primary goals of nonfiction writing is to inform. But I strongly believe that good writing begins in the mind, long before pen touches paper, or fingers a keyboard. Writers must learn to think like writers. I find this is a point I need to stress over and over again with my students. For thinking like a writer turns out to be a very radical change from what most of us have been taught and conditioned to do over our entire lifetimes. At first it feels very uncomfortable. In some ways it reminds me of learning to speak a foreign language. Conversation in the language requires intense concentration. It's such a relief to lapse back into English, which flows effortlessly in the mind and over the tongue. But as the grammar and vocabulary of the new language become familiar, conversation becomes easier. If one is immersed in a foreign culture for long enough, speaking its language becomes almost second nature. For most people, thinking like a writer is not nearly so difficult as learning a foreign language, but it requires effort, concentration, and discipline. It's a relief to revert to our usual patterns of thought. Over time, thinking like a writer becomes almost unconscious. In a few cases I've seen it all but transform someone's personality. For a desirable side effect of thinking like a writer is that it makes you more interesting to others. It enhances one's appreciation of life.

The essence of thinking like a writer is the recognition that what's most interesting is what's unknown, not what is known. Thinking like a writer prizes the question more than the answer. It celebrates paradox, mystery, and uncertainty, recognizing that all of them contain the seeds of a potential story.

At first encounter, it is probably hard to recognize how radical a notion this is. But consider: in ways large and small, subtle and unsubtle, overt and hidden, we are rewarded from childhood on for providing answers to questions posed by others. We are taught to process information by memorizing and retaining it, not by questioning it. Confronted daily by a mass of new information, we rarely stop to consider what is missing.

So many people seem to spend their lives in the inevitably futile quest for certainty. Often this takes the form of religion, which for many provides solace in the face of the unknown and the unknowable. But what may be entirely appropriate in the spiritual realm too often spills over into every other aspect of life. Patients expect certainty from their doctors; clients demand clear-cut answers from their lawyers; and voters want solutions from their politicians, however intractable the problems and far-fetched the proposed remedies. While managers may pay lip service to the notion that they welcome criticism and questions from their employees, the reality seems to be that they prize flattery and a parroting back of their own ideas. The more powerful they are, the more insulated they seem by yes-people. Questioners, by and large, are viewed as dissidents, heretics, and malcontents. It seems that the more we are confronted by change, the more we cling to the status quo.

No wonder the unanswered question prompts such a visceral reaction. Some people seem to panic, others suffer anxiety attacks, and most people feel uncomfortable. To varying degrees, all of us react this way. But instead of repressing or fleeing from such feelings, writers need to embrace them and explore their causes. They are important clues. All of them can be harnessed by the writer to make people want to read his or her work. For the fundamental paradox of the unknown is that even as most people flee from it in their own lives, they are fascinated by it. Even though people spend much of their time reading things that do nothing but reinforce what they already know and believe, curiosity remains irrepressible in the human spirit.

In my view, curiosity is the great quality that binds writers to readers. Curiosity sends writers on their quests, and curiosity is what makes readers read the stories that result. These days, when there is increasing competition for people's time, writers cannot count on anyone to read their work out of a sense of obligation, moral duty, or abstract dedication to "being informed." They will not read because someone else deems a subject to be important. They will read because they want to, and they will want to because they are curious.

While editing the front page of the *Journal*—a newspaper with as educated, affluent, and sophisticated a readership as any writer could hope for—I had to confront and accept the fact that the average reader isn't interested in much of anything outside his immediate self-interest. This is, of course, an exaggeration. Any given individual is interested in *something;* some people are interested in many things. But the odds that someone shares those interests with anyone else, let alone with all of the two million people who subscribed to the *Journal,* seem quite remote. The *Journal* conducted periodic reader surveys to determine what, in fact, people said they were interested in. A large portion, something in the neighborhood of 70 percent, indicated an interest in national macroeconomic data and trends, which isn't surprising given the makeup of the *Journal's* readership. The next-highest-ranking topic, but garnering less than 50 percent interest, was local business news, obviously of interest only to those in the same locality. Nothing else—not national political news, foreign news, legal affairs, religion, or editorial opinion— registered even a one-third interest level. And in surveys that revealed what *Journal* readers actually read, it was clear that when these broad topics were reduced to specific stories—say, oil production in Libya—there was no measurable interest at all. I never had the heart to tell some reporters that these surveys suggested that no one had read their published stories.

There are, of course, prominent exceptions to this general

level of lack of interest. During one week when such a survey was conducted, the front page ran an obituary of Sam Walton, the legendary billionaire founder of Wal-Mart Stores. As I recall, that story attracted an astoundingly high 80 percent readership, even though there was nothing particularly surprising or newsworthy in it. But during that same week in 1991, a group of dissident Communists attempted a coup in the Soviet Union, kidnapping Mikhail Gorbachev and trying to reinstate the repressive militaristic regime that had so long threatened the West. I couldn't imagine a much more dramatic or important story. The characters—Gorbachev, a heroic Boris Yeltsin, the vodka-saturated dissidents—were great; the action and intrigue was out of a Le Carré novel; and the day-to-day suspense was intense. Our Moscow correspondent, Peter Gumbel, handed in the best work of his career, and the front-page staff worked night after night to perfect it. As I recall, the largest readership achieved by any of those stories was a meager 36 percent.

These results were of less concern to the paper as a whole than they were to me as the front-page editor. On any given day, there was a broad enough range of news that something in the paper appealed to just about everyone in the *Journal*'s constituency. But the front page carried only three stories a day, stories that received dramatic display, took up a lot of space, and demanded a far greater commitment of time from readers. On average, only about 17 percent of the readers were reading these stories in their entirety, which meant that 83 percent were not interested enough to bother. Although these same studies showed a high level of satisfaction with the front page—a sign that sooner or later readers found something that interested them —I thought we could do much better. For from the point of view of the reporter and writer, who might write only a handful of front-page stories in the course of a year, I found the surveys dismaying. I myself didn't want to write a story that would be read by only 17 percent of the paper's readers.

When thinking about potential stories, I began to focus on what I estimated to be the 90 percent of readers who were *not* interested in the proposed subject. Indeed, I consciously tried to ignore my own particular interests, finding that I was far more effective if I could act as a surrogate for readers who weren't interested. After all, I wasn't worried about losing the readers who were interested in a given subject, but in attracting those who weren't. This exercise didn't prove necessary for those stories of obvious universal appeal to *Journal* readers, such as Walton's death. (At general-interest publications, the phenomenon is similarly seen with respect to topics that excite national hysteria, such as Princess Diana's death, the O. J. Simpson trial, and the Clinton-Lewinsky scandal—topics that are often, and mercifully, ignored by the *Journal.*) But universally fascinating stories are few and far between. And they are hardly a boon for most writers. I have found nothing more daunting, in my own experience, than trying to compete with a national press corps in full hue and cry. In this process, I tried to pay close attention to what I read, noting particularly those stories on subjects I hadn't realized I was interested in. I talked to others, as well, about what they read and why. I found the exercise so revealing that I have tried ever since to pay close attention not only to what I read but why. I also consider what I skip, and try to analyze that as well. Indeed, I have found these exercises to be an essential part of learning to think like a writer.

Take a week or so and keep a record of what you read and what you skipped over. Look with particular care at stories you read that covered topics in which you are not inherently interested. Try to analyze why.

What conclusions can be drawn? While the answer is usually implicit rather than explicit, the stories I read are rooted in questions rather than answers. News itself is a response to the question "What happened?" I rarely read a news story if that question has already been answered, usually by the previous evening's television broadcasts or, increasingly, on a Web site on the Internet. It used to be that the question "What happened yesterday?" was enough to sustain readers' curiosity, but now the question is more often "What happened today?" or "What happened during the past hour?" This doesn't mean that the traditional written news story is obsolete. Some stories are sufficiently important and dramatic that I read news stories to answer questions like "What did the *Times*'s (or *Journal*'s) reporter find out about this topic that I don't already know?" or "How are they interpreting this information?" But it seems increasingly clear that news stories are an endangered species. It's not surprising that the readership and circulation of major mainstream newspapers and magazines are in decline.

By contrast, magazines have long relied on feature stories, as has the *Journal's* front page, to provide a reading experience that can't be duplicated elsewhere. The so-called news magazines —*Time, Newsweek, U.S. News & World Report*—long ago turned into feature publications. Other major newspapers, such as *The New York Times*, the *Los Angeles Times*, and *The Washington Post*, are running more and more feature stories on their front pages, even though they retain a traditional news format. Such stories are often labeled "news analysis" or are set off visually by boxes or special column heads. The classic inverted-pyramid news story—the "who, what, where, when, why" that editors could cut from the bottom—is what passed for writing at most newspapers. It became a habit with many reporters, who rarely gave a second thought to the subject of writing. Unfortunately, they are now ill prepared for what is happening in print media.

The irony is that feature stories and books are now routinely breaking news, so much so that magazines like *The New Yorker* issue press releases for many of their stories, as do all major publishers for many of their nonfiction books. When writing germinates as an unanswered question, the likelihood that the attempt to answer the question will generate news is quite high. In part this is because, in the vast majority of cases, if you already know something, so do many other people; hence, your knowledge will seem stale. By contrast, if you discover something, it is bound to be fresh. This can be true even with respect to events that happened some time in the past. The attention span of many writers and journalists strikes me as far too short. They abandon a story long before all the important questions have been answered. This is especially true of the networks and daily papers, which have the opportunity, by virtue of their frequent broadcasts or publications, to scoop just about anybody. Yet that very ability, and the rush of daily events, often lead them to move on too quickly, leaving a tremendous amount of news to be broken by magazines and books, which have lead times of months, even years.

The stories I read with interest manage to convey their questions with greater specificity, even if those questions were implicit in the headline. For example, about two weeks after the crash of an Italian cable car, *The New York Times* ran the following headline: "Death in the Alps: How Wayward U.S. Pilot Killed 20 on Ski Lift." Even apart from sounding like a mystery starring

Hercule Poirot ("Death in the Alps"), this piqued my curiosity. I found myself reading the entire story. The headline could as easily have been stated with a question mark as without one. I had read the original news report with moderate interest: a ski lift car had crashed, killing twenty people, because an American military plane had clipped the cable suspending the car. On the scale of international disasters it wasn't particularly large, but it had an American angle. Was I naturally interested in an Italian ski slope calamity? Not really. But even though it appeared more than a week after the accident, and hence wasn't "news" in any traditional sense, the follow-up feature was far more interesting, because the event was now presented as a mystery: Why was the U.S. plane flying in the vicinity of a cable car? Why was it flying so low? Why didn't the pilots see the cable car? Who was responsible? All this was information missing from the news report I had read a week or so earlier. I read the story because I was very curious to know the answers. The main "news" contained in this story was that the pilots were using standardized American military maps that didn't include the cable car, whereas Italian maps did. Imagine if the headline had been "U.S. Pilots Used Maps That Omitted Cable Car." Put aside the question of whether the maps had anything to do with the accident (the story was unconvincing on this point); thanks to this headline, my interest in that story nose-dives. The explanation—the "answer" to the questions that had so intrigued me—turned out to be rather banal. Yet I read the entire story, thus demonstrating that the question is often more interesting than the answer.

Disasters, in particular, seem to lend themselves to this approach, often because disasters spawn mysteries. Bill Carley, a reporter at the *Journal,* has built a distinguished career by writing principally about air crashes. I'm not particularly interested in air crashes, but he always manages to pique my interest. A recent headline of his read, "Crash of Executive Jet Leaves Trail of Clues but Very Few Answers." What could be more mysterious? My interest is aroused even though the headline suggests the mystery won't be solved.

Compare my reaction to a front-page story that ran in *The Wall Street Journal* the same day as the cable car story. "Difficult Times Drive India's Cotton Farmers to Desperate Actions/Some Have Killed Themselves as Pests Ravage Fields and Banks Seek

Payback." I didn't read it. Am I inherently interested in Indian cotton farmers? No. But am I any less interested in Indian farmers than Italian skiers? Not really. And for all I know, these "difficult times" in India have killed far more people than perished in the Italian accident. Yet nothing about this story stirs my curiosity. "Difficult times for farmers" is as old a story as the weather. While I may have been briefly curious to know just what these "desperate actions" turned out to be, the headline answered my question: some people are committing suicide. In fact, the headline pretty much does tell the whole story. So why would anyone want to read more? I often warn my students that if they can tell their story in a headline, that's about how long the story should be. More fundamentally, I wonder what prompted the reporter to undertake this story in the first place. In other words, what didn't he know before he started working on it that he subsequently learned? My suspicion is that the writer already knew virtually everything in the story before he began thinking of it as a story, an approach that is often fatal to reader interest.

What's sad is that I've been told by some people who read this story that it was a fine piece of writing and reporting. Obviously the headline didn't discourage those readers inherently interested in the plight of India's cotton farmers, though I assume the number of such readers is rather small. If the story was a good one, there should have been a way to prompt reader curiosity in the headline, not extinguish it.

By contrast, a front-page story in the next day's *Journal* carried the headline "Ignoring All Problems, Most People in Business Glow with Optimism." The mood among businesspeople is a staple of economic statistics and reporting. While surveys suggest this is an intrinsically interesting subject for *Journal* readers, to a general audience it is about as dull as they come. Am I interested in the mood among businesspeople? No. Does this story promise any of the life-and-death drama of a cable car crash or suicides by Indian farmers? No. Was I interested in reading the story? Yes. Why?

Consider if the headline had simply been "Most People in Business Glow with Optimism." That's mildly interesting, but it tells me all I want to know. It's only when I read the contrasting phrase "Ignoring All Problems" that my curiosity is aroused. What are these problems? How could businesspeople be "glowing" if they're experiencing such problems? What's the explanation for such a seeming paradox? I suspect that similar questions motivated the writer of this story. Confronted with routinely reported events and statistics that seemed contradictory—in this case, trouble in Asia, Iraq, and Washington on the one hand, yet buoyant business confidence on the other—he asked how that could be. As is so often the case, the story itself didn't really answer the question it posed. It explored possible explanations—that businesspeople are simply irrational these days; that people tend to have short memories; that business confidence depends more on a healthy job market than on international incidents—all or none of which may explain the paradox. Indeed, if there were a simple and easy answer, it isn't clear that the topic would warrant a story of several thousand words. But the point, again, is that this story began with a critical way of thinking: the writer looked at some economic statistics not for what they told him, but for what they didn't. The story couldn't have been triggered by what he already knew, for the answer to the question he posed ultimately proved elusive.

The broad conclusion I have drawn is that we read for one reason: curiosity. And curiosity is stimulated by questions. This is true of news articles, of self-help and "how-to" articles, of longer feature stories, of books, even of fiction. To think like a writer is to learn to be always curious, to react to any event with one or more questions. This may sound simple, even obvious, yet I have found that for most people, it is a very foreign way of viewing the world. It requires constant vigilance, an alert mind, considerable energy, and a willingness to live with, even to embrace, uncertainty.

I have made the point that learning to think like a writer, by focusing on the unknown, the uncertain, the unusual, the curious, the paradoxical, all of which spawn questions before they provide any answers, enhances many aspects of one's life beyond writing. This occurred to me recently while watching CNN's coverage of the "town meeting" staged by the Clinton administration to explain its policy toward Iraq, which at the time was frustrating UN efforts to monitor its production of weapons.

Top administration officials, including Secretary of State Madeleine Albright and Secretary of Defense William Cohen, were plainly unprepared for the barrage of skeptical questions they received from a cross section of Americans. How does the United States know that Iraq possesses deadly biological weapons? What threat do these weapons, if they exist, actually pose to the United States and other countries? How likely is it that American military action can actually eliminate such weapons? And even if a military strike does succeed, how will Iraq's compliance be monitored in the future?

These were good questions, even obvious ones, yet I was struck by how little press coverage of the Iraq crisis had addressed them, and how any one of them could itself be the basis for a good story. (Indeed, William J. Broad and Judith Miller of *The New York Times* did publish such a story, not long after the town meeting.) I was also dismayed at top officials' inability to provide thorough answers, which led me to wonder how much they had been focusing on what military intelligence purported to know, and how little on what remained unanswered.

2
IDEAS

No MATTER HOW CURIOUS and alert one's mind, life can seem a confusing, nearly overwhelming array of undifferentiated bits of information. Each and every one of these could be the seed of a story, but the vast majority, of course, are not.

Facing this paradox can be one of the most daunting aspects of writing, for very few writers, in my experience, have any real understanding of where their ideas come from. The postpartum depression that many writers experience after completing a story arises in large part, I'm convinced, from anxiety about where the next story is going to come from. During the heyday of the mergers-and-acquisitions boom on Wall Street, a character in my book *Den of Thieves,* one of the most successful investment bankers on Wall Street at the time, told me he was consumed by anxiety about where his next big deal would come from. Though my work as a journalist seemed far removed from his world, I knew what he was talking about. While I don't believe I ever experienced the phenomenon as intensely as he did, it took me years to get over the same feeling about stories.

The reality is that good story ideas are abundant. Once one begins to think consistently along the lines explored in the last chapter, they will manifest themselves at a rapid rate. That doesn't mean that all of these ideas will—or should—turn into stories, but they will provide a pool of possibilities from which the best can be culled. Here's an illustration: The front page of the *Journal* ran fifteen feature stories a week, fifty-two weeks a year, except on occasional holidays. That's over 750 feature stories a year. To ensure that supply, my staff and I generated at least that many ideas, which we farmed out to reporters and other editors. Yet even our best writers were expected to produce only a tiny fraction of the stories we needed. A writer who publishes ten to twelve feature stories a year is working at an amazingly productive pace. One good book idea can occupy a writer for much more than a year, and usually does. A writer can build a career around surprisingly few ideas, as long as they are good ones.

. A good story idea is a precious thing. Some ideas are so good that I have pronounced them foolproof, meaning that I believed it impossible that the resulting story could be a failure. (I admit I was proven wrong on occasion, demonstrating that there are no certainties in writing.) Sometimes an idea was so good that I could approve a proposal after hearing a single sentence. As a rough estimate, I tell my students that a good idea constitutes about 50 percent of what makes a successful story.

When seeking story ideas, it is important to sweep aside one's own ego. I have known many writers who sneered at any idea they didn't conceive themselves. They seemed to take particular pride in spurning anything suggested by an editor. Some of the best story ideas are generated by writers, of course, since they are often in the best position to see what is going on around them, unlike an editor desk-bound in New York or Washington. But the generation of an idea is almost always a collaborative process. It is extremely difficult for even the most experienced writers to evaluate their own ideas. I encourage my students to discuss ideas among themselves as much as possible, for ideas are often honed as they are verbalized. I have never gone forward with a major story without gauging the reaction of someone I trust, usually my editor.

Whatever the source, good story ideas should be received like the precious gifts they are. What does the source matter? I have seen good ideas emerge from the unlikeliest places. After all, when the story is published, the writer gets all the credit. A gracious acknowledgment or two may be all that's required. (I might add that there is nothing less gracious than taking credit for someone else's idea.)

The underlying sources for stories are surprisingly few. There is, most obviously, direct observation or experience. Then there are other observers or participants, commonly called sources. Finally, there are other published accounts. These three categories cover nearly all story ideas.

As for direct observation or participation, we can naturally start with ourselves. If you had been a member of the Heaven's Gate cult (most of whose members died as they tried to shed their earthly bodies to join a passing comet), you would almost certainly find a publisher for your first-person story. If, on the other hand, you were in San Francisco during the 1989 earthquake, and hope to write about your experience, you will be competing with millions of others with similar accounts. I describe people who undergo such experiences as witnesses to history, and a witness to history always has a potential story. But the reality is that most of us will never be such witnesses, and certainly not often enough to build a career around them.

I can recall only one instance when I found myself a witness to history, and the experience was so unusual that at first I didn't even recognize it as a story. I find this is a common reaction among professional writers: we are so used to seeking out the stories of others that our own rarely strike us as possible stories. (This is in contrast to many nonwriters you have probably met, who find virtually anything that happens to them to be newsworthy, and are eager to tell you about it.) In this case, I was planning a trip to my hometown of Quincy, Illinois, during the summer of 1993 to help cope with the flood that inundated much of the upper Mississippi basin that summer. Quincy is located on a bluff above the river, and while its elevation protects it, the surrounding farmland and towns were all threatened. While I was a high school student there we would pile sandbags on the levees nearly every spring, and I knew from my parents that volunteers were needed for the dire threat that had materialized that summer.

A flood is not an easy story to cover. For one thing, it moves slowly, the water often creeping up just an inch or two a day. It also covers a huge geographic area. Only when a levee breaks is there a dramatic surge of water. That summer, television had begun devoting more airtime to the disaster, but only when it reached historic proportions did print journalists start arriving in the Midwest. (Indeed, I remember hearing that at the American

Society of Newspaper Editors convention in Chicago that summer, the flood had been cited as a story best left to the electronic
media.) *The New York Times* was an exception, sending numerous reporters to the area. Among them was Sara Rimer, a Boston-
based reporter who was dispatched to Quincy. Sara happens to
be a friend of mine, and when I learned she was heading to
Quincy, I arranged for her to have dinner with my parents and
suggested people in town she might want to meet. That hardly
proved necessary, since I was soon receiving reports that Sara
had become the toast of Quincy.

When I arrived in town, I went to see her at the Holiday Inn,
and she was filled with enthusiasm. "You have to do a story about
this," she insisted. The idea hadn't even occurred to me, though
of course it was staring me in the face. Listening to Sara, I realized
that so much about Quincy and the area that I took for granted
struck her as exotic and colorful: the Green Parrot, a bar in
the lowlands; the local sheriff and his deputies; the antebellum
architecture and timeless feel of Quincy itself. While I'm sure she
didn't anticipate this, I could easily see Sara herself as a character
in the story: the big-city reporter who comes to the small Midwestern town. "But surely you're writing the story," I protested.
She shrugged: she was filing daily copy, but couldn't get the time
and the space to do something sweeping that would capture the
immensity of the disaster and the human stakes. The next day,
when I called my editor at *The New Yorker* to say I was heading
down to the levee and thought there might be a story, he was
enthusiastic.

Nothing I said in that conversation was a fully developed
idea. The Midwestern flood of 1993 is what I call a topic, and a
topic is not an idea. I have had to make this point to students
and writers on countless occasions. Topics are inherently boring,
because they pose no questions and incite no curiosity. They are
like encyclopedia entries: interesting only if that happens to be
what you want to look up. "Women in law" is a topic. "Welfare
cheats" is a topic. "South Africa" is a topic. Reporters would
come to me with the most earnest demeanors, and say something
like "I want to do a story about how oil companies are causing
explosions at natural gas facilities." When I stifled a yawn, their
outrage would be apparent: "How can you not care about something so important?" The answer was simple: anytime someone

had to use the word "about" I knew we were discussing a topic, not a story. I would urge the reporter to come back with something more specific: What company? What explosion? Some topics are more interesting than others, but they should never be mistaken for ideas.

How the Midwestern flood metamorphosed from a topic to a story idea I will later describe in detail, but the point I am making here is that it originated in my own experience. Even so, it took another writer to prompt me to recognize the story. Quincy had earned its single footnote in history when it hosted a Lincoln-Douglas debate over a hundred years before. It had simply never occurred to me that anything happening in my hometown would ever again warrant national attention. I was wrong, and I was blind to the resulting possibilities. I should have been constantly asking myself whether what I was experiencing might be of interest to others.

Not only being a witness to history, but any personal experience that is sensational or bizarre enough will rather obviously yield a potential story. I am not going to dwell on this, for the likelihood of these things happening to us is extremely remote. Moreover, I often wonder how many of these alleged experiences have ever been fact-checked, though they are routinely treated as nonfiction. But if you have actually been abducted by a UFO, conversed directly with God, or danced with an angel on the head of a pin, you may as well write about it. Someone, no doubt, will publish it.

But the possibility that lightning will simply strike and embroil you in a potential story is relatively remote. For that reason, many writers and reporters try to engineer such experiences by moving into the path of the storm, so to speak; then, they write about what happens. This may be the most common source of ideas that spring from direct observation or experience. During the 1991 Gulf War, for example, every major news organization sent correspondents to observe the action (though they were so tightly controlled by the military that what they saw yielded little worth reading). As far as I know, no writer actually joined a branch of the military, planning to fight in the war and then write about it, but that approach, too, is time-honored. Journalists routinely rush to witness wars, disasters, crises of every sort. Tiananmen Square, the Berlin Wall, the Soviet coup against Gorbachev

—all were major events to which I dispatched *Journal* reporters, so they would be there to witness the story. I remember sending Jane Mayer, one of my favorite reporters, to Cairo during the Gulf War. Cairo seemed rather far from the action, but at the time there was concern that Saddam Hussein would unleash his Scud missiles on Arab nations supporting the United States, and Egypt seemed a likely target. Jane was willing to go. After a few days she called me wondering if something she'd noticed at her hotel might be a story: wealthy Kuwaitis were whiling away their time at the hotel disco until the war was over, leaving the fighting to others. Of course it was a story. The piece Jane wrote revealed more about Kuwaiti attitudes than anything I read from the front lines. It was a brilliant observation on her part, one that many reporters would have missed.

At a much more mundane level, reporters would often come to me with an "opportunity" to, for example, accompany the chairman of Procter & Gamble on a trip to Venezuela, with the hope that something might happen worth writing about. I was cool to such suggestions, since nothing usually happened in a reporter's presence, or if it did, it was staged for the reporter's benefit. If something spontaneous and interesting did happen, it could usually be reported in the ordinary manner, with far less expenditure of time and resources. Reporters were invariably disappointed by my response, especially when these opportunities involved trips to places like Hawaii and Paris. Still, these were all attempts by reporters to put themselves in a position to see a story in the making. And occasionally they do pay off: Jon Krakauer participated in an expedition to Mount Everest that resulted in the deaths of several participants. His resulting book, *Into Thin Air*, was a national best-seller.

Another popular genre is the reporter as direct participant, what I sometimes call the George Plimpton approach. These stories are generally triggered by the question "What would it be like to be . . . ?" The blank can be filled in by just about anything: "a pro football player," "a Radio City Rockette," "a stock-car driver," "a participant in a tractor pull," "a beauty-contest entrant," "a Playboy bunny," to cite several that have resulted in stories I've seen. Any wacky activity pursued by someone—bungee jumping, walking on hot coals, playing the violin in the subway (all actual stories)—can be indulged in by a writer who brings a man- or woman-on-the-street perspective, sometimes to humorous effect. I believe a fair amount of discretion needs to be exercised when evaluating this kind of story. I find that many end up being tedious, because the writer's experience is just what the reader would expect. Why not simply interview a participant, instead? I believe a question worth asking when considering whether to pursue such a story is "What unique qualities do I bring to this?" In some cases the unique quality will be nothing more than one's own ordinariness, which makes the writer a surrogate for readers who can live vicariously through the experience. The danger is that the resulting story may be just as ordinary. I find a good rule of thumb in this area is to consider whether you, as a writer, actually want to undertake the experience that is the subject of the story. If so, it probably isn't risky enough, daring enough, unusual enough—in sum, surprising enough—to pique a reader's curiosity.

Travel writing often falls into this category, and in doing so highlights another pitfall of the first-person story: all too often, it becomes autobiography. As the writer experiences one ordinary, predictable event after another (room service, a little sightseeing, some light entertainment), concluding the account with a description of the bed linens, readers learn more about the writer than the place visited, and few of us are interesting enough to sustain this.

A variation that poses some special problems is the so-called undercover story, in which a writer poses as someone he or she is not. *Black Like Me,* in which a white man posed as black, may be the best-known example. Undercover work was once a staple of investigative journalism, particularly consumer stories, but since an adverse verdict against ABC News in the Food Lion case, in which ABC reporters took jobs as workers at a large grocery chain and then reported on unsanitary conditions, there has been a cloud over the genre. The reporters' failure to disclose their true identities was deemed fraudulent. Many First Amendment lawyers don't expect this verdict to be upheld on appeal (it was reversed recently by an appellate court), but it has at least temporarily chilled undercover reporting and writing. Legal issues aside, this kind of journalism has always raised moral and ethical problems; in my view, it's always worth pondering whether the story is fundamentally fair.

Years ago, when I was working at *American Lawyer* magazine, we wondered whether personal-injury lawyers would allow their clients to lie in order to enhance the likelihood of a favorable verdict or large settlement, and thus a large contingency fee for the lawyer. We devised a scenario in which one of our reporters would claim to have tripped and been injured near a Consolidated Edison repair site. She would emphasize that Con Ed had nothing to do with the injury, but would wonder whether she might still have a claim. To pull off such a story required a fair amount of dramatic skill, poise, and courage, and none of the reporters wanted to do it. An editor, Jane Berentson, volunteered, and ultimately took her story to about a dozen lawyers in New York. Fully half of them did tell her to lie, even when she protested that she didn't feel comfortable doing such a thing.

As a story idea, this passed several of my informal tests: no one wanted to do it; it was risky, which brought with it a certain suspense (would the reporter pull off the deception, or be unmasked?); it posed a question to which we didn't already know the answer; and we believed it would be a public service. At the same time, we wondered if it was fair. None of the lawyers knew they were speaking to a reporter. While Jane was careful not to encourage anyone to ask her to lie, the experiment nonetheless had overtones of entrapment. Ultimately Steve Brill, the magazine's editor, decided to withhold the lawyers' names. He reasoned that the purpose of the "Integrity Test" wasn't to expose individual lawyers, randomly selected, but to assess the overall integrity of the malpractice bar. The story itself proved a huge success, was much talked about, and was reprinted in numerous publications.

I myself have done only one first-person undercover story, "My Life in an Unaccredited Law School," for which I enrolled in Golden West College of Law in Los Angeles and showed up for the first week of classes. California was one of the few states that permitted such law schools, and they were flourishing there at the time, 1978. It was a relief to discover that I could tell the truth in response to every question on the application. (It did not, for example, ask whether I had attended any other law school or received an advanced degree, in which case I would have had to reveal that I had already graduated from law school.) I am, in fact, a terrible liar. I was once hauled in for questioning at the Canadian border while trying to stammer out an answer to the question of whether all the passengers in my car, who were then asleep, were U.S. citizens. (They weren't.) I also believed I would be terrible at using an assumed name, so I used my real name on the application and at school. I found it relatively easy to maintain the deception, though my fellow students must have found me a little aloof. I wasn't eager to discuss whatever had brought me to Golden West or where I lived (a hotel). I recall only one moment of panic: I was driving a rented car, and a fellow student asked me why my car had Nevada license plates. I hadn't even noticed. I stammered again, and finally told the truth: that I was driving a rented car. Fortunately, that satisfied his curiosity; he didn't ask why. My departure after a week caused no comment that I know of.

The resulting story was written in a humorous vein, trying to capture the "Animal House" feel of the place, and it was enlivened by some very clever cartoons. Readers seemed to love it. In this case, all the names used were real, including those of faculty members who had made some blatant misstatements of the law in class. I felt that Golden West was holding itself out to the public as a legitimate law school and that there was no plausible expectation of privacy in a crowded classroom. Hence, real names were appropriate. But to be honest, I felt a little queasy about the experience. I was glad I didn't have to misrepresent myself more than I did, and I don't plan to do any more undercover operations.

Still, as an idea the unaccredited-law-school operation met my tests. What was life like in an unaccredited law school? I had no idea. While the schools turned out to be even more chaotic and shoddy than I might have guessed, the story might have been even better if they turned out to be good schools, kept out of the mainstream by a hide-bound profession's efforts to restrain competition. But what's important was that curiosity drove the story from the outset. As an undercover operation, this wasn't something I particularly wanted to do; indeed, I was very nervous because of the chance that I might be exposed. So I assumed readers would get at least a small vicarious thrill from experiencing this apprehension with me. Finally, as I've already noted, I felt the story would serve a public interest.

By far the most common type of story that results from direct observation or experience is the memoir, a first-person account that generally doesn't rely on any event of national interest. In recent years there has been a near explosion in the publication of memoirs, not all of them by celebrities. Indeed, in what seems to be our confessional era, almost nothing seems to be off-limits. I even suspect some writers of exaggerating their afflictions in an effort to appeal to talk-show hosts and hostesses or, in the case of self-help tomes, to make their turnarounds or makeovers all the more impressive. This trend will surely peak, and despite many successes in this genre, the everyday experiences of most of us are unlikely to turn into national best-sellers. Still, what seem to be ordinary experiences may indeed be the raw material for good stories. How does one know?

I find the simplest test, again, is to ask a question: What about my experience might interest someone else? Even better: What about my experience do I myself find puzzling, and what might I better understand given additional reflection and research? This latter question is particularly significant, since a disadvantage of first-person ideas is that self-knowledge leaves relatively little room for the kind of curiosity that yields the best stories. Often we already know too much about ourselves.

The broad themes that emerge from such stories are often more important than the immediate subject matter. Any story, for example, in which someone overcomes significant adversity appeals to an almost universal interest in suffering and redemption. If that adversity is something little written about or understood, but widely shared, so much the better. Many successful memoirs have been written in recent years in which the nominal subject matter has been taboo—alcoholism, spousal abuse, incest, a husband with AIDS, and so on. Indeed, it is hard to imagine anything today that would be both widely experienced yet still shocking. (Sensationalist talk shows seem to be turning ever more desperately to situations so aberrant as to be freakish.) In my view, the potential universality of an experience is far more intriguing and compelling than sensationalism. Jessie Lee Brown Foveaux, an elderly woman living in Kansas City, wrote an account of her troubled marriage to an alcoholic. After it was featured in a front-page *Wall Street Journal* story, her story sold to a publisher for a million-dollar advance. The bidding war may be highly unusual, but her experience was not.

Another question to ask is whether one's own experience embodies some broader trend or condition. If, for example, you were thrown off welfare because of the Welfare Reform Act passed by Congress in 1997, you might very well write about the experience, because many people similarly situated were having to cope with the same crisis.

Another category of memoir succeeds less because of the significance of the writer's experience than because of its setting. In these cases, the writer is a guide to another time and place about which readers may be curious. The enormous success of Frank McCourt's *Angela's Ashes* is due not only to McCourt's beautiful writing but also, at least in part, to its setting in Depression-era Ireland, a time and place significant for many Americans with Irish roots and, indeed, for many with immigrant ancestors. Much highly autobiographical fiction, such as Jay McInerney's *Bright Lights, Big City* and Bret Easton Ellis's *Less Than Zero,* succeeds for similar reasons. One is a guided tour through the demimonde of Manhattan, the other of Los Angeles.

Most memoir stories are far more modest in scope. I have written one such story myself, about being audited by the Internal Revenue Service. The fact that I was subjected to a full-scale audit, in a year when my income as an author and journalist was exceedingly modest, seemed at first to be nothing but a source of annoyance and anxiety. But in pondering whether it might make a story, the thought occurred to me that money and taxes are subjects of nearly universal interest that do remain something of a taboo. How many other people would be foolhardy enough to bare their experiences with the IRS? Not many, I suspected. Last year, more than a decade after the story ran, someone came up to me and said the story was one of his all-time favorites. I had all but forgotten it.

It should be obvious by now that our own experiences provide a wealth of possible story ideas and that we should be vigilant in spotting them. But it is also true that I would never have a career as a writer if I had depended only on direct observation and experience. Stories that began in this manner account for only a tiny fraction of my own output. And if you work as a journalist, you will soon learn that you were not hired to write about yourself. I mentioned in the previous chapter that, as an editor, I distrusted my enthusiasm for stories about subjects that

I personally found interesting. It is even more difficult to be objective about first-person stories, and for that reason it is essential to discuss these ideas with someone else, preferably a respected editor. The tests I have outlined need to be applied rigorously, and if you so apply them, you will discover that most of your own experiences, however fascinating to you, hold little appeal to a wide readership. Fortunately, the universe of story ideas is much broader.

Other people possess a wealth of story ideas, if only you can get them to share those ideas with you. Such people are usually referred to as sources. If you are known as a writer or journalist, you'll find that almost everyone has a story he or she wants to tell you. Most of them—the overwhelming majority of them— are bad stories. When I was a fledgling reporter working for the summer at my hometown newspaper, the *Quincy* (Ill.) *Herald-Whig,* one of my jobs was to entertain story ideas from our far-flung "local correspondents" in places like Cherry Box, Missouri, and Lima, Ill. I recall accounts of a tick being extracted from a boy's forehead and a traffic back-up caused by a broken stoplight. I have listened to so many bad story ideas that I can usually recognize one after a single sentence. But I keep listening, and my phone number is listed. I do sometimes ask people who embark on long and convoluted stories to put them in writing, because I find it helps them organize their thoughts. I read my mail. Just when I think I can't bear one more bad idea, something wonderful surfaces, for instance, the fact that inmates were growing marijuana right under the sheriff's nose outside the Palmyra, Missouri, county jail—a story I did write for the *Herald-Whig.*

More recently, I received a newspaper clipping from a restaurant owner in Carlisle, Pennsylvania. I had never heard of him, but he had read a recent story of mine in *The New Yorker* and thought I might be interested in the article. The possibility that I might be interested in writing for a national publication about anything happening in Carlisle, Pennsylvania, seemed remote. The clipping, from the local paper, was brief; it described the trial of an accountant, Dan Miller, who had been fired from his job for being gay. Afterward, his former employer sued him, alleging that he had stolen clients. The jury had ruled against Miller, assessing $150,000 in damages. On its face, this seemed inexplicable to me, and I have learned that anything that seems inexplicable is a potential story. I called the restaurant owner, assuming he knew more, but he did not. He simply thought there had been a miscarriage of justice and, as an immigrant from France, he didn't understand how such a thing could happen in America. He said he wouldn't want anything like that to happen to either of his two sons. He was asking the same questions I was. I ended up pursuing the story: total strangers can turn out to be sources.

Friends are often sources, and I'm often struck when I talk to other writers by how many of the characters I've read about in their stories turn out to be known to them. This is often the case when writers search for someone to illustrate a broader theme.

I recall, for example, discussing the AIDS crisis with Jane Berentson, who wrote "Integrity Test" and worked as my deputy Page One editor at *The Wall Street Journal*. A made-for-TV movie broadcast the night before had focused on mothers whose sons had AIDS. I mentioned that I liked the movie, that the subject would have been a good one for the front page, and that it was too bad mothers and sons was a subject that had been dissected so thoroughly elsewhere in the media. Jane mused that the topic of fathers whose sons had AIDS seemed virtually unexplored. The idea appealed to me instantly; among other things, the *Journal's* readership was overwhelmingly male. We had a computer search done, and indeed, it turned up virtually nothing. Why was everyone writing about mothers, but not fathers?

The upshot of this conversation was a story about a father coming to terms with his gay son's fatal illness. Judy Valente, a *Journal* reporter covering the airline beat in Chicago, wrote one of the most moving stories I've ever read, which was a finalist for a Pulitzer Prize. She knew the son slightly from the church they both attended, and she became very close to the family as she did the reporting. So her "sources" were known to her apart from her work as a journalist. Reporting and writing this story was emotionally draining for Judy, especially since the young man died.

I am reluctant to write about people who are my friends. I know too well what can happen with even the best-intentioned stories: they almost never appear as the subjects would have written them. A few years ago, *The New Yorker* was planning a fiction issue and asked me to think about writing a nonfiction piece on the subject. I told the issue's editor, Dan Menaker, that I didn't really have any ideas, but that I had been recently struck by how little money my friend James Wilcox made, although he was quite a successful novelist. Dan responded immediately that I should write a piece about Jim, but I demurred; I didn't feel comfortable writing about someone I knew personally.

At the time, I didn't know Jim all that well. One day while visiting Amanda Urban, my agent, I noticed a collection of Jim's books on her shelves. I had read several and was a big fan, and I told her so. When Jim's next book, *Polite Sex,* came out, she invited me to a dinner party and sat me next to him. We had since gotten together several times to play some piano duets.

Dan dismissed my concerns, saying I should just disclose our friendship. I felt I should discuss the prospect of doing the story with Jim, who, I thought, would resist the idea. To my surprise, he readily agreed. Needless to say, his editor was thrilled at the possibility of publicity. Still, none of us was prepared for the to-do that followed. Jim's books vaulted onto paperback best-seller lists. We were both interviewed on public radio, and Jim found the exposure so painful and humiliating that he canceled all other appearances. I think he was somewhat traumatized, and the episode could easily have damaged our friendship.

I feel I was right to be cautious about writing about Jim, but it's another example of a story that was right under my nose. I wouldn't have recognized it if Dan hadn't prodded me and then been so enthusiastic. What made it a promising idea? The notion that a novelist would have to struggle financially was hardly a new or surprising one. But the extremity of Jim's circumstances was surprising. He was, after all, a critically acclaimed writer, the author of seven books. His astonishing candor about his life and financial circumstances brought his plight to life in a way that hadn't been done before. Yet this was never an idea that I believed to be foolproof, and without Dan's encouragement, I doubt that I would have pursued it.

Most sources are known to the writer, but except for out-and-out publicity hounds like Donald Trump, relatively few propose stories about themselves. What's scarce is a good source, particularly one who thinks like a writer. Such a source is to be cherished. Among the virtues of hearing a potential story from a source is that you may be uniquely privy to the information, which means that you won't be competing with the rest of the world's writers on the same story. It is a great luxury to be able to work on a story alone, without the pressure of competition. In such cases, many writers get their sources to pledge that they will tell no one else. This I have always found difficult to do. But I have found that most sources understand the writer's need for exclusivity, and I have rarely had to make the agreement explicit.

What makes a good source? Good sources share an enthusiasm for stories. Like good writers, they love to read. They seem to love the idea that they are contributing to stories others will enjoy. "Gossip" has a pejorative tone, so perhaps I should simply say that good sources love to talk and exchange information. They are hungry for it.

The best source I have ever encountered is James J. Cramer, who runs his own investment partnership and founded The Street.com, a successful Web site on investing. I first met Jim long before he became a celebrity personal finance guru, when he came to *American Lawyer* to work as a reporter. We became friends, and remained friends when he went on to Harvard Law School and then to a job on Wall Street. In this respect, he was triply unusual: he was a personal friend, he thought like a journalist, and he worked on Wall Street, one of the most fertile sources of story ideas that interest me. Jim has a naturally curious mind, he seeks out paradox and contradiction and looks for explanations. He had his own far-flung network of sources. He positively percolated with story ideas—some of them, naturally, better than others. It was Jim who pointed out to me the mysterious rise in a key futures index the day after the market crash in 1987, a rise that proved critical in avoiding a complete market meltdown. Given investors' state of mind at the time, the rise made no sense. Could it have been manipulated, albeit for benign reasons? Pursuing this question was one of the factors that led to a *Wall Street Journal* story by Daniel Hertzberg and me, "Terrible Tuesday," for which we later won a Pulitzer Prize.

In that story, we turned the day after the crash, which had received almost no attention in the media, into a suspense-filled narrative of how disaster was averted. We provided an hour-by-hour account showing how serious the danger became, how close to panic many participants were, and how the sudden reversal in the Major Market Index offered a psychological boost that caused the market to recover. We never proved there was manipulation, but made a strong circumstantial case for it.

Another terrific source was Martin Siegel, who for a time was head of mergers and acquisitions at Kidder, Peabody and then, briefly, at Drexel Burnham Lambert. Siegel didn't give me confidential information about his own clients. But, like many good sources, he told me plenty about clients of other firms. (Siegel later got caught up in the insider-trading scandal and became a major character in my book *Den of Thieves*. It is naturally awkward when someone moves from being a source to a subject, a topic I'll discuss later.)

The best sources need to be sought out and cultivated, which is why I always encouraged people who worked for me to use their expense accounts and take people out to lunch and dinner. But many sources are readily available. One category needlessly shunned by many writers is public relations agents. It is true that PR people are often fundamentally at odds with journalists, since journalists are seeking the facts and PR people are often trying to conceal them, or at least to distort them in a way favorable to their clients. And some PR people manage to be exceedingly annoying, beginning their conversations with "How are you today?" in that mock-sincere, time-wasting tone perfected by telemarketers who call you at home during the dinner hour. But in my experience, a good PR person can be a good source. Some are former journalists themselves, so they recognize a good potential story. A prejudice against PR agents—or any other category of person, for that matter—should never stand in the way of a good story. Our job as writers is to listen, not to judge.

That doesn't mean that a source's motive shouldn't be considered in assessing whether something might be a story. Journalists often, and rightly, worry about being manipulated, and PR agents are especially likely to try to use journalists for their own purposes. But far more important than someone's motive in providing information is whether the information is true. And a virtue of conceiving stories as questions is that the outcome of the story is unknown. It's impossible to say ahead of time whether the piece will be favorable or unfavorable to its subjects, whether it will affect a stock price or not, or whether it will have any intended result at all. Good sources understand this.

Writers need to spend a lot of time talking to people. Colleagues of mine at *The Wall Street Journal* often marveled at how much time I spent on the phone, laughing and talking, often with my feet propped up on my desk, rarely taking a note. This didn't seem like "work" to them, and they sometimes asked how I got anything done. In fact, it *was* work. Oil drillers sink plenty of dry holes before they hit a gusher. I was simply prospecting for possible stories. Did I enjoy myself? Yes, and why not? The grim earnestness with which some writers tackle their work is only too evident in the resulting stories. Good sources can tell if you genuinely enjoy talking to them. If not, you're wasting your time and theirs.

I have found that the most fertile category of story ideas is one of the most readily accessible: other news accounts. By this I emphatically do not mean stealing someone else's idea, or rewriting a story that's already been done. But the fact is that most news accounts raise more questions than they answer, thus leaving room for a much more thorough and enriching account. Many news articles cover a brief, finite period of time, and are actually fragments of much longer stories. Journalists who write only news stories think differently from the kind of writers I am trying to encourage. Their focus on the traditional "who, what, where, and when" of news often distracts them from the deeper resonance of their stories. I have often seen the most eye-popping stories reported in a few deadpan, matter-of-fact paragraphs, usually buried deep inside a paper, or appearing in a publication with little circulation.

If you have been exercising your curiosity as I recommended in the last chapter, recognizing the potential stories lurking behind news reports will become almost second nature. You should realize at once that myriad questions remained to be answered about the cable-car accident, the Monica Lewinsky brouhaha, or Congressman Bill Paxton's sudden, mysterious decision to resign from Congress, to mention just a few recent cases. Another revealing exercise is to look at what kinds of feature stories and nonfiction books are being published: almost all of them derive from events that were originally covered as news stories. Even John Berendt's phenomenal best-seller *Midnight in the Garden of Good and Evil* was based on events widely reported in the Savannah, Georgia, press.

Let's consider some examples of this process.

On November 11, 1992, *The New York Times* ran this story on the third page of the Metropolitan section, without a by-line:

> A partner in one of Manhattan's most prestigious law firms was found stabbed to death early Monday morning in a motel in the Bronx, the police said yesterday.
>
> The victim was identified by the police yesterday as David L. Schwartz, 55 years old, the head of the real estate section of Cravath, Swaine & Moore.
>
> Sgt. William Larkin, commanding officer of the 45th Precinct Detective Squad, said investigators were still seeking a motive. Lieut. Richard Kuberski, a Police Department spokesman, said some of Mr. Schwartz's personal effects had been stolen. He would not reveal what they were.
>
> Mr. Schwartz's body was found by a night clerk at about 1:30 A.M. in a room of the Hutchinson River Motel at 2815 Westchester Avenue, described by the police as a transient motel near the Hutchinson River Parkway in the Pelham Bay section of the Bronx. He had been stabbed several times in the chest and neck.
>
> Mr. Schwartz, who lived on Park Avenue in Manhattan, had registered under the name Lou Rathmayer.
>
> Mr. Schwartz was married and had three grown children. He had joined Cravath after graduating from the University of Virginia Law School. He became a partner in 1969.

What an extraordinary story, positively shouting with unanswered questions. It concerns a murder of a prominent person, and death is inherently dramatic. Yet note the flat, uninflected, style embraced by the *Times*—almost as if, in deference to the sensibilities of the victim's family, the paper wanted to suppress readers' curiosity. At the same time, the anonymous writer was clearly aware of the sensational aspects of the story and chose to highlight the most incongruous details.

From the first paragraph, it's obvious that something curious has happened. Many people, no doubt, were stabbed in the Bronx that year, but none of the others was "a partner in one of Manhattan's most prestigious law firms." What was such a person doing in a Bronx motel, and why was he stabbed?

This question highlights an issue often discussed in journalism classes: why is it "news" when an Ivy League student, an honor student, a partner in a law firm, to cite a few examples, is murdered, but not when a drug dealer is? The discussion inevitably turns to whether coverage of such events is racist or sexist or betrays class prejudice on the part of editors and writers. The answer, I believe, is far simpler, and rooted in human curiosity: murders of such people (or by them) are surprising. While our surprise as readers may in fact be rooted in stereotypes, it is also backed by evidence: most partners in upscale law firms do not become murder victims; for drug dealers, the risks are obvious. In any event, while writers, in my view, shouldn't reinforce stereotypes by pandering to a prejudice, it is futile to try to suppress readers' curiosity by ignoring them. Indeed, as we shall see, it is often the writer's task to heighten curiosity. Anything surprising is a potential story, and the more surprising the better.

Later in the *Times* story, we learn that the reporter has asked the obvious question about motive, but has no answer. The mystery deepens. Clearly, robbery is suspected, since we learn that "some" of the victim's personal effects were missing. Still, we have no explanation of what Mr. Schwartz was doing in a Bronx motel. Only in the last few paragraphs does the writer reveal the most suggestive details: this was a "transient" motel, located off a major highway; Mr. Schwartz had registered under an assumed name and was found at the unlikely hour of 1:30 A.M.; he was a resident of tony Park Avenue, which makes it even more mysterious that he was found in the Bronx. Finally, Mr. Schwartz was married and had three children, facts whose relevance isn't immediately apparent. There the story ends.

Asking questions about a news story usually involves speculating about the answers as well, drawing on our everyday knowledge of the world and our common sense. This doesn't mean that such speculation will turn out to be correct, but it is a good exercise in deciding whether certain questions, if pursued and answered, are likely to result in an interesting story. Read between the lines of the *Times* story. Most readers would know that "transient" motels are often used for sexual assignations. It is probably no accident that the writer included this fact in an otherwise very brief report. And if Mr. Schwartz was stabbed during such an encounter, what was the sex of his assailant? It is, of course, possible that a woman could stab a man "several times in the chest and neck," but is it likely? If the assailant was a man, the fact that Schwartz had a wife and three children takes on new significance. Is it possible that Mr. Schwartz was gay? Such questions lead to even more questions—always a sign of a good potential story.

I was among the people reading the story in the *Times* that morning, and all of these thoughts occurred to me. I do not scour the third page of the Metro section every day looking for obscure crime stories, but this one caught my attention for a particular reason: I knew David Schwartz, because I had worked as a lawyer at Cravath for three years. I never worked with him, and probably had exchanged only a few words with him, but I certainly remembered him, and my memory made the story all the more puzzling. He was hardworking and disheveled, and seemed socially ill at ease, with one exception: I vividly recall him and his wife as excellent ballroom dancers at the firm "prom" held every winter, and I could still picture them on the dance floor of the Pierre Hotel, he in his tuxedo, she in a flowing, full-skirted gown. It was frankly hard to picture him having any outside sex life at all, let alone arranging assignations at a Bronx motel. The idea that he might have been gay, or interested in having sex with another man under any circumstances, seemed ludicrous.

I called a friend of mine at Cravath that day. The firm's phone lines were, predictably, humming. He told me that the firm had issued a brief statement, and that the suspect was male. Raymond Childs, a young black male, was soon arrested and charged with the murder. This was dutifully reported in the *Times,* and more gleefully in the tabloids. Then the story quickly died, none of its incongruities having been explored, much less explained.

This, obviously, had all the elements of a fascinating story. Indeed, it's hard to think of a much more obvious example. So did I immediately propose the story and start work? No. I was busy talking about it, speculating about it, another sure sign that something is at least interesting. Yet I did nothing. Why?

Looking back on my reaction, I see that my failure to grasp the potential story was in part due to its first-person element. As I've mentioned before, it is often very difficult to recognize a story when you are in the midst of it. I knew David Schwartz, and I knew other people who knew him, so of course my curiosity was high. When I have a personal interest in something, my confidence that others would also be interested erodes, so I sometimes tend to miss those stories. But in this case, there were more fundamental, but quite common elements to my obtuseness. Basically, I wasn't entirely sure I wanted to pursue this story.

This lack of desire stemmed partly from my having worked at Cravath. I had an excellent experience there, I was grateful to the firm for educating me and paying me, and I liked many of my co-workers. In my first book, *The Partners,* about big law firms, one chapter was an unvarnished account of Cravath's intense and ultimately successful defense of IBM, one of its biggest clients. I had never worked on the IBM case or any other IBM matter, I was careful to use nothing that I had learned while in Cravath's employ, and the firm's partners cooperated in my research, allowing me to interview them. Given Cravath's success in the case, I always assumed the chapter would be viewed as positive from a PR perspective, though that was not my concern in writing it. Still, some of the anecdotes I included, such as the time a lawyer at the firm billed twenty-seven hours in a single day by flying to California, changing time zones, and working on the plane, were distinctly double-edged. Some lawyers at the firm felt I had betrayed them, and were furious with me (one has never spoken to me since). With that experience still in mind, I wasn't eager to revisit the place, this time in the context of a lurid murder.

Even more fundamentally, the whole subject made me squeamish. I was admittedly interested, but I didn't necessarily want to proclaim that to the world by writing about the matter. The very thought of calling Schwartz's widow and children made me almost physically sick. To probe a dead man's sex life and then share it with the public struck me as repugnant. It often surprises people when I say this, and I doubt many believe it, but like many writers I know, I am actually a rather shy person. I also grew up in a typical Midwestern family, where sex and religion were not discussed. Besides, I was worried about my reputation as a writer of "serious" nonfiction. Wasn't this kind of story better left to the tabloids? Although I was not consciously thinking along these lines at the time, such were the feelings that blocked my thinking of the Schwartz murder as a story.

So why, one might wonder, did I nonetheless find myself having an animated conversation about David Schwartz with Tina Brown the next time I dropped in at *The New Yorker*'s offices? It's obvious that on some level I *did* know that this was potentially a good story. As she often does, Tina had asked me what was going on, what were people I knew talking about, and I had told her about the murder. I knew she'd be interested. One of Brown's strengths as an editor—the greatest strength, I think, an editor can have—is her unabashed curiosity. She wasn't fazed by the subject matter. She wanted to know what had really happened— and she suggested I write that story for *The New Yorker.*

I didn't immediately agree, but I did think about it. I focused on the elements of the story—the crime, the unanswered questions, the seeming paradox—and recognized that the answers I sought probably lay in the personality of David Schwartz and the world he inhabited. He had obviously been a far more complicated and desperate man than anyone realized. I thought the resulting story didn't have to be lurid or sensational. In fact, how could the truth be any worse, or more embarrassing, than the speculations swirling among everyone who knew him? Someone was likely to write this story, and couldn't I handle it as responsibly as anyone? I decided to go ahead.

I experienced another attack of squeamishness when I met with Hillary Clinton, at her behest, before beginning work on *Blood Sport,* my book about Whitewater and the Clinton White House. The first lady's confidante, Susan Thomases, had approached me, saying the Clintons were interested in cooperating in a book that would get at the truth of all the scandals swirling around the presidency.

News of Paula Jones's allegations of sexual harassment had just broken, and I felt obliged to ask Mrs. Clinton whether she would be willing to have me investigate the matter. The very idea of such a question made me anxious. Here I was, on my first visit to the White House, meeting the first lady for the first time, and I was going to ask her about an alleged sexual impropriety by her husband? But I did, and Mrs. Clinton seemed unfazed. "Of course" I should investigate Paula Jones, she replied without any hesitation. "She's part of the right-wing conspiracy to destroy my husband." Then I thought I detected tears welling in her eyes. "You have no idea how humiliating it is for me to have to read these stories," she added.

Since then—and after I did, in fact, investigate the Paula
Jones case and find it far more complicated than I assume the
first lady did—I have often wondered about those tears. I am
sure they were genuine. But whether they flowed from hurt,
from a belief that her husband was incapable of the sexual behavior alleged, or from sheer frustration that her own will had been
unable to intimidate the Paula Joneses of the world, I cannot say.

I have come to recognize that my own aversion to a story or
a question is often a positive sign. Readers, in effect, pay writers
and journalists to ask the questions they themselves are too
squeamish to ask. I have also come to recognize that silence
about subjects "that dare not speak their names" perpetuates
ignorance and fear. Schwartz's patronage of a male prostitute
made him no less of a human being. And didn't my own fear of
talking to his family mirror society's prejudice and sense of taboo,
rather than my compassion? Was my reluctance to ask the first
lady about Paula Jones rooted in a belief that the subject was
irrelevant to my book? Or was it that on some level I wanted Mrs.
Clinton to like me, so I didn't want to offend her? I have often
had occasion to reflect on my reactions to these stories, and I
now urge my students to do the same whenever they recognize
similar signs in themselves. Like avid curiosity, reluctance is a
possible sign of a good story.

That doesn't mean caution should be thrown to the winds.
Recently, someone suggested I write a story about the religious
convictions of Whitewater independent counsel Kenneth Starr.
This person told me that Starr sometimes began staff meetings
by holding hands and praying, and had been spotted singing
hymns in his backyard. I asked what relevance this information,
if true, might have, and the person replied that Starr was on a
witch-hunt against the Clintons, inspired by religious zealotry. I
immediately felt reluctant. The reasoning, I suppose, was that
Starr was a religious conservative; religious conservatives are intolerant of sexual infidelity and hate Bill Clinton; and therefore
Kenneth Starr is improperly motivated by hatred of Bill Clinton
rather than allegiance to the truth.

As I ask my students to do, I held on to my reluctance and
tried to think about its source. The fact that Starr came from a
religious background (his father was a minister, and Starr himself
once sold Bibles door-to-door) was something I had reported in
Blood Sport as part of a portrait meant to emphasize how differ-

ent Starr's upbringing was from that of Bill Clinton. But I had encountered absolutely nothing in my reporting on Starr's conduct of the Whitewater and Lewinsky investigations to suggest that his religious background had anything to do with the decisions he was making as a prosecutor. Some of those decisions could be criticized on strategic grounds, and were, but the motivation for them was obvious and had nothing to do with religious zeal. I recognized that I was apprehensive about asking Starr his religious views because if he in turn asked how my questions were relevant, I had no good answer. I opted not to pursue the story, and not out of any personal fondness for Starr.

I don't cite any of these examples to prove that I have superior judgment in such matters, only to show my reasoning. The case could be argued that I shouldn't have done the Schwartz story, should have kept all references to sex out of *Blood Sport,* and should have pursued the Starr story. But too many writers and journalists flee from their emotions, and never stop to reason at all. Often writers fear the impact a story will have on its subject. This is perfectly appropriate, and I warn students that the day they stop having feelings about the subjects of their stories is the day they need an extended vacation from journalism. But our ultimate duty as writers is to our readers. To subjects I pledge to tell the truth, to be fair, to act in a way consistent with ethical standards. I do not, and cannot, promise they will like the story.

Consider the following news story, which ran in *The New York Times* on December 11, 1992.

It was September 1990, and Hollywood was about to be shaken by the news that the Matsushita Electric Industrial Company of Japan was buying MCA Inc., the entertainment industry giant, whose president was the blunt, bare-knuckled Sidney Sheinberg.

On the evening of Sept. 21, 1990, with the pending purchase still secret, Mr. Sheinberg's son, Jonathan, visited the family home and heard his father discussing the deal on the telephone. That overheard conversation formed the basis for civil insider-trading charges filed yesterday by the Securities and Exchange Commission against Jonathan Sheinberg, who is 34 years old, and three other men.

The scene in the Sheinberg home was detailed in documents filed in Federal District Court in Los Angeles by the S.E.C.'s regional office. The commission said that Sidney Sheinberg, after realizing that his son had overheard him, had sternly warned Jonathan not to trade in MCA stock or disclose what he heard to anyone else.

Nevertheless, the commission charged, Jonathan Sheinberg told at least three other people in the next 72 hours, and those three men quickly purchased MCA stock or options. When the deal became public later in the month, the stock soared from the mid-30s to nearly $60 a share. The S.E.C. calculates the three men's improper profits at $417,000.

The three men accused along with Jonathan Sheinberg were Richard G. Ursitti, his father-in-law; Richard E. Shephard, his business manager, and Barry C. Fogel, an acquaintance. The elder Mr. Sheinberg, who confirmed last year that the commission was examining trading in MCA stock, was not accused of any wrongdoing.

All four men named in the complaint agreed to settle the charges, with no admission or denial of guilt, by paying a total of $1.3 million in disgorged profits and insider-trading penalties. Of the penalties, $416,000 was assessed against Jonathan Sheinberg, although he did not personally trade on the information. Lawyers for all four men said their clients had settled to avoid the expense of a trial.

Celebrity status aside, the case is being parsed and puzzled over in legal circles, lawyers said yesterday.

The story went on to discuss legal issues in so-called "family-circle" insider-trading cases.

Crime has offered writers fertile ground for centuries, and not just because it is often a lurid and violent subject. Crime stories present themes of law, justice, order, and morality. They embody the inherent and constant conflict between the individual and society. To the extent that crime is aberrational, it helps define what is considered normal or acceptable. For these reasons, I often urge my students to consider writing crime stories.

The Sheinberg story immediately caught my attention. I have long been intrigued by insider-trading cases, and not just because I wrote *Den of Thieves,* about the Ivan Boesky case, which roiled Wall Street in the 1980s. In my view, insider trading is the perfect white-collar crime. It seems irresistibly tempting to otherwise

law-abiding people. Even more puzzling, its perpetrators tend to
be affluent. They don't need the illegal profits. So why do they
do it?

This curiosity about motive, not any inherent interest in the
stock market, largely drives my interest in insider trading. This is
an often frustrating element of insider-trading cases, since prosecutors are concerned only with proving the elements of the
crime; motive, however fascinating, is not always legally relevant.
Years ago, while a reporter at the *Journal,* I was assigned to cover
the trial of Foster Winans, a fellow *Journal* reporter accused of
leaking information slated to appear in his "Heard on the Street"
column to a stockbroker, who in turn earned illegal profits and
paid Winans for his information. For obvious reasons, this was an
extremely sensitive story for the *Journal.* I was told to cover it
as I would any other story, and I did so, though it was hard to
ignore the fact that my copy was sent each day to the chairman
of Dow Jones for review. (No changes were ever made.) I still
consider the Winans case to have all the elements of a great story,
but attending the trial each day was often frustrating, because
the prosecutors didn't ask the questions *I* wanted to ask. It was
all I could do to stop myself from jumping up and continuing the
questioning.

In reading the Sheinberg story, I was immediately struck by
the opportunity to explore the questions that most interest me
about insider trading, because the case posed those questions
starkly. Sidney Sheinberg, as the story makes clear, was one of
the most powerful and wealthy men in Hollywood; his son shared
in that wealth. Jonathan surely had no financial motive for what
he did; indeed, he himself didn't even trade on the information
or profit from it. The case had another interesting dimension.
The story reports that Jonathan's father warned him not to use
the confidential information he'd overheard. Yet he did, defying
his father's injunction. Why? What was the relationship between
Sidney and Jonathan? What, in other words, was Jonathan's motive?

These questions make clear another point I often make to
my students, which is that a good story idea is "about" many
things. On the surface, this story is about insider trading. But
is it really? I was relatively uninterested in much of the *Times*
story, which explored the implications of the case for insider-

trading law. To me, it was immediately apparent that the *really* complex, rich story would be about the Sheinberg family, the relationship between a rich and powerful father and a less well-known son, about family relationships in Hollywood, about an Oedipal conflict, and ultimately, about human nature. Indeed, I've come to believe that nearly every good story is ultimately about human nature—a subject that comes as close to any as being universally interesting. What the completed article might ultimately say about these far-flung subjects, of course, I did not know—which only added to the story's appeal, since it fueled my curiosity.

News stories often raise more questions than they answer, and the *Times* account is a textbook example. Note how the writer has used some very specific, colorful anecdotal detail: the reader is in the Sheinberg home; Jonathan overhears his father "discussing the deal on the telephone"; his father "sternly warned" him. The presence of such detail implies that the writer knows a great deal about the subject—yet not even the basic questions are answered, let alone more minor ones. What did the father actually say, both on the phone and to Jonathan? Such details as the *Times* article offered whet a reader's appetite, but hardly satisfy it.

The *Times* item illustrates another important point about good feature-story ideas: they are less time-bound than typical news stories. Indeed, for what is essentially a news story, this one begins with a distinctly "feature" lead: "It was September 1990 . . ." In other words, even when the *Times* article appeared, the events were two years old. Yet I was considering it as a possible inspiration for a story that would obviously be published even longer after the events in question.

When is a matter *too* old? That's not often an easy question to answer. But too often possibly good stories are dismissed because they didn't happen yesterday, or the day before, or last week or month. If the question is compelling enough—say, "What caused the Big Bang?"—the events can be as old as the universe itself. A good rule of thumb is that if there's still a mystery, there's still a story. On the other hand, some unanswered questions clearly lose their appeal as time passes and curiosity is dulled by the sweep of more recent or more important events. I like to illustrate the phenomenon with a graph:

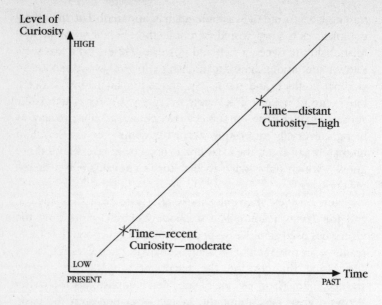

So freshness is an advantage, all else being equal. When I remain curious about events that happened some time in the past, I try to examine the source of my curiosity. If it is highly idiosyncratic, rooted in my own particular interests (e.g., why did my ancestors migrate from Scotland in the seventeenth century?), I tend to be skeptical. If it touches on broader themes (e.g., was Alger Hiss a Communist spy?) I'm enthusiastic. It's important to remember that exploring a still-unanswered question will almost always yield news, even if that news relates to events in the past. News is something we don't already know, not necessarily something that just happened.

In the Sheinberg case, I wasn't at all troubled that the events had happened several years earlier. Sidney Sheinberg was still a powerful figure in Hollywood, and his son was working there. If I could obtain answers to my questions, they would be fresh information. I recognized that not even people in Hollywood were desperate to know the details of the case; many had probably never heard of it. But, as I've already mentioned, my curiosity was rooted in broad questions about human nature, a subject that never becomes stale. Would the Sheinberg case stay fresh forever? Probably not. But I was confident I could still kindle reader interest for quite some time, because I was interested myself.

On August 2, 1994, the following story ran in *The Wall Street Journal:*

WHITTLE PULLS PLUG ON MEDICAL NETWORK, AMBITIOUS NEWS SERVICE IN DOCTOR OFFICES

By Patrick Reilly

Whittle Communications L.P. said it will shut down its Medical News Network, a costly interactive news and information service in doctors' offices.

The failure of the ambitious interactive service, which had been tested in 5,000 doctors' offices and was scheduled for a nationwide launch this fall, is another indication that Whittle Communications' founder and chairman, Christopher Whittle, is coming up short on raising the funds necessary to keep the company's media ventures alive. In the face of uncertainty over health-care policy, Whittle couldn't get major drug companies to sign long-term contracts to advertise on Medical News Network.

Whittle has already closed two media properties this year —Special Reports video and magazines for doctors' offices, and advertiser-sponsored books. Whittle is now said by people familiar with the talks to be negotiating the sale of about half of its interest in Channel One, the advertising-supported news program broadcast in 12,000 schools, to the merchant-banking arm of Goldman, Sachs & Co.

Now "Whittle, at this point, has really got only one platform, and that's Channel One, but that's it," said Michael Wolf. . . .

Whittle said yesterday it will focus on the education business, including Channel One and the Edison project. Edison, which is headed by Mr. Whittle but financially independent of Whittle's corporate operations, aims to run for-profit public schools and has already lined up schools in several cities to support its plan. There, too, however, Mr. Whittle is in need of new funds to support his ambitious plans beyond this year.

The story went on to detail, at considerable length, Whittle's recent business problems. In short, it was a typical well-reported business story, written in pyramid style. All the bases seem to have been covered, with no obvious questions.

What was my reaction to this piece? Surprise. I was very

surprised, though I knew next to nothing about the Medical News Network, nor was it something I was particularly interested in. Like curiosity and queasiness, surprise is an emotion that should be embraced and examined whenever it arises, for surprise contains the seeds of a story. The more surprising, the better. Why was I so surprised in this case? Chris Whittle had been the subject of immense publicity, nearly all of it flattering. The tale of how he and Philip Moffitt had come from the backwoods of Tennessee to rescue *Esquire* magazine and take Manhattan by storm had been told and retold, and it was a great success story. Even though the pair had broken up in what seemed an acrimonious parting, Whittle had launched numerous innovative ventures and continued to court the media. His charm, coupled with his revolutionary ideas, made him irresistible. Yet, without exactly saying so, the *Journal* story made it clear that the Whittle empire was rapidly collapsing. This conflict between expectation and reality is often at the root of surprise. It is also almost always the root of a story, because it gives rise to a very common question: How could someone like So-and-So fail? Surprise often spawns a question beginning with "how" or "why," and if it does, there may be a story.

In this case my surprise was heightened because I knew Chris Whittle slightly. When I first worked at *American Lawyer,* the magazine shared office space with *Esquire.* I was invited to *Esquire*'s fiftieth-anniversary party at Lincoln Center, which was in reality an extravagant tribute to Whittle and Moffitt's success. While at *The Wall Street Journal,* Whittle had been invited to lunch with the paper's top editors and the chairman of Dow Jones. Whittle was charming, as usual, but brash, ridiculing the way the *Journal* sold advertising and predicting the demise of traditional media in favor of his newer, advertiser-friendly publications. He seemed cocky. I could see why he had a reputation as a legendary salesman. He had some people around the table nodding in agreement even as he insulted them and scoffed at the notion of editorial integrity deeply ingrained in the *Journal* culture.

I was also familiar with and intrigued by another aspect of Whittle's life, though it didn't involve me personally. I knew he had a keen interest in architecture and design, and I had seen magazine photos of his extravagant Dakota apartment, designed by the interior decorator and architect Peter Marino. He had no sooner completed that apartment than he bought a newer and larger one, launching another renovation and decoration. He had a spread in East Hampton, Long Island, and he had commissioned Marino to build a lavish headquarters for Whittle Communications in Whittle's hometown of Knoxville, Tennessee. These were more than the usual accoutrements of success. Whittle lived on a scale that was both romantic and extravagant. What drove him to such lengths of connoisseurship and consumption? How would his love of luxury be affected by his recent setbacks? Had it contributed to them? In other words, I sensed in Whittle broader, universal themes of—again—human nature.

I hasten to say that I bore Chris Whittle no personal animus. If anything, I liked him. While I didn't share his views about editorial integrity, I admired his grandiose ideas and his courage, even foolhardiness, in pursuing them. I admired his energy and his drive. I thought he had good taste. Having grown up in a small city in a rural area myself, I suspected Whittle and I were alike in many ways. But none of those feelings were very strong; if they had been, I might have hesitated to pursue the story.

Thinking of this story in terms of Chris Whittle's personality made a huge difference, for it was no longer just a business story but a tale of personal success and failure. I sensed that if I could understand what had happened to Whittle, readers would learn something they could easily relate to in their own lives. This is one of the reasons, I believe, that biography has always been so popular. People want to know why someone else succeeds or fails, even if they aren't inherently interested in what that someone has done.

To illustrate the role that surprise often plays in story ideas, consider this item, also from *The Wall Street Journal:*

WORKPLACE: AT CHRYSLER, DEBATE GROWS ON GAY RIGHTS

By Nichole M. Christian

While attention is focused on General Motors Corp.'s labor negotiations, Chrysler Corp. is facing allegations from some workers that it is antigay.

The No. 3 U.S. auto maker has come under fire from gay and lesbian employees over its recent refusal to include the words "sexual orientation" in its antidiscrimination policy. General Motors added such language to its antidiscrimination policy years ago. But Ford Motor Co., like Chrysler, said it hasn't done so because it feels its antidiscrimination policy covers everyone. . . .

The story went on to discuss the issue at other companies, then returned to Chrysler:

Even with the contract talks now concluded, Chrysler's failure to adopt the nondiscrimination language has ignited the gay community. A few workers picket at different times each day outside Chrysler's sprawling headquarters in Auburn Hills, Mich., and some of them show up at Chrysler dealers from time to time . . .

The reporter then briefly quoted two gay Chrysler workers, one a tool-and-die maker, the other an electrician.

It's interesting to consider how *Journal* editors must have struggled with this story. It ran in the "B" section of the paper and, lacking an obvious news peg, it was tucked into the paper's "Workplace" column. Even so, the article's first words are about the now long-forgotten GM talks presumably taking place at the time; whatever was happening at Chrysler had been going on for a while and hadn't reached any obvious resolution. The traditional news format invariably has trouble conveying this kind of story, since it lacks the "news" that can be summarized in one or two sentences. I'm sure the eyes of most readers glided right over this item, and that it didn't make much of an impression.

So what caught my attention? Not the lengthy discussion of how companies are or are not codifying nondiscrimination policies toward gays and lesbians—that's the kind of subject I consider a topic rather than a story. The notion that well-educated white-collar employees at, say, IBM, were organizing for gay rights wouldn't have come as any surprise. But blue-collar workers, in the auto industry? I was surprised.

I readily admit that this feeling was rooted in stereotypes, both of gay and lesbian workers and of the auto industry. I've been interested in cars since I was a kid, and used to keep scrapbooks of the new models I clipped out of ads every fall. As Page

One editor of the *Journal*, I made a point of visiting Detroit each January for the North American auto show, which I both enjoyed and found to be a fertile source of story ideas. I got to be friendly with a few high-ranking auto executives. So I was reasonably familiar with the culture of the auto industry, and I have to say it's one of the most macho, for want of a better word, I've ever encountered. If anyone I met on any of those visits was gay, he or she did a good job of concealing it. So when I read the *Journal* article, I was doubly surprised: first, that there were gay workers on the assembly line; second, that they were willing to identify themselves as gay, even willing to picket outside Chrysler's headquarters.

However hard we try to free ourselves from stereotypes, we inevitably absorb them, or are at least aware of them. I believe this can be a virtue in thinking of story ideas: when we respond with surprise to facts that defy stereotypes, we have an opportunity to explore those stereotypes and perhaps debunk them. As Page One editor of the Journal, I heard regularly from an organization at the journalism school of the University of Missouri that annually graded national publications on the degree to which its articles perpetuated racist, sexist, homophobic (etc.) stereotypes. This group purported to analyze the stories by counting how many were about blacks, Hispanics, gays, and so on, and then deciding whether they were "favorable" or not. I got a failing grade every year. I was always bewildered by this exercise, though I had no objection to such groups evaluating our performance on the basis of whatever criteria they chose. I remember the group was especially incensed at a front page story we ran about a black contractor in New Orleans who was convicted of substantial fraud, arguing that this portrayed a black person in a negative light. That this might perpetuate a stereotype had never occurred to me, but when I thought about the matter, it struck me that I would have been patronizing not to run such a story. Shouldn't all potential subjects be held to the same standards of interest and newsworthiness?

In any event, the Chrysler story not only surprised me but also triggered a bit of squeamishness. Homosexuality still wasn't a subject of polite conversation in Detroit, and I knew it would cause embarrassment to bring up the subject with auto executives. As I later learned firsthand, some executives even had trouble saying the word "gay." So the story idea had this going for it as well.

I sometimes tell my students that I can sometimes sense that a story proposal's good just by hearing a sentence fragment. In this case, when asked what story I was working on, all I had to say was "Gay auto workers."

As I hope even these few examples make clear, to recognize a good story idea requires self-awareness. In my experience, most people are uncomfortable with most of their emotions, and are happy to push them aside and forget about them. Writers need to embrace their feelings and study the origins of them within themselves. Surprise, shock, outrage, anger, disgust, squeamishness, embarrassment, nervousness, anxiety—all are signals that a story may be at hand. This kind of self-analysis takes practice. But eventually it becomes second nature. It's also interesting. Otherwise unpleasant feelings can be recognized for their potential as inspiration.

3
PROPOSALS

Nearly every good story idea begins as a question. But some ideas are better than others. Most good writers have more ideas than they have time to turn into stories. So how does one discriminate among them? More practically, how does a writer persuade an editor to commission a story when the writer has nothing more to show than an idea?

In shaping a proposal, I find it helpful to place my idea into one or more categories. In my years of writing and editing, I've discovered that six broad categories account for a large percentage of all published non-news stories. It isn't necessary to explicitly label an idea as falling into one of these categories, but it's often helpful, and I've found that most editors at least subliminally respond to proposals that promise a kind of story with which they are familiar, and which has proven successful. (As I'll demonstrate later, these categories also help dictate a story's structure.) Categorization is nothing more than an analytical tool: obviously, the world of stories isn't so simple or scientific, and many good stories embrace more than one category.

The first three, which are both more common and generally easier to report and write than the others, are the trend, the explanation, and the profile. Any one is a good place for new and unpublished writers to begin.

THE TREND

This is a staple of nonfiction writing; there seems to be an inexhaustible demand for trend stories from newspapers, magazines, and even book publishers. What is a trend? My dictionary defines it as "a vogue, or current style, as in fashions." In other words, the essence of a trend is multiplicity.

Trend stories often have a simplicity that makes them easy to conceive, execute, and read, for the question that prompts a trend story is almost always a variation on the same theme: Are others doing X? Is X happening to other people? I have already mentioned that with the best story ideas, it doesn't matter what the answer to a question is. This rule rarely applies to the trend story; if the answer is no, there is no trend. But it should come as no surprise that the answer is rarely no. If one person is doing or experiencing something, there is almost always someone else in the same or similar circumstances.

On some days, it strikes me that fully half the stories I see featured on the front pages of major newspapers are trend stories. Why are they so popular? Why are people so willing to read them? My theory is that because we are inherently social creatures, however interesting or odd we find a single occurrence of something, we only relate to it if we recognize that others are subject to it as well. We then ask ourselves: Should I be doing this—or not doing it? Why are so many others doing it? Some trend stories comfort readers by describing something they may have experienced or witnessed themselves, but never thought of as a trend. Or a single occurrence of something may seem commonplace, but the existence of numerous examples is startling. In that case, the trend story functions much like a news story: the element of multiplicity is itself news, prompting surprise and related questions. One of the most memorable examples I recall was a *Newsweek* article saying that the likelihood of a single woman over forty getting married was less than the likelihood she would be killed by a terrorist. Obviously, a single instance of a woman over forty failing to find a spouse would not be noteworthy, but the trend, especially when stated in such extreme terms, created a furor. (The statistics on which that story was based, by the way, turned out to be defective, a point eloquently expressed by Susan Faludi in her best-selling book

Backlash.) Here is a random sample of trend stories I recently spotted in a single week's worth of *The New York Times:* (1) people are eating more fat; (2) more young people are sporting goatees; (3) rap lyrics are increasingly glorifying murder and other violence; (4) more people are having unsafe sex. Examples 1 and 2 prompted me to wonder how much fat I'm eating (not too much) and whether I should grow a goatee (no). Examples 3 and 4 both struck me as news stories. My reaction was surprise and dismay.

Certain topics seem to lend themselves to trend stories, fashion and style being the most obvious. But I see a plethora of trend stories on religious beliefs and practices; on business and economics; on politics. All the social sciences, in fact, seem to lend themselves to trend stories.

Spotting the trend story is not as easy as it might seem, and speed is important: being the second person to tell a trend story is inherently dull. Trend stories are often staring us in the face, yet we fail to recognize them. How many times have you read a trend story and said to yourself, "Of course"? Our own observations tend to be limited geographically, and by the time we see multiple examples of something in our own neighborhood, chances are it's too late to be the one who spots the trend. In any event, waiting for confirmation that something is a trend violates my experience that good stories begin with unanswered questions. The best trend stories are uncovered by writers who, wondering or suspecting that something might be a trend, try to find out.

Writers and reporters have often asked me how many examples of something are required to classify something as a trend. To this question there is no simple answer, but by and large, it is a function of how startling a single instance of something is. The more startling, the fewer examples are needed. A year or so ago there was a spate of trend stories about female genital mutilation. The idea that such a thing was happening in the modern age was inherently startling, but I noticed a distinct lack of example, when coverage inevitably shifted from Africa to Africans living in North America. I recently noticed a front-page story in *The Wall Street Journal* suggesting that passengers were increasingly having sex on commercial airliners. But a close reading showed a paucity of examples, and even those were hearsay accounts from stewardesses. For a reader, it is sometimes easy to be cynical about trend stories, for if the subject is sufficiently bizarre or sensational, even two examples seem to constitute a trend. I would urge writers to avoid the glibness so characteristic of this genre, and instead to concentrate on the vivid storytelling I explore throughout this book. It is often a mistake, in my experience, to proclaim a trend; it can be far more convincing simply to explore the possibility of a trend's existence.

THE PROFILE

If the trend story has a rival for ubiquitousness, it is the profile. What is the almost universal appeal of the profile? I believe it's quite simple: More than any other category of story, the profile engages our inborn curiosity in our fellows. The profile's appeal mirrors that of biography. We are all interested in human nature, even if we aren't interested in the profile's subject per se. Consequently, profiles cover a surprisingly wide range. I have written profiles of people who are very well-known, somewhat well-known, and not well-known at all.

Celebrities, of course, account for an immense amount of coverage. I will touch only briefly on the celebrity interviews that dominate magazine covers, most of which might just as well have been written by the star's press agent for all the insight they provide. I'm told that extensive negotiations typically precede such interviews, with every detail, from photographs to editorial content, worked out. When *Esquire* magazine ran a cover profile of Kevin Spacey, a star of *L.A. Confidential,* that evidently contained material that offended the actor, his agent at William Morris ordered his colleagues to reject any request by *Esquire* to interview the powerful agency's other clients. *Esquire* apologized. And Spacey, however appealing as an actor, wasn't even a first-tier star at the time. Imagine the reaction if the subject had been Tom Cruise. Such sorry episodes suggest to me that celebrity journalism is rarely journalism.

Nonetheless, the appeal of the celebrity profile is easy to understand, and it suggests some useful lessons. People are naturally curious about people they know, or feel they know. In the much-touted global village, there are a finite number of famous people at any given moment, and the rest of us are as interested in reading about them as we are in gossiping about our neighbors. This interest is still driven by curiosity, but the curiosity is enhanced by familiarity. One of the questions underlying our interest is "What is So-and-So really like?"

Hollywood celebrities are a poor example of the genre because they exist as much in fantasy as in reality, given that they are visible primarily as fictional characters. They are important more as images, as symbols, than as people who wield power and influence and therefore warrant investigative profiles. (There are exceptions, of course, such as John Travolta in his attempt to influence government policy toward the Church of Scientology.) People may want to know what stars are really like; then again, they may only want the illusion of knowing. This may be why very few serious profiles of actors and actresses are written.

Still, the public's interest in "stars" mirrors their interest in other well-known people. This is especially true with respect to people who have a vested interest in creating a false or highly selective persona for personal gain—politicians, for example. While this can be fertile terrain for an investigative approach, the result doesn't need to be sensational or scandalous to be effective. If the answer to the question turns out to be that someone is, in fact, very much like his or her image, the resulting article can be just as satisfying as long as the underlying curiosity can be evoked. There were numerous flattering profiles of Secretary of State Madeleine Albright, for example, after she revealed her discovery that her family heritage was Jewish.

Any well-known person can be a legitimate subject for a profile, but the appeal of the story is significantly enhanced if public curiosity has been heightened by a recent event, as in Albright's case. Here, the inherent curiosity to know someone better is intensified by questions about how the person will react to a particular event. With respect to Albright, in addition to wanting to know more about a recently appointed secretary of state, readers were probably even more curious about how she reacted to the discovery that she was Jewish. In this respect, the curiosity is rooted in the public's interest in human nature, which is far broader than its interest in diplomacy. All of us can imagine the shock of discovering we are not quite the person we thought we were.

Any event that disrupts the status quo will heighten curiosity about someone who is affected. Such events trigger inevitable questions: How will the person react? How will equilibrium be restored? Any dramatic incident triggers a simple narrative question: What happened next? For these reasons, I tend to wait to profile people until a sufficiently dramatic incident has affected their lives. It's true that by then, other publications have done profiles of the same people. But these pieces are usually dutiful, and often quickly forgotten. While I was covering Wall Street for *The Wall Street Journal*, I had numerous chances to profile Martin Siegel, who was the head of mergers and acquisitions at Drexel Burnham Lambert when the firm was at the height of its powers. But I waited, and eventually he was served with a subpoena in the Ivan Boesky insider-trading case, an incident that turned his world upside down. That's when I decided to propose a front-page profile. Of course, I had had no idea such a thing would happen to Siegel, and it is an unusually dramatic example. Still, I knew that sooner or later something would happen to someone as prominent, visible, and wealthy as he. Patience is often rewarded, even though we usually have a knee-jerk impulse to be first.

Another example, one I mentioned in the last chapter, is Chris Whittle. He had been covered in many profiles. Yet he became a subject of much greater interest once his business empire began to falter. I often adopted this approach as Page One editor, sometimes to the dismay of reporters. Confronted with a serviceable but uninspired profile of one business or political figure or another, I'd suggest we hold it until something interesting happened to the subject of the piece. Angry as reporters and editors sometimes were, something interesting almost always did happen eventually, and when the story ran, more people read and remembered it.

Recent news events affecting a person have the added advantage of raising that person's visibility and recognition, sometimes dramatically so. Who had heard of Monica Lewinsky before the sex-in-the-Oval-Office scandal broke, let alone such subsidiary characters as her confidante, Linda Tripp, or the literary agent Lucianne Goldberg? Yet all now became the subject of numerous profiles. Depending on the magnitude of an event, virtually anyone connected to it is a potential subject, the O. J. Simpson case being the most extreme, even absurd, example. These people need not be particularly well-known, as long as they play some role in events that are in the news. In these instances curiosity doesn't take the form of wondering what the person is really like, since most readers have no preconceptions. They simply want to know who these people are and what they've experienced.

Indeed, many, many profiles are published about people who are unknown. This is the premise of the "witness to history" story idea I mentioned in chapter 2. A major news event, whether it's the pro-democracy stand-off in Tiananmen Square, the fall of the Berlin Wall, the Gulf War, or the end of apartheid, involves people whose experiences make compelling stories. Again, it is essential that the events in question have an impact on their lives. I recall that when the Wall fell the *Journal* didn't have a reporter in Berlin, so we dispatched a European *Wall Street Journal* reporter based in Bonn. I had never worked with him and wasn't familiar with either his writing or reporting. But I liked an idea he had, which was to accompany an elderly couple on their first visit to their former home in East Berlin. Despite what I said earlier about such on-the-spot situations rarely yielding material of interest, this was an exception: the couple were not media-savvy people seeking publicity; they were unlikely to perform for the benefit of a reporter; and the situation was so inherently dramatic that I was confident it would yield a poignant story. No one had ever heard of these people. Indeed, their very ordinariness made them appealing.

So the reporter joined the couple on their trip, and I came into the office on a Sunday morning to read the resulting story. It was all that I had hoped for, at least as far as I got. Weaving in their past experiences, the reporter followed the couple from their home in West Berlin as far as the center of a bridge that had once demarcated the division between East and West. I called to find out when I could expect the rest of the story. "That *is* the rest," the reporter said, causing me near apoplexy. He explained that he'd had to rush back to file the piece in time for our deadline. I don't recall exactly what I said, but it was something to the effect that I didn't care if he had to tie them up and drag them back to their former home. I wasn't serious, of course, and in any event drastic steps proved unnecessary. The reporter was still able to join them for the last stage of their stroll, witness the tearful reunion, and complete an extremely charming and moving profile of the couple. I don't think anyone noticed that there was something of a gap in the narrative.

More often, unknown or little-known people make good profiles when they embody some issue or trend of interest, or when they provide a specific and dramatic example of a broader phenomenon. The story I mentioned earlier about the father whose son contracted AIDS is an example, as are the accountant in Pennsylvania who was fired for being gay, and the financially struggling novelist. In another instance, *Journal* reporter Joanne Lipman wrote a brilliant profile of a young financial whiz who had flattered and charmed his clients, then used them to advance to wealthy and more powerful benefactors. This story might have been just another profile of a successful young Wall Street tycoon, except that Joanne shrewdly focused on the most enthralling element in his success: his ability to suck up. The story was called "The Climber," and it was immensely popular with everyone but its subject. All Joanne had to say to sell me on it was that title. Everyone knows a climber, but rarely are such a character's ambition, methods, and insincerity dissected so thoroughly. (The nasty on-the-record comments by discarded mentors enlivened the piece considerably.)

I once wrote a piece for the *Journal* about a young lawyer who was a landlord's nightmare, withholding rent and suing at the drop of a hat—in one instance, over an allegedly chipped soap dish. He was all the explanation needed for a broader phenomenon: landlords were increasingly reluctant to rent to lawyers because they were so litigious.

In these two examples, the subjects were very unhappy with the stories. But both Joanne and I stressed to the unhappy participants that as long as the stories were accurate, we couldn't be responsible for how they were perceived by readers. Indeed, I suspected—and subsequent letters confirmed—that many readers were favorably impressed with the drive and tenacity the stories' subjects displayed. Still, when people I've written about to illustrate a broader trend ask me why I chose them, I often don't have an answer they find satisfying. I could probably have found many other people to illustrate the same point, but I didn't. For this reason I try to suggest to people, especially those who aren't sophisticated about the media, what the impact might be on their lives before they agree to be the subject of a major story. At a minimum they are likely to lose a fair amount of privacy, for at least a brief time. Sometimes a crush of media people, especially television reporters, descends upon them. But nothing I say can fully prepare them, and no one has ever refused anyway after I've given my rundown. On the contrary, quite a few people have asked me if I think they might get a movie deal, and however much I try to make clear how unlikely that is, they seem disappointed when none materializes.

THE EXPLANATORY STORY

I mentioned in the last chapter that whenever news triggers surprise or disbelief, writers should react by asking questions. The result generally falls into the category of the explanatory story, one that answers the question "How could that have happened?" or "Why did that happen?" For the explanation of an event can often be more interesting than the event itself.

Several of the story ideas I mentioned in the last chapter fall into this category: the cable-car crash and the puzzling level of business confidence, for example. Paradox and mystery are the essence of the explanatory story—the more paradox and mystery the better, for they generate curiosity in readers. The explanatory story need not solve the mystery or resolve the paradox, as long as it brings all available evidence to bear on it.

The possibilities in this category are virtually limitless. Any news event whose causes are not self-evident is a candidate. So is any development that defies predictive models and expectations, or anything that defies conventional wisdom. As I write this, for example, there has been a spate of stories in magazines and newspapers exploring the paradox of Bill Clinton's continued strong poll ratings despite repeated allegations of crude sexual infidelities. None that I've read has offered a convincing explanation. Yet I keep reading them with interest.

I mentioned that stories often fall into more than one category, and this seems particularly true of explanatory pieces. The profile of the novelist Jim Wilcox, for example, was also meant to explain the seeming anomaly that a highly acclaimed novelist would be living in near poverty. The Whittle profile was intended to explain the decline of his business empire. To the extent that trend stories are surprising, they, too, try to explain the paradox that triggers the surprise.

THE POINT-OF-VIEW STORY

Any article that advocates a belief or opinion can be characterized as a point-of-view story. While this definition can encompass everything from editorials and polemics to far more subtle "news analyses," I tend to use the category for stories in which a point of view arises naturally and inevitably from the presentation of facts. While virtually every story gives rise to *some* point of view, I reserve the category for stories whose point of view is their primary reason for being. In both respects, I take a far narrower view than do many writers, some of whom have made careers out of nothing more than expressing their own point of view on a myriad of topics.

I hasten to say that many great works have been polemics, from *Uncle Tom's Cabin* to *Silent Spring*. Many such books and articles are published. But I find most of them tedious, and am at a loss to explain why some touch a nerve and vault to prominence and popularity, while others go largely unread and are soon forgotten.

Perhaps that's because I classify myself more as a "fact" person rather than an "ideology" person. I find, generally, that the world's population can be divided along these lines, which run very deep in the human character. Fact people want to know where the truth lies before forming an opinion or judgment. Ideology people, conversely, tend to hold strong opinions and judgments and seek facts to confirm them. Fact people tend to be far less predictable, since their views derive from ever-changing facts, and less judgmental, since they are accustomed to waiting before forming opinions. They tend to be more open to new experiences, more comfortable with change and uncertainty, and more willing to embrace contradiction and complexity. They are often, by nature, agnostic. Many scientists are fact people.

Ideology people tend to reason from a fixed set of principles;

they prefer order and certainty, are capable of ignoring or ratio-
nalizing conflicting information, are comfortable with the notion
of faith, and are willing to believe in something before it can be
proven. While each category of people no doubt believe their
view of the universe is better for mankind as a whole, they take
a dim, and sometimes surprisingly hostile, view of the other. I
have heard some ideology people denounce fact people as weak,
amoral, and lacking backbone. Fact people, in turn, can be
equally intolerant of what they perceive as stupidity, blindness,
hypocrisy, and a primitive need for myth on the part of ideology
people. Most of us, of course, display aspects of both personali-
ties, depending on the circumstances.

Ideological writers, in my experience, are destined for disappointment unless they confine their work to like-minded editorial
pages, editors, and publishers, because the truth has a way of
confounding their expectations. A recent case in point is David
Brock, who came to prominence as the conservative author of
The Real Anita Hill, an attack on the credibility and character of
the woman who accused Clarence Thomas, then a nominee to
the Supreme Court, of sexual improprieties in the workplace.
Brock, a writer for the conservative *American Spectator* magazine, went on to produce an account of then-governor Bill Clinton's sexual infidelities in Arkansas, based on interviews with a
group of state troopers who worked for Clinton. The story set in
motion the Paula Jones lawsuit against the president and, in turn,
the Monica Lewinsky investigation. But the conservatives who
he thought were his friends, who had lionized him for his stand
on Anita Hill, abandoned him after he wrote a book about Hillary
Clinton which in many ways came to the first lady's defense.
Then Brock went even further, publicly apologizing in *Esquire*
magazine for writing the trooper story. Now Brock has new
friends in the White House, who will no doubt prove as fickle as
his former friends on the right.

By no means do I disparage the power of ideological writing,
which can be immense. During the nearly ten years I worked at
The Wall Street Journal, I often watched my colleagues on the
editorial page with awe and admiration, even though I differed
strongly from time to time with the views they embraced. They
were consistent, persistent, and courageous—all qualities that
fact-oriented writers would do well to emulate. When the truth

conformed to their ideology, they were fearless in pursuing it, even at the cost of ridicule. In the area of economic policy, their impact on U.S. and global capitalism has been profound and underappreciated.

That said, they also displayed some of the qualities that drive fact people crazy. They ignored contradictory evidence. They rarely, and then only grudgingly, conceded error. They could never accept my view of Michael Milken—a self-acknowledged felon and monopolist—whom they saw exclusively as a hero of free-market capitalism. Having thus categorized me as some kind of "liberal," they seemed quite baffled by my subsequent investigation of the Whitewater scandal, which lent credence to much —though by no means all—of what the *Journal*'s editorial writers had been saying about Bill Clinton.

In any event, I find that the successful point-of-view story tends to be subtle in its approach. I recall from my college psychology classes that people remember their own conclusions far better than what they are told, and I try to use this insight in my own writing. As I've said repeatedly, good stories begin with questions, and that's just as true for the point-of-view story as for any other. The question is usually "How should I feel about this?" or "What should my reaction be?" It might also be "How important or significant is this?" or "What are the implications?"

While point-of-view stories often have ideological underpinnings, they often do not. The reaction triggered in the reader may be shock, outrage, or concern, caused by injustice, negligence, or wrongdoing, all of them nonpartisan in nature. Point-of-view stories can also describe intellectual debates and conflict, which may or may not have ideological underpinnings. One of my favorite series while I was Page One editor of the *Journal* was called "Thinkers Who Shaped the 20th Century." Reporters reexamined the teachings and writings of Marx, Freud, and Einstein to see how their work had influenced our times and how their theories had held up in the academic community. As with many good story ideas, we didn't know the answers before we started, but had I guessed, I would have said that Marx was thoroughly discredited, Freud was flourishing, and Einstein had been eclipsed. Almost exactly the opposite turned out to be true. Despite the collapse of Communism, Marx still commands great respect and has had enormous influence on modern capitalism;

Freud has been largely discredited, though his legacy is important; and Einstein's theories have fared best of all. So the stories had the added virtue of surprise. To judge by the letters we received from readers, the series generated immense interest.

THE INVESTIGATIVE STORY

As the name implies, the investigative story turns the reporter into an investigator, someone who, according to my dictionary, undertakes "a detailed inquiry or systematic examination." As the definition's use of the word "inquiry" makes clear, the investigative piece makes explicit what is usually implicit: it begins with a question. "What caused the cable-car crash?" might trigger an investigative piece. So might "Who shot down Korean Air flight 007?" or "Did President Clinton tell the truth in his Paula Jones deposition?" The fruits of such inquiries form the substance of the investigative story.

Steve Brill used to argue that the phrase "investigative reporter" is redundant, and, of course, he was right. Reporters should be investigating things all the time; they should always be skeptical. But the category has come to be used for stories in which what is being investigated includes at least the possibility that wrongdoing will be found; as a result, the reporter assumes something of the role of a prosecutor, bearing in mind that prosecutors may exonerate their suspects as well as bring charges. In situations that don't include the possibility of wrongdoing, the investigative piece is probably better categorized as explanatory.

Probably no other category of writer has given rise to as much romantic imagery as that of the investigative reporter. Investigative reporters are loners; they engage in clandestine operations to gather information; they are secretive; they are willing to put their own lives at risk; they wear trench coats. Seymour Hersh and Jeff Gerth come to mind. Or they may be young, idealistic, headstrong, willing to tilt at power and authority. Think Bob Woodward and Carl Bernstein in *All the President's Men*. In my own experience, there is a kind of writer who gravitates to investigative work, though the image they project may be far less romantic. These writers are not only skeptical; they are passionate in their belief that things are seldom what they seem. They are willing to entertain seemingly preposterous explanations for puzzling events—and, lo and behold, they sometimes turn out to be right. They may not be conspiracy theorists themselves, but they are comfortable with people who are, and take them seriously. They are courageous, indifferent to the opinions of others, self-motivated, highly principled, and some of the most difficult people to edit I have encountered. When they write a great story, I forgive them everything.

Investigative reporters are not often known as prose stylists, in part because the fruits of an investigation are often written as a news story. As we shall see, that need not be the case. Investigative work is often inherently dramatic, which should be captured in the resulting story. But it's true that a successful investigation almost always produces news, sometimes news that is quite significant. The successful investigative story packs a double appeal to readers: it engages their curiosity and surprises them with the results.

Even when the personal pronoun "I" is never employed, the reporter often emerges as a character in the investigative piece. A hallmark of the genre is the reporter's confrontation of the accused with hard-hitting questions. Television has given such confrontations a bad name with an ambush approach that startles but gives the subject little opportunity to respond. Ambushes not only seem unfair but also deprive viewers of a kind of interview that I've found is often fascinating and revealing.

It sometimes takes reporters years to become comfortable with asking difficult questions—and beginners sometimes indulge in the potentially fatal step of failing to conduct a confrontational interview at all—because to do so flies in the face of everything we've been raised to believe about politeness and social discourse. Perhaps that's why readers seem to so enjoy the process vicariously. And in any event, it helps to think about the interview as less a confrontation than an opportunity, both for the subject and the writer. I cannot emphasize enough how many times I have felt there could be no explanation for the facts I had uncovered, and the subject has produced one. Invariably, such interviews enrich a piece dramatically.

The potential subjects of investigative pieces are legion, and they have the virtue of not needing to be in the news already, since an investigative effort usually generates its own news. I have often told reporters and my students to look for a person or institution with three qualities: wealth, power, secretiveness. The questions are obvious: "What have they done to generate such wealth?" "How did they gain their power, and how do they wield it?" and "Do they have something to hide? If not, why are they so secretive?" From this angle, secretiveness can be seen as a virtue. Writers are often deterred by someone who won't talk, yet closemouthedness should be a signal of something worth discovering. As we will see, what people do say is often far more surprising than what they don't.

I believe every writer should attempt an investigative piece at some point in his or her career. There is simply no experience that compares in terms of developing reporting skills, learning to be accurate, handling the consequences of one's work, mustering one's courage. Rich, powerful, and secretive subjects have the resources to challenge your work if they don't like the results. They can hire lawyers and publicists; they can advertise; they have access to powerful people in the media. (At one point, Michael Milken was spending $3 million *a month* on lawyers and publicity.) In short, they can fight back.

I will never forget one of my first investigative pieces for *The Wall Street Journal.* I was covering the law beat, and I wrote an article about how many law professors were supplementing their teaching with lucrative outside work, sometimes at the expense of their classes. My lead example was Harvard's Alan Dershowitz, then well-known but not yet the celebrity he would soon become. He was absent and working on the Claus von Bülow case, his students told me, while a tape recording of a police interview played in his criminal law class. I asked Dershowitz about this and included his denial in my story.

The day the piece ran, the managing editor called to report that Dershowitz was furious. Dershowitz was so insistent that the piece was inaccurate and that I had misquoted him that I was left with the impression that he might have taped my telephone interview with him. He demanded a meeting and said he would fly down from Boston for it. The meeting, duly scheduled for the next day, was to include not only Norm Pearlstine, the managing editor, but also the *Journal*'s publisher, Peter Kann. It was perfectly clear to me that my job and reputation were on the line. I checked and rechecked my notes. They were accurately reflected in the story, it seemed to me, but how could I say for sure? What if Dershowitz had tape-recorded my call to him, as some interview subjects do, and the tape somehow showed that the quotations were not completely accurate? I researched the legality of one-party taping and learned that it was illegal in Massachusetts, though not in New York. (I remembered this research when I first heard about Linda Tripp taping Monica Lewinsky, and knew that the law in such cases is very unclear.) But that would be scant comfort if a tape proved me wrong.

The morning of the meeting arrived. I wish I could say I was serenely self-confident, but I hadn't slept the night before, nor had I been able to eat any breakfast. When I entered the conference room there was no sign of Dershowitz. Blaming the bad weather, he had stayed in Cambridge and arranged a conference call. Once he was on the phone, Norm Pearlstine immediately demanded to know what was inaccurate. Dershowitz attacked the fairness and accuracy of my story, but he didn't claim that he was misquoted. I was so relieved that I remember little else about the call. I'm sorry to say that this was not my last encounter with Dershowitz, but I emerged from the experience tougher and better prepared for the kind of controversy that almost always accompanies successful investigative writing. For that, I suppose, I have Alan Dershowitz to thank.

The Narrative

The narrative is what we usually mean by the word "story." A narrative has a beginning, middle, and end. It is organized chronologically, though not necessarily strictly so. One of the most useful and simplest pieces of advice about writing I ever received was the time-honored adage "Show, don't tell." The narrative shows readers what happened, often in vivid detail. Of all the forms of writing, it is the one that strives to re-create reality for the reader.

I find the narrative to be the most challenging and satisfying kind of writing by far. Perhaps this is because, within the confines of nonfiction, it draws upon the skills of the novelist. It calls upon the writer to develop characters, set scenes, structure and pace plot, establish point of view, write dialogue, even develop symbols and metaphors. Because it creates a world and invites readers to enter, as if the experiences described were the readers' own, it can be the most memorable kind of story. Humankind has traditionally passed on its collective wisdom and knowledge in the form of narratives, be they cave paintings or the Bible. The comments I receive from readers, sometimes years after a story has run, are almost invariably about a narrative story.

At the same time, the narrative poses some special obstacles. It is a time- and space-consuming way to tell a story. I would estimate that what could be told in a 3,000-word explanatory story might easily take 10,000 to tell in narrative form. In our age of shrinking attention spans, this can be a serious problem. Narrative requires more effort from the reader. Many people want to be told what to think. I recall being confronted by an angry reader, a stranger to me, at a Christmas party one year not long after my story about David Schwartz appeared in *The New Yorker.* "I read your story from beginning to end," he began, "and I only have one question: What was the point?" I pondered that for a moment, then replied that if I had to tell him the "point," I had failed as a writer. I was pleased that he had read to the end, but I asked him to take my word that the story did have a point, and then reflect on what that point might be. If he still couldn't come up with an answer, I said, he could call me. I never heard from him again, but I sensed that he found my reply most unsatisfying.

You may recall from the last chapter that I had spoken to my editor about a Midwestern flood story before I went down to work at the levee near my hometown. Once I was there, it didn't take long for the "topic" of the flood to metamorphose into an actual idea that I could suggest. For I was struck by how interesting were the characters gathered together at this one small spot in the vast Mississippi River levee system: the local farmers, both the old-timers who knew the river, and the green newcomers; the city people who had come to help but had never gotten their hands dirty in the bottomlands near the river; the "experts" from the Army Corps of Engineers; and the national press corps. While the immensity of the flood was difficult if not impossible to capture in print, the story of the struggle to save one levee was manageable—and inherently suspenseful, since while I was there it wasn't clear whether the effort would succeed.

When is a narrative story appropriate? If the question underlying a story is "What happened?" then a narrative may be the answer. This was obviously the case with the flood story, even though the answer wasn't yet clear and I wouldn't be able to finish the story until it was. But I was reasonably sure it would be possible to declare victory within a matter of weeks, if the levee held. If the levee broke, that, too, would provide a conclusion. So I proposed the flood story as what I call a pure narrative, one in which the curiosity of the reader would be generated solely by the question "What happened?"

Many stories written in a narrative style, however, are not pure narratives, and may better be classified as explanatory, or as profiles. If to explain what happened requires an analysis of cause and effect, then a narrative is almost certainly appropriate. Narrative stories are often explanatory stories told in chronological order. If the focus of a story is a single character, a profile may best be written in a narrative fashion. I have already mentioned that sometimes story ideas have large ripple effects, touching on themes of human nature that extend far beyond the literal subject of the story. These themes are often best explored in a narrative context. And complexity lends itself to the narrative, since chronology is an ordering principle that is inculcated in children from the days of their first fairy tales. It clarifies complex events without oversimplifying them.

For that reason, although books usually combine several of the categories I have mentioned, they are best written as narratives. Both *Den of Thieves* and *Blood Sport,* for example, are extended narratives. But they are also explanatory and investigative, and each conveys a distinct point of view. Indeed, if an idea can be classified in only one of these categories, chances are it will make a better magazine or newspaper feature than it will a book. This, indeed, is one of the best pieces of advice I've received from my book editor at Simon & Schuster, Alice Mayhew; I have found it an excellent rule of thumb when other writers seek my guidance about turning their stories into book proposals.

When all is said and done, in my experience there is nothing to rival the sheer joy and satisfaction of reporting and writing the narrative story, whatever its length. Whenever I can, I embrace the narrative form. It provides a reading experience that cannot be rivaled by the ephemeral work that increasingly dominates television, the Internet, even newspapers and magazines, and as a result, it will never be obsolete.

Even the best ideas need to be "sold," in the sense that editors have to be interested and ultimately readers must be persuaded to read. I find that many writers resist the notion that they need to sell their work, as if to do so were inherently distasteful, vulgar, and commercial. And it is true, in my experience, that the kind of person who's attracted to writing isn't necessarily a natural salesperson. But the fact remains that most writers want to be published and have to support themselves. Publishing is a business. For writers who want to pursue the unorthodox, the avant-garde, the esoteric—anything that is not on its face likely to attract a broad readership—selling is even more important. Even for writers who write only for themselves, the discipline of working to interest others can be beneficial. I find that shaping an idea into a concrete proposal, far from vulgarizing or cheapening it, actually helps sharpen and clarify my thinking, which ultimately results in a better story that is, as a result, more marketable.

By and large, my goal in shaping an idea into a proposal is to evoke in an editor the same curiosity that inspired me in the first place. If possible, I try to make that curiosity even more intense. This is an extremely important task, since I will have the same goal with respect to readers. For that reason, I insist that my students submit written story proposals in class. *The Wall Street Journal* requires written proposals for most front-page stories. *The New Yorker* prepares story assignments which contain a written summary of a story proposal. Freelance articles are generally commissioned on the basis of written proposals, as are nearly all nonfiction books. I myself always jot down my ideas in proposal form even when I will be making the proposal orally. I cannot stress how important this exercise is, for it is amazingly easy during the days, weeks or sometimes months of ensuing reporting to forget why I undertook a story in the first place. As will be seen, it is essential to be able to re-create the elements that launched a story. This is so important that I'm going to repeat it: Write down the questions that generated your story.

The timing of a proposal can be critical, for speed is often of the essence. If you're thinking of a story, especially if it's triggered by a widely known news event, chances are that someone else is thinking along the same lines. Since the goal is to kindle curiosity, it is usually not necessary to embark on extensive reporting and fact gathering before you submit a proposal. It isn't necessary—or even desirable—to answer any of the questions being posed, but you may want to suggest what you think the answer might be, especially if the story is one whose answer will affect how good the story is likely to be, or even whether it's a story at all. Nevertheless, sometimes a modicum of information is necessary to sell an editor on an idea. Here are the classic elements writers use to sell proposals:

TIMELINESS

As I mentioned in the previous chapter, good stories can encompass a much broader time horizon than most writers recognize. But readers and editors still want to know why they should want to read something *now.* (Note that this is an entirely different matter from when the events in the story occurred.) As I mentioned before, the sooner a story appears after the events that triggered our interest in it, the better. Any story that is likely to yield news—for instance, to explain a still-unsolved mystery—is in itself timely. And the fresher the events, the more likely that numerous unsolved mysteries remain. (I noticed with interest, for example, that the creators of the movie *Titanic*—a much-examined subject concerning which few historical mysteries remain—felt they had to frame their story with a contemporary mystery, that of an elderly woman who held the clue to the whereabouts of a precious necklace.) Current events and issues, like Independent Counsel Kenneth Starr's investigation of Bill and Hillary Clinton, often trigger interest in analogous past events, such as what happened during Watergate. People often read history to better understand the present, and a proposal should make this explicit if the events in the story aren't recent. Even if events are recent, it is best to address the question of timeliness, since the attention span of the reading public seems to be shrinking. Events that consume the nation on Monday can seem distant by Friday.

UNIVERSALITY

If a subject happens to be of broad public interest, that should be mentioned. I have said that relatively few people have a wide array of interests; nevertheless, it's safe to say that certain subjects appeal to almost everyone. Stories with celebrities as the subject or as principal characters will generate wide interest; that is usually so obvious it need not be mentioned. But far more people are important but not so universally known or recognized; their importance may need to be explained in the proposal. I've also mentioned that good stories touch on themes of human nature that may be far from their immediate subject matter. The likelihood that a story will have that kind of appeal should be made explicit.

SIGNIFICANCE

Reading a story should never feel like taking medicine, but some stories matter because they do touch on subjects that readers should be informed about. If a character is famous or important, even if within a limited audience, say so. If something is dramatic and interesting, and also happens to be about a subject of importance, this enhances a story and should be mentioned.

EXCLUSIVITY

Writing remains an intensely competitive field. If you can deliver something of interest that no one else can, editors, and ultimately readers, will salivate in anticipation. This should be stressed in any proposal, whether the exclusivity comes from the writer's enterprise in examining something no one else has noticed, or is based on a source's promise to speak only to the writer, or is based on experiences that can't be duplicated by anyone else. In this regard, elements that might seem like deterrents can be used to advantage. The "squeamishness" factor that I mentioned in the last chapter, for example, can be used to suggest that few, if any, other publications will have the nerve to undertake the same story; that enhances the likelihood of exclusivity. Similarly, if a story seems difficult to report or write, others will hesitate to attempt it.

SIMILARITY

Every editor likes originality—unless the story promises to resemble something else that has already succeeded. (That's why Hollywood loves sequels.) This is why it's often useful to mention what category your planned story falls into. It's even more helpful to compare your proposal to something wildly successful, like a popular book or movie. I should emphasize that this doesn't mean—nor should it mean—that the resulting story won't be original. Who, after all, really wants to write sequels or remakes? But such a comparison is a useful sales tactic.

FEASIBILITY

Though your proposal needn't answer the questions being posed, editors need some assurance that there's a reasonable chance they *will* be answered and often want some indication of how a writer intends to pursue a story, including estimates of travel and related expenses. (I usually address these issues at the end of a proposal—when, I hope, an editor has already developed an interest in the story.) But, as I mentioned above, if a story seems risky or difficult, convert that potential defect into the element of exclusivity. Still, as a rule of thumb, the less feasible a story is, the better the idea has to be.

How do I put these sales elements into practice? Here's an example—the proposal I wrote concerning an idea I discussed in the previous chapter, the exploration of the insider-trading case involving Jonathan Sheinberg:

Tina:
    In a quiet settlement that included few details, Jonathan Sheinberg just admitted to an insider trading conspiracy involving the takeover of MCA by Matsushita. All Hollywood is buzzing. Jonathan's father, Sidney, is legendary, MCA's president and one of the film industry's most powerful executives. He's also

a self-proclaimed model of rectitude, so he must be dying of embarrassment. I don't know much about Jonathan, except that he works in the film industry and has produced several movies.

I'm baffled and intrigued by the story. What really happened? Why would someone as rich and privileged as Jonathan resort to insider trading, especially with the Milken case still fresh in Hollywood? Who are the co-conspirators and what's their relationship to the Sheinbergs? How did Sidney react? What role did Sidney play in resolving this?

I sense that at its core, this could be a classic drama of a father-son conflict set in the glamorous upper echelon of the film community. I can picture the scene where Jonathan "overhears" his father. How? What ensued? What is their relationship like? Has Jonathan, despite his famous name, had problems growing up in the shadow of so prominent a father? What kind of father is Sidney?

This should also be a good detective story, tracing the unraveling of the case from the SEC's perspective. It should also shed light on the law of insider trading, especially in family situations, and might help explain why so many insider trading violations are committed by people who really don't need the money.

I believe this story has the potential to be a rare look into the privileged but troubled world of one of Hollywood's most prominent families, a revealing account of how the film industry does business, and how it reacts when government authorities uncover evidence of wrongdoing. I'd try to write it as a fast-paced narrative, an *Indecent Exposure* set in today's Hollywood.

I think I can get the story. Obviously the Sheinbergs are trying to keep this quiet, but the case has been resolved, so someone will want to talk. There's also the possibility of getting SEC documents and transcripts, if not directly, then through an FOIA request. I'll probably need to travel to Washington and Los Angeles.

Let me know what you think; I'm excited and would like to jump on this while it's hot.

This memo is almost shamelessly promotional. But remember, the reader never sees the proposal; what counts is the finished story. And if a proposal is unsuccessful, then there won't be any finished story.

Let's look at how I structured this pitch. First, I provided a modicum of information, in this case the news that Sheinberg had settled insider-trading charges. But in the very first sentence I have planted many of the "selling" elements I've just described. The settlement was "quiet," which hints at exclusivity and secrecy; Hollywood is "buzzing," which suggests continuing curiosity and surprise; Sidney Sheinberg is "legendary," so this is about an important person; and he must be embarrassed, which makes us slightly queasy but even more curious.

With the editor's interest piqued—this must be done quickly, given the demands on the time of most editors—everything that immediately follows is meant to heighten curiosity. My questions are openly stated or implied. None are answered. Jonathan is relatively unknown—who is he? And the critical question is meant to underscore the paradox: Why would a presumably rich and privileged person commit such a crime? Note that I didn't have to say this is paradoxical. It's obvious, a matter of common sense.

In the third paragraph, I turned to the element of universality. This is not, I suggested, a story just about insider trading, a subject that few people are really interested in. It's a story about an Oedipus complex. Everyone has or had a father. Conflict with one's father is the stuff of Greek tragedy. It's one of the most universal of all themes. I posed a series of questions, with no idea what the answers were, intended to hint at the rich material that might be mined. For good measure, I mentioned the setting for this drama: the "glamorous" upper echelons of the film industry. This would be a good story even if it were taking place in a coal mine, but most readers like a little glamour.

The rest of it is pretty obvious; I may even have gilded the lily a bit. I mentioned—though I underplayed—elements of significance, including the law of insider trading. Note that I mention a best-selling book I knew Tina would have read: *Indecent Exposure.* I'm sure no one who read the finished story even thought of this book, but the analogy wasn't far-fetched. If I neglected any element that I might have stressed more, it was probably exclusivity. For the story did turn out to be exclusive—something I might have foreseen, for reasons that I'll discuss in the next chapter. I concluded with a paragraph on feasibility, here, to be honest, I glossed over the likelihood that reporting the story would be quite difficult, which turned out to be the case.

I didn't actually submit this proposal to Tina Brown; I wrote it before meeting with her. When I actually proposed the story, I didn't have to say more than a couple of sentences. Brown knew who Sidney Sheinberg was; she immediately saw it as a family story; she instinctively understood the paradox and knew there would be immense curiosity. In this respect, I must stress how important it is to have a good editor. There is probably no more important element of an editor-writer relationship than the discussion of story ideas. In my experience, good editors think along the lines I have described here, whether consciously or not. Naturally, I'm biased, since that's how I think. But most of what I've learned, I've learned from good editors. There's nothing better than an editor who intuitively understands what you're suggesting and who responds with encouragement and, above all, enthusiasm. I am sometimes amazed at how little I need to say when I have a good relationship with an editor.

I've also worked under bad editors. It is an extremely demoralizing experience, which should be avoided if possible. I recall writing a front-page story for the *Journal* about the takeover of an old-line industrial company in the Midwest; a poodle featured prominently in the first paragraph. My editor called me into his office, threw the pages of my story onto the floor, stamped on them, and said he had no idea what the story was about. He sent me to the "remedial" writing coach, Ellen Graham, who said she thought the story was fine. It ran on the front page pretty much as I wrote it, with the poodle intact. (Despite what I said about avoiding such editors, this man and I eventually developed a quite congenial working relationship, in which he pretty much let me write whatever I wanted.)

I have also had the experience of proposing what I thought was a good story, then watching the blank look of incomprehension on an editor's face. It must be what a comedian feels when he delivers a punch line and no one laughs. As I told the party guest I mentioned, if I have to explain the meaning of a story, I've probably failed. Not being understood is dispiriting and exhausting. I don't know why this is such a widespread problem, but I'm sorry to say that there are many bad editors. In my experience, they are hostile to almost everything I have to say about storytelling. They don't like surprise; they don't like unanswered questions; they don't understand notions of universality; and they certainly don't grasp metaphor or symbol. They don't read or like narrative nonfiction, which they dismiss as "arty." They never read novels, and they're proud of that. In my experience they like hard news and, for some reason, stories about mountain men in the wilderness.

Find good editors. And when you do, stay with them, treasure them, and thank them.

Of the story ideas I mentioned in the previous chapter, probably the most difficult to sell was the one about gay auto workers at Chrysler. The events described in the news article weren't that recent by the time I got around to my proposal. The story lacked marquee names, unless I could make Chrysler chairman Robert Eaton a major character, which seemed unlikely. What the story had going for it, however, was timeliness and universality. The question the story posed and proposed to explore was: "Is Chrysler homophobic?" Ongoing discrimination against any minority has been a topic of significant and widespread interest, especially since the civil rights movement of the sixties transformed American society. Discrimination against gays, in particular, has been a major battleground of late. Chrysler had recently withdrawn its advertising from the episode of the sitcom *Ellen* in which the title character identified herself as a lesbian. That had generated a storm of mostly superficial media coverage, which nonetheless significantly enhanced interest in a deeper story like the one I was proposing. Naturally, I made much of *Ellen* in my proposal, even though it was tangential to the story.

As I mentioned in the last chapter, the idea also depended on the seeming paradox of gay auto workers to heighten curiosity. The notion that an embattled minority was standing up for its rights in a hostile environment touched on issues of human rights and personal courage far removed from gay rights per se. And, pulling out all the stops, I mused in my proposal that this story probably would not be a "gay *Norma Rae*," *Norma Rae* being the movie in which Sally Field gave an Academy Award–winning performance as a textile-industry worker. I knew very well that by saying the article was *not* a gay *Norma Rae* I was planting the idea that it was—or, at least, had such inherent drama that it could be made into a movie. The proposal was approved.

This story also entailed a potential problem, which I would classify in the "feasibility" category: at the time, Chrysler was the nation's fourth-largest advertiser. I wish I could say that this thought never crossed my mind, and that no one should have to fear the power of advertisers over the content of what we write and read. But there's no point in pretending that the once-impregnable wall between "church" and "state," as the division between editorial and advertising was memorably described at *Time* magazine, has not eroded. That Chrysler had canceled its ads on *Ellen* and that a gay-themed short story in *Esquire* magazine had recently been spiked for fear that Chrysler would cancel its ads there, made me especially sensitive to the issue. Editors, of course, almost never admit that advertiser concerns might dictate their decisions about stories, but I have heard enough anecdotal evidence to convince me that they do, sometimes even at the most respected publications. (Indeed, after this incident, *Wall Street Journal* reporter Bruce Knecht wrote a front-page story documenting the startling degree of influence Chrysler and other major advertisers wield at many publications.) So I told Tina Brown point-blank that I didn't want to go to all the trouble of reporting and writing the story only to have it killed because Chrysler was an important advertiser at *The New Yorker* or in other Condé Nast publications. She assured me it would not be. I felt better, having gotten the issue out on the table.

By contrast, the David Schwartz story didn't need to be sold to an editor at all; I was the one who had to be persuaded to do it. But it had all the elements necessary to pitch it to just about any editor: it was timely, since the murder had just happened; it featured an important New York lawyer from what was arguably the city's most prominent law firm; it reeked of paradox, in that a wealthy Park Avenue denizen had been found dead in a transient motel in the Bronx; it was a mystery that, even when the murder was solved, cried out for further explanation. While the ultimate theme that would emerge wasn't immediately apparent, it was almost sure to be universal, given the issues of life and death, concealed identity, and desperation that were so plainly elements of the story. I suspect that Tina also found the story appealing because it was one that many genteel publications— probably including *The New Yorker* itself under her predecessors —wouldn't have touched. This is an example of the "squeamishness" factor being turned into a virtue.

Good proposals are sales documents. They should emphasize

the positive and, I hope it goes without saying, they should never be fraudulent or duplicitous. One of the most annoying syndromes I encountered as Page One editor was that some reporters and editors would consistently oversell their proposals, promising a level of reporting and information—even, in some cases, presenting specific facts—that never appeared in the finished story. A writer must never lose credibility with an editor, though honest mistakes are sometimes made. My approach, which emphasizes curiosity and questions rather than the results of reporting, should help to minimize this problem.

Good proposals should not seem labored or forced; in many cases the elements that make them appealing are so obvious they needn't be stated. When I proposed my story on the Midwestern flood, for example, it was the major story of the day; everyone was looking for a way to tell it. That it was a classic man-against-nature struggle, in which themes of human nature would prove far more important than the details of the natural catastrophe, was implicit, something that any reasonably competent and sensitive editor would immediately recognize. Yet I always find it helpful to remind myself of the elements that made an idea a good one. No matter how discouraging the reporting or writing may sometimes seem, I can go back and reassure myself that the original idea was sound. And, as I often tell my students, a good story idea is half the battle.

Although selling an idea is a practical necessity, it should never obscure what is most important: the writer's own enthusiasm for a story. No clever sleight-of-hand, however successful with editors, will ever fool the author—nor, ultimately, will it fool readers. Don't waste your time working on stories in which you aren't really interested. Life is too short; there are too many good stories to be written; and your lack of enthusiasm, I can almost guarantee, will be painfully apparent in your finished work. Writing is never entirely painless, but satisfying one's own curiosity should certainly be one of its greatest pleasures.

4
GATHERING INFORMATION

However intense one's curiosity, the time comes when it needs to be satisfied. Information gathering begins in earnest. I often liken the process to prospecting for oil: many wells are drilled, and then I wait to see if oil trickles—or gushes—out.

When I first began teaching my writing course at Columbia, I spent very little time discussing the reporting and information-gathering process. This was a writing course, I explained, and I assumed my students learned reporting somewhere else. It was, in any case, too vast a subject to cover in just one or two classes. I should have known better. For no story is any better than the facts within it. No writer can cover a paucity of information with a veneer of brilliant prose (though many try.) The writing process itself is often a function of the success of information gathering. Reporting is dictated by knowing what kind of writing will result. Writing and reporting are, in sum, inextricable.

An entire book could easily be written on the subject of reporting. In this chapter I will concentrate on aspects of reporting that are especially important for successful feature writing, especially narrative articles or books. Many of my students assume, erroneously, that it is news stories that rely most heavily on facts and information gathering. In reality, the opposite is true. I have often been able to construct a news story around just a few facts, but even simple feature stories require a multitude. Many also assume that anything written in the first person, in the nature of a memoir, requires no reporting or information gathering that extends beyond the writer's own memories. That, too, is a mistake, in my experience.

Reporting can be an immensely pleasurable process, once anxiety is overcome. Almost every writer I know experiences at least some anxiety at the outset of reporting, rooted in the suspicion that no one will talk. In extreme cases, I have seen people become all but paralyzed. I find it soothing to contemplate the obvious: If you know nothing when you begin, you have nothing to lose, and everything to gain, by trying. If someone rudely hangs up on you, you are no worse off than you were before you made the call. When you do succeed, you are that much further ahead. Invariably, a point comes where you know that you have enough to write a good story. How you will wrestle that information onto the printed page may yet seem murky, but you know it can be done—even if every person you contact from now on shuts you down. Then any remaining anxiety lifts, leaving you, blissfully unencumbered, to satisfy your curiosity. How many other people actually get paid to so indulge themselves?

The vast majority of my information gathering has taken the form of interviewing witnesses and participants in the events that are the subjects of my stories. Since I have written primarily about contemporary events, traditional research—the kind most people learn in college and graduate school—hasn't figured prominently in my own work. Nor have other published and written sources, though they have been important to some stories and I obtain them whenever I can. Interviewing is at the heart of most nonfiction reporting, and it is usually essential if a story is to be vivid and true-to-life.

Probably the question I hear more than any other is "How do you get people to talk?" In fact, I don't feel that I "get" people to talk. Writers don't have the subpoena power—which, in any event, doesn't ensure you're going to get the truth. Reluctant or recalcitrant sources are rarely of much value, even if they are forced to talk by the legal process. People talk because they want to talk. The best I can do is to create a conducive environment.

I often tell my students that what continues to surprise me in my work is not what people don't tell me. It's what they *do* tell. Perhaps that's because I am by nature somewhat shy and often cannot imagine myself answering the questions I ask other people, usually virtual strangers. I have had the most extraordinary telephone conversations with people I have never met. While working on the David Schwartz story, I spoke to a professor who confided that, though he had been married for over twenty years and had five children, he was gay; that no one else knew; and that he was growing increasingly desperate as he saw life passing him by. People have told me about their most intimate marital problems, their children's drug habits, their crises of religious and political faith. Several sources mused that they had come to think of me as their psychiatrist, a notion I tried to dispel by gently reminding them that my primary professional responsibility is to readers.

I have learned that no matter how hopeless the prospect might seem, it is always a mistake to assume that someone will not talk. Probably the most tedious but common exercise I went through as an editor was to ask reporters if they had called someone to get his or her side of the story. "No," the reporter would say. "Why not?" The answer, invariably, was "I know they won't answer," or "They never return my call." Just as invariably, I had to say, "Make the call and then tell me they didn't return it." Predictably, at least half the time the supposedly reclusive source did make a comment. In their anxiety that sources won't talk, reporters often all but guarantee the failure they fear.

Over the years I have often paused to reflect on why so many people talk to reporters. The main reason, I believe, is that no one else ever listens. Just as we live in an age of know-it-alls, we live in an age of talkers. Radio and TV talk shows are filled with people who talk, shout, and scream, often at the same time. Talking all the time, yet feeling that no one listens, paradoxically increases feelings of isolation. The supposed cure—more talking—only makes things worse. Many people, as a result, are lonely. They are waiting for you to call.

I believe that nothing is so important in my own efforts to get people to reveal information than a willingness to listen without judging. I constantly remind my students that in reporting, our only goal is to learn. It is not to browbeat, to argue, or to proselytize. Yet I have seen reporters lose control and engage in all of those tactics, which are invariably counterproductive. I know firsthand that the degree of self-control required can be immense.

I have had sources say outrageous things to me; offer opinions, for example, with which I violently disagree, make factual asser-tions that border on lunacy, present wild theories concerning conspiracies in which I am alleged to be a participant. Yet I bite my tongue. I remind myself that I should be grateful they're talking. No matter what the source says, it is likely to enhance my story.

On many occasions, I have assumed that someone is unlikely to talk, or might do so only reluctantly, and have prepared a detailed argument about my planned story and its importance to the public interest, or some other high-minded appeal to civic virtue. In fact, most such speeches go unsaid. Surprisingly often, people simply begin talking, evidently having already resolved whatever qualms they may have harbored.

That said, there are any number of things I can say or do to try to improve the odds that someone will talk to me. There are as many styles of reporting as there are reporters. I tell my stu-dents that there is no one model for success, and therefore they should be themselves. Steve Brill once took me along on an interview, and his performance was mesmerizing. He pounded the source with hostile questions and left him reduced to a quiv-ering bowl of Jell-O. This was effective for Steve, but I couldn't do it. I prefer a quiet, understated, nonjudgmental if not sympathetic approach. Unlike many reporters I know, I tend to say little about myself. This doesn't mean that I don't engage in the usual pleas-antries, or mention biographical facts the source and I may have in common, such as where we grew up or went to college. But beyond that, I tend to be very cautious. This allows my potential sources to project onto me whatever qualities they want, and indeed, they have often done so. I don't believe it is my obligation to affirm or contradict their projections. Sometimes sources ask me questions about myself point-blank, most often about my political views. While working on *Blood Sport* I was asked by almost every source whether I voted for Bill Clinton in 1992. I almost always refused to answer. On more than one occasion, I have gone so far as to curtail such questioning by reminding the source, as politely as possible, that as a journalist, I'm the one who's supposed to ask the questions, and to assure my interlocu-tor that whatever my own views, they will have as little effect as is humanly possible on my work. My political views, consequently, are irrelevant. As far as I can tell, no one has taken offense.

While I avoid personal subjects, I am willing to discuss, at whatever length a potential source wants, qualities of mine that I believe are relevant. Indeed, I invite such questions because they give me the opportunity to stress something that may reassure sources and encourage them to talk: my commitment to fairness and thoroughness. To make this clear can also be effective at defusing potential disappointment once a story appears. In this connection, I have learned over the years that it is always best to be honest about what I believe the story will be like. Almost everyone asks, "What kind of story is this going to be?" and, more directly, "Is this story going to be positive or negative?" I generally answer, truthfully, that I don't know. But when I approached Chris Whittle about my story on his crumbling empire, I was candid about what had triggered my interest. Conversely, when I asked lawyers at Cravath, Swaine & Moore about writing a chapter on the firm's work for IBM in the government's long-running antitrust case, I said I didn't know how the firm would be portrayed but that it would be impossible for me to ignore the fact that IBM had won, and surely that was positive for the firm.

Beginning reporters seem to have trouble being honest about their interest in a story, evidently because they fear they might alienate potential sources. Like most forms of dishonesty, this is invariably a mistake. At the very least, being misled can enrage a source or subject when the story appears. And, although I could be wrong, I believe candor enhances a subject's respect for a writer and therefore makes him or her more likely to cooperate.

This was much on my mind when I met with Hillary Clinton to discuss hers and the president's cooperation in what became *Blood Sport.* After we had discussed the vexing Whitewater affair at some length, I asked Mrs. Clinton whether she had any questions for me. Expecting the usual queries about how I thought the book would turn out, what scope it would have, how I would approach my work, and so on, I was surprised when she didn't immediately respond. She even seemed somewhat baffled by my suggestion. So I told her that while I wasn't a public relations expert, I thought there were some things she should consider. Among them, I said, was this: I would approach this story as I would any other; there was no predicting where my research would lead me, what I would uncover, and whether she would in the end be pleased with what I wrote. I stressed that neither she nor the president would have any control over what I wrote, nor would they be permitted to review the manuscript in advance of publication.

It was not easy for me to say these things. Meeting a first lady for the first time, I wanted to make a positive impression, and on some level, as I've said, I hoped she would like me. Though it might seem paradoxical, I made these points in the context of a discussion I hoped would persuade the Clintons to carry out their promise of unprecedented candor and cooperation. I emphasized the positive elements of these conditions, stressing that if the final work was to have credibility with the public at large, the Clintons could not receive any special treatment. I said that if they had something to hide, this venture was a mistake—but I quickly added that if they did not, then they had nothing to fear from my investigation. As for me, I didn't want to drop all else that I was working on and embark on this project only to have the Clintons later change their mind, and I said so explicitly. I recognized that there were certain risks in my approach, but I wanted to respond in keeping with the spirit of candor with which the Clintons themselves had set this project in motion.

Did I succeed? I suppose only Mrs. Clinton could answer that. At the time I thought I had, for I subsequently received encouragement to proceed, if not from Mrs. Clinton herself, then from her chief of staff, Maggie Williams. But the cooperation I was led to expect never did materialize. Someone working in the White House during that period later told me that despite my protests of independence, the Clintons had believed that I would write something favorable to them; immersed in a political world where everyone is partisan no matter what they say, the president and first lady cynically assumed that my comments were just window dressing. In that they were mistaken.

Just as being candid about the nature of one's work helps, so does stressing—without being embarrassingly immodest—whatever positive attributes you bring to a project. I do not recite a list of journalism prizes I have won, nor do I mention my education and related distinctions and awards. I do stress that I try to be fair and thorough, and I refer people to published work, in-

cluding some of my investigative pieces. I have been fortunate
enough to write for publications such as *The Wall Street Journal,*
The New Yorker, and *SmartMoney,* and stressing their virtues has
often persuaded people to talk. (I can't tell you how often someone would agree to speak to me after commenting of *The Wall
Street Journal,* "I just love your editorials." This was never the
time, in my view, to launch into a lengthy explanation of the
separation between the paper's news and editorial staffs.) Indeed, a publication's reputation is often crucial, as some reporters, accustomed to routine access to everyone in positions of
power and authority, discover when they quit the institution and
go out on their own: their phones suddenly stop ringing. But no
one who writes for less famous publications should be discouraged. When I began writing for *American Lawyer,* the magazine
hadn't even published its first regular issue and was all but unknown. People talked anyway.

In every writer's career, with persistence and a modicum of
success, the time comes when his or her reputation is more
important than any other factor. By then, one hopes, the quality of the work speaks for itself. There is no doubt in my mind
that the more well-known I have become, the more willingly people seem to talk to me, even though my reputation largely rests
on my books and my magazine, and newspaper articles, which
have been investigative and have described some prominent
cases of wrongdoing. People seem to be, at the very least, curious
to meet me.

I hope others attest to my fairness, objectivity, willingness to
listen and consider various points of view, even though I am not
so naïve to believe that my work has left no disgruntled participants in its wake. Not infrequently, prospective sources talk to
other subjects of my work, which is a point worth remembering
by journalists who take a "scorched earth" approach, assuming
that once a story is done, they'll never need to talk to a source
again. In this connection, I sometimes think of the commence-
ment speech given at the University of Arkansas by Vince Foster,
Clinton's deputy White House counsel, shortly before Foster
committed suicide in 1993: "There is no victory, no advantage,
no fee, no favor, which is worth even a blemish on your reputation for intellect and integrity."

I emphasize not only my character and reputation, but also

the practical benefits of cooperating with a reporter. The best position is one of strength: "I already know so much that I'm going to write this story whether you cooperate or not." This argument demolishes what is often the strongest deterrent to a prospective source's opening up: the belief that if he or she simply remains silent, you and the contemplated story will go away. It is important to try to deflect this thinking in any event, but you'll be far more persuasive if you can demonstrate some knowledge of crucial elements of the story. Then you can argue that a source can only enhance how he or she is treated by granting an interview, avoiding errors, rebutting the impressions of others, and putting the information you have in the most favorable light. Nine times out of ten, I find this approach works. In many cases, I need reveal only a few key details, and then the source assumes, sometimes in error, that I know virtually everything. Sometimes, I admit, what I purport to know is actually something I have inferred.

As I hope I've already made clear, I don't find threats very effective, because a good source cooperates not under duress, but voluntarily. Still, one admonition that, *if true,* is sometimes effective is the pledge that you will write the story whether the source cooperates or not. I stress "if true," because someone who threatens this repeatedly and never follows through will soon lose credibility. I can recall just one instance when I made such a claim and then didn't write the promised story, but that was because another story intervened, not because I gave up due to a source's lack of cooperation. Almost anyone can be profiled, almost any story can be written, without the subject's cooperation. Indeed, the story may be better off, for an uncooperative subject forces the writer to report much more thoroughly. And as word reaches the subject that others are talking, cooperation often ensues.

I sometimes further enhance the argument that someone should cooperate by mentioning that I myself have been the subject of quite a few articles, and that with only one exception, I have always followed my own advice and cooperated. I note that even though the resulting articles have not always been what I'd hoped for, I considered the time well spent. Although it may seem self-serving, since I'm a reporter trying to persuade people to talk, this claim has the virtue of being true. I recall spending hours with a reporter from *Institutional Investor* who was writ-

ing a cover story on me after the publication of *Den of Thieves*.
I began to suspect this would not necessarily be a flattering article when the photographer went to great lengths to get me to
pose behind the bars of a stair railing and used a filter on the lens
that was so dark it looked as if I hadn't shaved in days. The
reporter was nothing if not persistent; I remember at least five
in-person interviews. She later told me that the editor had insisted that the theme of the article be that I had succumbed to the
same deadly sins as the characters in my book—namely greed,
gluttony, and conspicuous consumption. The absence of a new
home or a new car, and my failure to take exotic vacations or
spend lavishly in any way, came as a great disappointment to her,
I could tell. That didn't eliminate the negative article's slant, but
I can only imagine what it would have said if I hadn't invested
the countless hours with the reporter.

The only time I refused an interview was with the author of
a book on *The Wall Street Journal*. The book's catalogue description had already appeared by the time the author called me, and
it said that the *Journal* had actually been scooped by others on
the insider-trading scandal; that I had stolen my material on Michael Milken from writer Connie Bruck (who happens to be a
close friend of mine and whose help I acknowledged in my
book); and that *Den of Thieves* was, in any event, biased and
inaccurate. I asked the writer, whom I had never met, whether
he would grant an interview if our roles were reversed. He acknowledged that he would not. Looking back now, I feel I was
mistaken. I should have suppressed my indignation and spoken
to him. For the book itself contained some inaccurate comments
about me that had nothing to do with Milken or insider trading,
and perhaps I might have warded those off.

So when I tell sources that it's in their interest to talk to me,
I believe this to be true. I know it's not what many PR agents
advise their clients. The conventional wisdom, for example, is
that someone should not talk about matters under investigation
or subject to litigation, although the O. J. Simpson case seems to
have stood that notion on its head. I now sometimes cite that
case to emphasize the point that talking to the press has become
an inextricable part of any successful lawsuit, for better or worse.
And I'm not sure the conventional wisdom ever made much
sense, as many lawyers recognized long before the Simpson case.

The one exception to my own belief that it's always in a

source's interest to speak to the press is the very rare case where without that cooperation, the story would be impossible. I once sought to write about a deposed head of a Hollywood studio. My goal was to write a very detailed and personal account of the experience of suddenly being deprived of power in Hollywood. After initially being interested, and despite my efforts at persuasion, the subject of the story declined to cooperate. It's true I could have gone ahead and done a story *about* him, and maybe he would have changed his mind as he realized others were talking. But the heart of the story had to be his experiences, feelings, and reactions, as only he could describe them. So I saw no point in going ahead without him. On the other hand, the Sheinberg family managed to silence almost everyone involved in the Jonathan Sheinberg insider-trading case. This—in itself, an interesting measure of Sidney Sheinberg's power in Hollywood —did not stop me from reporting and writing a very detailed story. While I was ultimately indifferent to whether the Sheinbergs cooperated, I continue to believe their silence was a mistake.

If I sense that a potential source is hesitating, I may make two further points. I will often say something to the effect that "I want to assure you that whether you do or don't talk with me I will not let that decision affect how you are portrayed in the story, to the best of my ability." I sometimes add that I respect people's right to remain silent as much as I do their right to talk. These assertions also have the virtue of being true. I myself have been offended by reporters who demand that I answer their questions, as if, being a reporter myself, I have an obligation to talk about everything they may chose to ask, no matter how irrelevant, personal, or private. I try to state, politely but firmly, that I won't answer those questions, which is an approach I respect when the roles are reversed and I'm the reporter. What annoys me is when sources hide behind some irrelevant claim of grand jury secrecy, or claim not to know or remember something, when it's patently obvious that's not true. They simply don't want to answer, which is their right. Still, even as I'm trying to defuse a source's anxiety and be reassuring, I recognize that in saying that someone's refusal to cooperate won't affect his or her portrayal, I am planting the idea that it might. However, most sources seem pleasantly surprised that I'm not out to retaliate, and the statement buttresses my argument that I try to be fair.

Another point I sometimes make is that the earlier someone cooperates, the more influence he or she ultimately has over the scope of the story. I've realized, over the years, that inevitably the course of reporting and the final story are disproportionately influenced by the people who are interviewed first. This isn't because I'm trying to favor these people, or because I'm grateful for their early cooperation (though I may well be); it's inherent in the process. By the time a reporter approaches a subject with a final round of questions, the story is probably all but written; in many cases, it is written, awaiting only specific responses. By then it is too late for that set of answers to make much difference to the structure of the story. I made this point to Mrs. Clinton and her staff on several occasions, and it obviously had no effect. But I'm confident that sophisticated PR advisers and sources know it to be true. Chris Whittle responded to my interest in writing about him by all but overwhelming me with cooperation, using the opportunity to try to shift my interest away from his earlier business ventures to his newer Edison project of for-profit schools. It was a shrewd approach, though I'm not sure it had much effect on the final story. In *Den of Thieves,* Martin Siegel was by far the most cooperative of the major characters. As a result, he emerged as the book's central figure, not because I favored him but because he gave me by far the most material to work with. I didn't minimize his criminal culpability, but his early and uninhibited cooperation made it possible to put those actions in a much broader, and ultimately more sympathetic, context.

This is a point that I find many reviewers of nonfiction fail to understand. They seem peeved if they detect that someone who cooperated ended up being treated more sympathetically than someone who did not. To some extent, that result is inevitable, as I've already explained. But it has nothing to do with rewarding or punishing anyone. And for examples to the contrary, I would refer them to the Whittle story, in which Whittle did cooperate, or to the Sheinberg story, where no one cooperated, yet Sid Sheinberg emerged in a sympathetic light, at least from my perspective.

I will briefly mention one common tactic: flattery. I have often heard reporters lavishing praise on a potential source to a degree that makes me cringe. All I can say is that insincerity is usually quite transparent and rarely effective. If I like someone, and I often do, I assume that becomes apparent one way or another. If I don't, I figure there's little point in pretending otherwise.

Finally, I cannot stress enough the virtue of persistence. Our natural tendency is not to be rude and, once rebuffed, to stop trying. But I myself have often found myself talking to reporters I had hoped to avoid, simply to get them to stop calling. Persistence is effective. It took me months of trying to finally make contact with Susan McDougal, who was the Clintons' partner in Whitewater and is a central character in *Blood Sport.* Susan had fallen on difficult times; she was moving from place to place, and she was difficult to track down, let alone persuade to talk, given that she was under investigation and was soon to be indicted. But finally we spoke on the phone (she returned one of my calls) and she agreed to an interview. She was living in California at the time, and said that if I flew out there, she'd meet with me. Hoping for a specific appointment, I asked where and when; she said— in a maddening way that I often encountered in Arkansas—"Oh, just give me a call when you get here." I told her the day I expected to arrive and the approximate time of my call. Imagine my frustration when I flew to California, checked into a hotel, and called the number she'd given me, only to get the answering machine of someone she was then living with. I called constantly for two days, trying to control my mounting panic, when the friend finally called me to say that Susan had gone back to Arkansas and didn't know when she'd return. I flew back to New York dejected and empty-handed.

I was angry and disappointed at being stood up, and I'm not sure why I persisted. But I kept calling, and finally one day Susan returned another call. She admitted she'd gotten cold feet, but said she was now prepared to meet me. I asked for an appointment, but she demurred, again insisting that I simply call upon my arrival. I flew to California as soon as I could. This time she was at home and she answered the phone. And the next morning she did show up at my hotel—wearing, I will always remember, a purple cocktail dress.

Early discussions with potential sources inevitably cover the terms on which the interview will be conducted. Even relatively unsophisticated sources are now familiar with the notion of "off the record" and will usually bring it up. If they don't, I consider it my obligation to discuss such terms and explain what I mean by them.

One reason this subject almost always arises is that sources are understandably apprehensive about what the consequences to them might be if they talk. We should always remember that candor is not necessarily viewed as a virtue in America—especially if it clashes with loyalty. Indeed, I am often struck by what seems to be a quality inherent in human nature: people frequently want to tell the truth even when it is not in their narrow self-interest to do so. It may well take considerable courage for someone to talk.

The three basic terms I use are "on the record," "not for attribution," and "off the record." Some reporters insist on putting all interviews on the record, which in my view is often a mistake. I only want a source to be on the record if he or she is comfortable enough with the idea that I am likely to get the whole story. Especially early in the information-gathering process, the important thing is to learn what happened; who can be quoted and identified as a source is a subsidiary question. So, in the early stages of a story, I will sometimes ask a source willing to speak on the record if he or she might not be more comfortable speaking "not for attribution."

Most sources assume that "off the record" accords them the highest degree of protection, but I have not always found this to be the case. By "off the record," I mean that what a source tells me cannot be used in my story or book, whether or not it is attributed to anyone. But it *can* be used—and this is crucial—in gathering information. So sometimes I will call another source, ask a question, and realize that the person is obviously omitting some crucial details. Then I might say, "But someone else already told me that . . ." and proceed to provide a detailed account. While I have honored my off-the-record commitment, it is often quite obvious who the source was, usually because the universe of possibilities is quite small.

And in the overwhelming majority of instances, only a very small number of people care who a source is—and they are usually contacted in the research phase of my work. I usually try to explain these risks if a source insists on speaking off the record.

I find that "not for attribution" provides most of the protection that sources want while giving me the flexibility I need to use material. By "not for attribution" I mean that I can use the information, but not by attributing it through direct quotation and not in a way that allows others to deduce the source's identity. "Not for attribution" actually provides a higher degree of protection in some ways than "off the record" does, because in using "not for attribution" information in the reporting process, I consider it part of my obligation to protect the identity of my source. So if there is only one possible source for information that contradicts what another source is telling me, I don't mention it. In the narrative writing that I prefer, direct quotations are rarely necessary anyway, and the facts imparted can be used. On the other hand, I always make it clear to sources that narrative quotations and the thoughts of the source can be stated as fact in my writing. In other words, if a source says he felt sick at a certain time and place, the story might say So-and-so "felt sick," but without attributing that information. (This point is addressed in greater deal in chapter 10.) Even though the identity of a source of unattributed information often seems obvious in the completed piece, I have never had someone decline an interview because I reserved the right to use the information they imparted, including their statements and thoughts.

I should mention the "confidential source," who seems to be surfacing with increasing frequency. So far, the only sources who have demanded such protection from me are lawyers, which suggests that this development is emanating from the legal profession. A "confidential source" is one who may not be identified in any way, either in a story or in the reporting process, and, most important, may not be identified in litigation, even if under a direct court order to do so. In other words, this is the kind of source a reporter is expected to go to jail to protect. I am not entirely sure what the point of this level of protection is, since I would refuse to disclose the names of unidentified sources whether or not they were accorded "confidential" status. On the other hand, I know that many news organizations are in fact disclosing sources to protect themselves from libel suits, so perhaps this is a legitimate concern.

I have found that many of my students are reluctant to conduct interviews on any but an on-the-record basis. While this is understandable, and in some ways admirable, given the media's frequent abuse of unattributed quotes, it isn't necessarily conducive to the level and depth of reporting needed for feature writing. I remind my students that the reporter's goal is to obtain information, not to enforce a moral code. Often sources of mine will speak only after being given some assurance of protection. In many cases, a degree of trust develops, after which they agree to abandon such constraints. Or they agree to let me quote specific statements I later find I want to use.

Whatever the arrangement, it needs to be taken seriously. I don't know that it needs to be treated as a contract, enforceable in court, as at least one judge has ruled. But the potential for disputes between reporter and source is vastly reduced if such agreements are honored.

Once someone has agreed to an interview, the first meeting is crucial. I say "meeting" because, in my experience, the level of detail required for a successful narrative requires a relationship that, with rare exceptions, can only be established in person. Witnessing firsthand a source's demeanor is also essential to assessing credibility (which is one reason I believe even presidents should be made to testify in court, in person, rather than on videotape). I will go anywhere at any time for an initial interview, a willingness that I think underscores the importance I place on our interview and my willingness to accommodate a source.

Perhaps the most peculiar such occasion came when someone who was a potentially valuable source for *Den of Thieves* agreed to meet me at the University Club in Manhattan. It was an eminently respectable venue that gave rise to no apprehension on my part. But when I arrived, he told me that he had booked side-by-side massages for us, and that I would be allowed to ask questions while the massage was in progress. Odd? Perhaps, but it seemed harmless enough. I had already agreed that this would be a "background" interview but this unorthodox configuration —we were both on our stomachs, clad only in towels—certainly guaranteed that I would not be taking notes.

I have gone to Paris, the Costa del Sol, and Australia just to interview people in person; I once waited for Adnan Khashoggi while he had his hair and nails done in his penthouse suite at a

Honolulu luxury hotel (he had his hair cut every day, I was told). If you think this kind of travel is glamorous, I should mention that I have also gone to Mamou, Louisiana, where the hotel—the *only* hotel—turned out to be a brothel, and I have driven over what seems like every paved road in the state of Arkansas. I believe I would draw the line at anything that seemed to put me in physical danger. But a friend of mine, a woman, once agreed to meet a potential source alone at midnight in Central Park. As I recall, the source used the occasion to make an amorous advance; with benefit of hindsight, my friend agreed she'd been foolhardy to agree to the meeting.

I rarely come to a first interview armed with an elaborate script, the way lawyers often do when they take a deposition in a lawsuit. It's an ominous sign when a source begins, "What are your questions?" Such interviews require you to know almost everything already, which certainly gets in the way of learning something new. I usually respond by saying that I'm there to listen and learn, and that I will probably only occasionally interrupt to ask questions. My goal is to get sources to narrate—to simply tell their stories in their own ways, in their words. It's often fascinating, for example, to see where a source begins a story—often much further in the past than I might have guessed. Most people soon relax and come to enjoy this approach, which is so much less adversarial than most seem to expect. And let's face it: most people find themselves interesting, and are pleased when you do, too.

Some people are born storytellers, and others, I'm sorry to say, are the opposite. It's often impossible to predict which category a source will fall into. Martin Siegel and Robert Wilkis, two characters in *Den of Thieves*, are probably two of the best narrators I have ever encountered. They can think chronologically, they have fantastic memories, they have a visual sense, and they intuitively discard irrelevancies. These skills and sensibilities rarely coalesce in one person, but when they do, it is relatively easy to bring such characters to life on the page. By contrast, one of the worst narrators I have ever met was Fred Joseph, the former chief executive of Drexel Burnham Lambert and another character in *Den of Thieves*. Let me hasten to say that I like Fred very much and don't hold this against him; he wasn't deliberately concealing information or, worse, trying to deceive me. Simply, his mind is analytical, and he seemed unable to put events into a chronology. Rather, he would move from concept to concept without any regard for time sequence or cause and effect. There was a logic to his narration, but it was of scant use to me. When I reread portions of *Den of Thieves,* I still lament how flat some of the narrative is because I couldn't get more from Fred.

One of the most taxing interviews I ever experienced—I should say, several of the most taxing—involved Ron Woods, the electrician at Chrysler who protested the company's policies toward gays. I flew to Detroit for our initial interview and met him at his well-kept home in a nearby suburb. We spent five or six hours together—and only got as far as Ron's performance evaluations during his first year at Chrysler, of which there were many, each and every one of which he had saved and each of which he insisted I review with him. I heard in excruciating detail about his early years, his parents and family, his elementary school education . . . virtually none of which, I knew, would make it into any story. Woods, too, would often stray from the chronology, one incident reminding him of another, sometimes separated from the first by years. He often apologized, and told me everyone told him he talked too much. I can only guess at how many hours I spent with Ron before his debriefing was complete—hundreds. I can honestly say I have never had an interviewing experience that even remotely compares to this. I could easily have filled a book on his life.

How do I handle such situations? As gently as possible, I interrupt and try to bring the speaker back to a specific date or event, in some cases all but forcing him or her to focus on chronology. In Woods's case, I had to be as blunt as I've ever been, sometimes telling him point-blank that a story he'd embarked on was irrelevant or boring or both. But a great deal of patience is often required. The expenditure of time may be inefficient, but I usually consider it a small price to pay for someone's heartfelt cooperation.

It may seem that allowing someone to talk with little interruption, especially if the narrator is a good one, leaves the interviewer without much to do, but the opposite is true. Listening is hard work, and I find I don't have the stamina for much more than three or four hours at a time. Particularly in early interviews, I'm looking for clues that go well beyond the surface of what someone has to say. What emphasis does someone place on certain events? What details are remembered? What does this signify? I am often asked by some readers and my students why I chose certain events to illustrate in great detail, while all but ignoring others. In most cases, I chose events because a source, while narrating, emphasized them by dwelling on them, without any prompting from me. Similarly with remembered conversations: sources usually narrate them; I don't have to interrupt and ask, "And what did you say then?"

Another important goal I have in early interviews is to identify other potential sources, including people or documents that might corroborate what someone is telling me. So perhaps my most frequent reason for interrupting is to ask for other people's names and find out where they might be reached, even get their phone numbers if these are readily at a source's disposal.

Especially for important sources, I find it is helpful to conduct a series of interviews, which gives them time to react and absorb the experience of the first interview. This is an advantage of working on a longer-term project, whether a book or an article. Many times in my experience, sources come to second and third interviews more relaxed and talkative. I suspect that, having approached the initial interview with some apprehension, they found the experience less onerous than they expected; furthermore, no adverse consequences ensued. Since I hadn't yet written anything, the consequences of talking weren't yet apparent. Indeed, on occasion I have come to the end of a lengthy series of interviews, only to hear the source express surprise that what he or she said was going to appear in print.

These follow-up interviews can often be conducted on the phone, or, I suppose, by e-mail, though I haven't yet tried that. I find that once a level of familiarity is established in the initial interview, most sources are quite comfortable on the phone, sometimes more so than in person. Only for the most important sources, usually major characters in a book or story, do I try to conduct all, or at least most, of the interviews in person. There is no substitute for personal contact, and for the ability to see and sense a source's reactions.

As interviews progress, they tend to become less narrative in style, and my questions may become somewhat more pointed. I never consider the interviewing completed until a story or book is published. Invariably, the process of writing triggers additional questions, and I often find myself typing a source's answers right into a manuscript. This is particularly true of the kinds of details that bring a scene to life, for it is often only in the writing that the need for such a level of description becomes clear. (Obviously, if the weather, say, was reported for every day that figured in a story, the reporting might never end.)

It is a common practice to save the most sensitive questions until the end, in case they will cause the source to stop cooperating. In my experience this is a legitimate concern, and I have on occasion saved the "hard" questions until a story is nearly complete. But sometimes that isn't an option. It's essential, in my view, that a source be given the time and opportunity to respond to such questions, outside of a last-minute "ambush" situation. That's not only because it seems the fair and decent thing to do, but because incorporating a source's responses to such questions invariably improves a story. And in most instances, if the hard questions are handled forthrightly, the source doesn't stop cooperating, even when it's clear the story is going to raise some troubling issues and may be far from flattering. This was the case with the Chris Whittle story I described earlier, and I remember my interviews with him toward the end of my reporting as some of the toughest I've ever conducted. Yet we remained in contact until the end. Even though the story was a highly unflattering account of his business practices—it detailed questionable accounting practices and a failure to pay state taxes—and no doubt caused serious disruptions in his career, we remained on cordial terms, at least as I saw it. Whatever else I had to say about Whittle, my description of him as a gentleman proved to be correct.

The last phase of reporting usually comes in the context of fact-checking, which is usually done after a story is written. I cannot stress how valuable this process can be, whether it is performed by a professional fact-checker, as is often the case at magazines, or whether you do it yourself. Knowledge that particular information is actually going to appear in print almost invariably triggers an outpouring of additional information. Many writers I know are reluctant to fact-check, for fear that knowledge of impending publication will alienate sources or give them reason to retract what they said. Surprisingly, though the concern is understandable, I've never known it to be borne out. For both *Blood Sport* and *Den of Thieves*, I hired fact-checkers to work with me. Fact-checkers have contributed greatly to the quality of

my work for *The New Yorker.* At *The Wall Street Journal,* as at
most newspapers, there were no fact-checkers, so I did my own
checking. The benefit was twofold: not only was additional information uncovered, but my work became more accurate. Nothing
makes a story more vulnerable to attack than a factual error, even
if minor. Something that is demonstrably wrong can undermine
the credibility of an entire story or book. I have sometimes been
amazed at how errors crept into my work, despite my diligence
and care. Fact-checking helps minimize this possibility, though it
can never eradicate it entirely.

While I have emphasized in-person interviewing, I don't
mean to ignore documentary sources. Computer search mechanisms, especially Nexis, have been a godsend to researchers, and
I have used them extensively. While many reporters and writers
disdain any reliance on anyone else's work, I have no qualms
about doing so, and am flattered and pleased when others use
mine, as long as it is acknowledged. I have often incorporated
the publication of other stories into my own narratives, especially
Blood Sport, in which other members of the press, especially Jeff
Gerth of *The New York Times,* figure prominently as characters.
Obviously, I wasn't going to pretend to have discovered Whitewater, a story broken by Gerth.

Originality is an important virtue, and any story worth writing
should include an abundance of new information. But while other
journalists and editors often obsess about who was first to report a
particular fact and what is "new" in an article or book, I find that
readers rarely do. Indeed, they tend to extend credit to the writer
even when something is attributed to someone else. An enthusiastic reader of *Blood Sport* came up to me after one of my bookstore
appearances to praise a section of the book about Lisa Foster, Vince
Foster's wife. As graciously as I tried to accept the compliment, I
pointed out that I had attributed that passage to an article by Peter
Boyer in *The New Yorker.* Sometimes I've gotten misplaced credit
for my own work. Someone complimented me on a revelation in
Den of Thieves that had actually appeared years before in one of
my articles for *The Wall Street Journal.*

Besides published material, original documents are often a
treasure trove. Letters, diaries, financial records, engagement cal-
endars—any written, contemporaneous evidence—is invaluable

and, I might add, usually far more dramatic and persuasive than verbal summaries. Whenever a source refers to a written record of some sort, I try to get the original document. Sources who are cooperative will usually try to oblige. For *Blood Sport,* after strenuous efforts, I was able to get from First Ozark National Bank in Flippin, Arkansas, the original Whitewater lender, the file containing correspondence between Hillary Clinton and the bank's officers. Far more persuasively than anything Jim or Susan McDougal might have said, it established that Mrs. Clinton was effectively handling Whitewater's affairs and thus undercut her public statement that she and the president were just passive investors. I found those letters so significant that I included photocopies of them as an appendix to the book. Such documents often go a long way toward corroborating sources' accounts, and thereby establishing their honesty and reliability, or conversely, undercutting them. Many writers shy away from "document" stories, evidently finding documents tedious to pore over. I find this is a mistake, for they sometimes reveal rich dramatic material.

In the case of the Sheinberg story I mentioned earlier, almost the entire narrative was constructed from the paper trail — transcripts and documents from the SEC investigation into insider trading in the MCA deal. The fact is that almost no one was willing to speak with me on any basis after the Sheinberg family apparently put out the word that they wanted no one to talk. I could never have written the story on the basis of my interviews. But I made a successful Freedom of Information Act request for transcripts of all the depositions taken in the case before it was settled. They were a trove of revealing, dramatic material. The testimony had the added virtue of having been given under oath.

The Sheinberg story is a good illustration of why I love lawsuits — at least, lawsuits in which I'm not a defendant. Lawsuits spawn an avalanche of material, much of it tedious and irrelevant, but much of it immensely valuable to a reporter. It was enormously helpful to me that many of the events described in *Den of Thieves* were the subject of both civil and criminal litigation. I would go so far as to say that any lawsuit is worth considering as a story simply because it yields so much information. I should point out that I am hardly the only person to have recognized this; lawyers themselves have become increasingly aware of the publicity their efforts can yield, and so have been moving to place court materials under seal, which prevents their disclosure to the public. Judges seem to be all too willing to grant such requests, both because no one is ever in court to speak on behalf of the public interest (most litigants are happy to keep materials in confidence, so they don't object) and because judges, like society at large, seem to be developing a growing disdain for the press and the public's right to know. (Judge Susan Webber Wright's opinions in the Paula Jones lawsuit against President Clinton displayed a barely concealed hostility toward the press, and she made numerous rulings placing materials under seal.)

As I mentioned earlier, I don't consider my reporting to be finished until a story or book is published. (Even then, I have occasionally had people call with even more information—which, in a few cases, led to sequels.) But a point invariably comes when I know it is time to start writing my story. How do I know? Generally it's because the curiosity that drove the story in the first place has been satisfied, or, in other words, the mystery has been solved. This doesn't mean that every loose end has been pinned down, just that, overall, I have a sense that I know what happened and why, at least as far as such things can be determined. At this point, I go over a mental checklist: Have I interviewed or tried to interview all possible sources, particularly those likely to appear as major characters? Even if I don't have everything that is to be known, do I have a critical mass of information that I find interesting? If, for some reason, I can't answer the questions that triggered the story, do I have a good reason why not, and can I still alert readers to some interesting new information? Sometimes I have begun to write too early in the reporting, which is a harrowing experience—the major cause, I believe, of so-called writer's block. The solution for me is simply to stop, clear my head, throw away whatever I've written, and go back to reporting.

At some point well into my research I develop something like impatience to get to the keyboard. Standing in the shower, going for a run in Central Park, I find myself fantasizing about possible leads. My friends find me preoccupied and absent-minded. That's generally a sure sign that it's time to write.

5
LEADS

THERE ARE FEW THINGS more intimidating than a blank computer screen, or more difficult psychologically than writing the first words of a story or book. Why is this? In part, it's because so much seems at stake. The beginning of any work is in many ways the most important, for if it fails to engage the reader, whatever follows may be written in vain. Beginnings are also a reminder of the daunting amount of work that goes into writing. First sentences take tremendous effort and concentration, and yet are only the first of thousands to come. When I finally finish the first few paragraphs of a book, then consider that hundreds of manuscript pages remain to be written, the task seems so monumental that I'm tempted to retreat to my bed.

But I try to start by relaxing. Bear in mind that first sentences can always be rewritten or even discarded altogether; they frequently are. The important thing is simply to get started. And never is it more important to remind yourself to take a project one day at a time than at the beginning. If you work diligently, eventually you will complete the task, no matter how long it is. A day's work is a day's work, whether your finished piece runs to twelve paragraphs or twelve chapters.

With that in mind, it is also possible to eliminate almost all the anxiety about beginning to write by following the few precepts I'm going to discuss in this chapter. Over the years, I've gotten to the point where the beginning of a story or book is pretty clear in my mind before I ever sit down to write. I've learned that if the structure of a story is clear to me, then the specific words aren't terribly important.

That doesn't mean that writing the beginnings of stories, usually referred to at magazines and newspapers as leads (or "ledes"), isn't a challenging task. On the contrary, I often find that I ultimately spend as much time writing and rewriting the lead as I do on the rest of a story. Virtually every word of the lead is important and must be carefully considered. But this part of the process can be fun and stimulating. It need have none of the terror associated with the blank page.

The key to a successful lead is quite simple: it must attract and hold readers by re-creating in their minds the same curiosity that drove you to undertake the story in the first place.

Let's ponder the implications of this, for, simple as it sounds, it is one of the most radical things I have to say in this book. It is the opposite of what most journalism students learn, and it stands the traditional pyramid style—the "who, what, when, where, why"—upside down. This lead seeks to inspire and inten-sify curiosity rather than to satisfy it. It invites readers on a jour-ney, but only hints at the destination. It must never give the ending away.

This point was driven home to me early in my time at *The Wall Street Journal*. Bill Carley, who has made a career writing excellent, suspenseful narratives, wrote a front-page piece about an oil executive who was kidnapped in South America. The inci-dent had happened perhaps a decade earlier, but Bill was able to re-create the experience in fascinating detail because of newly released transcripts. (This illustrates my precept that something can be "new" even though it happened years ago.) The incident and its aftermath had been reported at the time, but virtually no one remembered anything about it ten years later. Bill began the story by narrating the kidnapping—but then, in the third or fourth paragraph, just when suspense was at a peak, with the executive's life in peril and his future uncertain, Bill assured the reader that the executive was ultimately released unharmed. I told him I thought he'd written a terrific story, but said I was wondering why he gave away the ending so fast. Seeming puz-zled, he answered that he hadn't given it much thought—that was the way page one editors always made him write his stories. Years later, when I became Page One editor myself, I vowed to free Bill and everyone else from a rigid style that, out of a misguided sense of duty, drained suspense and killed readers' curiosity.

Before even contemplating the opening of a story it is helpful to review your initial idea, which I hope you jotted down, and then the story proposal, which should also be in writing. Even if you don't have these materials, you must somehow firmly resurrect in your mind why you began the story, and how you sold the idea to an editor. For readers aren't all that different from editors. They, too, need to be sold an idea if they're to invest time, attention, and money in reading your story or book.

It isn't easy to re-create your initial curiosity, because the information-gathering process has intervened. You may know too much. I find it surprising, the degree to which subsequently acquired knowledge can distort memory.

The initial story idea, which can usually be expressed in the form of a question, was inspired by some set of facts or observations. The simplest and often the most effective way to begin a story is to illustrate what inspired the question, then pose the question. This is generally done through implication, but there is nothing wrong with baldly stating the question. It is better to be too explicit than too indirect. Readers, most of them not being writers and journalists themselves, may not be as naturally curious as you are, so sometimes they need some prodding.

Let's briefly consider each of the broad story types I mentioned in chapter 3, for the type of story often dictates the lead. For the trend story, generally the simplest of those models, what caused you to identify something as a trend? Once you have the answer in mind, illustrate it in your lead. To take a very simple example, you may have been riding the New York subways when you noticed that more than half the men in the car were wearing earrings. Bring that scene to life, then ask if what you saw was a representative sample; if so, ask why so many men are wearing earrings.

If you are writing an explanatory story, you would illustrate whatever presented a conundrum or paradox that needed explaining. In a point-of-view story, you might illustrate a scene that first made you feel a sense of outrage. If you investigated a subject because an institution or person was secretive and powerful, begin by illustrating what made you suspicious—bring the power and secrecy to life. If you're profiling someone whose image you're going to debunk, illustrate the myth; then plant something that caused you to doubt its validity. Note that I have often resorted to words like "illustrate." This is simply a reflection of one of the simplest but best rules of writing: show rather than tell.

The narrative story poses some distinctive issues and opportunities, which I will discuss in greater detail later, but the principle is the same. Since a narrative is, by definition, a story told in chronological order, and is generally used when the explanation or answer to your question lies in the realm of cause and effect, then the beginning should be the scene that gave rise to the question underlying the story. Sometimes that question is quite simple. In the story of the kidnapped executive I just mentioned, for example, the question is "Did he get out alive?" Bill quite effectively began the story with the scene that put the executive's life in peril. The scene that most often gives rise to questions in the nature of "What happened?" is an event that destroys the status quo. Readers are inherently curious to know how someone regains equilibrium when the status quo has been shattered.

Establishing curiosity in the reader's mind is the primary goal of the lead. But a lead can accomplish much more than that. Indeed, if possible, it should touch upon all the points you used to "sell" your story in the proposal. To reiterate, they are timeliness; universality; significance; exclusivity; similarity; and feasibility.

This is much more complicated in the abstract than it is in reality. Many writers understand this process instinctively, but are at a loss if asked to put their approach into words. I find it easier to illustrate with some actual examples. Do you recall the questions that triggered my interest in the Sheinberg insider-trading story? After months had elapsed, during which time I made my Freedom of Information Act request and sought and conducted interviews, I went back to the original article that had prompted my curiosity and reviewed the proposal. The simplest and most important question, to me, had been why a rich person like Jonathan Sheinberg would get involved in insider trading. I also wondered why he would defy his father, and what light, if any, that shed on the father/son relationship in Hollywood. The proposal cited several additional selling points: that Sidney Sheinberg was important and well-known; that the story was set in the glamorous upper echelons of Hollywood; that I might get exclusive access to information; and that a reader might gain broader insights into both the law and psychology of insider trading. I thought of the story as an explanatory piece, but one that could be best written in the form of a narrative, because the explanation, which was quite complex, could best be understood in a sequence of cause and effect. So where would I begin?

I wanted a scene of the status quo being upended for Jonathan Sheinberg and his father, the story's two main characters, and that would naturally give rise to the questions that motivated my interest. Three possibilities were almost immediately apparent. First, there was the scene where Jonathan learned he was under investigation for insider trading. That was the moment when the status quo for Jonathan was shattered. A second possibility was the moment when Jonathan learned the secret information that MCA was going to be acquired by Matsushita. That information needn't have shattered Jonathan's status quo, but as events unfolded, it did. And a third possibility was the conversation in which Jonathan told his father that he was under investigation—a moment that shattered the status quo for Sidney Sheinberg.

After a little further thought, I discarded the first option. As the reporting had unfolded, my interest in the SEC lawyers, the investigators, had been eclipsed by my interest in Jonathan and his father. It had become pretty clear to me early on that the material would not lend itself to a classic detective-story approach, appealing though that might have seemed. The main problem from a narrative standpoint was that the case had been settled; consequently, the outcome of the investigation was an anticlimax. The most interesting aspect of the case was how the SEC had become suspicious. The investigation itself was more routine. Besides having the goals I've already mentioned, the lead introduces the reader to one or more characters and, by doing so, foreshadows a story's themes and emphasis. Though it's not essential, it helps if those characters are the main characters in the story. To have introduced one of the SEC lawyers as a main character in the lead made no sense once I had determined that the investigation would not be the principal focus of the story.

What the reporting had underscored was the importance of

the father-son relationship in understanding Jonathan's behavior. Indeed, the "slug," or shorthand title I used in submitting my draft of the story, was "Father." For that reason, I wanted an opening scene that would introduce both Jonathan and Sidney Sheinberg. The approach had the added benefit of touching on the "significance" aspect of the story, since the only really well-known character was Sidney. Either the second or the third option would work.

In many ways I preferred option 3. The moment when Jonathan had to confront his father was inherently dramatic. It was also intimate, a conversation the likes of which readers would have rarely, if ever, been privy to. This would have conferred an aura of exclusivity and reportorial authority. It would have clearly established the centrality to the story of the father-son relationship—a theme as old as *Oedipus Rex*—immediately broadening the story beyond the confines of Hollywood. There was only one problem, and it was substantial. This scene, so pivotal from a narrative standpoint, had been touched on in passing by the SEC questioners, since it had little, if any, relevance to anyone's legal liability. It was a classic instance of the frustration I often experience when lawyers are the ones doing the questioning; if only I could have conducted the Sheinbergs' depositions! But I was stuck with what was in the transcript, since neither Sidney nor Jonathan was willing to recount the scene to me. (For this reason alone, the Sheinberg family may very well have concluded they made the right decision in refusing to talk.) I tried to use the material I had to reconstruct this scene, but too much was lacking. It raised more questions than it answered. It implied an intimacy with the facts that I simply did not possess.

That left option 2. The scene in which Jonathan overheard his father on the telephone had been explored in much greater detail by the SEC lawyers conducting the depositions, so there was more material to work with. There had also been testimony about a father-son walk on the beach in Malibu after the phone call.

Let's look closely at the unedited lead I turned in for the Sheinberg story, using the second option:

> On Friday, September 21, 1990, Jonathan Sheinberg, then president of Lee Rich Productions in Hollywood, arrived with his daughter Thea for a weekend at the Malibu beach house of

his parents, Sidney Sheinberg, president and chief executive of MCA Corp., and his wife, actress Lorraine Gary. Sid Sheinberg and Lew Wasserman, MCA's chairman, rank as two of Hollywood's living legends, having transformed MCA from a small music-publishing and talent agency into the owner of Universal Studios and one of the nation's leading entertainment companies. Given their prominence, the Sheinbergs are besieged with invitations, and had bought the Malibu house as a retreat from their Beverly Hills mansion, a place where they and their two grown sons and their wives and children would gather for quiet family weekends.

The Sheinbergs have long prided themselves on their dedication to family. In a town and an industry where conventional values fare better on screen than in real life, their reputations had never been sullied by affairs, separations, divorce, or even rumors. Lorraine, in particular, had devoted herself to family-oriented causes, assuming the vice-presidency of the Westside Children's Center in Los Angeles, and, together with Sid, helping launch the Children's Action Network, which has made promotional films devoted to such issues as childhood vaccinations.

When Jonathan, thirty-three, and his daughter arrived that Friday afternoon, entering through the back door, Sid was on the phone in the next room. Like many of the multimillion-dollar houses that crowd the hillside above Malibu's Broad Beach, the Sheinberg house is relatively narrow, about thirty feet wide, and Jonathan could hear his father on the phone. Though Sid Sheinberg can be charming and gregarious, he has long been notorious for yelling at executives, even when he isn't angry. On this occasion he was shouting excitedly into the phone about the prospect of selling MCA to the Japanese in a $6.6 billion transaction that would, among other things, transform the already wealthy Sheinberg into one of the richest men in the country. His MCA stock alone would be worth $92 million, paying a dividend of $28.6 million a year. In addition, he was due to receive a $2.1 million "bonus," $9.6 million to replace various "incentives," and an annual salary of $8.6 million. Jonathan not only stood to inherit a large part of that fortune, but he too owned MCA stock. Some had been bestowed upon him as a child; some he'd bought on his own over the years.

Though MCA stock had appreciated handsomely over the years, recently it had proven a disappointing investment. Despite such hits as *Jaws* and *E.T.,* MCA had had its share of bombs, such as the ill-fated *Howard the Duck,* and its stock had languished. In the wake of Sony's purchase of Columbia Pictures from Coca-Cola for five billion dollars the year before, and the much-talked-about synergy between hardware manufacturers and the producers of programming for all those VCRs and TV sets, deal makers were frantically trying to match nearly every studio with a cash-rich Japanese conglomerate. The languishing Universal seemed especially attractive.

Superagent Michael Ovitz, a Sheinberg neighbor at Broad Beach and the matchmaker for Sony and Columbia, had in fact already initiated secret talks between Matsushita and MCA just a month before Jonathan's visit, when he approached Felix Rohatyn of Lazard Frères, who was a member of MCA's board and the company's principal financial adviser. Ovitz met with Wasserman and Sheinberg in early September, and just two days earlier, they and Rohatyn were told that Matsushita was definitely contemplating a bid for MCA. But investors not privy to this top-secret development had grown impatient by the lack of any concrete developments, and the stock was sliding to new yearly lows.

As Jonathan passed through the house, he bumped into his mother, who looked alarmed at Jonathan's untimely arrival. She knew what her husband was discussing, and she assumed Jonathan had overheard the conversation. "Those discussions are obviously secret," she said, or words to that effect, warning Jonathan not to mention the information to anyone. Then she rushed into the study, and as soon as Sid hung up the phone, she told him she thought Jonathan had overheard, and that Sid had better talk to him.

Sid agreed. As much as he loved Jonathan—and he always insisted he did—he had come to distrust his older son. Sid has described Jonathan as "vocal" and "gregarious"; someone, who at the least, might be indiscreet. Jonathan is highly excitable, almost compulsively talkative, given to bursts of enthusiasm but with a short attention span. ("I always thought it was hereditary," observes one former colleague.) Sid knew that what he'd been discussing on the phone was classic inside information, and that he had a legal duty to keep it confidential. Sid himself is a lawyer; early in his career, he was a law professor first at Columbia and then UCLA before launching his career at MCA as a young in-house lawyer. Moreover, public awareness of the insider-trading scandal that had rocked Wall Street was then at its height. Michael Milken, whose infamous trading desk was in Beverly Hills, had pleaded guilty to six felonies that spring, and Ivan Boesky, who owned the Beverly Hills Hotel, had been fined $100 million and was at that moment lodged in a federal prison at Lompoc, California, not all that far from Malibu. Discussions with Matsushita had been cloaked in extreme secrecy to preclude any taint of scandal in what was already likely to be a politically controversial purchase of an American studio by the Japanese.

Sid was about to embark on a walk along the beach (he walks every day he's in Malibu to "amortize" the high cost of the house, he has said) and he asked Jonathan to come along so they could talk without being overheard.

On the walk, Sid took Jonathan into his confidence, mentioning that Lorraine had told him he'd overheard the conversation. He filled in some details, identifying the likely buyer of MCA as Matsushita. Jonathan had never heard of the Japanese company, and Sid said it was best known in the U.S. for its consumer electronics brands, including Technics, Panasonic, Quasar, and JVC. While Sid was trying to confine his disclosures to what he thought Jonathan already knew, Jonathan managed to get both a good sense of the price per share of the deal (upward of eighty dollars) and its timing (imminent). Then Sid got to the real point of the conversation: he warned Jonathan that he must not trade in MCA stock, he mustn't do anything with the information, and he must keep it secret. "Keep that to yourself," he said. "For God's sake, don't trade on the stock."

Months after this walk along the beach, Sid was asked whether he believed his son would obey these admonitions. "I would have bet anything on it," Sid replied.

The first two paragraphs briefly identify a specific time and place. It is a variation of the "once upon a time" introduction; it is a shorthand way of saying "I'm going to tell you a story." The setting for this story happens to be Malibu, a wealthy, exclusive enclave, which is mentioned immediately. Most readers understand from this signal that a narrative story will unfold in a location of considerable interest, which is important, because the information immediately following doesn't advance the story. Rather, it serves other functions: it identifies Sidney Sheinberg as an important person, a "living legend." And it foreshadows an intrafamily conflict by emphasizing the Sheinbergs' reputations as champions of family values. Most people reading this lead don't need to be told explicitly that the Sheinbergs' reputations will turn out to be, to some extent, at variance with reality. Thus, the elements of significance and universality are planted in the very beginning of the story. I felt this was important in this story, because, as I've mentioned, Jonathan Sheinberg isn't widely known, and the opening scene concerns insider trading, a topic of limited popular appeal.

The third paragraph returns to the plot, and quickly establishes the story's central conundrum by emphasizing that the Sheinbergs are a wealthy family. Note that for a dramatic moment in the story, there is a paucity of actual description. What room is Sidney in? What does it look like? How did Jonathan overhear his father without Sidney noticing it? These are details I might very well have included—had the SEC lawyers elicited testimony that included them. But I had to work with what emerged in the deposition transcripts I had obtained. Note, too, that I went on in some detail about the financial aspects of the MCA deal for Sidney Sheinberg. These specifics speak more persuasively of the Sheinbergs' wealth than if I had simply said they were rich, or that they stood to make money on the deal. Here is another small example of showing something rather than telling it.

The next two paragraphs provide background necessary to understand the deal (we'll see how this was edited in the final story) and then the plot resumes, with Jonathan bumping into his mother. She talks to her husband, and we learn something of Sidney's state of mind, enough to understand why he might be concerned about Jonathan's having overheard the conversation. All of this information came directly from Sidney's deposition. This is a crucial paragraph, and it was somewhat difficult to write. That's because I wanted readers to know enough to understand why Sidney would have the ensuing walk on the beach and conversation with his son, yet not so much that they would lose their curiosity about why Jonathan would defy his father.

Finally we reach the dramatic climax of the opening scene: "For God's sake, don't trade on the stock," Sidney tells Jonathan. This quotation was available to me from the deposition transcript, and was enormously helpful in establishing a sense of immediacy and exclusivity.

At this juncture, it is important to recognize what is *not* included in the lead. Beginning writers, especially in their leads, are tempted to include information that the characters themselves could not have known at the time that is being described. The date of the opening scene is September 20, 1990. Anything that happens after that date would be unforeseeable by Jonathan, Sidney, or Lorraine, and thus should not be mentioned. You want readers to place themselves in the story, as though they were eavesdropping on the conversation between Jonathan and his father. Readers cannot be omniscient, or else they will know the ending or wonder why they aren't being told. This is essential to establishing narrative suspense. I have noticed in my own reading that even when the ending is known, the technique effectively establishes suspense. *The Day of the Jackal,* a suspense thriller about a plot to assassinate Charles de Gaulle, is a classic example. Every reader knew that De Gaulle had not been assassinated but died a natural death. Yet the plot was suspenseful because, in context, the characters themselves didn't know the outcome.

Sidney's admonition to Jonathan could easily have been the ending of the lead, and I pondered whether it should be. Chronologically, the story has progressed with only minor interruptions for additional information. Yet in the last paragraph ("Months later . . .") I jumped forward in time, violating the rule I have just cited about using nothing that happened after September 20. This upsets the chronological order of the story. It also risks giving away a crucial element of the plot, since the obvious inference is that Jonathan did violate his father's orders. Both of these are things I would ordinarily try to avoid. Why did I use the last paragraph?

I mentioned earlier that the primary goal of the lead is to instill curiosity in the reader. Perhaps I would have succeeded without that last paragraph. Indeed, I often tell my students that there is no one way to tell a story. But recall that my own interest wasn't in finding out whether Jonathan had leaked confidential information. I already knew that he had. My curiosity concerned why he had done so. Even at this early point in the story, it would be clear to most readers that Jonathan is going to do something wrong; otherwise there wouldn't be a story. Note, however, that I never actually say what Jonathan did—I leave that to the reader's imagination, which preserves at least a little suspense. Sidney's comment helps to heighten curiosity by making it seem even more improbable that Jonathan would have defied him: "I would have bet anything." That is a strong statement. That makes the ensuing events more surprising, more of a paradox, and thus more puzzling to readers. It heightens curiosity, and focuses that curiosity on "why." This is exactly the frame of mind I want readers to have as they embark on the rest of the story.

Did I succeed? Probably not with every reader. I can only hope that I did the best with the material I had to work with. And, as you can now see, I had a reason for writing the lead as I did.

Let's look at another example, the lead to the profile I wrote of the successful but impoverished novelist James Wilcox. Recall from my earlier discussion that my interest in the subject was kindled by the paradox of an acclaimed and critically successful writer who seemed barely able to make ends meet. I knew the story would be a profile, using Jim as a window into the workings of the publishing industry. Here is the lead I turned in:

> When James Wilcox is working at the St. Francis Xavier "welcome table," as its soup kitchen is called, as he does on the first and second Sundays of every month, it's hard to tell he's an acclaimed novelist. It took his fellow volunteers years to figure it out. No one there had read "Modern Baptists," his first novel, published in 1983, hailed in a front-page New York Times book review by Anne Tyler as "startlingly alive, exuberantly over-crowded." Nor were they familiar with its five progeny, three of them set in the fictional Tula Springs, Louisiana, a venue compared by more than one critic to William Faulkner's Yoknapatawpha County.
>
> Wilcox himself was much too shy to tell them. He looks younger than his age, which is forty-five, with his slightly ruddy complexion, medium build, and sandy hair. He's nice-looking, though he agonizes over his author photographs and didn't want one on his last book. Yale-educated, he speaks with no trace of an accent. His Southern roots are evident only in the elaborate courtesy with which he waits on the soup kitchen's "guests," as he unfailingly calls them when dispensing juice and coffee. He betrays little reaction when something really grabs his attention, like the saga of a woman plagued by the stench from a neighbor who kept twenty-two cats in her Murray Hill one-bedroom apartment.
>
> "For years I never knew what he did," says George Deshensky, a lawyer and one of the directors of the soup kitchen. "Then one day someone said, 'He's a published author.' So we'd introduce him that way. We didn't know what he published

or where." Deshensky began relying on Wilcox as a "calming influence" when altercations threatened to break out in the line, as happened with some regularity. Since then, during the eight years Wilcox has been working at the soup kitchen, he and Deshensky have become close friends and Deshensky has read his books. Still, it came as a surprise to Deshensky when he complimented Wilcox on the empathy he shows their impoverished patrons. "I'm only a check or two from being in the line myself," Wilcox replied.

This lead takes up only three paragraphs. In many ways, this is a much simpler story than the one about the Sheinbergs. The opening paragraph uses a common introductory device: a character or characters who act as a surrogate for the reader in that they know no more (and sometimes even less) about a subject than the reader does. Here those characters are Jim's fellow workers at the soup kitchen. Through their eyes we meet Jim, learning that he's an acclaimed novelist, and see some of his physical characteristics. This is a particularly useful device when the main character, like Jim, is probably unknown to readers. While they don't know Jim's reputation, the implication is that they should (as should readers) since he has been hailed in a front-page *New York Times* review by Anne Tyler. He has been compared to William Faulkner. Each of these details is important: Everyone knows Faulkner is a great American writer. Most readers will recognize the name Anne Tyler. Notices on the front page of the *New York Times Book Review* are highly coveted, and any readers familiar with the publishing industry will know that. And the review was a rave. Thus, the first paragraph introduces the main character and establishes him as an important writer, someone readers should know about. This helps to establish the "selling" qualities of significance and similarity (to Faulkner), which are especially critical when the story is a profile and the subject is little known.

But the main goal of the lead is to establish the paradox that gives rise to our curiosity about Wilcox: that an acclaimed novelist is nonetheless barely able to make ends meet. This is done in the last sentence of the lead, which serves as the punch line for the opening anecdote. By suddenly juxtaposing Wilcox's acclaim, which has been established at some length, against the reality that he's only a check or two away from a soup kitchen, I was trying to jolt readers into asking how this could be, without having to state the question myself. As I mentioned earlier, the power of the story is much greater if readers ask and answer these questions in their own minds, without much prompting from the author.

The lead in this story consists of a single anecdote, which, like all anecdotes, is a highly compressed narrative in its own right. Unlike the lead to the Sheinberg story, this mini-narrative is complete at the end of the third paragraph. So it doesn't establish the dramatic tension that arises in a narrative lead. The reader isn't left to wonder what happened next; there is no "next" in the story of Jim's work at the soup kitchen. Readers' curiosity must be aroused solely by the paradox. I hate to lose the opportunity to further heighten curiosity, given the proven willingness of most readers to stop reading with the slightest provocation. But the loss of narrative suspense is inevitably the case in all non-narrative stories, which is one reason I try to use the narrative form when possible.

Before leaving the Wilcox lead, note a few other details that are included: the anecdote about the twenty-nine cats, the altercations in the food line. What purpose do they serve? Keeping twenty-nine cats in a one-bedroom apartment is absurd, which foreshadows that this story may have some humorous elements. That Jim is a calming influence in a tumultuous environment foreshadows a major theme in his works—salvation through good works. By hinting at aspects of the story still to come, the ripple effects are produced in readers' minds, however subliminally, and begin to introduce elements of universality into the story.

I suggested earlier that in writing a point-of-view story, you may want to begin with an anecdote that gave rise to the point of view in the first place. The newspaper clipping I received from a Carlisle, Pennsylvania, restaurateur had mentioned a lawsuit in which an accountant, fired by his employer, had been sued by the former employer and lost, in what seemed an obvious miscarriage of justice. Here is the resulting lead:

On the morning of October 17, 1990, Donald L. DeMuth, who runs a professional management consulting business in Camp Hill, Pennsylvania, just outside the state capital, asked one of his employees, Dan Miller, to step into his office. Miller didn't know why, but it was possible that DeMuth was going to raise again the possibility of Miller becoming a partner in DeMuth's firm, which specializes in financial matters for the medical and dental professions. DeMuth had never promised Miller a partnership, but he'd recently asked him if he wanted to invest with him in a new office building in anticipation of his becoming a co-owner of the firm. As professional relationships go, DeMuth and Miller had become close over the five years they'd worked together. DeMuth often asked Miller to join him at Harrisburg Senator baseball games (DeMuth is a baseball fan and co-owns the Spartanburg, Virginia, Phillies), the two sometimes traveled together to professional conferences, and Miller often joined DeMuth and his wife for dinner. Over the years DeMuth had had other employees who were candidates for partnership, but none had established the good rapport he had with Miller.

DeMuth's tone that morning immediately established that something was wrong. "I'm sorry to have to do this," DeMuth began. Then he fired him. "Why?" Miller demanded. "You know why," DeMuth replied. DeMuth told Miller he'd get no severance pay and his medical benefits were terminated. He was given the rest of the day to remove his belongings from the office.

After absorbing the shock—Miller had never gotten so much as a bad grade, let alone a summary discharge—Miller opened his own office across the river in Harrisburg. Several of his clients, baffled by his sudden departure, continued to send work his way. Some of them soon received a letter from De-Muth, which contained this passage:

> Engaging practice management consultants and accountants is generally with an eye on a long term relationship. If something happens to someone in my firm, clients are not left in a lurch, but will have continuity of service. Right now Dan is on his own. If he ever wants to grow, I question who he will be able to attract as an associate. While there may be other homosexual practice management consultants and C.P.A.'s, to the best of my knowledge I've never met one.
>
> It's well known that homosexuals are significantly at risk for AIDS. While I have no knowledge of Dan's medical condition, consider getting the results of a blood test from him, if you are considering using his services on a long term basis. . . .
>
> I believe if you compare what my firm offers with any other firm you are considering, we will be viewed favorably. I am enclosing a copy of my curriculum vitae.

DeMuth also took his concerns to the Institute of Professional Business Consultants, writing that "I am concerned that a former employee of mine, who I discovered was a homosexual, has attempted and is continuing to attempt to pass the CPBC exam," and the Society of Medical-Dental Management Consultants, an important organization and credential in the field, urging that Miller be barred from membership.

Miller was not, at the time, the kind of person who likes to make waves. But in the wake of his firing, the letters, and the attempt to bar him from the professional organizations, he was beginning to think seriously about filing a lawsuit against DeMuth, even though he knew that money for litigation was something he'd be hard-pressed to muster. But then DeMuth sued *him* in the Cumberland County Court of Common Pleas in nearby Carlisle.

DeMuth charged Miller with breach of contract, in that Miller's employment contract had contained a non-compete provision. Confronted with the suit, Miller counterclaimed for wrongful discharge, libel and slander, and interference with his efforts to earn a living. Last summer the jury reached a verdict. After considering the evidence, which established that Miller is gay, does not carry the AIDS virus, and was considered an exemplary employee by clients, co-workers and DeMuth himself, the jury ruled in favor of DeMuth, the employer, on all counts. It dismissed all of Miller's counterclaims. It awarded DeMuth $123,648—somewhat more than DeMuth had actually stipulated as damages.

Stunned by the verdict, Miller has been raising funds from friends and family members for an appeal and to pay his attorney's fees, which amounted to over $44,000. Because of his financial plight, he can no longer afford these lawyers and has turned to pro bono counsel. His appeal is scheduled to be argued this fall. In the meantime, he has had to pay over $150,000 —the full award plus 25 percent—to the court as a bond in order to assure DeMuth that the money will be there when, as DeMuth has every reason to believe, the jury's verdict is upheld.

This is another example of an anecdote in which I tried to show rather than tell, which I deem especially important in a point-of-view story. My reaction to this anecdote, though it inspired the story, is quite rightly of little interest or relevance to readers. Their reactions are what is important. That said, I tried to make sure that all the facts on which my reaction had been based were present for readers to consider. As in an explanatory piece, which in a sense this is as well, I tried to heighten curiosity about how such a thing could have happened by emphasizing those facts which make the result all the more surprising.

Thus, I mentioned the good working relationship between Miller and DeMuth, even that Miller thought he was being called in for a promotion. I included Miller's exemplary work record and his popularity with clients. Yet Miller is abrubtly fired. I did not mention in the opening paragraphs that Miller is gay—since DeMuth refused to explain his action, Miller himself didn't know that was a factor. The opening paragraphs are told from the point of view of Miller, and so must strictly adhere to what Miller knew at the time.

Could the lead have ended with Miller being fired? I considered that option. It was appealing because it gave away so little about what happened in the story, and it was confined to a single scene; the element of simplicity is always an advantage when you're opening with an anecdote. But consider the "selling" function of the lead. Both Miller and DeMuth were unknown to readers. They are accountants. A suburb of Harrisburg isn't a setting likely to generate much interest. However reliable an employee, would readers be all that curious as to why Miller was fired? Would they care about him? Not, I concluded, unless they knew he was gay, and thus a potential victim of prejudice.

The following paragraphs reveal how the issue of Miller being gay surfaced: somewhat obliquely, in DeMuth's campaign to keep clients from defecting to Miller. DeMuth never told Miller the reason for his firing, nor was he explicit to clients. (The inability to directly confront the issue spoke volumes about De-Muth's character and attitude.) Again, I attempted to *show* how the issue surfaced, by using the text of DeMuth's letter to clients rather than my characterization of it. Note how much more effective and persuasive is that letter than anything I might have said about it.

There, too, the lead might have ended, with Miller presumably a victim of antigay prejudice. That added the element of significance I felt the story needed. Yet it still lacked the element of outrage I felt the original news clipping had inspired. That depended upon knowing not only that Miller is gay, but that he was sued by DeMuth—and lost. This broadened the story considerably, suggesting that not only was Miller a victim of preju-

dice, but the discrimination against him had been compounded
by the legal system. This added the crucial element of universality. And it seemed to me to be the one fact that would jolt readers
into having a point of view. For, sadly, discrimination is simply too
routine to engender much surprise. But to suffer discrimination
and then be sued—that suggested a vendetta, and hence it was
much more puzzling and potentially troubling.

It was too bad, from a purely narrative standpoint, that virtually every key scene in the story—Miller being fired, DeMuth
writing his letters, Miller being sued, Miller losing the lawsuit—
had to be included in the lead. But each of them is seen through
the eyes of Miller, whose own surprise and outrage are intended
to trigger the reader's. The question the reader is meant to be
left with is how such a turn of events could have come to pass,
which shifts the focus from Miller to DeMuth. DeMuth is the
major actor in the story. When these events are revisited in the
body of the story, they are seen largely from DeMuth's point of
view. Miller is initially a somewhat passive victim, someone who
was not "at the time" likely to make waves. That sentence subtly
implies that there will be a time when Miller *does* make waves,
and thus suggests that he will be changed by the experience.
Being fired and losing the lawsuit are events that shatter the
status quo for Miller.

Did I succeed with this lead in generating reader interest in
two Pennsylvania accountants? Once again, there's no way of
knowing for sure. But I received a very high volume of mail from
readers, which in a sense isn't surprising—point-of-view stories,
not to mention editorials, always tend to generate more mail than
other types of stories. Most of the letters did express outrage and
admiration for Miller. Curiously, though, a fair number voiced
support for DeMuth. You may find this strange, but I was gratified
by that result. It suggested that I had been fair in presenting the
facts. Just as in life, responses to stories should be as varied as
the readers themselves. The fact that people who shared De-
Muth's views would even be talking about the rights of gay employees struck me as an accomplishment.

Having looked at an explanatory lead, a profile lead, and a
point-of-view lead, let's turn to the narrative lead, using my story
about the Mississippi flood as an illustration. Recall that I pro-

posed the flood story as a "pure" narrative, one in which the
reader's curiosity had to be triggered solely by the question
"What happened?" Both the Sheinberg and Wilcox stories, not
being pure narratives, had the advantage of paradox in triggering
curiosity. But the narrative usually rests only on its chronological
arc. As I pointed out in connection with the Sheinberg story, the
opening scene in a narrative lead is often the one that upsets the
status quo for the story's principal characters. In considering
the events in the flood story, I had a very limited range of possibilities. There was, first, the beginning of the flood, which certainly
upset the status quo and set the ensuing events in motion; there
was the moment when the main characters were in greatest
jeopardy, in which the imminent failure of the levee would have
drastically altered their lives; and there was the failure of the
levee, if that was the outcome. (If the levee held, the status quo
would obviously remain unchanged in that respect, and I'd have
only options 1 and 2.) Given that I arrived at the levee before the
outcome was clear—and left while it was still unclear—options
2 and 3 were hardly viable alternatives, since I didn't know for
sure if the participants had yet faced their greatest peril, or
whether the levee would hold.

Purely from a writing standpoint, this is a fairly unusual situation, one that generally only arises in the "witness to history"
stories I mentioned earlier. Usually a dramatic event is narrated
by a participant who has lived through the outcome, so the full
range of options is available to the writer. But in this case, I had
left the levee. To be honest, once I had done some work myself
and interviewed all the participants at length, I wasn't all that
eager to hang around. In midsummer the heat at the levee was
stifling, the insects were devouring me, and, more to the point,
nothing was happening as far as I could tell. It pretty much
looked like the battle of the Sny levee had been won. As measured by a yardstick stuck into the muddy water, the river was
slowly receding. Man, it seemed, had triumphed over nature. So
I came back to New York and started writing. Timeliness was,
after all, a consideration.

One of the advantages of writing the narrative story is that,
if no other option presents itself, one can always begin at the
beginning. Indeed, I've often counseled students and reporters
faced with writer's block to simply begin by writing the scene

that is first in chronological order. Even if the scene is later moved for literary effect, it is a starting place, it will lead to a coherent story, and, more often than many writers realize, it very well may be the best place to start. (Think how often biographies begin with the birth of the subject.) In my reporting on the flood, I'd asked just about everybody what had caused the river to rise in the first place. The consensus was that the culprit was the extraordinarily heavy rains throughout the spring and early summer, rather than the regular annual melting of the snowpack. In particular, just about everybody described a deluge that had struck Quincy at the end of June. Even though it was obvious that a single rainstorm couldn't have caused a flood of the magnitude that ensued, this was where the story began, from my point of view. And since it set in motion a sequence of events that changed everyone's lives, it also served the purpose of threatening the status quo. Here is how I began:

On Wednesday, June 30, at about ten P.M., as Alexander J. House turned in early for the night, he heard the first of the rain on the metal roof of the nineteenth-century farmhouse built by his great-grandfather. After House's father died and his mother remarried, the thirty-five-year-old House had come back in 1986 to the family home in Payson, Illinois, a small farm town located about five miles southwest of Quincy, the commercial hub of the area. Before going to bed, House had gazed out over his pond and the rolling fields to the west where the land descends toward the Mississippi. There, in a basin formed by the old Sny Channel, which runs parallel to the Mississippi, lies some of the richest farmland in the world, 1,400 acres of which belong to House and his family. Over the fields that night he'd seen an ominous bank of black clouds, confirming local forecasts of potentially heavy rains and thunderstorms.

House, tall, handsome, with dark blond hair—the New York *Times* magazine once ran a full-page photo of him in an article on bachelors (he has since married)—was hoping to fall asleep quickly, knowing he had only a few hours before he had to be up to help load trucks with calcium carbonate, a white mineral his company extracts from the high bluffs that define the floodplain of the Mississippi. Like many farmers in the area, House is also a businessman; he helped found and co-owns Quincy Carbonates. After graduating from Kenyon College and the Loyola University business school, he could have moved to Chicago, St. Louis, or another big city, but, he says, "I grew up in Payson and always knew I'd come back." Though he does a fair amount of farming himself, he rents out his Sny acreage to Kenneth Crim, a powerfully built forty-six-year-old who farms House's land and nearby land belonging to Crim's mother-in-law.

That night, as the thunder crashed and the rain beat more heavily on the roof, House found he couldn't sleep. Finally, around midnight, he got up to look outside, and saw a deluge like he'd never seen before. Worried about getting the trucks in for loading, he dressed, jumped into his Dodge Ram four-wheel-drive pickup, and headed west toward his plant. Along the way, he noticed that power failures had plunged the area into darkness. By the eerie, sudden flashes of lightning, he could see that ditches and creeks were overflowing. When he got to Illinois Route 57, which runs south from Quincy along the old Sny basin, it had turned into a rushing waterway. At one A.M., House got into a front-end loader and started digging a drainage ditch to protect his plant. "Basically, there was a wall of water coming at us," he says. Further south, on House's farmland, Ken Crim got up to watch the deluge, and says he had only one reaction: "Holy shit."

About eleven P.M. that night, in Quincy, Adams County Sheriff Robert Nall, seeing the torrential rains, got into his custom-fitted patrol car and headed out to some of the country roads north of town. Gazing up periodically through the windshield, the fifty-one-year-old sheriff saw what he describes as the "most spectacular show of lightning I've ever seen," which lasted not the usual minutes, but hours. As the severity of the storm became obvious, he headed down to his office on the first floor of the Adams County Courthouse and began calling his deputies, sending them out on the roads to look for dangerous conditions and for any cars that might have been swept off in the deluge. From around the county came reports that creeks had burst their banks, flooding roads, which had in turn all but formed small rivers. When Nall went home at about two A.M., with rain still falling, he had the ominous feeling that worse news was to come.

The next morning, Leo Henning, the operations manager for WGEM TV and Radio in Quincy, an NBC (television) and ABC (radio) affiliate, got up and checked out the damage in his basement, where several inches of water had collected overnight. Henning may have been one of the few people in town who slept through the storm. Like many people in Quincy, the Chicago native didn't ordinarily give much thought to heavy rains. Quincy's founders, back in 1840, had had the foresight to locate their river port on some the highest bluffs on the eastern side of the Mississippi. From the old dock areas along the riverfront where stern-wheelers in profusion once called, the streets rise steeply to the east. From buildings surrounding the old town square high above the river, and from WGEM's offices in the Hotel Quincy just around the corner, there are sweeping views that stretch for miles into the fertile lowlands of Missouri. Those lands, as well as vast tracts to both the north and south of Quincy, along with their farms and the towns and hamlets that dot the landscape, are protected by an elaborate system of levees and drainage districts along both sides of the river. So, too, are the two bridges that cross the Mississippi at Quincy. Despite mild annoyance at the water in his basement, Henning did recognize a story. WGEM radio had recently shifted to a twenty-four-hour news and talk format, and when he heard the numbers, he knew he had more than a routine weather bulletin.

Overnight, Quincy had received a record six inches of rain. Some areas to the north had been drenched even more. The Mississippi River, which typically rises or falls a tenth of a foot in a twenty-four-hour period, had risen a startling two feet. Coming as it had after an unusually wet spring, the downpour left Henning, Nall, House, and just about everybody else in and around Quincy with one major question: Would the levee hold?

Like the Wilcox lead, this opening is quite simple: a rainstorm strikes Quincy and the area around it, which imperils some of the local citizenry living behind protective levees. How inherently interesting is this?

Not very, you may be saying. Indeed, while punctuated with some visual pyrotechnics, a rainstorm is pretty commonplace, as far as natural disasters go. Nor did this tempest descend upon anyone the average reader could be expected to be even remotely familiar with. From a writing standpoint, this was a challenge. In a very short space, I had to try to make readers care about people they'd never heard of, so they would be curious to know whether the levee ultimately held. There was no paradox to draw upon, no mystery that needed explanation.

The lead begins with the story's main character, Alex House. In a short space, I crammed in quite a bit of biographical detail, a mini-narrative in its own right. House is someone who'd come home to the floodplain. He'd gone away to a good college, he'd lived in Chicago, but something about roots, family, and tradition

—he lived in his grandfather's farmhouse—drew him back to Payson. This vignette thus provides the outline of a biographical story that I felt would resonate with many readers—with anyone who has left home and felt the urge to return: in other words, most of us. What was at stake for House was not just his farm, but a way of life he had consciously chosen as an alternative to the more conventional, lucrative career in the big city he could have had. So the stakes for him were very high. House made an appealing character because he bridged the world of most *New Yorker* readers and the far less familiar world of Midwestern farming, personified by Ken Crim.

To the extent I could, given the facts, I made House seem as significant and interesting as possible. He had, after all, been profiled in *The New York Times Magazine* as a "bachelor," hardly a signal achievement in its own right, but one that many readers of *The New Yorker* might actually have remembered. (House is strikingly handsome; after his picture ran, he was deluged with marriage proposals from strangers.)

Within the brief span of the lead, I also tried to convey a strong sense of place and history: the town of Quincy's magisterial setting high above the river and the bottomlands of northeast Missouri; the old farmhouse set near fields rolling down toward the river. That this is a story as much about geography and nature as about people is foreshadowed; so, too, is my attempt to provide a "sweeping view" of the flood disaster. I do not actually mention the Midwestern flood; that this was my subject would have been self-evident to anyone reading the story at the time it was published, when news and images of the flood filled television broadcasts.

I could have ended the lead with House and a mention of Crim. But I also wanted to hint at the scope of the story by introducing two other characters, and through them, two other themes in the story: the sheriff, a representative of law and authority; and the radio manager, a Chicago native and outsider, a representative of the media. The story's point of view will shift among these three characters, for reasons that I'll discuss later. When that happens, readers are prepared, having met the three in the story's opening paragraphs.

In the last paragraph of the lead, the perceptions of the characters are made concrete, as I assume a certain omniscience and document the severity of the storm. I mentioned earlier that the question that triggered a story rarely needs to be stated explicitly. In this case, however, the lead ends with that question stated baldly. In a lead such as this, which depends so heavily on that question being triggered in readers' minds, I felt I could leave nothing to chance. But note that I placed the question in the minds of the main characters, thus keeping it within the narrative context rather than stating it in my own voice.

Let's consider how well this lead succeeded in selling my story to readers. The significance of the story is implicit in its subject matter, and given national interest in the flood at the time, I would rate that significance fairly high, even though all the characters are unknown. As I said, I didn't feel the need to mention the greater flood in the lead; I assumed that readers would be aware of it. What about someone reading the story now, or in years to come, when its relationship to a larger flood might not be remembered and would not be self-evident? I still think it is unnecessary to mention the broader event in the opening paragraphs. I wouldn't dream of making the claim that this story rose to the level of great literature, but literature generally doesn't need a news context in order to gain resonance, because it is about more enduring themes than today's news. *Moby-Dick* is not introduced with the news that the nineteenth-century whaling industry is in decline. To the extent that the broader context is relevant, it can be presented later in the story.

Universality is also self-evident, this clearly being a story of man versus nature. The ripple effects (pardon the pun in this context) are quite broad, ranging from the wisdom of even trying to control the Mississippi floodplain, to local resentment of outside experts, to the hubris of levee-building in the face of the river's immense power, to—at the farthest ripple of all—the place of man in the universe. Many of these themes, too, became more explicit as the story unfolded, but they are all foreshadowed in the lead by the storm that imperils the characters. On the universality scale, I rated the story quite high.

Timeliness? I was able to deliver the story almost within hours of its conclusion. ("And what *was* the conclusion?" you may, I hope, be wondering. As in the story, you will have to wait to find out.) Exclusivity? An advantage of writing about unknown characters is that there is little risk they will show up in anyone else's story. To the extent that other reporters were writing about the flood from Quincy, they became characters in my story. None of them was attempting a long feature. Nor were other reporters hanging out at the levee while I was there. The only risk in this respect was that a similar story—using one geographic spot as a microcosm for the whole flood—would surface in another publication. Oddly, none did, perhaps because the print media had ceded the story to TV.

Now that I think about it, I might even have suggested the story's similarity to other popular writing by mentioning that the Sny levee lies almost directly across the river from Mark Twain's boyhood home, Hannibal, Missouri.

Note that nearly all the conventional selling qualities are implicit in this example. If a reader doesn't recognize them, at least subliminally, my insisting that they're there will not be persuasive or memorable. And, I assume, most readers did read on, largely for one reason: they wanted to know if the levee would hold, and how the experience of battling the river would change the lives of these characters, people whom, however briefly, they had just met, and who might become their friends.

Over the years I have used the principles I've explained here on numerous occasions, both in my own stories and in those I've edited. I think I can say that they have never failed me, though the lead—indeed, the story as a whole—can never be better than the idea that inspired it. The same principles have worked for all kinds of stories, and I used them to begin both *Den of Thieves* and *Blood Sport.* I vividly remember when each opening scene came into my mind. In the case of *Den of Thieves,* I was jogging along the West Side Highway in Manhattan with a then-colleague at *The Wall Street Journal,* Steve Swartz. I was describing a scene in which Martin Siegel's secretary tells him someone has been arrested for insider trading, and Siegel thinks she's talking about him, since he knows he has been guilty of insider trading himself. Instead, the person turns out to be Dennis Levine. As I told Steve the anecdote, it dawned on me that the arrestee might as well have been Siegel, because that moment destroyed his peace of mind. From then on, he was sure he would eventually be caught, and indeed he was. I knew then that the arrest of Levine—which set the insider-trading scandal in motion—seen through the eyes of Siegel would become my opening scene. It shattered the status quo for Siegel. Note how analogous is this scene to the opening of the Sheinberg insider-trading story.

For *Blood Sport*, I was interviewing a young officer in the National Park Police when he told me of his experience of coming upon a dead body in Fort Marcy Park, outside Washington, D.C. He didn't know that he had discovered the corpse of Vincent Foster, whose suicide set in motion most of the events that have been grouped under the rubric "Whitewater." I knew immediately that this should be my opening scene, because it depicted Foster's death and because the event would be seen through the eyes of a charatcer who knew nothing about it, someone who could serve as a surrogate for readers.

Even though the term isn't usually applied to books, here are the openings to *Den of Thieves* and *Blood Sport:*

PROLOGUE

Martin A. Siegel hurried through Washington, D.C.'s, National Airport and slipped into a phone booth near the Eastern shuttle gates. For years now, phone booths, often at airports, had served as his de facto offices. He complained often about his long hours and frequent absences from his wife and three children, but the truth was that he thrived on his pressure-filled life as one of the country's leading investment bankers.

May 12, 1986, had begun much like any other day. He had flown that morning from New York to Washington to visit a major client, Martin Marietta, one of the country's leading defense contractors. A few years earlier, he had helped Marietta fend off a hostile takeover bid from Bendix Corporation, and the deal had launched Siegel's star. He became one of the country's most sought after takeover strategists.

The visit to Marietta had gone smoothly, with only one disturbing note. The company's chairman, Thomas Pownall, was upset about a recent insider-trading case. Pownall was set to testify as a character witness for Paul Thayer, a former deputy secretary of defense in the Reagan administration, who had been charged with insider trading for leaking top-secret information he gleaned while a director of Anheuser-Busch to, among others, his Dallas mistress. Pownall, along with most of corporate America, had been stunned. He had often done business with Thayer at the defense department, and the two men had become friends. "It's unbelievable, isn't it?" he had remarked to Siegel.

Siegel had nodded and quickly pushed any thoughts of Thayer aside. Handsome as a movie star, tanned, fit, Siegel, at 38, had recently moved to Drexel Burnham Lambert Inc., the powerhouse junk-bond firm. He was ready to vault to even greater stardom.

Now Siegel dialed his office in New York. It was just after 2:45 P.M., and he wondered what the stock market was doing. He hated being separated from his array of sophisticated news-delivery mechanisms, from computer screens to wire services.

His secretary, Kathy, briefed him quickly and then started ticking off the many calls that needed to be returned that day. Suddenly a rapid series of bells rang at the Dow Jones ticker tape just outside Siegel's office, a signal that a major news announcement was imminent.

Kathy moved to the ticker and gasped as the headline emerged. "SEC charges Drexel Burnham Lambert official with insider trading," she read aloud.

As Kathy waited for the ticker to resume its account, Siegel felt his almost perfect world collapsing. Everything he had worked for all his life. His $3.5 million compensation and his $2 million bonus he earned when he moved to Drexel from Kidder, Peabody & Co. earlier that year. The astoundingly lucrative mergers-and-acquisitions practice he was melding with Michael Milken's junk-bond money machine. The blue-chip clients, like Martin Marietta, Goodyear, and Lear Siegler, that were now flocking to use Drexel's and his services. The house on the beach in Connecticut, with its own tennis courts and swimming pool. The four-bedroom cooperative apartment in Manhattan's exclusive Gracie Square. The helicopter rides to Manhattan. The glowing newspaper and magazine profiles.

Suddenly the image of arbitrageur Ivan Boesky, once Siegel's confidant and mentor, flashed before him and he felt a sudden terror. He thought Boesky might have him murdered.

"Oh my God!" Kathy exclaimed as the ticker resumed. "It's Dennis! It's Dennis Levine! He's been arrested!"

Siegel told his secretary to keep reading. "The SEC charged Dennis Levine, a managing director of Drexel Burnham Lambert Inc., with insider trading in connection with an alleged scheme to buy and sell securities based on non-public information gained through his employment as an investment banker for a period of five years," she continued. "Drexel Burnham said it will cooperate fully with the SEC in the investigation. . . ."

Dennis Levine. Dennis Levine was the investment banker in the office next door. Siegel broke into a sweat. All he could think was this: A gun had been pointed at his head, the trigger had been pulled, and miraculously, the bullet had killed Dennis Levine instead. Overweight, overeager, self-promoting, ineffectual Dennis Levine.

In the Beverly Hills office of Drexel Burnham Lambert it was just before noon Pacific time, the peak of the trading day. Michael Milken sat at the center of a huge, X-shaped trading desk, his loyal traders and salesmen radiating out along the axes. As he avidly scanned the trading data on his computer screen, he reached for his two ringing phones—one for each ear.

This was the epicenter of the new economic order, the capital of the junk-bond empire that Milken had created. "Hey, Mike," called out one of the traders as the Levine news came over the wire. "Look at this." Just weeks before, Levine had debuted at Milken's hugely successful 1986 junk-bond conference, the "Predators' Ball," hosting a breakfast on mergers and acquisitions. Milken paused in his phone conversation, glanced at the news on his computer screen, then resumed work as though nothing had happened. "It's like a bad car wreck," one of the salesmen shrugged. "You slow down for a couple of days and then drive fast again." Nothing could stop the Drexel juggernaut.

Ivan Boesky, the legendary arbitrageur, emerged from the conference room at his Fifth Avenue offices and walked down the hall, trailed by several of his employees. Suddenly Jeffrey Hennig, one of Boesky's traders, rushed out of his office waving a piece of ticker copy. He shouted toward Boesky, "Did you see this about Dennis Levine?"

Boesky stopped abruptly and turned. "Dennis who?" he asked.

"Levine," Hennig replied. "Here." He showed Boesky the ticker tape announcing the SEC's charges against Levine.

Boesky read the item quickly, then handed it back. "I've never heard of him," he said, walking briskly away.

PROLOGUE

"We've got a DB in Fort Marcy Park."

John C. Rolla, criminal investigator for the United States
Park Police, suddenly looked up as the call came in over his
shortwave radio. "DB" meant dead body. It was just after 6 P.M.,
July 20, 1993. After five years of undercover work in the war
against drugs, posing as a busboy in Shenandoah National Park,
a drug dealer in Glacier, the athletic thirty-one-year-old Rolla had
graduated to the major crimes unit—robberies, rape, homicide
—that month and had just returned from a stint at "death investigation" school. This might be his first homicide.

He hurried to his car and drove from his office in the District
of Columbia to Virginia, where he turned north on the George
Washington Memorial Parkway. Fort Marcy Park, the site of a Civil
War fortification built to protect Washington from Confederate
attack, was part of the federal park system. Despite its historic
significance, the presence of two Civil War–era cannon, and several footpaths, it is now little more than a wooded roadside rest
stop. Rolla had patrolled the park a few times before, and he knew
it as a gay meeting place and cruising area convenient for com-
muters, the site of romantic trysts and an occasional assault.

As Rolla pulled into the parking area, emergency medical
technicians were driving out. He noticed a blue Mercedes with
its hazard lights flashing, a white Nissan, and a white or light
gray Honda Accord. Several officers were already on the scene.
Officer Franz Ferstle told Rolla that a body had been located up
near the second cannon, and that he thought the Honda might
belong to the deceased. A man and woman were in the Nissan,
and the owner of the Mercedes had called for a tow truck. They
looked in through the Honda's window. A dark blue suit jacket
was neatly folded over the back of the front seat. Ferstle thought
it matched the fabric on the corpse's slacks. A blue silk tie
dotted with swans was draped over the jacket.

Using his car phone, Rolla phoned in the number on the
Honda's Arkansas license plate to check the car registration on
the National Crime Information Center computers. The response: Vincent Foster, Little Rock, Arkansas. The name meant
nothing to Rolla or the other investigators.

Rolla walked uphill a fair distance to reach the cannon. It
had been a hot day, 90 degrees, and the dirt was dry and packed.

The body lay about ten feet from the cannon, the head near the crest of the embankment with the legs extending downhill, the feet resting on some exposed roots. There was no sign of a struggle, nor any indication the body had been moved. Rolla walked over and stood directly above the head, looking down into Foster's open, now lifeless eyes.

Blood, some of it still wet, ran from the right nostril and the right side of the mouth onto the dirt. Flies were crawling over the face. Rolla noticed how big the man was, probably six foot four. He was wearing a long-sleeved button-down white shirt, tucked in, but no tie. Rolla had to move the foliage of a small bush to see what looked like a .38 caliber revolver in the right hand, which was marked by powder burns. On his belt was a paging device, turned off, suggesting he didn't want to be disturbed. Rolla lifted the body's left hand. It was still warm.

When the medical examiner arrived, around 7 P.M., Rolla rolled the body over, struggling to keep it from slipping down the hillside. There was a small hole in the back of the head. Blood stained the back of the shirt. Wearing gloves, Rolla felt inside the wound. He noticed that the skull and brain were largely intact, though "mushy," and mixed with blood and hair. After taking several Polaroid snapshots, he searched the pants pockets, which seemed empty. He removed a watch, a ring, and the beeper. The beeper was marked with the letters "WHCS."

When Rolla got back to the parking lot, he opened the door of the unlocked Honda. The suit jacket did indeed match the trousers. Inside the jacket was a wallet, with $282 in cash and an Arkansas driver's license identifying the owner as Vincent W. Foster, Jr. As Rolla searched the jacket, his colleague, Cheryl Braun, noticed a plasticized identification card attached to a chain that must have been lying under the jacket. She looked at it closely. "Uh oh, he has a White House ID here," she said.

Rolla reached for the card. It had a photo of Foster, his name, and the phrase "White House Communications." "This looks like the guy, it must be the guy, it looks like him," Rolla said. He knew that plenty of people worked in the White House, many at relatively menial tasks. Still, this could be significant. Braun thought she recognized the name, and that Vincent Foster might be somebody important.

"We'd better notify the Secret Service," Rolla said.

There was an air of excitement at the White House as the president's staff checked final preparations for an interview with

Larry King. The talk show impresario was interviewing the president that evening, broadcasting live from the ground-floor library of the White House. It was Clinton's first appearance on Larry King since the inauguration, and the president and his staff saw it both as an opportunity to relive some of the talk show triumphs of the campaign and to put the recent snafus—gays in the military, the White House travel office—behind them. King himself seemed to be reveling in his access to the president and the unusual opportunity to broadcast his show right from the White House. He'd brought his wife along, and, assuming the interview went as expected, the couple was going to get a tour of the executive mansion after the broadcast.

Thomas F. "Mack" McLarty, the president's chief of staff, stopped in to make sure everything was set for the interview, then joined senior advisor George Stephanopoulos, counselor to the president Bruce Lindsey, and communications director Mark Gearan in the residence to watch the interview on television. But once it seemed to get off to a good start, McLarty excused himself and walked out into the broad corridor on the ground floor of the White House, planning to join his wife at home. He noticed Bill Burton, his staff director, hurrying toward him.

"Mack, I have tragic news," Burton began. "There's a body at Fort Marcy Park that appears to be Vincent Foster. It appears to be suicide."

McLarty was stunned. He'd known Foster practically all his life. They'd grown up together in Hope, Arkansas, Clinton's birthplace. Tall and thin as a teenager, Foster was still known to McLarty by his high school nickname, "Pencil." Though Foster wasn't much of an athlete, he and McLarty had played football together in junior high. Foster was president of the student body in high school; McLarty was vice president. McLarty had gone on to be elected governor of Arkansas Boys State,* and Foster had called McLarty "Governor" ever since. McLarty had gone on to head Arkla, the big Arkansas gas utility, and Foster had become a partner in Little Rock's Rose Law Firm. As chairman of the Arkansas Democratic party, McLarty had become close to Bill Clinton, and Foster had forged a closer relationship with Hillary Clinton, his fellow litigation partner and soul mate at the

---

* Boys State is an American Legion civics program for high school students organized in each state. Delegates may go on to Boys Nation in Washington, D.C.

Rose firm. They'd often bump into each other at Sunday buffets at the Country Club of Little Rock and at the Clintons' birthday parties.

It seemed impossible that Vince was dead. McLarty had gone over to chat with Foster that morning in the Rose Garden, when Louis Freeh was sworn in as the new FBI director. Vince had chuckled at something McLarty had said, as he often did. Surely there was a mistake, or at least the possibility of a mistake?

Burton allowed that the body hadn't yet been positively identified. Bill Kennedy, one of the White House lawyers and another former Rose partner, was on his way to the Fairfax County Hospital morgue to identify the body. Still, there was little likelihood that the identification by the Park Police had been mistaken. David Watkins, an Arkansas native who was head of White House management, was heading over to the Foster home.

Even as he continued to talk with Burton, McLarty found himself pushing his own thoughts and reactions out of his mind. Whatever had happened to Foster, his job now was to serve the interests of the president, who was being televised, live, down the hall. Was news of Foster's death about to go out on the news wires? Surely it was only a matter of time. Should he interrupt the Larry King interview?

Just then Stephanopoulos and Gearan noticed McLarty in the hall and came out from the room where they were watching the interview on television. McLarty broke the news, and the two men gasped. McLarty asked for their views on whether the interview should be interrupted; they agreed that it was better to wait. But they asked that incoming calls to the show be screened, so the president didn't learn the news on live television.

McLarty's next priority was to reach the first lady. He stepped into an adjacent room and asked the White House operator to locate her, saying it was urgent. Moments later McLarty was connected to the Rodham home in Little Rock, where Hillary was visiting her mother and father, who was ill, after a trip to the Far East and the West Coast. The first lady's press secretary, Lisa Caputo, answered the phone in the kitchen.

"I need to speak to Hillary right now," McLarty said. He wanted to make sure she heard the news from him, and not from a news bulletin. He knew that Foster was probably Hillary's best friend in the White House. Caputo was struck by the urgency in his voice.

"I have some tragic news," McLarty began when Hillary took the phone. Then he told her that Foster was dead, an apparent suicide.

There was silence. Then, "I can't believe it's true," Hillary said. "It just can't be true." She began to cry.

McLarty said there hadn't yet been a positive identification of the body, but that it most likely was true. "All we can do is hope and pray that there's been some mistake," he said.

"What about Bill, does he know?" she asked. The first lady hadn't been watching TV, and didn't seem to know that the president was being broadcast live at that very moment. McLarty explained the situation, and said he'd be told at the earliest opportunity. He told her he'd keep her apprised of developments, and the two hung up. The conversation had lasted just a few minutes.

While McLarty spoke to Hillary, Stephanopoulos called Webster Hubbell, another former Rose partner, now associate attorney general. He knew the Hubbells and Fosters had been best friends. McLarty also spoke to Hubbell, urging him to join Watkins at the Foster home. Just then, Stephanopoulos came rushing up with the news that Clinton had spontaneously agreed with Larry King to continue the interview for a half hour beyond its scheduled conclusion. "You've got to stop him," Stephanopoulos urged, anxious that the Foster news would break at any moment. "You're the only one who can stop this."

McLarty hurried into the library during the commercial break. Clinton looked ebullient, pleased with the interview.

"Mr. President, we need to quit while we're ahead," McLarty said, trying to appear grave without alarming King. "We've done the hour interview, It's been a fine interview."

"Oh, Mack," King replied, "it's going great." Clinton, too, resisted the idea of interrupting.

"Larry, I agree with you," McLarty continued, more firmly, "but the president has to conclude the interview at this point."

Clinton sensed that something must be amiss. "Mack is right," he said to King. "I'll be back in a few minutes."

As the two men walked into the hall, Clinton could barely contain himself. "Mack, what's wrong? What's up?"

"It's not a national emergency or crisis, but it's a very serious matter," he said. "Let's go upstairs where we can sit down." Clinton continued to press McLarty as they walked down the hall, but he held off until they were seated upstairs in the living quarters.

"Mr. President, Vince Foster has committed suicide."

"Oh, no," Clinton cried. Tears welled up in his eyes. "I want to call Hillary. Have you told Hillary? Does she know?"

After a few moments to collect himself, Clinton said he would call Hillary and then visit the Foster home himself. While Clinton got on the phone to the first lady, McLarty arranged with the Secret Service to get the president to the Foster residence safely while attracting minimal attention. No press were notified. They set out from the White House without the usual motorcade, traveling in a Chevy Suburban van, accompanied by two unmarked cars.

Leaving the other investigators at Fort Marcy Park, Rolla and Braun got into their car and phoned headquarters to get Foster's address. This would be Rolla's first death notice to the next-of-kin, and he was a bit apprehensive. As they drove to the Foster home, a three-story townhouse at 3027 Cambridge Place in Georgetown, Rolla got a call from his office asking him to phone someone named Bill Kennedy. Rolla reached him, and Kennedy said he was a personal friend of Foster's and worked at the White House. He wanted to see the body, and Rolla said he could go to the morgue at Fairfax County Hospital and help with the identification. Rolla was barely off the phone with Kennedy when he was told to contact another White House official, David Watkins, who was described as an even closer friend of Foster's. Watkins had grown up with Foster in Hope, and Watkins had dated Foster's sister Sharon. Watkins's wife had played tennis with Lisa Foster, Foster's wife, that morning, and the Watkins house was close to the Fosters in Georgetown. Watkins asked if he could join Rolla in breaking the news to the Foster family. Rolla agreed to pick up Watkins first; Watkins's wife would follow in their car.

Rolla was glad to have a close family friend on hand, but as word spread at the White House, things threatened to get out of control. First Watkins had wanted to wait until Foster's sister could join them; Rolla had said no. Then, as they pulled up at the Foster home, several other people converged, introduced to Rolla as Sheila Anthony and Sharon Bowman, Foster's sisters, and a tall heavyset man who seemed to be always talking into a cellular phone. He, too, was introduced as a close friend of Foster's from Arkansas: Webb Hubbell. Rolla didn't want a crowd standing on the porch when a family member came to the door; he asked them to stand back.

Rolla, accompanied by Watkins, knocked on the door. Twenty-one-year-old Laura Foster answered. "I'm John Rolla, with the United States Park Police . . ." Before he could finish he saw Laura looking behind him at her aunts, Hubbell and his wife, Watkins's wife, Braun, all of them looking stricken.

"What's the matter?" she cried. "What's wrong? Mother," she yelled. Then, screaming, "Mother! Something's wrong."

Lisa Foster, clad in a bathrobe, her dark blond hair carefully coiffed, looking tanned and slender from her frequent tennis outings, hurried down the stairs. She paused on the third step as she saw Watkins and Rolla. "What's wrong?" she asked. "Is it something about Vincent?" She meant her son, Vincent III.

"Sit down," Rolla urged her, taking a deep breath. "I am very sorry to tell you that your husband, Vincent, is dead."

Lisa Foster screamed and slumped to the stairs, clutching her arms around her and sobbing. Watkins's wife rushed to comfort her. Laura, too, was crying uncontrollably.

"He shot himself," Rolla added. Laura screamed and ran upstairs.

Lisa, between sobs, managed to ask: "Did he put it in his mouth?"

"Yes," Rolla replied. He was startled by the question. Had Lisa had some indication, some premonition, that Foster planned to shoot himself? Lisa rose and rushed up the stairs after her daughter.

Everyone now pressed into the living room, and Rolla and his colleague, Braun, began trying to gather some information from the distraught members of the group, now talking quietly among themselves, many still fighting back tears. He knew this was the time when people were least likely to have their views of events colored or tainted by exchanges with others. This was still an open investigation. Though suicide seemed by far the most likely cause of death, murder remained a possibility that would have to be investigated. "Did you see this coming?" he asked. "Were there any signs of this?" Everyone insisted no. Hubbell declined to answer questions, spending his time on the cellular phone. Rolla called headquarters and said Foster's White House office should be sealed. Braun told Watkins the same thing.

After about fifteen minutes, Lisa returned, dressed and looking more collected. Braun tried to ask a few questions, but Lisa wouldn't answer. Rolla seemed to manage a better rapport with her. "Were there any indications of depression?" Rolla asked her.

"No, nothing," she said, her eyes brimming with tears. "He was so happy."

"Did he own a gun?"

"I don't know," she replied. "What kind was it? What did it look like?"

"It was a .38 caliber revolver . . ."

Suddenly she seemed agitated, even angry. "How would I know? I don't know what guns look like." She turned and stalked into the kitchen, terminating the interview. She and Hubbell began searching the house, looking in vain for a suicide note.

Neither Rolla nor Braun, who was also working the room, made much headway with any of the others. The phone began ringing off the hook. The investigators felt Hubbell, in particular, was discouraging people from saying anything; as Braun tried to question Sheila Anthony, the heavyset Hubbell pushed Braun out of the way and led Sheila out of the room. Some people seemed more concerned with publicity than with what had happened. Watkins asked Rolla and Braun not to issue any press release until Foster's elderly mother in Hope could be notified in person. A devout Catholic, Lisa worried that if it were known her husband had committed suicide, he couldn't be buried in a Catholic cemetery. The officer said they'd hold off as long as they could, but that they'd have no choice but to make a statement fairly soon.

The group's collective denial that anything was upsetting Foster didn't ring true to Rolla and, in any event, flew in the face of the apparent suicide. Lisa Foster's insistence that her husband had been "so happy" seemed forced. Was she in some kind of denial, brushing any problems under the rug to put a more acceptable face on the tragedy? Was she withholding information? How did she know to ask whether Foster had shot himself in the mouth?

Any hopes for further progress were soon dashed. At 10:50 P.M., the front door suddenly opened and a Secret Service agent walked in, followed by the president and McLarty. "Oh my God," Rolla thought, as the realization finally sank in that Foster was a member of the White House inner circle. Clinton looked haggard, his eyes red, visibly upset. He glared at Rolla, giving him the impression that Clinton thought it inappropriate for a law enforcement officer to be intruding on their privacy. The president hurried toward Lisa. Clinton put his arms around her, then sat between her and Laura on the sofa in the living room. He spoke quietly with Lisa and her daughter.

Rolla hovered in the background, trying fitfully to ask a few more questions, and was reduced to handing out his business card. "Please call me if you learn of anything . . ." More people poured into the Foster home: David Gergen, a White House advisor; Vernon Jordan, the Washington lawyer and close friend of Clinton's; Arkansas senator David Pryor and his wife. Rolla felt shunted aside. He'd never sensed that President Clinton was much of a friend to law enforcement, and this experience didn't change that impression. Finally Braun turned to him. "John, we might as well come back tomorrow, because we're not going to get any more information tonight."

Rolla stayed another ten minutes. No one seemed to pay him any attention. All eyes were on the president.

Even though these passages are the openings of books that run hundreds of pages, they are concise, barely longer than some of my leads for feature articles, and they function in the same way, with the same goals. By now, the points I've made in this chapter should be fairly clear. In *Den of Thieves,* much as in the flood lead, the book's four major characters—Martin Siegel, Dennis Levine, Michael Milken, and Ivan Boesky—are introduced. At the time of the book's publication, all were household names, well-known to the general public as symbols of excess in the eighties. It was also widely known that all four had been brought to justice; I didn't need to say this. By writing that Siegel thought he had escaped the bullet; that Milken acted as if nothing had happened; and that Boesky purported never to have known Levine, I emphasized to readers the opposite of what they knew to be true. Thus, I underscored the paradox that despite their power and (false) confidence, these men were caught. I hoped to trigger curiosity not about the outcome, which I assumed readers knew, but about how the four men went from such defiant states of mind to getting caught. *Den of Thieves* is basically an explanatory book, trying to tell readers how and why the insider-trading and related scandals of the eighties happened. At the same time, from a narrative point of view, the opening scene was intended to plant curiosity about how Siegel would confront the reality he had feared, and how he would restore equilibrium in his life.

This was a difficult passage to write; I re-drafted it many times. I still believe it demands a lot from readers, asking that they understand why Siegel would mistakenly think that the news release was about him rather than Dennis Levine, without explicitly being told that Siegel, too, had been guilty of insider trading. But I was trying to write from the point of view of Siegel, who of course had no need to explain to himself why he would break into a sweat, as he had put it. The "gun to the head" analogy—the fear that Boesky would have him killed—might even seem melodramatic. But I vividly recall how Siegel used precisely that analogy and described that fear when he told me of his reaction to the announcement. It's with respect to just such issues that a good editor is essential. Alice Mayhew assured me that readers would be able to follow what was happening without my being more explicit, and she turned out to be right. At least, no one ever complained to me of being confused.

The *Blood Sport* lead is much more straightforward. In this example, the discovery of Vince Foster's body is seen from the point of view of John Rolla, the park police officer, who at the time has no idea of the significance or implications of what he's witnessing. He doesn't even know who Vince Foster is: "The name meant nothing to him." Cheryl Braun later muses that he "might be somebody important." By the time the book was published, of course, Foster was a household name and the subject of continuing controversy, so the reader would immediately know the significance of the unfolding events. But Rolla and Braun, as trained investigators, are filled with questions, and in that sense are meant to be surrogates for readers, whom I want to be asking the same questions.

The scene then shifts geographically (but stays in strict chronological order) to introduce the president and first lady, the book's two major characters; it then returns to Rolla and his arrival at the Foster home.

This is inherently dramatic material: the discovery of a dead body; the scenes of the president and first lady absorbing the tragic news; Lisa Foster's shock and her mysterious remark about the gun. All these lives have been dramatically changed—or, in Foster's case, ended. The lead is also a classic narrative lead: it is the traditional beginning of a mystery story. "All eyes were on the president," the lead concludes. Was he involved? What did he know? Was Foster's death a murder? If it was suicide, what was his motive? These are questions I hope readers are pondering at this juncture. All of them are implicit; they didn't need to be stated explicitly. At the same time, there is no hint of what the answers might be. As in far simpler stories, my goal is to make readers as curious as possible, to make them want to read on.

6
TRANSITIONS

ASSUMING THAT READERS' INTEREST has been captured in the introduction, their curiosity aroused, what comes next? In traditional nonfiction, the lead is followed by a transition, which is meant to serve several purposes. To the extent that the lead itself has failed to accomplish the task of selling the story to the reader, the transition should do so. It also provides a bridge from the opening to what follows. As we've seen, the shift from the opening scene may involve an interruption in chronology, a change in point of view, or the introduction of entirely new characters and settings. All of this is potentially unsettling to the reader and offers an all-too-ready excuse for abandoning a story altogether.

Under the leadership of Barney Kilgore, who became managing editor of *The Wall Street Journal* in 1941 and was later president and chairman of Dow Jones, the front page of the paper developed its unique format, which continues today. The *Journal*'s front page consists of concise news summaries, a column, and three feature stories, which continue inside the paper. The style and structure of the *Journal*'s front-page features have had enormous influence on nonfiction writing, especially with respect to transitions, or, as they are called at the *Journal,* nut grafs (invariably spelled with an "f").

When I arrived at the *Journal* as a new reporter in 1983, the nut graf was an institution unto itself. When I turned in a draft of my first front-page story, my editor exclaimed, "But there's no nut graf!" *Journal* features typically began with an anecdote, then moved to a nut graf. I don't recall anyone actually telling me what a nut graf was or what it was supposed to do, but it was easy enough to draw those inferences. In those days, nearly every front-page story had a nut graf or grafs, so I learned by example.

The nut graf performed the "selling" function I've already described. In essence, it told readers why they should take the time to read the article. It tried to make the story seem important, timely, topical. It frankly acknowledged that most readers of a daily newspaper were probably looking for reasons to skip a long, time-consuming story, and it tried to address that reaction. In this, the *Journal* was ahead of its time.

But over the years something had gone wrong, in my view. As I've already mentioned, reader surveys demonstrated that the nut grafs were not selling readers on a story and encouraging them to read on. Instead, a huge percentage of readers stopped reading after the nut grafs! In an increasingly desperate effort to rationalize the use of readers' time, the nut grafs were becoming summaries of the story. They often betrayed the endings of suspenseful narratives. They were wooden and didactic. Conclusions that should have been left to readers were made explicit. The nut grafs told the reader so much that they left no reason to read on. And if this was the case, I often wondered, why not just end the story right there? A large chunk of the paper's resources, from reporters' time to newsprint, was being spent on that tiny percentage of readers so interested in any given topic that they would read the entire story even though they'd been told everything they really needed to know in the first few paragraphs.

I often found myself locked in arguments with editors for whom the nut graf had become more important than the story. They always wanted to move the "good" material, the "news," as they often called it, from deep in the story into the nut grafs, without regard to the story's overall structure or even chronological order. "No one will read that far," they would tell me. "Why *would* anyone read that far," I countered, "if they've been conditioned to expect everything of significance in the first few paragraphs?"

As an editor, I noticed that this problem would surface when reporters had written their leads and nut grafs, then found they were stalled with nowhere to go. This, I usually found, was because there *was* nowhere to go. They had already revealed everything of significance.

Many of the arguments I had over nut grafs were never fully resolved, and believe me, I wrote my share of nut grafs, both as a reporter and editor. Indeed, nut grafs continue in the ascendancy at many publications, including the *Journal*. They are no longer transition paragraphs at all; they have become the leads.

Here's a recent example from the *Journal*, a front-page story about turmoil at Deutsche Bank. The story begins: "When in Germany, do business as the Germans do." That is the entire first paragraph. It is also the "moral" of the story, as storytellers would say. It is a conclusion. It is, in a sense, a nut graf. After a brief anecdote, the story reverts to another nut graf in the third paragraph: "And now the Germans are taking back the reins of their far-flung operations, ending an expensive three-year effort to build a global banking powerhouse. . . ." This continues for numerous paragraphs, but the "ending" of this story has already been fully revealed—that Deutsche Bank is asserting more control from headquarters.

Beginning with a nut graf is still unusual. That same day's *Journal* contains a more typical example in a front-page story about PhyCor, a health-care provider. After an anecdote, the story continues, "PhyCor's troubles illustrate how hard it is to run medicine like a normal business, even when there is no calamity to complicate matters like the fraud investigation at Columbia/ HCA." Telltale nut graf verbs are "illustrate," "show," "demonstrate," and, that hoary chestnut "is the story of . . ." All are too often used in stories that do exactly the opposite: they tell rather than show, demonstrate, or illustrate. This paragraph also all but goes out of its way to discourage the reader, assuring us that nothing so dramatic as a "calamity" will enliven the article, and further draining the story of whatever suspense might have been engendered. Isn't whether or not something amounts to a calamity a conclusion, or even an opinion, which in any event might better be left to readers to decide?

Today even a narrative piece, which you'd expect to begin with a scene from the story, might instead begin with a nut graf. Here's an example, a recent front-page *Journal* story about the making of ABC's documentary *The Century.* The story begins:

"ABC News's effort to tell the story of the 20th century has become an epic drama in its own right." We finally get to the beginning, chronologically, of this "epic" story (which was, by the way, quite an interesting one, though hardly, in my view, epic) in the fourteenth paragraph! Shouldn't readers be allowed to decide whether a story is in fact "epic"?

I single out these recent examples from the *Journal* only because its feature stories are rightly regarded as among the nation's best. The rise of the nut graf is even more prominent in other newspapers, and it is beginning to creep into magazines. What accounts for the dominance of nut grafs in journalism today? In my view, they cater to and mirror broad trends: People want the whole story in a nutshell; they want it fast, and they want it to be conclusive. Nut grafs simplify the experience of reading. They are perceived by many editors as a way to compete with TV.

My own bias is probably apparent by now, so I will admit it: If I could put a stake into the heart of the nut graf, I would. And yet I would have to almost immediately reinvent it, for I use it myself. Indeed, it is possible to go too far in the opposite direction, shunning nut grafs. This was arguably the case in what has become known as the "old," or pre–Tina Brown, *New Yorker,* where the magazine's persistent refusal to explain itself, even in headlines, was viewed by many as arrogant and elitist.

Like so many conventions that have become ossified almost beyond recognition, the nut graf serves a useful purpose. Readers must understand why they are being asked to read something, and if you need a nut graf to accomplish this, then you need a nut graf. Leads usually do need a transition, a term I prefer to "nut graf." Long stories, and certainly books, do need to be sold to readers, who rightly want reassurance that they are not being asked to waste their time and money. And much as I might bemoan the current state of affairs, we live in a world dominated by television, which constantly summarizes and simplifies. Yet I am confident that readers will readily respond to being allowed to draw their own conclusions and think for themselves, that they will remember the experience long after most nut grafs have been forgotten, and that they appreciate being treated with the respect implicit in such an approach.

A transition can be written so that it accomplishes all the

goals of the nut graf while preserving every bit of the suspense and curiosity so carefully cultivated in the lead. Indeed, I believe this is taking the nut graf back to its roots as something that genuinely enhances a story rather than crushes it. Here are some guidelines I find useful in crafting such passages:

> Never give away the ending of a story.
> Never state the conclusion of a story.
> Foreshadow, but do not make explicit, the broader
> themes in a story.
> Anticipate the questions a reader might be asking early
> in a story, and address them.
> Give readers a concrete reason or reasons to read on.

Bear in mind that a transition can never substitute for a good lead. It should only reinforce the lead. As I hope I've made clear, the lead should have already sold the story by addressing as many of the selling points I've identified as possible. If you have truly succeeded, and readers are eager to get on with the story, any transition should be brief, because otherwise it will annoy readers impatient to satisfy their curiosity. Often, no transition at all is needed. Oddly, given that so many view a function of the nut graf as being to save time, the nut graf can rightly be judged as wasting it.

For this reason, I find it useful to write the story first without the nut graf, and then read it over. How does the story fare, standing alone? Is the lead effective? Can I, in short, dispense with the transition? This is often a difficult judgment to make; a good editor is enormously helpful. In many cases, almost always in collaboration with my editor, I have decided that any transition would only get in the way, seem didactic and patronizing, and drain the story of suspense. This proved to be the case in more than half the stories we have already discussed in detail, including those of Sheinberg, the flood, the Cravath murder, and the fired accountant.

Even if I conclude that a transition is warranted, writing it after the rest of the story is finished avoids cannibalizing material that belongs elsewhere in a story, especially at the end. As we shall see, nut grafs and endings actually share many characteristics. As an editor, I often found it necessary to move material

from the nut grafs to the ending. Writing the transition last miti-
gates this problem.

There are no hard-and-fast rules about whether transitions
are needed, so writers and editors usually rely on intuition. But
the need for a transition is often a function of how compelling the story idea was to begin with. Even if there is no nut graf,
the information that would ordinarily be included in it must be
implicit. I find that such a transition is least often necessary in the
narrative story, where readers' desire to find out what happened
should be so strong that they need little further encouragement.
In nearly all the stories I've discussed where I didn't use a transition, I relied on narrative suspense to propel readers forward.
But a transition is often necessary even in narrative stories, if the
characters are little known and the significance is not immediately apparent from the context. Transitions are often needed in
explanatory stories, where the paradox or conundrum must be
made explicit. I find it is almost always necessary in trend stories,
where the question of whether something is a trend needs to be
made explicit and put in context. And I have included something
resembling the nut graf in all of my books, primarily because
works of such length need to be sold to readers more explicitly
than shorter magazine or newspaper stories.

Let's look at the transition I wrote for the profile of Jim
Wilcox, the critically acclaimed but struggling novelist. The lead,
you will recall, consisted of an anecdote that showed Wilcox
working at a soup kitchen, musing that he himself was just one
check away from being in the line. Then came these paragraphs:

> There have always been struggling novelists, of course, as
> well as a handful of best-selling, highly publicized multimillion-
> aires. But in the past twelve years James Wilcox has published
> six novels to rave reviews. While his books are classified as
> "literary fiction" by the publishing industry, they aren't inacces-
> sible or highbrow. He has been described as a "comic genius"
> (*Vogue*), "a master" (*Kirkus Reviews*), "a natural . . . One of
> the most promising fiction writers on the national scene" (Los
> Angeles *Times*) "among the classic American humorists" (*News-
> day*), and "Dickensian in [his] wealth of eccentric charac-
> ters" (New York *Times*). He has a high-powered agent, Amanda
> (Binky) Urban, of International Creative Management, who has
> consistently got him advances that were larger than could be

justified strictly on the basis of the number of his books sold. In other words, among novelists Wilcox counts himself one of the lucky ones. Even so, the current state of publishing has consigned him to a life of near-poverty.

At my insistence, Wilcox, who is single and lives alone, showed me his tax returns for the past ten years. His best year was 1988, when he had a gross income of $48,600 before agent commissions (of ten percent) and expenses. He now remembers that year as an aberration—a time when he could eat out occasionally, and even take a cab. And since that time, as the market for trade-paperback fiction has shrunk and authors' advances have declined, his income has dropped accordingly. In 1992, he earned twenty-five thousand dollars. Last year, it was fourteen thousand dollars. The advance for his current novel was ten thousand dollars; in a concession, his publisher gave him two-thirds up front, rather than the customary half. When I visited him recently, he had just finished the last of three meals he'd extracted from eighteen pieces of chicken he bought at Key Food for three dollars and forty cents.

Nor is Wilcox's plight confined to making ends meet. HarperCollins, which published his last five books, didn't exercise its option for his current project. Only Hyperion, the Disney publishing subsidiary, showed any interest in the manuscript, and then mostly because Rick Kot, the editor who championed Wilcox at Harper, had recently moved to Hyperion. Hyperion is a smaller house, less able than HarperCollins to indulge a distinguished but unprofitable author. In Wilcox, commerce and art are now at a standoff, with Wilcox's future as a novelist at stake. At a time when some unpublished first novelists are igniting bidding wars and hauling down advances of half a million dollars, "we were lucky to get ten thousand dollars," Urban says of Wilcox's current contract. "This book is absolutely critical. Something has to happen."

What was implicit in the lead is now made explicit, beginning with the story's central paradox. There can now be no doubt that Wilcox is a highly acclaimed writer, given the lengthy string of review comments. This reinforces the notion that he is a character of significance (though no number of reviews can turn him into a celebrity, or even a character sufficiently well-known to carry the story on his own). Nor can there be any doubt that he is struggling financially, given his tax returns and the need to extract three meals from a single purchase of chicken pieces at the distinctly downscale Key Food supermarket. Wilcox is a writer facing a crisis. And then I state the story's central theme: "Art and commerce are at a stand-off." In other words, this isn't just a story about a struggling novelist; it's about the publishing industry and the paradox that an unproven novelist can garner a $500,000 advance while Wilcox is lucky to get $10,000. Finally, I plant some narrative suspense: "Something has to happen." "Like what?" I hope readers are asking.

But note what is *not* included in these paragraphs. There is absolutely no hint as to what might explain the paradox. On the contrary, everything in these transition paragraphs is meant to make the paradox seem more acute and more puzzling. No mention is made of what happens to Wilcox by the end of the story. And several important questions remain implicit, to emerge more distinctly in the course of the story: Why does Wilcox do what he does, given how little remuneration he receives? Why doesn't he try to write something more commercial? I left these unstated, partly because I was opting for simplicity, and partly out of a sense that readers' curiosity had been sufficiently engaged.

Yet the reader is told much of what might have been left implicit. The importance of Wilcox to the reader is that he represents something much larger: the relationship of art and commerce. This is an age-old theme and has been the subject of debate going back at least to the Renaissance. This makes the story's significance and universality explicit in a way that was impossible in the anecdotal lead.

At this point, who did I think would read this story? There were obviously Wilcox's fans and readers—say, 10,000 people. That didn't get me far. There were presumably people interested in literary fiction, even if they'd never heard of Wilcox. That probably added 100,000. The transition paragraphs broadened that potential readership, by adding people who work in publishing and anyone interested in the business of publishing. Finally, I hoped I attracted anyone interested in the relationship of art and commerce, which might be any reasonably thoughtful and well-educated person, a group, I hoped, that would number in the millions. Even for those uninterested in any of these things, the transition paragraphs provided reassurance that I, as the story's author, had a reason for writing it that went beyond what might be construed as my own narrow interest in a little-known novelist.

In chapter 2 I mentioned my interest in the news that gay autoworkers were organizing at Chrysler and picketing company headquarters. You may also recall that I had some difficulty persuading Tina Brown that this story would meet the high standards of *The New Yorker* and was worth pursuing. In my reporting, I had focused on one of those workers, an electrician named Ron Woods, and had decided to use his story to explore the surprising rise of gay activism in such a traditional and male-dominated industry. The lead I later wrote introduced Woods and the world of the engine factory in which he worked, concluding with a graphic account of Woods being attacked by a homophobic co-worker while his supervisor looked the other way.

The lead clearly established several important selling points: that Woods was gay; that workers on the auto factory floor were conservative and often homophobic; that Woods had tried to fit in, that he had been persecuted in a dramatic fashion. I felt it succeeded in establishing surprise, in raising a significant subject of current interest, and in triggering curiosity about what would happen to Woods. But, as I mentioned above, the idea for this story had to be a good one to stop there. And I had had some difficulty selling the editor on the story proposal. For those reasons, I felt I had to write a transition to place the unknown Woods in a broader context, to establish the story's universality, and to heighten readers' curiosity. (In effect, I had had to do the same thing to get approval to do the story.) After briefly summarizing Woods's transformation from meek electrician to activist, I wrote:

> Ron Woods's visibility, if not always his confrontational tactics, has encouraged others. Chrysler now has another gay employees' organization, People of Diversity. Composed mostly of non-union, managerial employees, it was modeled on a similar organization that had been formed recently at Ford. Perhaps most startling was the decision of a much admired vice-chairman of Ford, Allan Gilmour, to disclose his homosexuality in an interview last winter with *Between the Lines,* a Detroit monthly. Gilmour had already retired from Ford, but continues to serve on the boards of five major corporations.

Many people in Detroit are astounded that gay ferment has reached the auto industry. Car and truck manufacturing is "probably the most conservative industry in the country," says Jeff Montgomery, whose father, a Chrysler executive, warned him that being gay could ruin his career. Montgomery heads the Triangle Foundation, a lesbian-and-gay civil rights group in Michigan. Phill O'Jibway, who is the managing editor of *Cruise*, a Detroit-area gay-and-lesbian weekly, says, "I'm astonished that any of this is happening in Michigan. I thought this would be the last place on earth. I grew up here. . . . It has a lot to do with the conformist corporate culture that this area is famous for, as well as the heavily blue-collar conformist culture."

Nevertheless, most gay and lesbian autoworkers remain in the closet, for fear of discrimination and even violence on the factory floor, if not in executive suites. Michigan is one of thirty-nine states with no job protection for gays and lesbians; federal legislation to extend job protection to gays and lesbians failed in the Senate last year by a single vote. Despite Woods's success in obtaining union support, Chrysler refused to include sexual orientation as a protected category in a new three-year contract it entered into with the U.A.W. last year, and the U.A.W. capitulated. Though People of Diversity has adopted a policy of non-confrontation, Chrysler has yet to sanction the group as an official employee organization—a sanction that would entitle members to meet on company property and use company resources such as bulletin boards. (Its counterpart at Ford has company sanction.)

Even as Chrysler earlier this year issued several statements pledging non-discrimination, the company got caught up in two public controversies that brought into question the company's stance. *Esquire* cancelled publication of a short story by David Leavitt planned for the April issue—a story that contained explicit gay material—after its publisher warned the editor that Chrysler would withdraw its advertising. In March, Chrysler cancelled its previously scheduled advertising on an episode of the ABC series "Ellen" in which the main character would reveal that she is a lesbian.

As the fourth-largest advertiser in the country, Chrysler is highly visible, and its status as a major consumer-products firm makes it especially averse to controversy that might trigger the kind of boycott recently proclaimed by the Southern Baptist Convention against the Walt Disney Company, because of the company's perceived support for gay and lesbian employees.

(Disney owns ABC, the network that airs "Ellen.") In addition, many Chrysler executives are simply squeamish when it comes to homosexuality, a topic that remains off limits in polite Midwestern society, and thus they were unprepared for the idea that gay-rights advocates would prove to be as zealous and well organized as the religious right.

Based on his experience at Ford and as a corporate director, Gilmour says that in most old-line, conservative industrial companies, homosexuality "is an issue that is never brought up." By contrast, many high-technology, media, and entertainment concerns have prohibited discrimination against gays and lesbians for years; I.B.M. has had such a policy since 1974. Of Ford, Gilmour said, "If I'd taken a poll of key people, many of them would have been very uncomfortable about homosexuality, the subject in general. They would wish the subject would disappear."

The paradox that gay ferment has reached the auto industry is heightened with the comments of Montgomery and O'Jibway, who is "astonished." Many people, I noted, are "astounded." This invites readers to share the same reaction, which mirrored my own surprise when I first learned of Woods's activities. Nor is Woods an isolated example: even a high-ranking Ford official has come out of the closet, albeit after retiring. Then a new element of significance is introduced: national legislation banning employment discrimination on the basis of sexual orientation, which might have applied in Woods's case, failed in the Senate by a single vote. In other words, the plight of gay workers is a current issue of national significance. The transition quickly shifts to a secondary paradox: Chrysler management, while paying lip service to nondiscrimination, seems to be acting in the opposite manner, refusing to grant protection to gay workers and pulling its advertising from the coming-out episode of the TV sitcom *Ellen*. This adds an element of timeliness—the *Ellen* episode had been getting saturation coverage, and any mention of it was likely to generate considerable interest. Finally, I used the squeamishness factor I discussed earlier as a selling point. Clearly the subject will not "disappear," and this sentence suggests the awkwardness with which Chrysler executives will be seen handling an issue they can barely bring themselves to talk about. In just five paragraphs, this transition highlights every aspect of the story I had used to sell the proposal to my editor.

You may be surprised to learn that this story does not turn out to be exactly what you expect—that Woods comes in for criticism for taking a legitimate issue too far. Many readers found that both the lead and transition paragraphs suggested that Woods would be a hero, a valiant champion for civil rights; that Woods's co-workers would be hostile, even violent homophobes; and that Chrysler management would be stocked with bigots. But do the transition paragraphs actually imply any of that? While that's one possible explanation of what has befallen Woods and Chrysler, those expectations are, in my view, fueled by the conventions of modern storytelling, not by what I wrote. As I said before, Woods turned out to be no "gay Norma Rae," even though I'm sure many readers found it impossible to see beyond that particular role model.

That readers were surprised by the story even after the lead and transition paragraphs was immensely reassuring to me. That meant I had succeeded in provoking their curiosity and interest, but not at the cost of giving away the ending. The convention of the nut graf has become so widespread that it is very tempting to summarize a story's conclusions, since many writers and editors have come to believe that conclusions are what gives a story significance. This is a temptation that should be studiously avoided.

I applied these same principles in writing the passages that functioned as transitions in both *Den of Thieves* and *Blood Sport.* A book, of course, attempts to do much more than an article, even a long one. In the transition sections of my books, I've tried to draw attention to the dimensions of the story—investigative, explanatory, point-of-view. This is more than any single lead could do, however effective it is at provoking curiosity.

Here are those passages from *Den:*

Years later, looking back on that day, Siegel realized he had been wrong. The bullet that killed Levine killed him, too. It killed Ivan Boesky. It killed Michael Milken.

The same bullet shattered the takeover craze and the greatest money-making boom in Wall Street's history, and it exposed the greatest criminal conspiracy the financial world has ever known. The Greed Decade may have taken four more years to play itself out, but after May 12, 1986, it was doomed.

Even now it is hard to grasp the magnitude and the scope of the crime that unfolded, beginning in the mid-1970s, in the nation's markets and financial institutions. It dwarfs any comparable financial crime, from the Great Train Robbery to the stock-manipulation schemes that gave rise to the nation's securities laws in the first place. The magnitude of the illegal gains was so large as to be incomprehensible to most laymen.

Dennis Levine, the small fish, confessed to $12.6 million in insider-trading profits. Ivan Boesky agreed to pay $100 million in forfeitures and penalties; no one pretends now that that is anywhere near the total of his illegal gains over the years. And then there is Michael Milken, whose crimes were far more complex, imaginative, and ambitious than mere insider trading. In 1986, Milken earned $550 million in salary and bonus alone from an enterprise that had been tainted with illegal activity for years. When he finally admitted to six felonies, he agreed to pay $600 million—an amount larger than the entire yearly budget of the Securities and Exchange Commission.

Nor were these isolated incidents. Only in its scale and potential impact did the Milken-led conspiracy dwarf others. Financial crime was commonplace on Wall Street in the eighties. A common refrain among nearly every defendant charged in the scandal was that it was unfair to single out one individual for prosecution when so many others were guilty of the same offenses, yet weren't charged. The code of silence that allowed crime to take root and flourish on Wall Street, even within some of the richest and most respected institutions, continues to protect many of the guilty.

To dwell on the ill-gotten gains of individuals, however, is to risk missing the big picture. During this crime wave, the ownership of entire corporations changed hands, often forcibly, at a clip never before witnessed. Household names—Carnation, Beatrice, General Foods, Diamond Shamrock—vanished in takeovers that spawned criminal activity and violations of the securities laws.

Others, companies like Unocal and Union Carbide, survived but were nearly crippled. Thousands of workers lost their jobs, companies loaded up with debt to pay for the deals, profits were sacrificed to pay interest costs on the borrowings, and even so, many companies were eventually forced into bankruptcies or restructurings. Bondholders and shareholders lost many millions more. Greed alone cannot account for such a toll. These are the costs of greed coupled with market power—

power unrestrained by the normal checks and balances of the free market, or by any fears of getting caught.

Nor should the financial implications of these crimes, massive though they are, obscure the challenge they posed to the nation's law-enforcement capabilities, its judicial system, and ultimately, to the sense of justice and fair play that is a foundation of civilized society. If ever there were people who believed themselves to be so rich and powerful as to be above the law, they were to be found in and around Wall Street in the mid-eighties. If money could buy justice in America, Milken and Drexel were prepared to spend it, and spend it they did. They hired the most expensive, sophisticated, and powerful lawyers and public-relations advisors, and they succeeded to a frightening degree at turning the public debate into a trial of government lawyers and prosecutors rather than of those accused of crimes.

But they failed, thanks to the sometimes heroic efforts of underpaid, overworked government lawyers who devoted much of their careers to uncovering the scandal, especially Charles Carberry and Bruce Baird, in the Manhattan U.S. attorney's office, and Gary Lynch, the head of enforcement at the Securities and Exchange Commission. Their efforts did not succeed perfectly. The pervasiveness of crime on Wall Street after a decade of lax enforcement sometimes overwhelmed their resources. Not everyone who should have been prosecuted has been, and mistakes were made. Yet their overriding success in prosecuting the major culprits and reinvigorating the securities laws is a tribute to the American system of justice.

This is the full story of the criminals who came to dominate Wall Street, how they achieved the pinnacle of wealth, power, and celebrity, and how they were detected and brought to justice. Despite the intense publicity that accompanied the charges against them, very little of this story has been made public. Milken, Boesky, Siegel, and Levine, by pleading guilty to reduced charges, avoided full public trials. This account is based on over four years of reporting, including scores of interviews, the review of voluminous documentary records, grand jury and other transcripts, lawyers' interview notes, and notes of various participants. In an era that purported to glorify free-market capitalism, this story shows how the nation's financial markets were in fact corrupted from within, and subverted for criminal purpose.

At the most basic level, American capitalism has flourished

because everyone, rich and poor alike, has seen the marketplace reward merit—enterprise, innovation, hard work, intelligence. The securities laws were implemented to help protect that process, to guard the integrity of the markets and to encourage capital formation, by providing a level playing field on which everyone might pursue their fortunes. Violations of the securities laws are not victimless crimes. When insider traders gain windfall stock profits because they have bribed someone to leak confidential business secrets, when prices are manipulated and blocks of stock secretly accumulated, our confidence in the underlying fairness of the market is shattered. We are all victims.

Why, you may be wondering, did I violate one of my cardinal rules? For in these passages I state explicitly that the main characters "confessed," were sentenced, and paid large fines. Isn't that the ending of the story, and am I not giving it away prematurely?

In a sense, I am, for those events are the dramatic ending of the narrative. But, as I pointed out when I discussed the lead to *Den*, I assumed that readers knew the outcome. Indeed, they *had* to know the outcome to recognize the conflict between the characters' professed self-confidence and denials and the reality that they were guilty of securities crimes and were soon to be caught. The mystery in *Den of Thieves* is how they committed their crimes and how they got caught, not *that* they did. This is made explicit in the second-to-last paragraph, where I also state that "very little of this story has been made public." In other words, "This is a mystery, and I am going to solve it for you with information that hasn't been revealed by anyone else." I was trying to excite curiosity and highlight the exclusivity of my information.

Den of Thieves is a long book, nearly 600 pages. This transition is an attempt to persuade readers that reading it is worth their time. The money involved in the scandal was huge, the impact on the economy significant. And, as the last sentence states, all of us have paid the price, and thus have a personal stake in understanding what happened and why.

What's important, however, is that the explanation for what happened is promised but not revealed; that I have a point of view is clear, but exactly what it is isn't explicit. I hoped that readers would be more eager to continue with the book when they finished this passage than they were before they began it.

The transition paragraphs in *Blood Sport* are even more

streamlined than those in *Den of Thieves.* After I'd opened with the death of Vince Foster, my task in *Blood Sport* was somewhat easier, since the events covered in the book were still a subject of national controversy (and remained so two years later). Thus, the significance of my account was implicit, and barely needed to be mentioned. Unlike the conclusion of the *Den of Thieves,* which was known, the ending remained a mystery in *Blood Sport;* indeed, the narrative was still unfolding when the book was published. So it was relatively easy to establish narrative suspense.

Here are those paragraphs in *Blood Sport:*

Vincent Foster, deputy White House counsel, lifelong friend, confidant, and counselor to the president and first lady, was the highest-ranking White House official ever to die under suspicious circumstances while in office. The only comparable incident seems to have been James Forrestal, secretary of the navy under Truman, who leaped to his death from a military hospital. Foster had led a sheltered life in Little Rock, a partner in Arkansas's leading law firm, a pillar of the state bar, chairman of the local repertory theater. He married his college sweetheart and raised three children. His world was pretty much bounded by the attractive white-columned home in Little Rock's Heights neighborhood, the Country Club of Little Rock, a modest walk down the street, and his office downtown at the Rose firm. He rode to work each day with Rose partners who lived nearby, often remaining silent during the ten- to fifteen-minute drive. He lived quietly, with dignity, with a reputation for integrity that meant everything to him. With minor variations, it was the life he'd chosen years before, when he opted to attend Davidson College, a highly regarded Presbyterian liberal arts college in North Carolina, and then returned to Arkansas for law school.

It is impossible to know how Foster himself would have reacted to the events his death set in motion. Given the pain he suffered at the attention of the *Wall Street Journal* editorial page, given his idealism and naïveté about politics and government service, he would surely be horrified. His friends believe that had he had any idea at all of what was going to happen, he would still be alive. Or perhaps in the hours and days before his death he saw his destiny as a political liability only too clearly, a realization that, in deepening his despair, made his death all but inevitable.

What is clear is that Vincent Foster's death has festered like an open wound on the body politic. To the extent the Clinton administration ever enjoyed a honeymoon, it ended on July 20, 1993. Among the confidential matters Foster was working on when he died was the Clintons' ill-fated investment in Whitewater, an Arkansas land development. A minor footnote to the 1992 presidential campaign, Whitewater was suddenly resurrected in the national press, and soon was as familiar a synonym for White House scandal as Watergate or Iran-contra. To a degree that left them stunned and at times depressed, the president and his wife were buffeted by what seemed an unending succession of scandalous allegations, from the first lady's profitable commodities trading to sexual harassment charges filed by Paula Jones.

These matters arose not in a vacuum, but in an environment of bitter partisan conflict primed by years of seething resentments lingering from past scandals. Republicans in Congress predictably fell with glee upon every allegation that could damage the Clinton presidency and legislative agenda, calling successfully for legislative hearings and the appointment of an independent counsel. Partisan members of the media, from conservative populist radio hosts to influential columnists, had a field day, keeping the scandals alive in the public mind and all but forcing the mainstream media to devote resources, print space, and airtime to exploring the most unsavory questions surrounding the Clinton presidency.

Yet, despite all these efforts and the attention, the mysteries surrounding Vincent Foster and the White House seemed only to deepen. In a climate of apparent obfuscation and half-truths, conspiracy theories abounded among a population jaded and skeptical from years of scandalous revelations at the highest levels of power. Was Foster murdered? If he did commit suicide, why? Do the answers lie in what Foster knew about the president and first lady? Were documents hidden or destroyed? Did top officials tell the truth? Was there a conspiracy to obstruct justice? If the Clintons had nothing to hide, why did they so often act as though they did?

As events unfolded, the mystery of Foster's death became inextricable from the Clintons' own lives, especially a past that, apart from the president's tortured effort to avoid being drafted and his relationship with Gennifer Flowers, has proven surprisingly elusive. It was only after Clinton's election and Foster's death that Whitewater was explored in any detail or gained a foothold in the American consciousness, that the first lady's handling of the couple's personal finances caused any suspicion, or that Arkansas troopers surfaced with disclosures that corroborated allegations of marital infidelity by the president. Mystery begot mystery. Apart from hardened conspiracy theorists and partisan zealots both for and against the president, most Americans were left to wonder: Where does the truth lie?

The main task in the transition is simply to guide readers from the death of Foster to the broader questions that will be addressed in the book. For I wanted to make clear that this book wasn't simply for readers curious about the death of Foster, but for anyone interested in the various inquiries triggered by Foster's death, including the Whitewater and Paula Jones matters, and, at the broadest level, the political culture—the "environment of bitter partisan conflict"—that found expression in those scandals. This, then, was an effort to get beyond significance, which seemed obvious, to universality, where readers needed guidance, in my view. Indeed, surprisingly few people, even when *Blood Sport* was published, recalled that it was the death of Foster that caused Whitewater to become the major scandal it did.

In this respect, I'm not sure I entirely succeeded. Somewhat to my dismay, public curiosity about Foster's death, and whether Bill and Hillary Clinton were "guilty" of some crime, were so intense, and political sentiment, both for and against the Clintons, so strong, that my attempts to focus readers' attention on the broader, nonpartisan issues of political culture and human nature at times seemed futile. Very few reviewers addressed what I saw as the most profound themes in the book; most contented themselves with a much more superficial examination of the Clintons' guilt or innocence and the immediate political implications of my findings.

Yet I remain convinced that it is the universal themes in any work, article or book, that provide an opportunity for longevity. I made this point explicitly when I met with Hillary Clinton to discuss the possibility of writing *Blood Sport*, saying that I hoped that, long after she and the president had left Washington, readers would still find the book a valuable portrait of American political culture at this juncture in our history. I was trying to appeal to Mrs. Clinton's interest in contributing to something that would be of enduring interest rather than just a passing political strategy. She didn't respond, so I have no way of knowing whether the idea held any appeal. Still, as years pass and the immediate urgency of the Whitewater affair recedes, those transition paragraphs will remain to put the narrative in a context that, I hope, will continue to interest future generations.

Besides wanting to establish universality, I intended the transition simply to heighten what I hoped was already a high degree of curiosity. Here I made no attempt at subtlety: I stated the unanswered questions explicitly, and I emphasized the mystery, not the solution, with phrases like "mystery begot mystery." Trying to reassure readers that I had approached the subject not as a partisan or zealot, but simply as a reporter, I concluded with the most basic question of all: "Where does the truth lie?" It is implicit that by the end of the book—but only by the end—I will have answered that question.

7
STRUCTURE

ALL GOOD STORIES have a structure, a backbone, which unifies even seemingly disparate elements. The presence of structure reassures readers that they are in the hands of a skilled storyteller, someone they can trust with their time and interest. They know they are going somewhere, which means they can relax and enjoy the journey.

Once a structure is established, the problem that bedevils every writer at one time or another—"Where do I go next?"—is largely solved. The logic that will reassure readers also guides writers as they work through a story to its conclusion. I have been amazed to discover how much time I have saved, and how much anxiety I have avoided, by having a clear structure firmly in mind, if not on paper.

It's surprising how few writers and reporters give this important aspect of their stories much thought. Armed with a good lead and a nut graf, they simply proceed to empty their notebooks, moving from one source to the next, ladling quotations directly into their text. When they run out of material, they simply stop. Or, embracing at least the vestiges of the traditional pyramid style, they dole out what they consider to be their best information and quotations first, assuming an editor will cut the story from the bottom (as, unfortunately, editors often do).

I still read many published stories that appear to be organized in this fashion. They have a meandering quality that invariably makes my anxiety mount. The unread text becomes an albatross. I rarely finish such stories.

The simplest organizing principle is often the most effective: chronology. While physicists and philosophers may debate the nature of time, the rest of us inhabit a world of simple linear chronology. It's no accident that most people say stories have a beginning, a middle, and an end. We mark our lives with time: in years, months, weeks, days, hours, minutes, seconds. Time is a universal organizing principle. More than any other, it clarifies and illuminates a chaotic universe.

While time itself may be a simple concept to most of us, using chronology to structure a story is not always a simple task. Using chronology as your paramount organizing principle doesn't mean simply telling a story in strict chronological order. Most stories deviate from strict chronology, often many times. Stories can even be told entirely in reverse chronological order, although time remains the organizing principle. Some writers treat chronology the way Picasso treated visual realism. Dream and fantasy sequences, popular in some circles, defy conventional chronology. But most nonfiction writing isn't, and should not be, primarily an experiment in literary technique. What I seek is a structure that will clarify the information I have to convey while at the same time heightening its dramatic impact, a structure that will help me make the most of the material I have gathered. As with so many other aspects of writing, there is rarely a single structure that will do this, and there may not even be a best one. But I always have a reason for choosing the structure I settle on, and it, in turn, reflects a consistent logic.

Chronology often solves the problem of how to organize a story, even if the story isn't a pure narrative. Profiles lend themselves to a narrative approach, as do explanatory and investigative stories. In the investigative piece, an effective chronology is often the progress of the writer's investigation, in which the author becomes a central character, implicitly if not explicitly. Even trend and point-of-view stories may lend themselves to a chronological approach, particularly if the subject of the story has evolved over time, as is often the case.

The enemy of chronology is analysis. Analysis focuses on meaning rather than on what happened. It is difficult to organize chronologically, because most often it takes place in the present, or in the very recent past. It is usually solicited by the writer in interviews, which may have no organizing principle other than the ability of the reporter to reach a subject at any given time. Analysis distances readers from the events in a story, which usually occur long before the analysis is rendered. It also tends to be didactic; it tells readers what to think rather than inviting them to form their own conclusions. There is nothing wrong with the "news analysis" that shows up so often in newspapers and on television, as long as it is intelligent, brief, and to the point. But, in my experience, it almost never provides memorable reading.

Nonetheless, most of the reporters and students I have worked with over the years are far more comfortable with analysis than with telling a story. This may be, in part, because an analysis can never really be factually wrong; it is akin to opinion. But I suspect it is also because analysis exists in the present, which is almost always easier to re-create than the past. Indeed, a challenge that must be confronted and surmounted in narrative writing is to distinguish memory and perception, which exist in the present, from events, dialogue, and states of mind that existed in the past. This problem invariably surfaces in the reporting process, when you're interviewing sources about events that happened in the past. People tend to tell you what they think now, rather than what they thought at the time of the event in question.

When I would ask people what they thought of Ivan Boesky, they almost always told me they thought he was a charlatan, a scoundrel and a criminal. I would have to ask again, urging them to share with me their thoughts when they first met Boesky, *before* he had admitted insider trading and pleaded guilty to securities fraud. So powerful is the effect of present impressions that many sources would insist that they immediately sensed something untrustworthy or shifty about Boesky, even though some of them had entrusted him with millions of dollars. Just as thinking chronologically becomes quite easy once a writer has become accustomed to it, sources adapt very quickly after being prodded a few times. What's important is that they put themselves back in time to the events being discussed, banishing everything they learned or thought since. Sources who are good at this (some are amazingly good) will naturally begin speaking in the past tense, recalling dialogue and states of mind.

The first task in organizing a story chronologically is to determine the time frame of the story. By this I do not necessarily mean the point at which the story actually begins—which, as we've seen, may fall in any number of places along the time sequence. What I mean by "time frame" is the range between the earliest event that will be depicted in the story, and the most recent. My students are sometimes confused by this seemingly simple exercise, because some information included in a story by way of background or as a postscript may fall outside the chronological frame. The birth of a principal character, for example, is rarely the chronological beginning of a story, however logical it might seem. While I will often refer to someone's age, the actual circumstances of someone's birth have almost never warranted inclusion. The events that make up this frame must be sufficiently relevant to warrant being depicted. In this respect, I find it helpful to visualize an event, almost as though I were watching a scene in a movie. Would I include such a scene in my story? If so, where does it fall in the sequence of events?

Until this process becomes almost second nature, as it does eventually, I encourage my students to write down the events of the story they plan to depict. This needn't be laborious. It's easy enough to add or delete scenes later. Arrange the scenes or incidents in chronological order. This doesn't mean that a specific date is necessary for every scene, but enough information is required to place an event in sequence. (It's surprising how often further reporting is necessary simply to establish chronological order, which is a useful exercise in its own right.) Be disciplined about this—do not let spurious notions of logic intrude upon the ordering process. Keep the events in strict chronological order.

Once this process is done, you have a workable story outline. Indeed, there are far worse ways to tell a story than in strict chronological order. There may be better ways, but it is hard to go wrong with a chronological approach. And chronology is always a useful fallback position if something more ambitious doesn't seem to work, or meets resistance from an editor. At the very least, all writers should be able to tell their stories in chronological order, even if that isn't the way they end up writing them.

Let me illustrate this important principle with the story I discussed earlier about the flood in the Midwest. As I said, I had decided to try to capture the human dimension of this immense natural catastrophe by focusing my attention on one geographic spot, the Sny levee south of my hometown of Quincy, Illinois. This was a narrative story, and I had chosen as the opening scene the rainstorm that was the immediate cause of the flooding around Quincy. What was the time frame for the flood story? Its beginning, chronologically, was the rainstorm. As is often the case, the starting point of any chronology is at least a little arbitrary. The argument could be made that there were earlier events that caused the flood. There was the spring thaw. There were other rains that spring leading up to the tempest of June 30. But did I want to show these events? None of the characters in the story had taken any special note of them at the time. Spring thaws are routine, as are spring rains. It was the rainstorm on June 30 that had caused everyone to worry and to take action. The longer-term causes could easily be accommodated in the story as background without having to illustrate melting snow. So the rainstorm served as one end of the chronological frame.

The element of suspense in this story came from the levee itself: Would it hold? The end of the story was pretty obvious: it either did, and the river would recede; or it didn't, and the land would flood. So the fate of the levee would be the other end of the frame. You will recall that I didn't know that fate when I began writing the story, so there might be a later scene—if, for example, the land flooded and one of the characters was injured, or showed heroism, or whatever happened. In that case the fate of the levee would be the climax of the story. But since I didn't yet know the ending, for purposes of organizing my material, the fate of the levee served as the end of my time frame.

Here are the "scenes" in the flood story, listed in chronological order:

1. Wednesday, June 30. Rainstorm inundates area.
2. The morning of the next day. Sheriff Nall meets with levee commissioners.
3. Noon, the next day. Alex House brings his bulldozer to the Sny levee.
4. Evening, the next day. Levee construction at the Sny is under way.
5. Saturday. Sheriff Nall arrives at the Sny with a contingent of prison inmates to help shore up the levee.

6. Tuesday. National Weather Service predicts flood crest for following Sunday; Nall and Leo Henning of WGEM-TV and radio react.
7. Friday, July 9. A major upstream levee breaks, relieving pressure on the Sny. The national media arrives in Quincy to cover the break.
8. The following Thursday. The Sny levee survives a thirty-two-foot crest.
9. The next day. The West Quincy levee breaks, a victim of sabotage. Pressure on the Sny is relieved again.
10. Saturday. President Clinton calls WGEM from Air Force One.
11. Sunday, July 25. The battle of the Sny ends.

These aren't the only events that take place in the story, of course, but they are the major ones, which provide the signposts to move readers toward the conclusion. They provide most of the action in the story, and most of them are easily visualized. (In the case of the inmates arriving at the Sny, I actually quoted the sheriff saying, "It looked like something out of *Bridge on the River Kwai*.") Some of the scenes are included in part to develop suspense as the river rises and reaches a crest, threatening the levee, then falls. The break in the West Quincy levee, a result of sabotage, provides highly dramatic material. Though it takes place away from the Sny levee, it is directly related to the Sny's fate, and in a marvelous coincidence from a storytelling standpoint, House witnessed the break from a helicopter. The phone call from Air Force One also added drama. Note that all of these events take place in a time frame that is actually quite brief: it spans less than a month, from June 30 to July 25, 1993.

As it turned out, this chronological list of scenes is exactly how the final story was structured. There were only two deviations. One was a section that served as a further transition, in which I appear as a character in the story, explaining that Quincy is my hometown and that I was returning to see the extent of the flood. This occupies only one fairly lengthy paragraph, and accomplishes two purposes: it establishes how I came to witness the events that unfold in the story, and I serve as a surrogate for the reader, someone aware of the overall extent of the flood but unfamiliar with the plight of any individual farmers or others whose lives were affected by it.

The other departure follows immediately, once the story has returned to the main characters, and it consists of the background necessary for a reader to understand how events have reached a crisis. In establishing the state of mind of the worried farmers calling Sheriff Nall, I wrote: "They'd been keeping an uneasy eye on the river since April. . . ." Then I filled in the weather developments leading up to the storm on June 30. Such deviations are usually signaled by the past perfect tense: "had been keeping . . ."

In general, I find that the simplest chronological approach is the best. Every time one scene ends and is replaced by another, readers are expected to shift their attention as well. Readers often continue reading because they want to know what happens next. "Next" is the key, a deeply embedded convention in storytelling. For that reason, I try to minimize disruptions in chronology. Readers do not generally want to move to the next scene or event if to do so sends them backward in time—if it, in fact, deprives them of finding out what happened next. Though flashbacks are a commonly used technique, and may readily be accepted by a sufficiently curious reader, they can be confusing. Use them only if you have a good reason. As I discussed in the chapter on leads, one of those reasons is to generate the curiosity necessary to sustain a reader's interest throughout a story. But to sprinkle interruptions in chronology through a story invites readers to quit.

Another reason readers keep reading is the pace of a story. Note that the time intervals are quite short in the beginning of the flood story, and tend to grow longer toward the climax. This helps give the story momentum, something I'll later discuss in greater detail. It's easier to introduce background information and anything else that falls out of strict chronology, early in a story. My editor at *The New Yorker,* John Bennett, likens a story to a train pulling out of the station: it starts slowly, gathers speed, then races down the track toward its destination. I try to keep that in mind as I write.

You may recall that this story had three main characters who were introduced in the lead: House, the farmer; Nall, the sheriff; and Henning, the radio station manager. As each character comes into the story, we see events from his point of view. In the lead, for example, where I wrote "House was hoping to fall asleep quickly . . . ," I am telling the story from House's point of view. This is clearly signaled by bringing the reader into House's mind: House is "hoping" for something. Until a clear shift is indicated by moving to another character's point of view, we see events through House's eyes. The reader is meant to identify with him.

This is an example of narrative point of view, which is, after chronology, the most important element of structure in a story. By "point of view" I do not mean an opinion to which readers are steered, as in the point-of-view story. I mean events as seen through the eyes of a particular character. Narrative point of view is essential in almost any story with multiple characters, unless a single character narrates. A story that shifts freely among points of view is usually described as having omniscient narration, since the reader can experience different characters' states of mind, as an actual participant could not. Omniscient narration is the most common form of story-telling.

Every incident described in a story, every scene, takes place at a particular time and is seen from someone's point of view. Shifts in time and point of view must be clearly established. Because such shifts require some effort on the part of the reader, because they break a scene and its mood, they are opportunities for a reader to lose interest and quit a story; as a result, they should be minimized. At the very least, there needs to be a good reason for the shift. This is especially true when chronology and point of view are interrupted at the same time.

As is the case with chronology, I recognize there are certain literary writers who deliberately shift point of view for particular effects. A case in point is the critically acclaimed novel *The English Patient,* by Michael Ondaatje. The Academy Award–winning movie adaptation eliminated many of the novel's shifts in chronology and point of view, greatly simplifying the narrative. Yet even the movie left some viewers puzzled. I loved *The English Patient,* but I would be highly reluctant to imitate its literary techniques in my own writing. It's hard enough to make a non-fiction story clear and dramatic, without compounding the difficulties.

Just as events and scenes in a story can be listed in chronological order, so the characters' points of view can be listed in a sequence that corresponds to each of those events, providing a given character participated in or witnessed the event being described. The process is somewhat analogous to how characters in a play may be on or off-stage at any given moment. After writing down the scenes or events in chronological order, I next record which characters are present in each of them; this presents the options for that scene's point of view. In the case of the flood story, these were the possibilities:

1. House, Nall, and Henning (indeed, any character in town at the time)
2. Nall
3. House and workers at the levee
4. House
5. House and Nall
6. Nall and Henning
7. Nall, Henning, Sara Rimer (*New York Times* reporter)
8. House and levee workers; Army Corps of Engineers captain
9. House, Henning, Nall
10. Henning
11. House and levee workers

We've already seen how three points of view were incorporated into the opening scene of the rainstorm. The next scene, which incorporates the background material I described earlier, is told from Nall's point of view, introduced with the statement that Nall's "phone was ringing with calls." In other words, we are going to listen in on Nall's conversations with farmers in outlying areas. When the scene shifts to the levee, there is a new paragraph, beginning "When House arrived at the levee . . ." We now see events through House's eyes, including the introduction of two secondary characters, both farmers—Ken Crim and John Guenseth, known as Peanuts. "About twenty farmers had gathered. . . ." Once the reader has met Crim and Guenseth, their points of view can be introduced within the same scene: "Peanuts knew . . ."

In the third scene, Nall brings the prison inmates to the levee, where House, Crim. and Peanuts are working. The paragraph begins, "With the inmates on their way, Nall jumped into his car and headed for the levee," which establishes Nall's point of view. Within this same scene, it is easy to shift the point of view to the other characters, so we see the same event through their eyes. A new paragraph begins, "Crim, House, and the others heard the new arrivals before they saw them. . . ."

It is always easier to shift scenes if the point of view remains the same, or to shift point of view within a scene. In the flood story, because the same characters were often present in successive scenes, it was relatively easy to minimize disruptions for the reader. Scenes three and four were connected by House, as were four and five. In both cases the scene could shift while the point of view remained constant. Nall was the common character in scenes five and six, and Henning in scenes six and seven. Scene seven introduces the character of Sara Rimer, the "outsider," a New Yorker who comes to town, which also enabled me to introduce the subject of a possible romance between Nall and Rimer. But this took readers away from the Sny, and left me with no common point of view with which to return to scene nine. In the text of the published story, this break was signaled with a space and a large capital letter to begin the next paragraph: "That Tuesday evening, thinking that the battle for the Sny was lost, Crim and House went home. . . ."

Use of a larger, boldface capital letter and a space is *The New Yorker*'s style; *The Wall Street Journal* typically uses a row of small stars set in the center of a column of type. Other publications use different devices, but the large capital letter, usually referred to as a drop cap, is common. All are used as graphic signals of a shift in chronology, point of view, or setting, or all three. But they should be used carefully, since even more than transitions within the text, they offer readers an opportunity to quit. Think how often you stop reading a book at the end of a chapter, rather than in the middle of one.

The flood story required relatively few such graphic breaks, because the events unfolded within a geographical frame that was almost as circumscribed as its chronology. Setting, or geography, is the third organizing principle, and is analogous to the scenes, or stage set, in a play. A change in location also asks a reader to make a shift, to visualize a new place. Here are the settings for the flood story, organized by scene:

1 and 2. In and around Quincy
3, 4, and 5. At the Sny levee
6 and 7. In an around Quincy
8. At the Sny
9. In West Quincy
10. At WGEM radio in Quincy
11. At the Sny

There are really only two significant settings: the Sny levee itself and Quincy and its environs. West Quincy and WGEM are brief diversions. Like the introduction of a new character, the introduction of a new setting calls for some descriptive writing to help readers visualize the scene. Here is my description of Quincy and the surrounding area:

Quincy's founders, back in 1822, had the foresight to establish their river port on some of the highest bluffs on the east bank of the Mississippi. From the old dock areas along the riverfront, where stern-wheelers once called regularly, the streets rise steeply to the east. From the buildings surrounding the old town square, high above the river, and from WGEM's offices, in the Hotel Quincy, which is just around the corner, one has sweeping views across the river of miles of the fertile lowlands of Missouri. Those lands, and also vast tracts both north and south of Quincy, with their farms and with the towns and hamlets that dot the landscape, are protected by an elaborate system of levees and drainage districts.

I recognize that this is a fairly lengthy passage of description. But it comes early in the story, when for reasons of pacing readers will accept such a level of detail, and it accomplishes several purposes: it provides some history, it describes settings that will recur, including WGEM and the lowlands in Missouri where West Quincy is located, and it puts the levee system in context. Occurring in a 10,000-word magazine story, this description doesn't seem excessive; it certainly wouldn't be in a book. Then again, it might in a 3,000-word newspaper story.

As befits the chief setting of the story, the Sny levee is described in even more detail. It is described again once the water rises:

In the best of circumstances, a levee in midsummer is a place to avoid. The moist bottomland breeds mosquitoes said to be the size of horseflies. There's no shade, and the sun, reflecting off the river water, is doubly oppressive. Humidity builds, and the levee deflects any river breezes. A few workers sought relief by plunging into the water, but most of them shunned the river, unwilling to risk floating debris and ever-present water moccasins.

Once you've described a place, little further description is necessary; it is relatively easy for readers to return to a setting they already know. As in the case of point of view, it is easier to make chronological and point-of-view shifts if the setting remains constant. Thus, even though there is a significant shift between scenes 1 and 2, the common setting of Quincy helps ease the transition. Even in the transition between scenes 7 and 8, the reader is returning to the Sny, which is at least a familiar setting.

Just as an audience enjoys the curtain rising on a stage set, and will sometimes gasp and applaud in delight, most readers enjoy descriptive writing, as long as it comes early in a story and doesn't interfere with pace. Bryan Burrough, a former colleague of mine at the *Journal* and an exceptional feature writer, often begins his stories with a physical description of the setting for the first scene, sometimes at considerable length.

It is also an advantage to minimize the number of settings in a story. Just as action in a play may take place offstage, action that is relevant to a story but that takes place in an entirely new setting doesn't have to be depicted in detail. This was an issue in the flood story for scene 9, the break in the West Quincy levee, which introduced an entirely new setting quite late in the story. As I mentioned earlier, the pace of a story ideally gains momentum toward the conclusion, and a new setting, requiring as it does considerable description and background, slows the story. I would probably not have made the West Quincy break a scene in its own right except for the extraordinary coincidence that House, one of my main characters, was watching from a helicopter at the moment the levee broke. This was not only great drama, but it enabled me to use a point of view already familiar to readers. Had that not been the case, I would probably have kept the story at the Sny or in Quincy, and readers would have learned of the West Quincy break and its significance as a character in one of those locations did.

With practice, it becomes possible to keep these principal organizing elements of chronology, point of view, and setting in one's head while writing. But to clarify the relationships among them, it can be very helpful to plot them on a single graph, which I do for complicated stories and for books. An example of such a graph for the flood story appears on the following page.

As I said earlier in this chapter, chronology is usually the most effective organizing principle, followed by point of view and then setting. The flood story was essentially told in chronological order, which minimized disruptions in the sequence of events. Nonetheless, in shifting between scenes, I used point of view to ease those transitions for readers. Finally, I used a common setting when possible, and minimized the number of settings, to further ease those shifts.

While that is the approach I almost always use in my own writing, it isn't the only option. It is possible, particularly in profiles, to use a single character's point of view as the major organizing principle in a story, relegating chronology to a secondary role. (In such cases, the order in which a character learns of events takes precedence over the order in which those events took place.)

It would have been possible to organize the flood story entirely on the basis of point of view. All the scenes with House as the main character could have been followed by those with Nall and then by those with Henning, requiring only two shifts in point of view. In telling the flood story such an approach would have been nonsensical, since it would have required several confusing chronological shifts and would have given away the ending prematurely. This was a narrative whose suspense turned on the fate of the levee. Nonetheless, point of view is an organizing principle that would be perceived by readers as having a logic unto itself, and the result would be more comprehensible than many stories that have no organizing principle whatsoever.

As narrative stories go, the flood story was relatively simple. This was because it could be told in straightforward chronological order. It was complicated slightly by the number of characters and by multiple settings. In my class, I encourage students who have never written a narrative story to begin with one that can

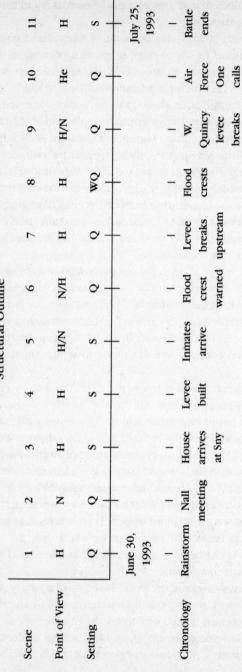

"Battle of the Sny"
Structural Outline

Scene	1	2	3	4	5	6	7	8	9	10	11
Point of View	H	N	H	H	H/N	N/H	H	H	H/N	He	H
Setting	Q	Q	S	S	S	Q	Q	WQ	Q	Q	S
	June 30, 1993										July 25, 1993
Chronology	Rainstorm	Nall meeting	House arrives at Sny	Levee built	Inmates arrive	Flood crest warned	Levee breaks upstream	Flood crests	W. Quincy levee breaks	Air Force One calls	Battle ends

Key

Point of view: H = House; N = Nall; He = Henning

Setting: Q = Quincy; S = Sny levee; WQ = West Quincy

be written in chronological order using one setting and a single point of view. If that isn't possible because of the nature of the story, I urge them not to worry at the outset about point of view and setting, but simply to put events in chronological order. Simply getting students to write down the events of their stories in chronological order works wonders.

In truth, few stories are as simple and easy to structure as the flood story. Many stories can be better told by deviating from strict chronological order. Others can't be told in strict chronological order. This is usually the case in stories with multiple characters who separate for extended periods. The characters are like pieces on a chessboard. One character advances through time; then the writer has to backtrack in time to another character and move him to the same point. In such stories, point of view assumes greater importance as an organizing principle. But the goal is the same: to make the journey as clear and dramatic as possible for the reader by minimizing shifts in chronology, point of view, and setting.

A good illustration of the more complex structure that is often called for in stories is the piece about insider trading involving Jonathan Sheinberg. It was obvious to me almost from the outset that the story should not be told in chronological order, because to do so would almost immediately undermine the suspense generated in the lead, which was based on the twin questions "What happened?" and "Why would someone as wealthy as Jonathan get involved in insider trading?" The answers to both appeared at the time of the trading, long before any investigation was under way, and far too soon to sustain readers' interest in what would remain of the story. Even so, I began by determining the time frame and arranging events in chronological order. I find that this exercise is even more important for stories that are not told in strict chronological order than for those that are, since chronology still forms the organizing principle.

In the Sheinberg story, the earliest event was plainly Jonathan's overhearing the phone call in which his father discussed the imminent acquisition of MCA by Matsushita. The most recent was Jonathan's agreement to settle SEC charges and end the case. This was the time frame for the story, and it didn't take much struggle to identify it. The first event took place in September

1990 and the last in December 1991, a span of about sixteen months. (I was working on this story in 1993, which illustrates another point: that a postscript can be used to cover a considerable period of time.)

Here is how I arranged the events of the story chronologically within that frame:

1. September 21, 1990. Jonathan and his father walk on the beach; Jonathan is told not to trade or talk.
2. Sept. 23. Jonathan calls his wife, Maria, and her boyfriend, Barry Fogel, with news of the MCA takeover.
3. Later that evening. Jonathan, Jonathan's girlfriend, Susan Ursitti, Maria, and Barry meet at Jonathan's to discuss trading in MCA stock.
4. September 25. SEC lawyer Andrew Geist hears a report on the radio of unusual trading in MCA stock just before the takeover was announced. Geist gets a summary of the trading.
5. Several days later. The SEC issues subpoenas. Jonathan's business manager, Richard Shephard, receives one.
6. The next day. Barry Fogel gets a subpoena. Maria calls, crying; Jonathan meets with her to reassure her.
7. March 25, 1991. Geist and another SEC lawyer contact Shephard.
8. April 24. Geist deposes Fogel, who denies everything.
9. Several days later. Jonathan faces his father, telling him he violated his strictures and disclosed the MCA deal.
10. May 1991. In a bid for leniency, Sid Sheinberg's lawyers call Geist and explain what happened.
11. Summer 1991. The SEC lawyers depose all the participants, including Fogel, who now agrees to tell the truth.
12. October 1991. Despite pleas from Sheinberg lawyers, the SEC decides to file charges.
13. December 1991. The Sheinbergs and all other defendants settle, ending the case.

Like the flood story's, the lead for this piece turned out to be the first scene, for the reasons I explained in chapter 6, and yet another example of the adage that the beginning isn't a bad place to begin. But, as I've mentioned, I couldn't proceed in chronological order, because the central questions of the story would have been answered in scenes 2 and 3, in which Jonathan plots strategy and carries out the insider-trading scheme; those scenes reveal what happened and shed considerable light on his motives. In order to sustain readers' curiosity, I wanted to place those scenes as late in the story as possible.

Point of view is the device that enabled me to do this. Before further discussing the chronology of the story, let's match the scenes to the characters, as I did in the flood example.

Scene 1. Jonathan and Sid Sheinberg
Scene 2. Jonathan, Maria, Barry Fogel
Scene 3. Jonathan, Maria, Barry and Susan Ursitti
Scene 4. Geist
Scene 5. Geist and Shephard
Scene 6. Geist, Fogel, and Maria
Scene 7. Geist and Shephard
Scene 8. Geist and Fogel
Scene 9. Jonathan and Sid
Scene 10. Geist, Sid, lawyers for the Sheinbergs
Scene 11. Geist, Jonathan, Fogel, et al.
Scene 12. Geist
Scene 13. Geist, Jonathan, and Sid

With the exception of scene 9, where Jonathan confronts his father, Andrew Geist, the chief SEC lawyer, appears in every scene after the first three. That means all of those scenes could be narrated from Geist's point of view. If scenes 2 and 3 were moved to the point in the story where Geist learns what happened, they would come after scene 11, for only in the depositions of the participants did Geist and his colleagues learn how the insider trades were planned and carried out. This came very close to satisfying my goal, which was to withhold the information in those scenes until near the end of the story.

Now let's briefly consider the settings for the story, which in this case are quite simple. All the scenes take place in or around

Malibu, Beverly Hills, and Los Angeles, except scene 4, which is in Geist's apartment in New York. In scenes 5 through 7, the action is bifurcated, with Geist and his colleagues in New York and Jonathan and his associates in Los Angeles.

You may recall that when I wrote the lead for this story, I considered using scene 4, in which Geist learned of the possible insider trading, as the opening scene; this would have been the classic approach to a mystery or detective story, which in a sense this story was. I rejected that option because the investigation itself wasn't all that dramatic and the Sheinbergs were the central characters. But that didn't mean I couldn't still use Geist's point of view to move readers through the story. Connecting the characters to the scenes made it immediately apparent that using Geist would suit my literary purpose, which was to heighten and maintain suspense and curiosity as long as possible. With this in mind, I was able to rearrange the scenes in the chronology in this order: 1,4,5,6,7,8,9,10,11,2,3,12,13.

Let's look at the chronology again. There are essentially three time periods that make up the story. First come the planning and execution of the insider-trading scheme, scenes 1–3. Jonathan and his associates are the characters; Geist is offstage. Then there is the adversarial stage of the investigation, when the SEC is issuing subpoenas and Jonathan and his colleagues are reacting with varying degrees of panic and obfuscation. This comprises scenes 4 through 8. Geist and Jonathan and his friends are participants, but it is important to recognize that these scenes cannot be presented solely from Geist's point of view, since at the time he was unaware of how the targets were reacting. As my analysis of the settings made obvious, in these scenes the SEC lawyers were in New York, although they were connected to Los Angeles by phone or mail. It is important to remember that information must never be imputed to a character that he or she could not have had at the time, even if it was later revealed. The same characters appear in the final stage, when what happened and why is revealed. This time Geist and Jonathan are onstage together.

Scenes 5 through 8 thus pose a problem, since the action is split between New York and Los Angeles, between Geist's point of view and those of the participants. Neither knows what the other is up to. My choice was either to leave those scenes in chronological order, with a point-of-view shift in each, or to shift point of view once, from Geist to Jonathan and his colleagues. That would require one additional chronology interruption, if scenes 5 and 6 were moved to follow scenes 7 and 8. I opted for the latter approach as the least disruptive for readers. Again, there is no right or wrong decision here, but given the need for shifts in either chronology or point of view, I chose the option that required only one shift of each kind, rather than four shifts in point of view. But I must admit that I agonized over this decision. Whereas I could justify the chronological move of scenes 2 and 3 on the grounds that Geist only learned the information at that point, I could not use the same logic with scenes 5 and 6. Geist learned that information when he learned everything else, during scenes 10 and 11. But I did not want to delay giving readers this information, since the efforts of the co-conspirators to evade capture generated much of the story's suspense. So I simply broke both the chronology and the point of view at this point, in service of the overriding goal of maximizing the reader's curiosity. This did require covering the Fogel deposition twice, the first time from Geist's point of view, and the second, much more briefly, from Fogel's.

So now the chronological order of the story looked like this: 1,4,7,8,5,6,9,10,11,2,3,12,13.

The corresponding points of view were:

1. Jonathan, Sid
4. Geist
7. Geist
8. Geist
5. Geist, Shephard, Jonathan
6. Maria, Fogel, Jonathan
9. Jonathan, Sid
10. Geist
11. Geist
2. Jonathan and the co-conspirators
3. Jonathan and the co-conspirators
12. Geist
13. Geist, Sid, and Jonathan

I now had two chronological shifts to contend with, one between scenes 8 and 5, and another between 11 and 2. Resuming an interrupted chronology, as between scenes 6 and 9, and between 3 and 12, doesn't in my view constitute a real break; readers are generally relieved to be back on track. And note that the breaks between scenes 1 and 4 and scenes 4 and 7 would not "read" as shifts because it wouldn't yet be apparent to readers that any scenes were being omitted.

These chronological interruptions enabled me to reduce the shifts in point of view to five: from Jonathan to Geist after scene 1; from Geist to Jonathan between scenes 8 and 5; from Jonathan and Sid to Geist after scene 9; from Geist to Jonathan after scene 11; and from Jonathan back to Geist after scene 3.

Let me illustrate how I wrote some of these shifts in chronology and point of view in order to minimize disruption for readers.

Here is the break between scene 8, in which Geist and his colleagues have just finished a frustrating deposition of Barry Fogel, and scene 5, in which Fogel and the others react to receiving the subpoenas.:

> Here the deposition ended, convincing Geist and Brotbacker [a colleague of Geist's] of only one thing: Fogel was lying. To keep the pressure on, they immediately issued subpoenas for all of Fogel's phone records. They sensed that they were on to something. But they were far from the breakthrough they'd hoped for. They still had no idea how a Beverly Hills restaurateur would have gained access to one of the most closely guarded secrets in corporate America.

There is a space, and the next paragraph begins with a large capital letter, visual devices that signal a shift:

> Just about everyone in Hollywood talks about how hard it is to be the son or daughter or the spouse of somebody famous.

After a lengthy discussion of Jonathan and his background, the story resumes:

> It was Shephard who got the first of the SEC's subpoenas, and one of his first thoughts that day was to speak to Jonathan,

who happened to call in on his cellular phone as he was driving to work.

It's no accident that the writers of serial novels tried to end each chapter with a cliff-hanger in order to entice the reader to return for the next installment. Every time a writer faces a break in chronology or point of view, the goal is the same. Thus, just before this break, I tried to heighten the suspense by focusing on how baffled Geist and his colleague were. Yes, they have made some progress—"they sensed that they were on to something"— but "they still had no idea" how Fogel had gotten the information. Obviously, the point of view is Geist's, but I hoped that readers would be just as baffled—and eager to satisfy their curiosity by reading on. I recognized that I was asking readers to make a big leap. The next paragraph shifts the setting to Hollywood, and focuses again on Jonathan. The chronological shift itself is fairly subtle, occurring after considerable background material on Jonathan, and when the chronology resumes, it isn't specifically dated. Most readers will not recognize, and probably wouldn't care, that Shephard's subpoena was issued some time before the Fogel deposition that ended the previous scene.

In the other chronological shift I used a similar tactic. By the end of highly condensed versions of scenes 10 and 11, Geist and his colleagues had learned what actually happened, though readers had not. Here is how I wrote the transition:

> The SEC lawyers were amazed. Despite the famously loose mores of Los Angeles, they thought it most unusual for an estranged husband and wife and their lovers to be so intimately involved in an insider-trading conspiracy. Levine and McCaw [the Sheinberg lawyers] described the fateful phone call that Jonathan had happened to overhear. More important, they announced that all those involved, with the exception of Ursitti, had agreed to cooperate and answer fully the SEC's questions in the upcoming depositions. In those sessions, beginning in late June and continuing into September, Geist and Brotbacker finally learned just what had happened.

There is again a space and a large capital letter. The story continues:

As long as Jonathan was at his father's house that September weekend of 1990 . . .

Finally, scenes 2 and 3 reveal what happened and why.

By telling readers that Geist and Brotbacker knew what happened, but withholding this information from readers, I have again tried to intensify curiosity so that readers will not abandon the story at this chronological shift. This time, the break is explicit, since I refer to the weekend at the beach house, which was described in detail in the opening scene, and date it as September 1990. This is the payoff, the satisfaction of readers' curiosity, and in that sense, it is the climax of the story. I doubt that many readers abandoned the story at this juncture, despite having to flash back to earlier events and accept a shift in point of view from Geist to Jonathan.

Note that scenes 10 and 11 have all but disappeared from the narrative. The *process* by which Geist learned what happened wasn't all that interesting; *what* he learned was. Scenes 2 and 3, told in rich detail using information from the deposition transcripts I had obtained, contained the most interesting information in the story.

Although this story required a complicated structure, these are the only two simultaneous shifts of chronology and point of view. The other point of view changes occur within scenes, or at least in chronological order—which, as I've noted, make them much easier for readers to absorb. Still, the other three shifts in point of view were signaled with a space and a large capital letter to begin the next paragraph. Since the paragraphs proceeded in chronological order, I relied on readers' interest in what happened next to propel them over those gaps.

As a final note, I should point out that the opening scene at the Malibu beach house had to be briefly reprised in scene 2. That's because what happened there was part of what Geist learned from the depositions of Jonathan, his father, and the co-conspirators. As we will shortly see, opening scenes are often revisited when the narrative overtakes them. One of the best narrative writers at *The Wall Street Journal*, Barry Newman, referred to this structure as an "inverted e." If you draw an "e" upside down, you will see what he meant: the story starts, drops back, returns to the starting point where the loop of the "e" connects, and then continues.

Point of view provides an effective vehicle for returning to scenes that have already appeared in the story. As in the Sheinberg story, where the Fogel deposition was seen first through the eyes of Fogel, and later through the eyes of Geist, another character can provide a fresh vantage on familiar material. This was the case in the story I wrote about the accountant who was fired for being gay, in which, as I mentioned earlier, nearly every dramatic turn in the plot had to be mentioned in the lead. Each of these scenes appeared again in the course of the story, this time in greater detail and from the point of view of the accountant's boss.

I used this approach in *Blood Sport* to reprise the scene at Vince Foster's home that opens the book. As I mentioned earlier, in the opening, readers see the events through the eyes of John Rolla, the park policeman who was investigating Foster's death. But then, in chapter 1, the narrative drops back to 1978 and the origins of the Clintons' Whitewater investments. Nine chapters and 290 pages later, the "e" is connected when the narrative again reaches Foster's death. This time events are seen from Foster's point of view, and after his death, from his wife Lisa's and daughter Laura's. Let's look again at how I described the scene in the book's prologue:

> Rolla, accompanied by Watkins, knocked on the door. Twenty-one-year-old Laura Foster answered. "I'm John Rolla, with the United States Park Police . . ." Before he could finish he saw Laura looking behind him at her aunts, Hubbell and his wife, Watkins's wife, Braun, all of them looking stricken.
> "What's the matter?" she cried. "What's wrong? Mother," she yelled. Then, screaming, "Mother! Something's wrong."

Here is the same scene in chapter 10:

> By 7 P.M. there was still no sign of Vince, so Lisa called his office again. He wasn't there, but she learned that the president was about to appear on *Larry King Live*. She figured her husband must have gone to watch the show with people from the White House. She and her daughter, Laura, went upstairs and turned on the TV.

The doorbell rang, and Laura went to answer it. Some Greenpeace volunteers were asking for a contribution.

The Clinton interview ended, and the doorbell rang again. Laura ran downstairs. Lisa heard the door open, and there were some muffled voices.

"Mother," Laura yelled. Then, screaming, "Mother!"

Note that the second version ends with exactly the same quotation from Laura that appeared in the first version. This signals to readers that the precise point in the narrative has again been reached, and then the scene ends, almost as though a director had yelled "Cut!" I felt there was no need to proceed any further, since readers knew from the prologue what had happened next. When a scene such as this is reprised, there's no need to repeat details, or even to introduce another point of view if that isn't relevant or significant to the story. Laura's statement ended both the chapter and part 2 of the book. When I resumed in the next chapter, the narrative leaped over the scene at Foster's home and moved forward.

The break in the narrative at this point, which involved a shift in point of view and in setting, is the equivalent of the large capital letter and space in a magazine or newspaper story. Even more significantly, the reader knows the answers to several of the mysteries with which I launched the story. They now know that Foster's death was a suicide, and they know the underlying causes of his depression. Yet more than 150 pages remain in the book. How could I expect readers to continue?

Had all the questions posed in the prologue been answered, that might have been a problem. But, as I briefly mentioned earlier, I had moved from the scene at the Fosters' home to a second scene inside the White House. I had carefully ended the prologue with questions about the president and first lady's possible involvement. Most of those questions remained unanswered, though readers would know at this point how far-fetched was the notion that either Clinton had plotted to murder Foster (a notion that was circulating widely at the time). To remind readers of these unanswered questions, I used "Shrouding the Truth" as the title of part 3, which hints at some involvement on the part of the Clintons, at odds with public claims that they had nothing to hide. In books, chapter and section titles offer a further opportunity to heighten reader interest, as do headlines, which I'll discuss in chapter 12.

As the previous paragraphs suggest, books can be structured just as articles are, by using the same approach. For *Blood Sport* I determined the time frame (1978, the date of the Whitewater investment, to 1996), sketched out the main scenes in chronological order, assigned points of view and settings to each, and then divided the whole into chapters at breaks in point of view and setting. *Blood Sport* is organized chronologically. With the exception of the prologue, it proceeds in strict chronological order, much as the flood story does. The three parts of the book—"The Road to Scandal," "A Death in the White House," and "Shrouding the Truth"—roughly correspond to three points of view and settings. Part 1 is Jim and Susan McDougal in Arkansas; part 2 is *New York Times* reporter Jeff Gerth and Foster in Washington; part three is White House counsel Bernie Nussbaum and others in the White House. The Whitewater saga and related stories were complicated enough, so I tried to keep the structure of the book as simple as possible.

Den of Thieves posed a far more daunting challenge, for the paths of the four main culprits, Milken, Boesky, Levine, and Siegel, didn't cross all that often, which meant that I rarely had all four characters onstage at the same time. The first half of the book, which I called "Above the Law," showed their activities before a federal investigation drastically altered their lives and Wall Street in the eighties. To outline the progress of the four characters through the years leading up to the insider-trading scandal, I had to make four separate chronologies. I wrote them on a large piece of paper, which I taped to the wall above my computer. After I had worked through a number of scenes for one character, I would have to break the chronology and point of view and bring another character up to that point in time, repeating the process with each character.

In part 2, "The Chase," I was able to shift to a unified point of view, that of investigators at the Securities and Exchange Commission and the U.S. attorney's office in New York. For this half of the book I could use a single chronology, which was much easier.

Here's a simplified version of the chart:

DEN OF THIEVES
Structural Outline

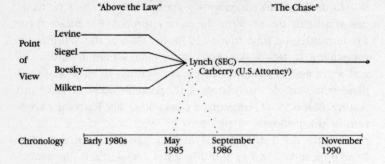

Because of their greater length and complexity, books may involve more points of view and more settings than articles. But the underlying organization, based on chronology, point of view, and setting, is the same.

Using these principles to structure stories may at first seem daunting. But over time, doing so becomes almost second nature, and eventually it probably won't be necessary to write down your lists in detail. I often jot down the main events in chronological order and rearrange them in the order I will use in the story; then, especially for stories with relatively simple structures, I can mentally work out what points of view will be necessary. When you read the finished stories at the end of this book, you will easily recognize the underlying structures. The complexity of a Sheinberg story is the exception; most stories can be told with very simple and clear organizing principles.

I find that analyzing the structural elements of a story, far from being tedious or anxiety-producing, is one of the most stimulating parts of writing. It engages the creative processes; it enables a writer to contemplate alternatives, even to experiment to see which options work better. It banishes most anxiety from the writing process—and, once a structure has been decided upon, the writing dramatically speeds up.

Indeed, I sometimes experience a creative letdown once a story's structure is in place. The work of converting a structure into the words of a finished story seems almost ministerial, a nonetheless labor-intensive task I sometimes wish I could assign to a stable of journeymen, much as Renaissance artists assigned parts of their paintings to apprentices. But that is a fanciful notion, even though some prominent authors (James Michener was one) are reputed to have created such workshops. It is not a practical approach for most of us; indeed, even as I occasionally have such thoughts, I banish them. For the task of actually writing the words invariably enriches the story and sometimes leads to changes even in a structure that had seemed flawless in the abstract.

Having a structure gives writers a concrete reason for the placement and inclusion of every element of a story. There may be other issues that override those reasons, but at least there *is* a reason, one that can be articulated if an editor asks questions. I have often seemed to surprise editors by actually being able to defend my approach to a story in logical, consistent terms. At the least, this elevates debate between editor and writer to a far more constructive plane than the test of wills into which such controversies so often devolve. And, more important, applying these principles can yield stories that are so clear and readable at the outset that editing and rewriting can be focused on perfecting a good story, rather than salvaging a near disaster.

8
DESCRIPTION

Descriptive writing is a component in almost every story, even if it is as simple as the insertion of someone's age after his or her name. Description is almost always present when characters and settings are first introduced. It is essential to help readers experience the events of a story, for it engages their senses: it enables readers to visualize events, to hear them, at times to feel and smell them. To do this, writers themselves must learn to engage their senses, not just their powers of memory and analysis. I often ask my students to visualize a scene, to place themselves in it, to experience it, for clues to the information they need to bring that scene to life for the reader. This in turn informs the questions they need to ask, often in follow-up phone calls or interviews. This doesn't mean that every detail or object in a room need be described (though excruciatingly detailed description is a hallmark of some literary writers). Usually a few brush strokes will do.

As I mentioned earlier, some writers like to begin with a physical description of a geographical place. I reserve this approach for stories in which the setting is highly relevant to the story, when it is more than just the stage set. For descriptive writing is time-consuming for the reader, it takes up space, and it is rarely essential to establish the curiosity that is the goal of the lead. I prefer to engage readers immediately in the action of a story. Yet some description is necessary, as I just mentioned, to engage readers' senses.

Any physical setting that appears in a story's structural outline needs at least some description so readers can visualize where a story is taking place. The story's structure will also usually suggest how much space and detail should be lavished on describing a setting. If a setting is important to the plot and the background for most of the scenes, it can sustain more attention than can the setting for a brief and minor subplot. There are no hard-and-fast rules, but I try to keep in mind the importance of pacing, a sense of proportion, and common sense. To the extent that the setting is inherently interesting—remote, unusual, colorful, exotic—so much the better. By this I don't mean the setting has to be Paris, Venice, Beijing, the Himalayas, or some other subject of travel articles. I'm sorry to say that few of my stories, and none of my books, have been set anywhere so glamorous. The hot, humid, muddy levee in the flood story is a place of inherent interest, one that few readers have probably visited. So, too, is the Trenton engine factory, the largest machine-tool factory in the world, where Ron Woods, the Chrysler electrician, worked. I described both settings in considerable detail. On the other hand, Harrisburg, Pennsylvania, and its suburbs, even though they made up the entire setting for the story of the accountant Ron Woods, required minimal description. And some places are so well-known they probably shouldn't be described at all: the White House, the Eiffel Tower, the Pyramids.

Lengthy descriptions are the exception. Even colorful settings can usually be described quite concisely. Descriptive words are often as important for what they imply as for what they actually say, and the implications of descriptive passages need to be carefully considered. Here is how I described Kingston, Arkansas, the town where Jim and Susan McDougal launched their ultimately ill-fated foray into banking:

> When Susan finally arrived in Kingston, she thought she'd been exiled. The day she arrived, a cow dung–throwing contest was in progress. Kingston is a tiny, old-fashioned town of two hundred people built around a dusty central square to which area farmers still brought their livestock for sale on weekends.

What do these few words convey, beyond the literal image of a cow dung–throwing contest, a dusty square, a weekend livestock market? Surely that Kingston is rural, provincial, largely untouched by modern highways and strip malls, a place where everybody probably knows everybody else and their business. Should it later come as any surprise that the McDougals' ambitious efforts to restore and redecorate Kingston and then turn it into a tourist attraction were greeted with something less than enthusiasm on the part of the Kingston natives?

The same principles apply to describing characters as settings. Any character, even a minor one, whose point of view is used as a narrative device should be physically described. Being able to picture someone invites the reader to see through that person's eyes. Other characters, too, may be described, often quite easily and concisely. As with settings, the more important the character, the more extensive the physical description. It is unusual, though not unheard-of, for more than three or four characters to receive physical descriptions in a magazine or newspaper feature story. More physical description than that in a relatively short space becomes confusing.

Even more than in the case of settings, many human qualities tend to be mentioned because they concisely imply a great deal. It is conventional to include a character's age, largely because age is a quality from which many other qualities can be inferred, including maturity, breadth of experience, and physical stamina. These are, of course, inferences derived from everyday experience and common sense; when they don't accord with reality, rebut them. Occupation is often mentioned; it provides clues to a character's education, level of responsibility, and economic status. Where a character was born or raised might be mentioned, in order to convey certain regional characteristics. The existence of a regional accent might convey the same information.

Oddly enough, while I find it relatively easy to write physical descriptions of places and things, I often find description of other people quite difficult; it is all too easy to resort to such clichés as "handsome," "beautiful," or "homely." I also find it awkward to describe characters who I know will be reading the story. It remains a taboo in polite society to comment directly on someone else's looks. I don't pretend to have mastered this skill. One of the exercises I assign my students is to write a description of someone they know well. It can be anyone: a roommate, spouse, lover, friend, teacher. I've been doing the exercise myself along with them, and I have found it helps. The physical description needed for most characters is mercifully brief, and I am always relieved if a story is accompanied by photographs. Yet photos should never be a crutch.

On a purely visual level, I at least consider mentioning those characteristics that I myself noticed in a person, or, if I haven't actually seen the person, those mentioned by others. These are the qualities, after all, that we notice simply in order to physically distiniguish one person from another: hair color, length, and style; facial hair; height, weight, build, and other physical characteristics; clothing style, jewelry, makeup, accessories, and other elements of appearance. I try to trust my own instincts. When I notice something about a person, I ask myself why that characteristic made an impression. Physical description need not be exhaustive; a few adjectives usually suffice. That a character is described physically at all is enough of a signal that he or she is important to the story (the next time you read a newspaper or even a magzine article, note how few people are actually described in the text). Generally, the more a character is described, the more important a role that person plays in the story.

Once someone's point of view is established, it is relatively easy to meet and describe other characters from that point of view. Of course, the first person a reader meets has to be described by the writer—unless, I suppose, that character happens to be examining his or her appearance in a mirror. An approach I often use at the beginning of a story is to combine description of a character and a setting, enabling the reader to see through the eyes of a principal character. This not only allows the reader to visualize the setting and the main character, but also establishes that character's point of view.

Let's look again at the first few paragraphs of the flood story, in which I introduced the central character of Alex House:

Before going to bed, House had gazed out over his pond and the rolling fields to the west, where the land descends to the Mississippi. There, in a basin formed by the old Sny Channel, which runs parallel to the east bank of the Mississippi, lies some of the richest farmland in the world, 1,400 acres of which belong to House and his family. Over the fields that night he'd seen an ominous bank of clouds, confirming local forecasts of potentially heavy rains and thunderstorms. . . . House, tall, handsome, with dark-blond hair—the New York Times magazine once ran a full-page photograph of him in an article on bachelors (he has since married.)

Note that I described the setting before I described House. The setting is far more important to the story, especially since this is some of the richest farmland in the world. We see the river basin through the eyes of House, who is looking to the west that night for clues to the weather—weather that will almost immediately figure prominently in the plot. This is a significant detail, since for some reason writers often describe the weather when they're trying to bring a scene to life—even when there is nothing noteworthy about it. In a similar vein, I once asked a writer who turned in a front-page story why he included the fact that the investment bankers involved in a deal had eaten shrimp scampi the night before the deal closed. He had no explanation beyond the fact that he knew the details of the menu. Such facts do establish that the writer has a certain intimacy with the material, and had the meal played a role in the plot, the menu might have been a detail that would help readers visualize the scene. But the meal didn't feature in the plot, and the inclusion of such trivia only invited the question of why the writer didn't know more about scenes that *were* important.

As for House himself, I resorted to the word "handsome" for want of a better adjective, though no doubt a better one might have been found. But House *is* handsome by any conventional measure. If he were going to be played by a Hollywood actor, it would be a younger Robert Redford. I thought it helped the story to mention House's good looks. All else being equal, a physically attractive hero is obviously something readers—and audiences—respond to. Surely we would all agree that this would not be the case in an ideal world, where physical appearance would be acknowledged as a superficial quality that has little bearing on virtue. But I suppose we like good-looking characters because as readers, and even more as viewers, we want to identify with them. If we identify with such a character more strongly, we will care more about his or her fate, and thus be more curious. Beyond that, I leave the explanation to psychologists and sociologists.

The first character a reader meets in *Blood Sport* is John

Rolla, the park policeman who examines Foster's body. Rolla is not a major character, nor do his physical characteristics play any significant role in the story, so his description is correspondingly brief:

> After five years of undercover work in the war against drugs, posing as a busboy in Shenandoah National Park, a drug dealer in Glacier, the athletic thirty-one-year-old Rolla had graduated to the major crimes unit—robberies, rape, homicide—that month and had just returned from a stint at "death investigation" school. This might be his first homicide.

In other words, Rolla is onstage when the curtain rises and I, the author, simply describe him. I provide just a few visual details; in fact, his appearance made little impression on me. What's important is that he is woefully inexperienced for the task that will soon confront him. Indeed, it struck me as extraordinary that someone who had never investigated a possible murder would stumble into the high-profile Foster case as he did. Hence, there is far more detail about Rolla's experience and background than there is about his physical appearance.

Once Rolla has been introduced and described, and his point of view established, it is easy to see events and other characters through his eyes. Here is my description of Foster's body, seen through Rolla's eyes:

> Rolla walked over and stood directly above the head, looking down into Foster's open, now lifeless eyes.
> Blood, some of it still wet, ran from the right nostril and the right side of the mouth onto the dirt. Flies were crawling over the face. Rolla noticed how big the man was, probably six foot four. He was wearing a long-sleeved button-down white shirt, tucked in, but no tie. Rolla had to move the foliage of a small bush to see what looked like a .38 caliber revolver in the right hand, which was marked by powder burns. On his belt was a paging device, turned off, suggesting he didn't want to be disturbed. Rolla lifted the body's left hand. It was still warm.

This is obviously a highly detailed description. Not only is Rolla's examination of the body a pivotal scene in the story, but every detail will later figure in controversies over whether Foster's death was a suicide or murder. Readers may not know that at this point, but the attention and space given the scene signal that it is significant, and that readers should pay attention.

Soon after these events, we meet Foster's wife, again through the eyes of Rolla, who has come to the front door of the Foster home to break the news.

> Lisa Foster, clad in a bathrobe, her dark blond hair carefully coiffed, looking tanned and slender from her frequent tennis outings, hurried down the stairs.

What do these few physical details say about Lisa? That she is attractive, goes to a hairdresser, and perhaps belongs to a country club; they further suggest that she lives in a sheltered milieu of privilege in which murder or suicide would hardly be expected, would not be something that she was prepared to cope with. All of these inferences, in my view, would have been both warranted and factually correct.

Later in this scene, we see the president through Rolla's eyes: "Clinton looked haggard, his eyes red, visibly upset." Extremely famous people, such as the president and first lady, like famous places, do not need to be physically described. It is safe to assume that readers know what they look like, and to provide generic descriptions seems patronizing. Yet their appearance in reaction to particular events may be significant. That Clinton seemed shaken by the news, that he had obviously been crying, and that he was upset, at the very least suggest that news of Foster's death came as an unwelcome surprise.

And even well-known people should be described when their appearance has changed over time, or when readers may not be familiar with their earlier appearance. For example, I introduced Hillary Clinton through the eyes of her future Whitewater partner Susan McDougal at an engagement party for Bill and Hillary soon after Hillary moved to Arkansas:

> Susan was introduced to Hillary Rodham, and it just didn't add up. This was Clinton's fiancée? The party was filled with people who were Bill's old friends. The women all seemed to be tall, blond or brunette, wearing lots of makeup and jewelry. Susan thought they were nearly all beautiful and sophisticated.

Hillary looked nothing like them. She seemed to pay little or no attention to her appearance. She wore almost no makeup, and it looked like she hadn't even been to the hairdresser the day of her own engagement party. She wore big, unattractive glasses that made her look bookish, which was poison when it came to men as far as Susan was concerned. Susan thought she would rather die than stick out like Hillary did.

This passage is fraught with significance, as much for what it reveals about Susan as for what it says about Hillary—another advantage of seeing one character through the eyes of another. For someone in Susan's world—Arkansas, 1978—it was probably only a slight exaggeration that she would rather die than "stick out." Most women, including Susan, tried to please men, blend in, suppress their individuality under elaborate hairdos and makeup. That Hillary would defy these deeply entrenched conventions not only astounded Susan, but suggests many traits that would later surface in Hillary's career: adherence to principle and a determination not to deny her own identity, certainly, but also stubbornness, self-aggrandizement, perhaps a lack of empathy and perception.

Four years later, Susan and Hillary are thrown together on the campaign trail, and readers are introduced to a very different Hillary Clinton, again through Susan's eyes:

Susan McDougal was amazed by the transformation of Hillary Clinton on the campaign trail. Suddenly she was being introduced, and even referred to herself, as "Mrs. Bill Clinton" rather than Hillary Rodham. Susan assumed that Hillary had gotten the message that Arkansas voters didn't like women to flaunt their independence, but still she was bewildered. Hillary had always been so militant about keeping her name, and it had made such an impression on her. Equally surprising, Hillary had acquired a new, tastefully conservative wardrobe. She had contact lenses now. She was even wearing makeup, and had had her hair styled. She looked much more attractive, Susan thought, far more like the conventional politician's wife.

What inferences might be drawn from this description? Obviously the changes in Hillary's appearance are at least partly motivated by political realism. Has she changed fundamentally, perhaps abandoning much of the feminist ideology that seems to have motivated her earlier defiance of Arkansas convention? Or is the change illusory? Is the image of Hillary beginning to diverge from the reality? More significantly, does this transformation suggest a willingness on Hillary's part to compromise in exchange for political survival?

All these seem to me to be legitimate questions for further reflection, but it's hard, certainly at this point, to draw any inferences. Indeed, Susan herself is "bewildered" by the changes, which suggests that readers, too, might reserve judgment. Nonetheless, even a brief description such as this underscores one of the most important themes of the book, which is the ways in which honesty is undermined in the quest for political power.

While descriptions may give rise to inferences that at least purport to be logically connected to the meaning of the words, words may trigger associations that have nothing to do with their literal meaning and signify something else entirely. At this point, words have become symbols.

Symbolism figures prominently in classes on literature; I remember a college professor grilling members of my introductory class in fiction on the meaning of the sea in Stephen Crane's short story "The Open Boat." We floundered until the professor decoded it for us, saying that water is understood by every literate person as a symbol for life itself. Based on my experiences in this and other literature classes, I concluded there must be some kind of Rosetta stone for writers, on which words such as "water," "snake," "cave," to mention just a few, were translated into their symbolic meanings.

To my mind, reading nonfiction should not be like struggling with a foreign language. The associations evoked by symbols should flow naturally. The reaction of readers to symbols can be even harder to anticipate than what inferences they draw from descriptive words, so symbols should be used sparingly. But when the opportunity arises, they can enrich a story.

Consider this passage from *Den of Thieves,* in which Ivan Boesky arrives for a tennis game at the Westport, Connecticut, home of Martin Siegel:

A pink Rolls-Royce turned into the driveway. It pulled quietly into the parking area, and a smiling Boesky emerged carrying a tennis racquet and, Siegel noticed with some curiosity, a leather pocketbook, the kind some European men carry.

None of this information is essential to the narrative, though the tennis outing was important to the story and had figured in my structural outline. Yet I found it interesting, even memorable. Boesky drives up in a Rolls-Royce—a pink one, no less. A Rolls-Royce is a symbol, one so familiar that it needs no further explanation. Boesky is the kind of man who would drive a pink Rolls-Royce and carry a purse. What kind of person is that? The answer is hard to put into words, really, and I suppose each reader would bring a different perspective. But to me, the Rolls and purse suggest that Boesky is eager to attract attention to himself and his wealth; they are, if not kitschy, then vulgar; they suggest someone who lacks self-confidence. None of this, of course, appears in the text: symbols lose their subliminal appeal if they have to be explained.

When the now-defunct magazine *Manhattan, Inc.* commissioned some artist's renderings of scenes from *Den of Thieves,* Boesky's arrival in the Rolls-Royce was one the artist chose to depict. I find that a surprising number of the book's readers remember this detail.

Cars often seem to function as symbols. In *Den of Thieves* insider trader Dennis Levine drives a red Ferrari Testarossa, which certainly has symbolic meaning. Interior decoration, architecture, consumer goods, clothing, and jewelry often function on a symbolic level. Indeed, their owners often intend them as symbols. Often the symbol is an object to which a character has attached some significance. Consider this passage from *Blood Sport,* which takes place while Hillary Clinton and Susan McDougal are campaigning together in the 1982 gubernatorial election:

> Much like Bill [Clinton], Susan loved campaigning—all the hugging and glad-handing and getting to know people from all over the state. Hillary, by contrast, looked slightly pained by the experience. On one occasion when the McDougals and Clintons appeared together, a woman came rushing up to Hillary. "I made these for you, honey," she said. "I just think so much of your husband." Beaming, she handed Hillary a pair of earrings in the shape of hogs—the Arkansas Razorback mascot.

Here the hog earrings work as a symbol not only for the donor, for whom the Razorback was a positive symbol of the ferocity and tenacity of Arkansas athletic teams, but also—in an entirely different way—for Hillary herself. ("This is the kind of shit I have to put up with," Hillary told Susan once the woman was out of earshot.) Those hogs symbolized everything that must have appalled her about Arkansas. Surely I didn't need to mention that no one ever saw the earrings again—certainly not on Hillary.

The earring incident made a great impression on Susan McDougal, who told me about it in considerable detail. In the context of the Whitewater saga, it was a trivial episode and could have been omitted. But as a symbol of the relationship between ordinary Arkansans and their First Lady, the earrings and Hillary's reaction to them spoke volumes. Like the pink Rolls-Royce, the Razorback earrings seem to stick in the minds of readers, who often mention them to me.

By now it should be clear that the way descriptive words resonate in readers' minds is at least as important as their literal meaning. While such associations enrich the reading experience, they also pose problems for the writer, for while we can control what words we use, we cannot determine what thoughts they will inspire. Sometimes we can't even anticipate them. Simple though the task of description might seem, it is fraught with peril, and has generated considerable controversy in my own work, most of which took me completely by surprise.

Race is perhaps the most obvious example. We invariably notice a person's race or skin color and use it as one of the identifying characteristics that help us recognize that person again. Yet as long as prejudice persists, some readers will undoubtedly draw stereotypical inferences if race is mentioned. Moreover, we tend to notice minorities more than we do the majority. Thus, I rarely find a character identified as white; that someone is white is assumed, unless another race is specified. It would have seemed absurd to mention that House is "white, tall and handsome, with dark-blond hair." Yet what if House had been black or Hispanic, with black hair? He would have been the only black or Hispanic farmer on the entire levee, so I probably would have included that physical detail even if it played no part in the story.

House was a hero of the story, and I doubt that anyone on the lookout for political incorrectness would have chastised me for portraying a minority person in an unflattering light. But what if the white person who sabotaged the West Quincy levee had been a member of a minority? Had I mentioned the fact, I would no doubt have been called upon to explain the "relevance" of his race. This is no doubt a result of our judicial system's sorry history of injustice to black suspects. Yet physical description is often no more than that—it isn't meant to convey anything beyond appearance.

Besides race, characteristics that provide distinguishing features but may also give rise to negative stereotypes include religion, ethnicity, sexual orientation, political affiliation, medical condition, obesity, disabilities or any physical infirmity, and physical unattractiveness. Some can't be avoided. The mere mention of a person's name generally conveys gender and often ethnicity. There is no easy answer for such situations. I try to be sensitive to possible inferences, to avoid making them myself, and to avoid mentioning characteristics irrelevant to the story. Characteristics that are relevant usually surface at some point anyway, and then the relevance should be obvious. This is no insurance against controversy, but it at least provides a principled defense.

In the story about Dan Miller, the accountant who was fired for being gay, the fact that he is gay is a central element of the story, so it obviously had to be mentioned early, as it was. But when the events described summarily in the lead are recapitulated in greater detail, I provided a fuller physical description of Miller, as seen through the eyes of his employer, DeMuth:

> Miller made a good impression on DeMuth. Miller is thin, sandy-haired and fair, a former intramural basketball player, perhaps best described as "clean-cut." His hair is neatly trimmed and parted and he wears white dress shirts to work. His desk is immaculate. His parents and three sisters live in the Harrisburg area; his father, a former professional baseball player with the Chicago White Sox, is an administrator at a local college, and his mother works at Sears.

In this descriptive passage, I was trying both to provide readers with a visual image of Miller and, at the same time, to point out those qualities from which DeMuth, rightly or wrongly, might have drawn inferences that pleased him. What inferences might DeMuth have drawn? Possibly that Miller had a somewhat anal personality, no doubt a virtue in an aspiring accountant. That he came from a stable family that embodied all-American qualities. That he would make a good impression on the conservative businessmen and physicians who made up DeMuth's clientele. And —to the extent that he gave it any thought, that Miller was straight. The possibility that a former basketball player, the son of a pro baseball player, might be gay had apparently never occurred to DeMuth.

All this, of course, is implied; I made no pretense of knowing precisely what DeMuth thought at the moment he met Miller, though he certainly described their meeting in similar terms during our interviews. Nor, by singling out these qualities of Miller's —all of which are verifiable facts—did I intend to convey that any inferences would be correct. Indeed, a major point of the story was that DeMuth was wrong about nearly every inference he seemed to have made.

It never occurred to me that in thus describing Miller I would run into a thicket of political controversy. Nonetheless, the story was denounced by some gay activists, including a columnist in a San Francisco-area gay newspaper, as demeaning to effeminate, unathletic, and non-clean-cut gay men—indeed, to all gay men who in some ways conformed to stereotypes held by the majority population. To me, this is "spin" run rampant, in which symbolism and inference have supplanted fact altogether. No doubt many gay men who conform to certain stereotypes do suffer employment discrimination, but Dan Miller wasn't one of them, and that wasn't his story.

As this incident illustrates, it is pointless to include or exclude anything with the exclusive goal of averting controversy; in my experience, almost any story worth telling generates some controversy. What's important is not to engage in or encourage inferences that perpetuate stereotypes. Then such criticisms may be justified, and the resulting controversy warranted. As I mentioned earlier, at the height of the Monica Lewinsky investigation by independent counsel Kenneth Starr, an editor suggested I undertake a story that would trace what was perceived in many quarters as Starr's excessive zeal in pursuing President Clinton to

Starr's fundamentalist Christianity and that of his chief deputy. Any attempt to link Starr's and his deputy's private religious beliefs to the public conduct of their jobs struck me as highly perilous, for it turned on the inference that devout Christians would be offended by the president's sex life. The case could as plausibly be made that devout Christians would be as likely to forgive transgressions in others. Moreover, Starr's zeal could as easily be attributed to his mandate to investigate perjury and obstruction of justice—as Starr himself repeatedly insisted it was. This isn't to say that the story idea wasn't a possible one, if there was evidence linking Starr's religious belief to the conduct of his job—if, for example, he had confided to a reliable source that he was conducting a vendetta to punish Clinton for his sins. Absent even a shred of such evidence, I found the inference indefensible, and I declined to write such a story.

That doesn't mean, however, that I wouldn't mention Starr's religious background. Here, for example, is a passage from my description of Starr in *Blood Sport:*

> He is deeply religious, philosophical, and moral, with a palpable reverence for the law. His worldview would never countenance the everyday compromises that characterize political careers; much less would it permit breaking the law. Though Starr was born in a small town in northwest Texas, not far from Hope, Arkansas, his upbringing is in stark contrast to Clinton's. His father was a Church of Christ minister; the young Starr sold Bibles door-to-door to put himself through college, and he grew up in a family where two staples of the Clinton family—profanity and liquor—were banned.

Why did I include such descriptive information? Not to suggest any sinister inference to be drawn from his religious views, or to promote any stereotypes of religious conservatives from the Bible Belt, but rather to underscore the contrast in religious upbringing between Clinton and Starr. In other words, it seems a reasonable inference to me that, steeped in a religious upbringing emphasizing clear distinctions between right and wrong, Starr would be unlikely to turn a blind eye to possible violations of law that some might prefer to dismiss as inevitable in politics, and inconsequential. To try to make sure that readers focused on this contrast, I introduced the description by suggesting that the danger to Clinton in the appointment of Starr as independent counsel lay not so much in Starr's conservative Republicanism as in a quality "deeply rooted in Starr's nature." Of course, there is no way I can control what inferences readers choose to draw from the facts I present. They bring their own experiences and common sense to bear—often, I have discovered, drawing inferences that seem far wiser than anything I had contemplated.

The worst experience I have endured in my career as a journalist and writer derived from what I deem to have been unwarranted inferences from descriptive passages in *Den of Thieves*. Just days after the book was published—the day of the book party, to be precise—my parents were in town. My mother had gotten up early and read the *Times;* when I came into the kitchen she was obviously somewhat shaken. She said, "There's a full-page ad for your book in the paper." I knew of no such planned advertising, so I rushed to the paper and discovered not an ad for the book, but a full-page ad taken out by Milken lawyer Alan Dershowitz, attacking the book as anti-Semitic because I had identified some characters as Jewish. The inference Dershowitz drew was that because some of the felons in the Wall Street scandal featured in *Den of Thieves* were Jewish, I was perpetuating the stereotype that Jews in the financial world are corrupt.

I had tried to anticipate every possible attack from the Milken camp, for I felt sure there would be attempts to undermine the book, but this had never crossed my mind. To write a book about Wall Street in the eighties without mentioning that Michael Milken and some other characters were Jewish would have been preposterous. It was generally known, whether or not I mentioned it. Having grown up in a small, homogeneous Midwestern city where such subjects were never mentioned, I had been startled by how much conversation on Wall Street turned on the ethnic and religious identities of its participants. Given the long and sorry history of institutional anti-Semitism and ethnic prejudice among some prominent Wall Street firms, this was no doubt inevitable. In any event, it was impossible to understand the dynamics of the financial community without acknowledging that history and the resulting sensibilities, resentments, and competitive impulses.

As I mentioned earlier, I often prefer to describe characters through the eyes of another character. In *Den of Thieves* I introduced Milken and Fred Joseph, the chief executive of Drexel Burnham Lambert, through the eyes of I. W. Burnham, then chairman of the firm. After noting that at the time Drexel was considered, at best, a second-tier firm, I wrote that the firm had resulted from a merger of Drexel Firestone, which traced its lineage to "the illustrious Philadelphia Drexel family and the unabashedly anti-Semitic J. P. Morgan empire," and the less prestigious Burnham & Co. Then I continued:

> The survivors of the two firms still mostly shunned one another, even now, three years after the merger. As they walked through the firm, Burnham told Joseph that when he first met the head of Drexel at the time of the merger, he'd asked how many of the firm's more than 200 employees were Jews. He was told that there were a total of three. One, Burnham said, was the man he wanted Joseph to meet: Michael Milken. Joseph shook hands with the intense, slender young man with dark, deep-set eyes.

There was much more description of Milken in the book, virtually none of it having anything to do with his religion, but this passage was one of those seized upon by Dershowitz. Yet it is a fact that practically the first thing Joseph heard about Milken from Burnham was that Milken was Jewish (as are Burnham and Joseph). Burnham had found this significant, as had Joseph, and it was for this reason that I included the information. If there was any inference to be drawn, I thought it would be that Milken might have been expected to suffer at least some discomfort as one of only three Jews in a firm with a history of anti-Semitism— which, if anything, would place him in a sympathetic light. As for the inference that I generally portrayed Jewish characters in the book as corrupt or criminal, neither Burnham nor Joseph was ever charged with any wrongdoing; Joseph, in particular, who was described as the "son of orthodox Jews," emerges as a pillar of virtue by the then prevailing standards of Wall Street.

I could continue in this vein with the few other passages deemed offensive by Dershowitz, but it would be largely beside the point; I'm convinced readers couldn't possibly have believed that either I or the book is anti-Semitic. I was later told that the Milken camp had hired a private detective to investigate me for evidence of anti-Semitism, among other possibly inflammatory qualities, but the detective came up empty-handed. The whole affair was part of an enormous and expensive extrajudicial public relations campaign to rehabilitate Milken and undermine his critics, which continues to this day. I was gratified that numerous Jewish organizations, including the Anti-Defamation League, rallied to my defense. Still, the experience was painful. On a radio call-in show in New York, a woman called and compared me to Nazi propagandist Joseph Goebbels. I asked her if she had read the book, and she said no; she didn't need to after reading the Dershowitz ad. But even at the worst of the Milken campaign, I comforted myself with the belief that truth ultimately prevails.

9
DIALOGUE

IF DESCRIPTION enables readers to visualize a scene, dialogue lets them hear it. Like description, it makes events immediate and accessible; it allows readers to absorb material into their own lives and reflect upon it. It "shows" rather than "tells," and is thus often far more persuasive and convincing than anything the writer can say. Consider the advent of "talking pictures," and the importance of sound to what is usually considered a visual medium. Dialogue has been an important component of storytelling from time immemorial. Yet I find it is used far too infrequently in most nonfiction writing.

In writing, the spoken word is indicated by quotation marks, but it is important to distinguish between narrative quotations—statements made at the time of the events being described—and remarks made later, usually in response to a reporter's questions. I call these contemporary quotations. Narrative quotations are statements that were made in the past. Their existence is a fact, like any other element of a story, such as the color of someone's clothing or the size of a bank account. Quotations elicited by a reporter usually reflect statements made after the events in question, in which the speaker looks back and, with benefit of hindsight, offers comments, usually in response to a question. Though readers understand that a reporter's research has taken place in the past, usually the recent past, such quotations are often framed in the present tense to distinguish them from narrative quotations.

To illustrate, consider these quotations from the lead paragraphs of the Sheinberg insider-trading story, in which Sid admonishes Jonathan not to trade on the confidential information he has just learned:

> "Keep that to yourself," he said. "For God's sake, don't trade on the stock."

This is a narrative quote. It is a fact that on the day in September 1990 when Jonathan learned the confidential information about MCA, his father walked with him on the beach and said those words. The speech happened in the past, at the same time as the walk.

The story continues:

> Months after this walk along the beach, Sid was asked whether he had believed his son would obey these admonitions. "I would have bet anything on it," Sid replied.

This, too, is a narrative quote, as the story later makes clear. Even though the statement is not contemporaneous with the walk on the beach—it takes place "months after"—it occurs during another event in the narrative, Sid Sheinberg's deposition, which occurred about two years before I reported and wrote the story. (The quotation is from his deposition transcript. I did not personally interview Sid.)

Toward the end of the story, Andrew Geist, the SEC lawyer in charge of the case, is quoted:

> "My own personal opinion is that everyone is surprised when people in Hollywood do things that seem weird and strange, but they're just like everybody else, if not more so." He is confident that "the right result was reached," he says.

This is a contemporary quote. Though as the reporter I am both invisible and silent, in an interview I had asked Geist to reflect on the meaning of the case. This happened during my reporting, in the recent past, long after the events of the story were over. I quoted his answer in the present tense.

Usually narrative quotes can be presented as contemporary quotes, but the result can be confusing. It is cumbersome, it injects quotes within quotes, and it interrupts chronology. Let's assume that instead of obtaining the quotes from Sid Sheinberg's deposition, I had gotten them in an interview with Sheinberg (which is how most narrative quotes are obtained). In that case, I could have written the passage as follows:

> Sid Sheinberg recalls that, while walking on the beach, he warned his son not to use the information. "I told him not to trade," Sheinberg says. "I said, 'Keep that to yourself. For God's sake, don't trade on the stock.'" And months later, when the SEC questioned him, Sheinberg told the lawyers he was confident Jonathan would obey him. "I told them at the time, 'I would have bet anything on it,'" Sheinberg recalls.

In this version, two narrative quotes are embedded within a contemporary quote. Narrative writing simply strips away the contemporary quote, leaving the dialogue intact.

I find that this distinction between narrative and contemporary quotes is often new to my students, most of whom have never used anything but contemporary quotations. The idea that the spoken word is a fact like any other seems never to have occurred to them, nor have they written conversation among multiple speakers, using the past tense. They seem to find this awkward at first, though they quickly overcome the difficulty with a little practice.

Contemporary quotations, by contrast, are a staple of journalism; simply look at yesterday's newspaper. I often wonder what some reporters would do if they weren't allowed to consult and then quote various "experts" on events in the news. Such quotations are overused, in my opinion, particularly in stories in which the writer makes a point, then quotes someone making the same point, then finds another source to say the same thing. All too often, this passes for good reporting and writing.

There's nothing wrong, of course, with the well-placed contemporary quote. The popular "Q and A" interview format pioneered by *Playboy* and now used by publications as varied as

Barron's and *Rolling Stone* is nothing but a dialogue between reporter and subject. But unlike these interviews, most contemporary quotations are in fact oddly disembodied, for readers are given the answers to questions, but rarely given the questions. Isn't that a curious convention? I suspect it dates from earlier days of "objective" journalism, in which the reporter had to be as invisible as possible. I have been quoted in enough articles to know what distortions can result when a comment, accurately quoted, is juxtaposed with a question, usually implied rather than stated, that was never actually asked in the interview. I try to avoid this myself, but in most of my magazine and newspaper feature articles I have used contemporary quotes, I hope judiciously.

It is important to keep in mind that every contemporary quote in fact interrupts the chronology of a story, because it takes place in the "present" in relation to the past events in the story. This would be clear if the interview between writer and subject were treated as one of the scenes in a story's chronology. The interview would be at the end of the chronology, and every time a quote from it was used, the scene would have to shift to that place and time. Fortunately, the use of contemporary quotations in the midst of a narrative is so commonplace that readers tend to accept them without losing their chronological focus. But the more contemporary quotations there are, the more difficult for the reader this becomes.

Another distinction that should be kept in mind is that while both contemporary and narrative quotes are attributed to a speaker, the source of a narrative quotation may not be immediately apparent, especially if the quotation is presented as narrative dialogue. The person reporting the contemporary quotation is presumed to be the writer, unless otherwise indicated. On the other hand, narrative quotes are almost never anonymous, whereas contemporary quotes often are.

The pure narrative story uses no contemporary quotations at all. To my mind, this is the best approach, one I have used in both *Den of Thieves* and *Blood Sport*. It is the most direct and immediate way of writing, since contemporary quotations tacitly insert the writer as a filter between the reader and the material. And it avoids the chronological interruptions I've just mentioned. Why, then, do I use contemporary quotes so often? Simply because the raw material for narrative quotes is often difficult to obtain.

As I mentioned in the chapter on reporting, to obtain the material for writing dialogue is usually a challenge, though such material proves to be available far more often than many reporters initially think it will be. The most accurate sources for the spoken word are tape recordings, and much of what is said today is, in fact, recorded: anything in the media; anything in Congress; much of what takes place in courtrooms and police stations; even one's brokerage transactions and catalogue orders, not to mention cellular phone calls. As Linda Tripp's recordings of Monica Lewinsky made clear, we live in an age of private surveillance. When such tapes or transcripts are available, they must be obtained and quoted accurately. They are the only conclusive source for what was said in an historical context.

Without tapes or transcripts, dialogue must be reported from other written records or from sources' memories. I have often been able to write dialogue based on notes of conversations made at the time they took place, or soon after. For instance, lawyers I have interviewed about what their clients might have said often turned out to have made notes of those conversations. Just as taping is increasingly widespread, note-taking is even more prevalent, especially in business and politics, as the raft of internal White House memos related to Whitewater demonstrates. Memory is the most common source for dialogue—as, indeed, for most facts contained in a story. As I mentioned in the chapter on reporting, most sources mention dialogue spontaneously, with a phrase like "And then he said . . ." Indeed, I find conversations are often remembered quite vividly. But if they're not, it rarely helps to ask people to try to reconstruct conversations from memory.

Despite these problems, even a minimum of dialogue can convey a sense of immediacy; often a mere snippet of remembered conversation will suffice. It is also quite easy to combine contemporary quotes and narrative dialogue in the same story, securing the advantages of both. Sometimes direct quotations aren't even necessary, and narrative paraphrasing will do. This is sometimes the only feasible way to convey the substance of a conversation when sources don't remember the words they used and there are no records of the conversation.

When is a narrative quotation appropriate? Assuming the reporting has yielded the raw material for direct quotation, I use the following guidelines: Anytime such quotations establish immediacy, especially near the beginning of a story. Whenever the substance of a quotation advances the plot of a story. Whenever the words used convey qualities of the speaker more effectively than direct description would. And always when the existence and substance of a conversation constitute a scene that I have included in my structural outline.

These elements were present in the flood story, and I used both narrative and contemporary quotations, as I often do. Here is the scene in which President Clinton called the local radio station:

> Quincians were also bolstered the next day by a phone call to WGEM. Steve Cramblit, a sales manager turned reporter, answered the phone at about 8:30 A.M., and an operator said, "This is Air Force One calling. Will you take the call?" Cramblit was so astonished that at first he thought the operator was asking him to pay for the call—would Air Force One call collect? Then an aide got on the phone and said, "The President would like to be on your radio station." Henning [the station manager] was connected via his car phone but opted to let his reporters in the studio handle the interview. Cramblit and three of his colleagues gathered in the studio, and at about 9:15 President Clinton, speaking from his plane en route to a governors' conference in St. Louis, came on the air. "I wanted to call you," the President said, "because your radio station has done such a remarkable job of coordinating the information, keeping people in touch, and keeping them up in the middle of this. I really respect your effort and appreciate it very much." . . . When the interview was over, the veteran reporter Bob Turek told Henning that it had been the proudest moment of his career. "I've done City Council meetings and zoning meetings and lost dogs for forty years," he said. "Finally, I got to say, 'Thank you, Mr. President.' "

All of the quotations used in that passage are narrative quotations. The words were spoken not in the course of my reporting, but at a particular time in the story and at a particular place. The first group of quotes is from conversations between Air Force

One and the radio station. The last quote is from a subsequent conversation between Turek and Henning. As I mentioned, a narrative quote is a fact like any other, and is verified in the same way. I had a transcript of the dialogue with Air Force One (the conversations were recorded and broadcast live) and both Henning and Turek described their conversation and remembered the words they used. This passage does not, strictly speaking, contain dialogue, since only one speaker is quoted at a time. But the effect of immediacy is almost the same.

Here, in a passage meant to convey the growing distrust between the farmers on the levee and the Army Corps of Engineers, is a passage that combines narrative dialogue with contemporary quotation:

> The day after the Sny levee survived the storm and the first thirty-two-foot crest, representatives of the Army Corps of Engineers descended on the levee. According to House, a Corps of Engineers captain had been there briefly the previous Friday, and had got off to a bad start by criticizing House for the way he was building the access road. "Are you putting down mats to keep the gravel from mixing with the mud?" the captain had asked.
>
> "No," House replied.
>
> "That's what the Corps recommends," the captain rejoined, in what House deemed an officious tone. "We have a supply at Rock Island."
>
> "I'll bet we'll have this road done before you find the matting," House countered.
>
> On this second visit, the captain had some new suggestions. Gazing along the length of the levee, which had taken such prodigious effort to build, he said, "We need to raise that board levee."
>
> Crim and House were stunned, but shrugged and said, "O.K., what's your suggestion?"
>
> "Well, we've got this giant dragline, and we'll just put it down there"—he pointed to the field adjacent to the base of the levee—"and get some dirt and make a new levee." Crim rolled his eyes in disbelief. There was no dry dirt within ten miles. And, even if there had been, anyone who tried to dig at the base of the levee would have just caused water to rush up, weakening the whole structure.
>
> Crim says, with some exasperation, "He stands there telling

218   FOLLOW THE STORY

us this, and about that time in came a National Guard pickup
and tried to pull up. He buried it. Then this character says,
'Mr. So-and-So, getting out of this truck, is an excellent dragline
operator. Excellent.' Now this numb-nuts just buried his pickup
in the mud. And *he's* going to run the dragline for us? I said,
'Whoa! This is a very dumb idea.' "

Shortly afterward, House says, he came upon two Corps
engineers bickering about the height of the river. "I can tell you
pretty close," House said. "Thirty point five."

"How do you know?" they asked skeptically. "My stick," he
said, pointing into the river's flow. "I marked it." One of the
engineers waded into the water. After examining the rudimentary measure, he infuriated House by pulling it out. He later
replaced it with a stick of his own, using the same principle as
House's, and said that it was a Corps device.

From then on, the farmers and volunteers on the levee
listened politely to the Corps's suggestions and then ignored
them. For what they all thought, and Peanuts actually said, was
that practically all the levees upstream to which the Corps had
lent its expertise had met the same fate: they broke.

The conversation between the Army Corps captain and
House is written as narrative dialogue. But Crim's recollection
of that conversation and his reaction to it are conveyed in a
contemporary quotation. Note that Crim's quotation is written in
the present tense to mark the distinction. I could have conveyed
his reaction as part of the narrative, avoiding the disruption in
the story's chronology. But I used this quotation as much for
what it said about Crim as for the substance of the quote. The
way Crim described this to me—the cadence, the words he used
—more effectively captured the absurdity he was experiencing
than anything I could say.

As this passage indicates, description of a character's
thoughts and state of mind is closely related to dialogue, and can
be handled in the same way. There are narrative thoughts—what
a character was thinking at the time—and contemporary
thoughts—what the character was thinking when interviewed.
Unlike quotations, however, a character's thoughts can only be
revealed by that character, unless he or she explicitly conveyed
them to someone else.

Here is an example of a passage that combines narrative

dialogue and narrative thoughts, in a scene from the Sheinberg
insider-trading story in which the SEC lawyers interrogate Barry
Fogel for the first time, and Fogel is trying to protect Jonathan by
pretending that he learned about the MCA deal from published
sources:

> Several days later, Brotbacker also heard from Fogel,
> through his lawyer, Roger J. Rosen. Like Shephard, Fogel had
> received a subpoena. When Rosen spoke to Brotbacker, he ar-
> gued that Fogel shouldn't have to testify, that turning over his
> trading records should suffice. Brotbacker said that that
> wouldn't do. She and Geist were eager to get his testimony as
> soon as possible, so they agreed that Fogel wouldn't have to
> come to New York: they would interview him over the tele-
> phone, even though they would have preferred to observe Fo-
> gel's demeanor during questioning. "After you talk to him, you'll
> see there's nothing there," Rosen told them, sounding blasé.
>
> On April 24th, Rosen and Fogel arrived at the S.E.C.'s offices
> in downtown Los Angeles; Geist and Brotbacker used a speak-
> erphone in Geist's New York office. Fogel was sworn in and
> began testifying. After some preliminaries, in which he said he
> had graduated from Beverly Hills High School, class of 1976,
> and had attended one quarter at Los Angeles Valley College,
> Brotbacker got to the point, asking, "Why did you buy MCA?
> What were your reasons for it?"
>
> "I had been following it for some time in the L.A. *Times,*
> and it seemed like a very good investment," Fogel replied. "It
> was at one of its all-time lows, as far as I could tell."
>
> "How long had you been following it?'
>
> "Well, I believe I started sometime in 1990, probably first
> part of the year."
>
> "How did you follow it?"
>
> "L.A. *Times.* . . . I followed the L.A. *Times* business section
> and occasionally I would see articles on it in periodical maga-
> zines."
>
> "What article can you recall seeing?"
>
> "I don't recall any. I don't recall a specific article."
>
> Shifting tack, Brotbacker asked him if there was any other
> reason he had bought MCA options, other than the vague sense
> that he'd read about the company somewhere.
>
> "I've been raised in Los Angeles, familiar with MCA/Univer-
> sal Studios. I know they have amusement parks and they make
> movies. And I've known from what I've heard and what I've

read . . . that entertainment stocks traditionally do best in recessionary times."

"Where did you hear that entertainment stocks do best in
recessionary times?"

"Wall Street Journal, L. A. *Times,* magazines."

"What magazines?"

"Time, Newsweek, I don't really recall."

Geist, who was listening in in New York, couldn't resist
interrupting. "Do you recall reading about that in *Time* magazine?" he asked, barely keeping the disbelief out of his voice.

"Not specifically."

"You were guessing when you said *Time* and *Newsweek?"*

"I have a recollection, I don't know if it would be called a
guess."

"Do you have a recollection of reading about it in a newsweekly magazine?"

"I believe so."

"You don't recall which one it was?"

"That's correct."

"Do you know when, roughly, in time it was?"

"No, I don't remember."

There had been no articles on MCA in any of the news
magazines just prior to Fogel's trading. In conducting an insider-
trading investigation, S.E.C. lawyers routinely examine any published reports referring to the company in order to anticipate
possible defenses and to be able to put further questions to a
witness who mentions them.

Most of my students have had scant experience writing dialogue, and they tend to struggle over what verbs to use, constantly looking for synonyms for "said," or for adjectives to dress
up such a straightforward verb. Generally, I either eliminate the
verb altogether or revert to "said," unadorned by any adjectives.
In my opinion, dialogue is not where writers' prose should compete with the speakers' words; after all, what the speaker's words
convey is the main reasons dialogue is being used. As this passage
indicates, simply separating the speakers by paragraphs is an
effective and conventional way to indicate the shift from one
speaker to another. While it is *The New Yorker's* style to use
quotation marks, I have seen such quotes introduced by dashes.
If this is confusing, it may be remedied by identifying the speaker
and using the verb "said," or, in this interrogative context, "asked"

and "replied." Once they have written a few passages, my students are quite comfortable with narrative quotations.

One way that I often combine narrative and contemporary quotes in the same story is to introduce contemporary quotes when they in fact took place—after the events of the story have occurred, near the end of the story. I did this with the Sheinberg story, turning at the end to the two major protagonists—Jonathan and Geist—and giving each the opportunity to reflect on the story:

> In a brief conversation, Jonathan displayed many of the characteristics I had heard described by others. He seemed immediately excited, saying that the MCA affair was "my story"; that "this isn't a magazine article, it's a book"; and that "if anybody's going to tell this story, it's going to be me." I offered him that opportunity, but he changed his tack. "Don't you realize how painful this is for me and my family?" he asked, adding, "You wouldn't be writing this except for my name." While his voice was still rising, he hung up.
>
> At the New York office of the S.E.C., Geist has been promoted to assistant regional director. Though he is limited in what he can say about the investigation, he says he feels little sympathy for Jonathan and the other defendants. "My own personal opinion is that everyone is surprised when people in Hollywood do things that seem weird and strange, but they're just like everybody else, if not more so." He is confident that "the right result was reached," he says. "It always struck me that what happened was improper conduct, and that this was the type of situation that was contemplated by the anti-fraud provisions. It would have been a great trial to do, and I'm confident that even in the Second Circuit we would have prevailed. Still, it's always good to have a case over with, with a good result."

This has the advantage of not giving away the end of the story prematurely, maintaining the suspense, and not interrupting the chronology, especially in a story such as this, which as I've pointed out, already had a chronologically complex narrative structure.

I remarked earlier that I always use dialogue if possible when the existence and substance of a conversation constitute a scene in my narrative, and also that dialogue sometimes makes a point

far more persuasively than anything I could say by way of para-
phrase. Both elements converged in an unusual way in a scene
I included in *Blood Sport,* in which an ABC producer, Chris
Vlasto, was conducting an interview of Buddy Young, a former
Arkansas state trooper who had been promoted by President
Clinton to head the Federal Emergency Management Agency office in Dallas. After the eruption of "Troopergate," in which Arkansas state troopers went public with allegations that Clinton
had extramarital affairs while governor, Young had become an
outspoken defender of the president and had worked assiduously
to undermine the credibility of his former colleagues on the
police force. The White House had maintained that it wasn't
coordinating Young's statements, and that he was simply speaking out on his own initiative because he was dedicated to the
truth. Here is what happened when Vlasto, in Little Rock, sent a
cameraman to interview Young in Dallas:

> Lindsey was also busy orchestrating damage control. ABC
> producer Chris Vlasto had arranged an on-camera interview
> with Buddy Young, with a camera crew in Young's office in
> Denton, Texas, while Vlasto asked questions over the phone
> from Little Rock. The interview was proceeding uneventfully,
> with Young insisting that the troopers couldn't be believed,
> when Vlasto heard a phone ring in Young's office. "Hold on a
> second, I've got another phone call," Young said, putting Vlasto
> on hold. Vlasto waited about forty-five seconds; then Young got
> back on the line.
> "Who was that?" Vlasto asked.
> "CNN wants to talk to me," Young answered.
> "I'm glad you're talking to me and not them," Vlasto said,
> half-seriously.
> The cameraman sent the footage by Federal Express to
> Vlasto. When he began editing it the next morning, he noticed
> that the tape had recorded the phone call Young received while
> Vlasto was on hold. Vlasto listened in amazement.
> "Buddy?"
> "Bruce. Yeah," Young said, as Vlasto heard Bruce Lindsey's
> voice—not CNN. Vlasto turned to a colleague. "My God, we've
> got the White House on here." The tape continued:
> "What do you know?" Lindsey asked.
> "I am on the phone right now in the middle of an inter-
> view."
> "With who?

"ABC." Young turned to the cameraman. "Is that right?"

"Okay," Lindsey continued. "We need you to do CNN at some point. Will you call me? Will you have them page me after you get off?"

"Have . . ."

"Call the White House and ask them to page me while you hold or have me call you right back."

"Okay . . ."

"Thanks."

Vlasto was amazed that a top aide to the president was apparently orchestrating Young's TV appearances. ABC News executives hadn't been sure they would even run the story, but when they realized how involved the White House was in controlling the story, they decided to air the segment.

This passage is also a relatively rare example of verbatim conversation, since I obtained the transcript of the incident from ABC.

I mentioned earlier that it is essential to quote from a transcript or recording if one exists, since even good memories are so often at odds with the actual words spoken. This posed a unique problem for me in a scene from *Den of Thieves.* One of the most dramatic and pivotal scenes in the entire story occurred when Ivan Boesky secretly tape-recorded Michael Milken while working as an undercover agent. It goes without saying that the conversation between the two of them was recorded. But because Milken ended up pleading guilty, this evidence was never made public. Nor could I gain access to it with a Freedom of Information Act request, since it was withheld under the "investigative" exception to the act. Indeed, it was no doubt in part to suppress and keep from public view such information that Milken agreed to plead guilty. On the other hand, the Milken camp had the transcripts, and I knew that if I relied only on the memory of witnesses to the conversation, Milken's people might produce excerpts from the transcripts to savage me for inaccuracy. But here is the scene that resulted:

In mid-October, Boesky and Tom Doonan, the investigator who was now assigned to handle him, met with Pitt in Pitt's small room at the Beverly Hills Hotel. They'd flown to Los Angeles separately so as not to attract attention.

Doonan asked Boesky to remove his shirt so he could attach a small battery pack and tiny microphone, but was disconcerted when he discovered Boesky wasn't wearing an undershirt under his expensive white dress shirt. Doonan didn't want to tape the microphone to Boesky's skin, so he shed his own clothes, offering Boesky his undershirt. Boesky hesitated. Doonan ordered him to put it on.

"Ivan breaks out in a series rash if he puts anything that costs less than $250 next to his skin," Pitt quipped.

Boesky donned Doonan's T-shirt, and Doonan hooked up the microphone. It would broadcast from Boesky's suite on the first floor, where he was scheduled to meet Milken shortly after one P.M. Pacific time, into a tape recorder in Pitt's room.

"What happens if I get caught, if he figures out I'm taping?" Boesky asked nervously. He was still terrified of Milken, who had close friends in the casino industry. Boesky feared that someone might try to rub him out. "Get the hell out of there" if anything goes wrong, Pitt advised. "Just run out."

Boesky returned to his own suite. While they waited for Milken, Pitt asked Doonan if he wanted to order lunch from room service. Doonan was shocked that a hamburger at the Beverly Hills cost $16. Government regulations prevented him from accepting a meal paid for by someone else, and his modest per diem wouldn't cover anything on the menu, so he declined, even though he was hungry. He watched as Pitt ate a hamburger.

Boesky waited anxiously in his suite. A room-service waiter knocked, then wheeled in a table laden with food. Milken arrived moments later. Boesky greeted him, then paced nervously as the black-jacketed waiter fiddled with the dishes, silverware, and ice. They didn't have much time to spare. "That's fine, just leave it," Boesky finally said to the waiter. "Would you please get out of here?"

Boesky and Milken chatted briefly about the market. Boesky seemed himself. He was ordinarily so stiff and awkward that any nervousness at being wired seemed natural. Then Boesky turned the conversation to its real purpose.

"The SEC subpoenaed my records," he confided to Milken. The commisson was "breathing down my neck." He indicated he was worried he was going to have to deal with the calculations of profts and losses on his "arrangement" with Milken, and wanted to make sure they had the same story.

"Well, my guy doesn't remember anything," Milken said, evidently referring to Thurnher. "Does yours?" Boesky took that as a veiled suggestion to have Mooradian destroy any records. Milken and Boesky went back and forth, with Boesky trying to get Milken to make a more explicit acknowledgment of their dealings.

"If we're asked, what will we say about the $5.3 mllion?" Boesky asked.

"We could say the $5.3 million outstanding was for investment banking services," Milken volunteered.

"What services can we say were included?"

Milken started mentioning some of the deals Drexel had explored for Boesky, but Boesky said he didn't have any documentation to back them up. Milken said he'd send Boesky some papers for his files. Then Boesky pushed the conversation a bit further, saying that he hadn't entirely made up for what he owed Milken with the $5.3 million payment. "You know, I'm still holding this for you," Boesky said.

"Keep it," Milken cagily replied.

Before Boesky could make further progress, Milken made a remark that startled him. "You've got to be careful," Milken warned Boesky. "Electronic surveillance has gotten very sophisticated." Boesky nearly panicked. Was Milken catching on? He quickly brought the meeting to a close.

Even at this date I am not at liberty to reveal how I was able to verify the precise words of some of the most significant passages in this dialogue. But I can say that it required one of the most intense reporting efforts I have ever undertaken. I never was able to determine everything that was said in the hotel room, but I'm confident I gained enough to give readers a sense that they, too, were eavesdropping on one of the most dramatic conversations in the history of the securities laws.

The fact is that almost no quotation, contemporary or narrative, represents precisely what a speaker said. Note-taking is naturally subject to human error and spontaneous editing. Even writers who record and transcribe their interviews correct sentence fragments and delete the "uh"s, "ah"s and other sounds so common in everyday speech. Publications use different standards, but all that I have worked for edit quotations for grammar and usage and simply to make sense of what was said. In fiction, too, no one actually speaks the way dialogue is written, in neat sentences and paragraphs. I believe that readers understand and accept this implicitly. The important thing is that the substance of what was said be conveyed accurately.

Narrative quotations, especially those drawn from a source's memory, are almost never exact accounts of what was said. I have seen this quite clearly when I've compared a source's memory of a conversation with an actual transcript of the same conversation. Such an exercise is a good test of a source's powers of recall. What I have found, almost without exception but for those few instances when a source was lying, is that memory of the substance of a conversation is quite accurate, though memory of specific words is often spurious. The degree of error tends to be a function of how much time has passed since the conversation being remembered, though as I mentioned earlier, I have encountered a few sources with phenomenal memories for dialogue. More fundamentally, the vicissitudes of the human mind always affect memory. This is the case whether it be memory of a conversation or of other historical facts, such as dates and days of the week (something I find sources are mistaken about much more often than they are about the substance of conversations). Like any other fact, narrative dialogue needs to be verified when possible. (It usually can be, since by definition there was at least one other participant, unless the person was speaking to himself, like Richard Nixon talking to the portraits in the White House.)

As I mentioned earlier, one of the main differences between contemporary quotations and narrative quotations is that the reporter is present to hear and possibly record the former, but generally is not present for the latter. Readers may trust the reporter to accurately present at least the substance, and probably most of the words, of the contemporary quotation; by using a contemporary quotation, the reporter is in effect telling the reader, "I heard this statement." But as for the accuracy of the *substance* of the statement, the reader must still rely on the source (when the source's identity is disclosed, which it may not be) and on corroborating information included by the writer. In the narrative quote, for which the writer wasn't present, the reader must rely on the speaker for both the substance of the statement and for the accuracy of the words used. If the source is someone who heard the remark, he or she must be relied upon. In a narrative quotation, incidentally, the speaker is almost always identified; there can be no "anonymous" narrative quotes, except in those rare instances where an unknown person yells "fire" in a crowded room, and the like.

I've dwelt on this distinction at some length because, for reasons I have difficulty fathoming, use of the narrative quotation in nonfiction writing is controversial in at least a few quarters. I have never encountered any resistance to it anywhere I have worked; on the contrary, most editors have been thrilled by the immediacy and vibrancy dialogue brings to a nonfiction story. But I have been taken to task by *New York Times* book critic Michiko Kakutani, whose work I otherwise much admire, for using narrative quotations, especially in *Blood Sport.* I hope I am fairly describing her position, which, as I understand it, is that narrative quotations are inherently unreliable, if not out-and-out fiction; that they imply the writer was present at events when he or she was not; that the source for the quotation isn't identified; and that thus they should be shunned in nonfiction writing.

In reviewing *Blood Sport,* Kakutani wrote that I had "created a novelistic narrative, filled with colorful scenes." Then, she continues,

> The problem is that this technique sacrifices verifiability for verisimilitude, and substitutes color for hardheaded analysis. Scenes that Mr. Stewart could never have observed firsthand are recounted from an omniscient viewpoint. Mr. Stewart rarely identifies the sources for such scenes; nor does he take into account the subjectivity and often self-serving nature of memory. The reader never knows whether the quotes Mr. Stewart has put in the mouth of an individual (whom in some cases he has not even interviewed) are from a first- or secondhand source.

That any writing that is colorful would be deemed novelistic is, to my mind, a sad comment on the dullness of much nonfiction prose. But, that issue aside, Kakutani has confused technique with substance. Whether a story is believable is not a function of literary technique. All reported events not directly witnessed by the writer—that is to say, most of what we read in Kakutani's own newspaper, the *Times*—suffer from the subjectivity of memory, the passage of time, and the reliability of sources, who may or not be identified, and even if they are, may or may not be reliable. Just because someone says something, and is identified as saying it, doesn't make it true. In the end, the reader has to rely on the integrity and reputation of the writer, since readers are rarely in a position to evaluate the credibility of most sources. What I say happened is what I believe to be true, and I try to provide as much corroboration as I can. This applies to narrative quotations as well as to any other facts in a story.

Just as readers know that quotations aren't exact reproductions of the spoken word, they know that the reporter wasn't present to hear narrative quotations any more than at any other event that happened in the past and is depicted in a story. I am at a loss to understand why using a narrative quotation falsely implies the contemporaneous presence of the reporter, but stating that the president wore a red tie and stood on the steps of the state capitol on such-and-such a date is acceptable reporting. In neither case was the reporter there; re-creating events that took place in the past is largely what reporting is about.

It is true that the narrative quotation doesn't usually identify the source, but under the circumstances it hardly seems necessary. The only possible sources are the speaker; someone who heard the remark; transcripts or recordings; or some combination of the three. In most instances, the source is obvious to the reader. If there are two parties to a conversation, and one refused to be interviewed, the source is obviously the remaining participant. In my experience, both parties to a conversation usually agree about its substance, even if one rather than the other recalled the precise words used. In such cases, it doesn't matter who the source was. In some instances—speeches, for example —the number of people who heard remarks may be vast. It hardly needs to be said that the sources for a quoted remark were "several people present," just as it is unnecessary to provide sources for every fact contained in a story. To do so would not only be hopelessly confusing, but would strike most readers as absurd. It elevates the information-gathering process—a topic of interest to journalists, but only rarely to readers—to at least the same status as the subject of the story.

Nonetheless, I have often—always, in my books—carefully addressed the use of narrative quotations, in case a reader doesn't understand their sourcing and inherent limitations. In *Blood Sport,* for example, I wrote:

> Quotations come from the speaker, someone who heard the remark, or from transcripts and notes of conversations. To the extent practicable, the substance of quotes provided by anyone other than the speaker was repeated to the speaker for comment or correction. Many sources not only demonstrated excellent memories, but kept extensive contemporaneous notes

of their thoughts and remarks. Still, readers should bear in mind that remembered dialogue, particularly when years have elapsed, is rarely an exact reproduction of a conversation, as comparisons with actual recording and transcripts often make clear.

Despite her stated concerns about anonymity, Kakutani herself deduced that Susan McDougal was a source for dialogue in my book, as I assumed most readers would. She described Susan as someone who had "reason to be resentful" of the Clintons and was "hardly the most reliable of sources." Those are factors to be considered, no doubt, as I assume readers would, but doesn't Susan's imprisonment for refusing to answer questions before the grand jury suggest that, far from being resentful toward the president, she is trying to protect him? And whatever Susan's credibility, she is in some cases the only source of information, as the eagerness of independent counsel Kenneth Starr to interview her makes clear.

Here is a passage from *Blood Sport* that illustrates some of these issues. At this point in the story, Jim and Susan McDougal, separated and with their real estate empire in ruins, have fled to California. Though Whitewater is all but worthless, Jim wants the Clintons to sign over their interest in it to him so he can use the corporation for other developments he hoped to undertake, and he asked Susan to try to persuade them to do so.

> Susan called the governor's mansion in Little Rock and asked for Bill, leaving her name. Late the next evening, Hillary returned the call. Susan said she was rescinding her power of attorney, and said she didn't understand why Hillary and Bill didn't just sign over their interests in Whitewater to Jim. There was nothing left of any value.
>
> Hillary was angry at the suggestion. "We own half of it, and we are not getting out of it," Hillary retorted. "It's incredible that partners would be asked to sign over their stock."
>
> Now Susan was angry. "This was Jim McDougal's project, his idea, his money!" She couldn't believe Hillary was insisting on retaining half of an empty corporation. "Don't you understand that I don't want anything. It's all going to Jim. It's morally wrong for you not to give it to him." Susan felt herself near tears. "You're terrible people, after all he would and did do for you, that you wouldn't do this."

"I will not be blackmailed," Hillary responded. "You can't force us by making some threat."

Suddenly Susan felt frightened. She wasn't making any threat—she was just emotional and upset. Why was Hillary using the word "blackmail"? Was someone else there on Hillary's end of the line? Or worse, was the conversation being taped? Susan ended the conversation.

Shaken, she immediately called Jim. "For what it's worth, I did everything I could" to get the Clintons to turn over their interest in Whitewater, she said. "They should do it. But I believe they were taping the conversation or someone was listening in. She used the word 'blackmail.' "

Jim commiserated with Susan. This wasn't Little Rock anymore. Bill and Hillary were headed to the White House.*

*The timing of these conversations is disputed by Hillary Clinton. David Kendall said that they must have occurred when Hillary sought a power of attorney in 1988. Susan McDougal insists that they occurred during the campaign.

Susan McDougal is obviously the source. But I do not rely solely on her recollection, though it was quite vivid and explicit. Her former husband, Jim, corroborated her account; she had told him the same thing in a contemporaneous description of the conversation with Hillary, as the text indicates. Finally, Hillary Clinton's lawyer confirmed the existence and substance of such a conversation, but disputed its timing, as I noted in a footnote. As a result, I have no doubt that such a conversation took place, and in more or less the words remembered by Susan. Specifically, all concerned, even the Clintons' lawyer, who I assume reviewed this with Hillary, recalled the use of the word "blackmail." Isn't this obvious? Would this passage have been any more credible had I taken twice as much space and cluttered the dialogue with contemporary quotations from Jim and Susan McDougal, in which they narrated their recollections of the earlier events? And doesn't Susan's accurate memory of this conversation attest to her powers of recollection, and to her credibility in general?

In my view, this is not substituting "color" for "hardheaded analysis." It is the reporting of verifiable facts and the trusting of readers to make their own analysis and judgments. This is the essence of effective nonfiction storytelling.

10
ANECDOTES

ANECDOTES ARE STORIES WITHIN STORIES, and as such, they draw upon all the storytelling skills we have already discussed. My American Heritage dictionary defines anecdote as "a short, entertaining account of some incident, usually personal or biographical."

As the definition suggests, anecdotes are often used to develop characters—to illustrate personal qualities, especially those that don't lend themselves to direct description, such as character and personality. But they may also be useful in establishing the character and quality of institutions, the ambience of places—virtually anything that can be described. For anecdotes are descriptive tools, and everything I've said about description —including the perils of inference—applies to anecdotes as well.

Like stories, good anecdotes show rather than tell. They require readers to think and draw their own conclusions as to their meaning. There's a reason the biblical prophets spoke so often in parables. They are persuasive to a degree that descriptive words alone rarely are. Indeed, whenever you're considering the use of an adjective, it's worth pondering whether an anecdote exists that would make the same point more convincingly. The same thing goes for the reporting process. When a source describes someone with adjectives, it's worth finding out why the source uses such words, by asking what incidents they're based on. Even without prompting, most sources readily introduce anecdotes into their oral accounts.

Anecdotes almost invariably take more time and space than a simple description. They are detours from the narrative, and hence should be used sparingly. Redundancy should be avoided. Anecdotes' relevance must be immediately apparent, and if it's not, they should be discarded. They are better used earlier rather than later in a story, for reasons of pacing. And, as the definition suggests, ideally they are entertaining for the reader. Whether something is entertaining or not is, of course, a subjective decision, but anecdotes that are memorable and entertaining do seem to share some characteristics: They are fresh rather than stale and recycled. They are often revealing in ways unseen by their source. They may be highly personal, even intimate. They catch their subjects unawares. They are often embarrassing, humorous, or poignant. Like good story ideas, good anecdotes often trigger emotions in the reporter, such as squeamishness and unease, which should never be a signal to flee the subject. (As an editor I was shocked to see how often the best anecdotes resided in a reporter's notes rather than the finished story.) Good anecdotes —which is to say, entertaining anecdotes—stick in the mind. I rarely need to resort to my notes to recall them. Like good description, they trigger inferences and often have symbolic value.

Since anecdotes are themselves stories, they have their own structure, but because they are so short, the structure must be as streamlined and simple as possible. They are almost always told in strict chronological order, with no flashbacks, interruptions, or recapitulations. Because they serve a descriptive function, however, they can be inserted almost anywhere in the overall structure of a story without triggering a chronological disruption. Indeed, multiple anecdotes can even be used sequentially. In order to minimize disruption in a chronology, the exact dates of anecdotes are rarely mentioned; "once," "years ago," and the like usually suffice to fix an anecdote somewhere in the indeterminate past.

At the same time, anecdotes may appear within the chronological structure of a story, if some event in the anecdote itself occurs in the course of a story's plot. Such anecdotes, however, shouldn't be confused with actual plot developments; an anecdote is not a "scene" in that sense.

Here is an anecdote from *Den of Thieves* that illustrates some of these principles. At this point in the overall narrative it is 1982, and Ivan Boesky will soon need another stock trader named John Mulheren to rescue him from a failed buyout. Mulheren hasn't yet appeared in the story.

West Sixty-seventh Street between Central Park West and Columbus Avenue is one of Manhattan's prettiest tree-lined blocks, home to one of its venerable eateries, the Café des Artistes. Ivan Boesky arrived at the restaurant in 1976 to meet, for the first time, a young Wall Street trader named John Mulheren. In keeping with the restaurant's genteel, old-world character, nearly all of its male patrons wear jacket and ties, as, of course, did Boesky.

Mulheren showed up in a bright knit polo shirt and khaki trousers. Tall, and solidly built, with tousled sandy-colored hair and a friendly Irish countenance, he looked, at age twenty-seven, like an overgrown college kid. . . . When the Café des Artistes waiter came to take their order, Boesky said he hadn't decided and that the others should make their selections. Then Boesky ordered: "I'll have every entree." The waiter's pen stopped in midair. Boesky repeated his order. "Bring me each one of those entrees."

Mulheren glanced at his wife, raising his eyebrows slightly. Seema [Boesky's wife] chatted on as though nothing unusual had happened. Mulheren wondered whether this was how rich people ate.

When the food arrived, the waiter wheeled a table next to them. On it were the eight featured dishes of the day. Boesky looked them over carefully, circled the table, took one bite of each. He selected one, and sent the rest back.

Boesky only picked at his food. Mulheren was relieved that he didn't have to pick up the check.

Although this incident takes up just a few paragraphs in a long book, it seems to be one of the things nearly all readers remember about Ivan Boesky. The behavior described, of course, is unusual and therefore memorable. But it also resonates on a symbolic level. The imperiousness of demanding all the dishes, the extravagant disregard for expense, the waste of throwing so much food away—this at a time when ill-fed homeless people were no doubt huddled in doorways just outside the restaurant

—says a great deal about the personality, character, and values of Boesky at the time. No wonder the incident made an impression on the young Mulheren.

That I would include this mini-narrative in the book was obvious to me from the moment I heard it from Mulheren. I was as riveted by it and as fascinated by the implications as many others have been. I didn't forget it, and while writing the book, I didn't have to look for Mulheren's account in my notes. But how would I use it? The date of the dinner, 1976, preceded almost all the events of the book; it did not fall within the narrative frame I had constructed. Even if my narrative *had* reached back to 1976, Mulheren would then have left the stage and not appeared again until 1982, when his business relationship with Boesky began in earnest. Using the story as an anecdote was the answer; it both explained how Mulheren and Boesky met and, more important, showed how Mulheren viewed Boesky and shed light on Boesky's character. So the anecdote is really a short flashback in the narrative.

This anecdote could have been told even more briefly, but given that it was memorable and entertaining, I felt it could support a good deal of description. So the beginning, a description of the setting, enabling readers to visualize the location, is detailed. Mulheren is introduced with a fair amount of physical description. Then the pace picks up, accelerating into the punch line: "I'll have every entree." Direct dialogue is used. If the waiter said anything in response, no one remembered it. The denouement is even briefer.

Like the writing of stories themselves, the writing of anecdotes requires an understanding of their chronological structure, their pacing, and the need to introduce characters and include descriptive material. Like that of most anecdotes, the chronological span of this one is brief: a single evening—indeed, a few minutes—at dinner in the Café des Artistes. The anecdote adheres strictly to chronological order: the guests arrive, the waiter comes, others place their order while Boesky muses; Boesky orders, the waiter reacts; the waiter brings the food; Boesky sends all but one dish back.

Because anecdotes should be short, there is no foreshadowing, there is no summary or nut graf, there is no need for any transition. If an anecdote needs to be explained, it shouldn't be used. This rule applies here even more strictly than it does in complex stories. There is nothing more deadly to a potentially good anecdote than to introduce it by characterizing it or, worse, giving away the punch line. Think of the dinner guest who prefaces an anecdote "I just heard the funniest story. . . ."

Had the Café des Artistes incident not been narrated as an anecdote, it might have read like this:

> John Mulheren says that Boesky was always a conspicuous consumer. At his first meeting with Boesky, a dinner at an expensive restaurant in Manhattan, the waiter recited the day's eight specials, and Boesky ordered them all. The waiter wheeled out a table with the dishes on them, Boesky examined each of them, then sent back all but one. Mulheren says he's glad he didn't have to pick up the bill.

This, unfortunately, is how anecdote is often used in nonfiction writing. Would readers still be talking about this incident years after my book appeared? I doubt it. The incident lacks drama, immediacy, and even a degree of credibility, for details lend credibility. Mulheren's characterization of Boesky as a conspicuous consumer foreshadows the punch line and limits the many other inferences a reader might carry away.

The reporting of anecdotes sometimes poses singular problems. As is often the case, Mulheren first told me this story in terms similar to the lackluster account I just provided. The moment I began to press for more details—How many entrees were there? How did the waiter react? What did Seema say?—he suspected I would use the story, and he wanted to know why. Sources often tell stories they believe to be unrelated to the story you're writing, and then perk up and become suspicious when you show an interest in them. The "point" of an anecdote, to which a source may have been oblivious, suddenly becomes clear. Obviously, the story of Boesky at the Café des Artistes was not flattering to Boesky. Mulheren was nonetheless willing to provide details to the extent he could remember them, and others present were able to add to his account. But that isn't always the case. An anecdote often takes an immense amount of reporting proportionate to the space it occupies in a story. It is essential that every detail be correct. Steven Brill, of the *Ameri-*

can Lawyer, CourtTV, and most recently, *Brill's Content,* took *The New Yorker* publicly to task when a "Talk of the Town" item about him incorrectly described the shape of a conference table at which he was seated.

By contrast to the Café des Artistes anecdote, here is an anecdote that fits entirely within the chronological structure of the book:

> Jim Dahl took a deep breath and walked into the conference room for his annual salary review. This year, 1986, he was prepared to insist on more than Milken offered. He never knew the exact size of the high-yield operation's bonus pool, but he knew it had to be big. Other employees, such as [Peter] Ackerman, had succeeded in wheedling large amounts out of Milken. This year. Dahl had been indisputably the top salesman, coming through in even the most difficult situations, as in the $100 million of Boesky debt he sold Charles Keating.
>
> Milken went right to the point. "You're going to be paid $10 million this year," he told the thirty-three-year-old Dahl. This was more than Dahl had ever dreamed of making, but he stuck to his resolution. "I really think I'm entitled to more," he insisted, ticking off his achievements. Milken listened sympathetically, but quickly disagreed. "Jim, I really can't pay you any more," he said in a soft voice, "or you'd be making more than me. Now that wouldn't be fair, would it?"

This incident, occupying just two paragraphs, appears in chronological order. Yet it isn't a scene in the story, because it does nothing to advance the plot. It is included only for the insight it yields into Michael Milken's values and character. One of the claims made by Milken's lawyer Alan Dershowitz was that Milken "never cared about money" and was solely concerned with the allocation of capital to worthy borrowers who otherwise couldn't get credit. Because the anecdote about Dahl's compensation is told in strict order, the punch line appears several paragraphs later, after some other events have intervened. By then, the point of view in this anecdote has shifted from Dahl to Fred Joseph, the firm's chief executive, who knows far more about the firm's compensation than Dahl did:

> Once Joseph approved the overall bonus pool of $700 million, it was up to Milken to divide it up as he saw fit. Milken

doled out about $150 million to his colleagues in Beverly Hills, including the $10 million he'd promised Dahl. But Milken didn't keep just $10 million for himself, as he'd implied. Nor did he plow the remainder into the firm's capital, as Dahl had surmised. Dahl had no way of knowing this at the time, but Milken bestowed $550 million on himself. That was more than the $522.5 million in profit that Drexel itself—the entire firm—had earned.

The fact that Milken earned $550 million in 1986 was one of the most widely reported facts from *Den of Thieves*. Years later, it remains a staggering amount of money for one person to have earned, and it is another anecdote I find readers of the book often mention. Told as an anecdote, in strict chronological order and using dialogue and a point-of-view shift, it's far more effective, in my opinion, than simply stating the facts would have been. Readers readily absorb the point of this story, and invariably draw their own conclusions. Need any more be said about Milken's alleged integrity and lack of interest in money? I doubt that the many millions Milken has spent on lawyers and public relations experts in an effort to change his public image will ever blunt the impact of this single anecdote.

Many feature stories begin with what is known as the anecdotal lead, in which, as I mentioned in chapter 5, an anecdote serves as the beginning of a story. In such instances, the point of the anecdote usually at least foreshadows the theme of the story; in many cases it *is* the theme. Anecdotal leads used to be so common at one time in the front-page stories of *The Wall Street Journal* that the device threatened to become a cliché.

Recall the anecdote that opened the story about the impoverished novelist James Wilcox. It occupies three paragraphs, and tells the story-within-the-story of Jim's work at the St. Francis Xavier soup kitchen:

When James Wilcox is working at the St. Francis Xavier "welcome table," as its soup kitchen is called, as he does on the first and second Sundays of every month, it's hard to tell he's an acclaimed novelist. It took his fellow volunteers years to figure it out. No one there had read "Modern Baptists," his first novel published in 1983, hailed in a front-page New York Times book review by Anne Tyler as "startlingly alive, exuberantly overcrowded." Nor were they familiar with its five progeny, three of them set in the fictional Tula Springs, Louisiana, a venue compared by more than one critic to William Faulkner's Yoknapatawpha County.

Wilcox himself was much too shy to tell them. He looks younger than his age, which is forty-five, with his slightly ruddy complexion, medium build, and sandy hair. He's nice-looking, though he agonizes over his author photographs and didn't want one on his last book. Yale-educated, he speaks with no trace of an accent. His Southern roots are evident only in the elaborate courtesy with which he waits on the soup kitchen's "guests," as he unfailingly calls them when dispensing juice and coffee. He betrays little reaction when something really grabs his attention, like the saga of a woman plagued by the stench from a neighbor who kept twenty-two cats in her Murray Hill one-bedroom apartment.

"For years I never knew what he did," says George Deshensky, a lawyer and one of the directors of the soup kitchen. "Then one day someone said, 'He's a published author.' So we'd introduce him that way. We didn't know what he published or where." Deshensky began relying on Wilcox as a "calming influence" when altercations threatened to break out in the line, as happened with some regularity. Since then, during the eight years Wilcox has been working at the soup kitchen, he and Deshensky have become close friends and Deshensky has read his books. Still, it came as a surprise to Deshensky when he complimented Wilcox on the empathy he shows their impoverished patrons. "I'm only a check or two from being in the line myself," Wilcox replied.

This anecdote takes place at an indeterminate time approximately eight years in the past. Although the incident falls within the chronological frame of Jim's career as a novelist, and thus could have been placed within the chronological order of the story, it is disembodied at the outset of the story because it establishes the paradox that is meant to propel readers forward. As I mentioned before, it creates no narrative suspense, because the mini-narrative of the anecdote ends with its punch line. We have no further need to see Jim working at the soup kitchen, and there is no further mention of the incident in the story.

There is a fair amount of detail in this anecdote, but words aren't wasted. When an anecdote appears in the course of a story, presumably enough suspense has already been generated to carry readers through it, even if, like the Café des Artistes example, it is fairly long and detailed. But the writer can't rely on this at the outset, because the anecdote itself carries the burden of establishing suspense and curiosity on the part of readers. This is a difficult task. The patience readers will often display once they have committed themselves to reading a story is, I find, in scant evidence when they begin a story and don't want to waste their time. Thus, I omitted any physical description of the St. Francis Xavier soup kitchen itself, and not just because there is nothing that visually striking about it. It is not a scene in Jim's story, and the action never returns to this location. Nor did I provide any physical description of Jim's friend, who makes his last appearance here as well. I explained in chapter 5 the reasons for nearly every other word in these paragraphs, which are used less to advance the anecdote than to establish the paradox. The anecdote is there only to provide a frame for this material, and for the punch line, which is meant to startle. And, as I mentioned earlier, the anecdotal lead never establishes narrative suspense, since the end of the anecdote is the end of the mini-narrative. Our curiosity about that incident has been satisifed. Readers presumably aren't panting to know what Jim's friend said after Jim disclosed that he was only one check away from the food line himself.

For these reasons, the anecdotal lead is in eclipse; I actually use few of them. Many leads that at first brush might seem like anecdotes, such as the Sheinbergs' walk along the beach at Malibu, are actually scenes from narratives. Yet they are still a staple of many feature stories. They are especially useful in introducing a narrative element into stories that otherwise lack one, as is often the case in trend, explanatory, and point-of-view stories. But anecdotal leads have to be good stories, preferably highly memorable and entertaining. They should be as concise and to-the-point as possible.

Remember the editor who threw my story on the floor and stomped on it? Here is the lead from that story, with a very brief anecdote embedded in it:

Secretive and rich, Allen-Bradley Co. was the epitome of the privately held corporation. Founder Harry Bradley identified so closely with his manufacturing-controls company that, during the early 1960s, he lived in a suite of rooms in the factory building. An insomniac, he spent long nights walking the factory floor with his pet poodle and chatting with members of the night shift.

Vowing that Allen-Bradley would never be sold, Mr. Bradley created an elaborate trust arrangement to safeguard the company after he died. But earlier this year, less than 20 years after Mr. Bradley's death in July 1965 at the age of 80, Allen-Bradley was auctioned to Pittsburgh-based Rockwell International Corp. for $1.65 billion, the highest price ever paid for a privately held U.S. company.

Most people in Milwaukee, a city that has lost one corporation after another to outside acquirers, are baffled by the takeover of the one local company they thought was safe. How it happened is a story of family rivalry and corporate intrigue more often associated with freewheeling Dallas than with staid Milwaukee.

So there you see the offending poodle. By now I'm sure I don't need to remark on the obvious "selling" points in this lead: the attempt to make an event seem as improbable as possible and to create a sense of mystery and curiosity. Let's just consider the anecdote about Mr. Bradley and his poodle.

Does it fit the dictionary definition of "short and entertaining?" Which do you find more interesting: that Mr. Bradley lived in the factory and walked his poodle on the floor, or that there was an elaborate trust arrangement? As so often happens with anecdotes, readers mentioned the poodle to me more often than any other aspect of the story. While the anecdote has some purely symbolic resonance, it conveys in very few words that Mr. Bradley was the embodiment of his company, so much so that he lived in the factory and knew individually even members of the night shift. It establishes that he was somewhat odd, even eccentric, and makes readers want to know more about him. It makes it all the more mysterious and poignant that this otherwise uninteresting machine-tool manufacturer would have been sold to an impersonal outside corporation. And it suggests that this will ultimately be a story about people, not machine-tools.

Here is a somewhat longer anecdote I used in a 1983 front-page *Wall Street Journal* story about sex discrimination in large law firms:

At a weekend outing held in North Carolina this past summer by the prestigious Atlanta law firm of King & Spalding, a group of lawyers decided it would be fun to stage a "wet T-shirt" contest featuring the firm's women summer associates.

But cooler heads prevailed. The lawyers had to content themselves with a more old-fashioned, and not quite so revealing, bathing-suit competition. As he bestowed first prize on a third-year law student from Harvard University, one of the firm's partners said, "She has the body we'd like to see more of."

Lawyers at King & Spalding dismiss the incident as an example of the rollicking good times that characterize the firm's social events and contribute to an unusually high esprit de corps among the firm's lawyers.

But some participants in the impromptu bathing-suit event say they felt humiliated and that they didn't protest only because they were candidates for year-round jobs with the firm. They say they were stunned that the contest occurred, especially since the firm was a defendant in a sex-discrimination lawsuit.

What made this an effective lead? As I discussed in the chapter on lead paragraphs, this incident—in which a large and prominent law firm was being sued for sex discrimination but held a bathing-suit contest for its female employees—is so staggering that it cries out for further explanation. How could such a thing have happened? What kind of people—lawyers, no less—would exhibit such poor judgment and such cavalier disregard for the sensibilities of its women lawyers? This generates the curiosity to propel readers into the story.

The power of this anecdote was such that years after the story ran I encountered readers who remembered nothing about it except the fact that King & Spalding had held the contest. Every detail is vivid: that the firm first considered a wet T-shirt contest, something even more vulgar; the words used to crown the winner. (The plaintiff's lawyer couldn't have drafted anything any more damning.) Is it any surprise that King & Spalding eventually settled the suit? Is there anything I could have said that would have better or more convincingly described the good-ol'-boy atmosphere at this large law firm?

While I have had cordial exchanges with individual King & Spalding lawyers in the years since the story ran, I have been told by colleagues who have had dealings with the firm that a sizable contingent of lawyers there will never forget nor forgive me for including this incident in my story. They felt I took a trivial incident and blew it out of proportion by putting it on the front page. But no one ever disputed that the contest occurred. While it may indeed have been trivial in the grand scheme of things, its symbolism was not, which would surely have been evident to anyone who considered the issue. In my view the lawyers' ire might better have been aimed at those who proposed the contest in the first place. King & Spalding remains one of the country's most successful firms, and like many large firms, has since become far more sensitive and hospitable to women and minorities. I'd like to think that my story hastened that improvement. But at the time, this incident seemed to have hurt the firm even more than the fact that it was sued for sex discrimination. Such is the power of anecdote.

As I mentioned earlier, anecdotes are especially useful for establishing character, and for that reason often accompany the introduction of a character in a story. In the Sheinberg insider-trading story, a series of anecdotes establishes Jonathan Sheinberg's personality and character and illustrates some of the characteristics mentioned by his friends and colleagues, such as his being headstrong and impulsive. Here is an anecdote about Jonathan's brief tenure as president of Lee Rich productions:

> At Lee Rich Productions, it became increasingly apparent that Jonathan's career had plateaued. Some friends say they warned Jonathan not to take the job at Rich, even though he was getting a substantial raise. Lee Rich, as a wealthy and powerful Hollywood legend in his own right (he is a co-founder of Lorimar), was similar to Jonathan's father, some felt, and had the reputation for being difficult to work with. Both Jonathan and Rich are often described as headstrong and impulsive, and they proved a mismatch almost from the outset.
>
> An executive from another company recalls a meeting with Jonathan and Rich. As Jonathan was making one of his typically animated presentations, Rich interrupted, told him, "Shut up. You're an idiot," and took over the presentation, while Jonathan obviously simmered. When Jonathan's contract at Rich expired in 1991, "I told him that he wouldn't be in my plans," Rich told the Washington Post. "Jonathan is tough to live with," he added. Friends of Jonathan's attribute the rift to jealousy on the part of Rich, because Jonathan was getting too much credit in the Hollywood trade papers.

This anecdote, narrated in just a single paragraph, falls out of the article's chronological span; it happened at an indeterminate time before the events of the story, while Jonathan was working with Rich. The source, "an executive from another company," isn't named; it would obviously embarrass him if Jonathan learned he had repeated such an unflattering tale. But the identity of the source, as is often the case, is irrelevant, since he is asserting facts, not opinion. There were multiple witnesses to the incident; either Rich or Jonathan could have denied it, which they did not, and others confirmed the incident or could have come forward to deny it. Facts have an inherent authority and can usually be independently verified, whatever their source.

The anecdote speaks volumes about Jonathan, his relationship with Rich, and his discretion. That Rich would publicly chastise the president of his production company is a fact that most readers found both memorable and entertaining, even humorous.

Most anecdotes take place before the events of a story, and are included by way of background. But sometimes anecdotes occur chronologically after the events of the story, and can be included as part of a postscript. Such an anecdote also appeared in the Sheinberg story:

> Jonathan's career hasn't been nearly so successful as MCA's. After Lee Rich declined to renew Jonathan's contract, in September of 1991, Jonathan said that he would become an independent producer. Instead, he landed a job as a literary agent at Triad Artists, which was acquired last year by William Morris. Starting without any clients, Jonathan has been slowly building a list, though it includes "no one whose name you'd recognize," one of his colleagues says. According to his colleagues, he raised eyebrows at Triad when he signed up a grade-school child as a director on the strength of the child's home movie. (That relationship lasted just three months.)

The anecdote about the grade-school director takes up a single sentence and a parenthetical conclusion. Yet it took immense effort on my part and even more on the part of the fact-checker to verify this information. While the story of Jonathan and the child director circulated widely in Hollywood, no one knew the crucial details, such as the child's name or exact age. Obviously, no one at William Morris was eager to call attention to such an absurd incident, nor were any friends of Jonathan's. Yet we persevered, because this snippet said so much about whether Jonathan had changed or learned much from the MCA experience. It was also entertaining, in my opinion.

In longer works, especially books, and with major characters, anecdotes can be effectively strung together to provide a detailed portrait of both a person and place. Here is a series of anecdotes that accompany the introduction of Michael Milken as a character in *Den of Thieves.* They reveal qualities about Milken's character and personality, even as they illuminate the high-pressure atmosphere of Drexel's Beverly Hills outpost:

> With Dahl, as with all his employees, Milken demanded total commitment and allegiance. No one left the office to eat; meals were catered every day for breakfast and lunch and often for dinner as well. To prevent any distractions, Milken hired several women to pick up dry cleaning for his traders and salesmen, go to the post office, wait at their houses for repairmen and deliveries, and take care of pets. Soon after he first came aboard, Dahl, still adjusting to the time change, started to leave the office after the markets had closed on a Friday.
>
> "Where are you going?" Milkin asked sharply.
>
> "I'm tired, and I'm going home to read research reports," Dahl replied.
>
> Milkin was appalled at such a lack of stamina. "Read here, then go home and take a nap," he said. Dahl meekly returned to his desk.
>
> On another occasion, Dahl was leaving the office after learning that his mother had been diagnosed with cancer. "Where are you going?" Milkin again demanded.
>
> Dahl said he was worried, his aunt and uncle had both died of cancer, he wanted to visit his mother. Milken looked disgruntled. "When are you going to be back?" he asked. He did not express any concern or sympathy.
>
> A few years later, when Dahl's wife went into labor prematurely and the baby died after two hours, a devastated Dahl was at his desk the next morning, determined that Milken wouldn't notice his grief. He had learned that Milken expected nothing less.
>
> No one had much private life. Ironically, given the lip service Milken paid to marital fidelity and family values, the intense,

hothouse atmosphere kept employees away from their families and spawned intra-office affairs between traders and secretaries, including one between Trepp and Milken's own administrative assistant, Jeannette. Milken seemed oblivious until they announced their engagement.

One of the office's secretaries kept a diary detailing her sexual encounters with men in the office. One of the most talked-about entries described in lurid detail how she gave one salesman fellatio and used drugs. Such incidents were commonplace. Some of the trading assistants in the office even had breast implants, paid for by Drexel salesmen and traders.

On one occasion in 1984, Milken's employees hired a stripper to celebrate his birthday. She arrived during trading hours, shed all of her clothing while dancing around Milken's desk, then leaned toward him shaking her ample breasts in his face. Just then, Milken's phone rang. It was a client wanting to do a trade. To escape the stripper, Milken ducked down under the desk, still gripping his phone. The stripper followed him on hands and knees as Milken completed the trade.

Milken rarely socialized with others in the office and, indeed, spent little time with his own wife and his two sons and daughter, though he did show up for important sporting events and school occasions and coached his sons' basketball team. On a family trip to Hawaii, Milken rented three suites in the hotel: one for him and Lori, one for the children, and a third that functioned as his office. He worked every day of the vacation from 3 A.M. until 8 A.M. Hawaii time, while the markets were open in New York.

With rare exceptions, Milken only left his desk during work hours for nonbusiness reasons once a year, when he took his wife to lunch on their wedding anniversary. He usually ate at his desk, mostly junk food. He never seemed to get any exercise. Even during off hours, he was usually in his home office; calls there, even late at night and on weekends, were answered promptly. On the rare occasions when he did attend parties, he seemed awkward. At birthday parties, he spent most of his time playing with the kids.

Milken was a perfectionist and could be relentlessly critical, questioning a trade over and over, fixating on a fraction of a point. He'd ask the same question over and over, badgering a trader to make the point that the trader had been foolish or stupid. But after Trepp demonstrated to Milken that he'd been right in five disputed trades, he told Milken to "stop nagging me," and for the most part Milken did.

Dahl once asked Milken why he criticized so much and never praised anyone. "There's not enough time in the day to sit around praising each other," Milken sharply replied. "We don't need to talk about our successes. We only need to talk about our failures."

In this atmosphere, what might seem ordinary gestures of kindness elsewhere seemed memorable. Once, when Winnick was getting ready for a rare vacation to Italy, Milken sent him a bon voyage package and a note telling him to have a great trip. When they moved to the Los Angeles area, Milken extended personal loans to nearly all the employees so they could buy nice houses. When Dahl and his wife celebrated their wedding anniversary in Palm Springs, they were greeted with a large bouquet and a card reading, "Happy Anniversary. Mike and Lori." Milken made a hospital visit and offered financial help to the dying brother of a member of the office's support staff.

Trepp was constantly amazed at Milken's obsession with squeezing more profits out of trades, and frequently had to remind him that securities dealers' guidelines permit only a 5% markup. Milken's power over the market was so complete that he frequently tried to mark prices up as much as 25%. One of Trepp's responsibilities as head trader was to sign the trading tickets; when Trepp saw what he considered an egregious ticket, he bounced it back to Milken. But at times, Milken did the trades anyway and someone else forged Trepp's initials; he doesn't know who.

On at least four occasions, Trepp threatened to quit over what he considered serious trading improprieties. He had loud fights with Milken, and in each case, Milken backed down. Milken never fired anyone. He was obsessed with the notion that anyone who left would reveal his secrets, the scope and success of his money-making activities.

The pressure took its toll, in varying degrees. Peter Ackerman was hired initially as a trader, but Milken's relentless criticism reduced him on one occasion to tears. Ackerman quit trading, and focused increasingly on cultivating clients, functioning more as an investment banker for Milken. He became so sycophantic toward Milken that others resented him. His nickname was "the Sniff," because, in the words of a colleague, "his nose was always up Mike's ass."

Trepp began smoking four packs of cigarettes a day. Another trader took to chewing rubber bands; another developed a serious drinking problem. Bruce Newberg, deemed a brilliant technician by many in the office, had to start taking blood pressure medication. One day Newberg started raving hysterically when his phone line went dead during an important conversation with a client. It turned out that he had chewed through the phone cord.

Winnick developed a reputation as the office hypochondriac, sometimes checking himself into the Scripps Institute in San Diego because he thought he had brain tumors and other serious ailments.

There are at least ten anecdotes in this passage, most of them extremely brief. I was struck, during my reporting, by what a negative portrait of Milken his colleagues presented, at least those who were willing to speak to me, and so I went back to many of them asking for any episodes they recalled that showed Milken in a positive light. I did include those, but as the material suggests, they weren't especially memorable or persuasive. But by using a heavily anecdotal approach I was able to avoid using anonymous characterizations of Milken. Nearly all of these episodes were witnessed by numerous people and could be verified.

For major characters, sequential anecdotes may be used to convey even single aspects of a person's character. In writing about Bill Clinton in *Blood Sport,* even long before the Monica Lewinsky allegations surfaced, it was impossible to explain the dynamics of the Clintons' marriage, which in turn affected their investment in Whitewater, without discussing Clinton's alleged womanizing. Whether he had had affairs was not within the scope of my book, but his fights with Hillary were, because they helped explain her anxiety about their marriage and, in turn, her need to invest to provide financially for her future and Chelsea's. This posed a peculiarly difficult problem of writing and reporting, for at the time Clinton staunchly denied having any affairs at all, even with Gennifer Flowers. (It was only much later that he admitted to a single sexual encounter with Flowers.)

Here is a series of anecdotes that addressed this aspect of Clinton's character:

By now, it must also have been obvious that Hillary couldn't count much on financial contributions from her husband, given his earnings prospects and lack of interest in making money. In his campaigns, Bill typically didn't even carry any money, leaving it to aides to pick up the tab when necessary (an approach he'd learned from McDougal and Fulbright). At semiannual meetings with Smith to discuss the discretionary account, it was Hillary who asked nearly all the questions and wanted explanations for various investment strategies. Bill, by contrast, showed little interest in the account's growth and would ramble on about political developments, comments that left Smith puzzled as to their financial relevance.

According to friends of the couple, it was also at this time that Hillary expressed doubts about the future of her marriage, and, as a result, whether she could count on Bill to support her and a child. Their marriage, now in its third year, was, by the Clintons' subsequent admission, at a low point. If Gennifer Flowers's account can be believed, she and Bill were in the passionate, early stages of their affair that summer. People close to the Clintons were aware of other women in Bill's life, too. They believed Bill had been unfaithful to Hillary even during their engagement, and moving to Little Rock as attorney general had only broadened his opportunities with other women. They were suspicious of Bill's "jogging" expeditions, especially on days improbably hot and humid for athletic activity. On one such occasion, an Arkansas trooper assigned to Clinton's security detail, Roger Perry, asked Clinton how far he'd run that day. "Five miles," Clinton replied.

"Well, sir. You need to see a doctor," Perry replied. "There's something wrong with your sweat glands." Later, Perry noticed that Clinton would sometimes use the troopers' bathroom to splash water on his face and shirt before he entered the governor's mansion.

To many of their friends, the situation seemed especially painful for Hillary. Bill seemed to flaunt his interest in certain women. One summer he liked to run with Pat Wyatt, who was locally renowned as a founder of the Marquis de Sade running club and who had helped carry the Olympic torch across the country in preparation for the 1980 Winter Games in Lake Placid. She later worked in Clinton's first administration as governor. When he'd return from their runs, he couldn't stop extolling her virtues to Hillary, with comments like "Isn't that Pat terrific?"[*] Hillary would typically say nothing then. But later there would be arguments, shouting matches, a thrown shoe or two. Both Bill and Hillary had volatile tempers, which they

---

[*] *Wyatt, now Torvestad, denies having any romantic involvement with Clinton. She confirms their jogging outings. "He can still sprint and drop me," she says.*

didn't hesitate to inflict on each other. To longtime observers, it was an essential dynamic of their relationship, and the fights were often followed by reconciliations that seemed loving and tranquil. But privately, Hillary expressed pain and dismay. She sought out the husband of one close friend, trying to understand why Bill would be so unfaithful. Did he cheat on his wife? Did he know other men who did? How should she react? How should she feel? Hillary seemed in equal parts puzzled and hurt.

Bill and Hillary's move to the governor's mansion in January 1979 did little to ease these anxieties. If anything, Bill's greater celebrity status opened up more opportunities. He confided in Susan McDougal that he loved being governor: "This is fun. Women are throwing themselves at me. All the while I was growing up, I was the fat boy in the Big Boy jeans." Women treated Bill like he was a rock star. When a group of Girl Scouts visited and Bill came out to greet them, they shrieked and screamed as though they were meeting the Beatles. Susan wasn't surprised that women seemed to be hurling themselves at him. Her brother Bill Henley had been elected to the State Senate. He had women around all the time, and he was just a state senator. Still, Susan felt bad for Hillary. At an inauguration party, Susan had seen Bill Clinton disappear from the party with a tall blond woman in tow. Hillary was putting on a brave face, but the incident was stirring up a buzz and Susan could tell she was upset. She went over to commiserate with the state's new first lady, sharing an observation she'd gotten from Betty Tucker, wife of Congressman Jim Guy Tucker. "Betty told me," Susan confided, "that it doesn't change from the local, to the state, to the federal level. The girls just get prettier."

This is essentially a sequence of three anecdotes, the first from Perry's point of view, the second from Hillary's, and the third from Susan McDougal's. The passage doesn't purport to state that Clinton had extramarital affairs, simply that many people, Hillary evidently among them, believed he did, and that there were incidents and remarks that fueled such speculation. In my view, the anecdotes are far more persuasive than anything I might have said, which might have seemed insinuating and unconvincing. Everything in the anecdotes could be verified, including the fact of the fights between the Clintons and the comments at the inaugural party between Susan and Betty Tucker.

Still, the inference most readers would draw seems clear—

that where there's this much smoke, there might be fire. This can present difficulties for writers, since the fact that someone made a statement may be relevant, even if the substance of the remark turns out to be false. Thus, writers should in some instances not only try to verify *that* a statement was made, but try to verify its substance as well. Failure to do so, especially if the writer has reason to doubt the accuracy of the statement, might subject the writer to liability. I find this to be a peculiar burden on writers, for surely most readers know that everything they hear isn't true, but nonetheless find it interesting that a statement was made. Even more burdensome, writers are sometimes expected to anticipate the inferences readers might draw, and try to verify those as well. Hence the footnote to the anecdote about the Marquis de Sade running club, in which the participant denies having an affair with Clinton. Simply tracking her down took enormous effort, since she had subsequently married and changed her name. And in those days, before Clinton's sex life was a staple of every talk show in America, it wasn't easy to call a total stranger and ask point-blank if she'd had an affair with the president. But she took the question with evident good humor.

Anecdotes may also be widely separated in both time and space within a story, especially when they are used to show character development. As I mentioned earlier in discussing plot, a character who changes over time, and in response to specific events, is an important vehicle for storytelling. In the chapter on description, for example, I included a passage in which Susan McDougal noticed changes in Hillary Clinton: that she had changed her name, started using makeup, and wore more attractive clothes. Much later, both chronologically and within the book—109 pages later, to be precise—another anecdote appears that explores the issue of image and reality with respect to Hillary Clinton. This is my account of a widely reported incident from the 1992 campaign:

> The next morning, Bill and Hillary, campaigning in Illinois, dropped in at the Busy Bee restaurant in Chicago. NBC reporter Andrea Mitchell, after getting Bill's approval to ask Hillary a question, plunged into the propriety of Hillary's representing

Madison before a state agency. Hillary's famously acid wit immediately surfaced. "I suppose I could have stayed home and baked
cookies, and had teas," she retorted. Off-camera, campaign strat-
egist Paul Begala quickly intervened, urging Hillary to soften the
comment. "I'm going to say what I feel," she insisted. "That's all
there is to it." That flash of candor proved short-lived. As a result,
enormous efforts were expended to reposition Hillary as more
of a traditional wife and mother. She even participated in a
"bake-off" with Barbara Bush, organized by *Family Circle* magazine.

In other words, the "real" Hillary, by her own admission,
would not have been home baking cookies. Once Hillary has
been "repositioned," can anything she says really be trusted? This
anecdote and the others like it prepared readers for a much later
scene in the book, when Hillary is asked about her extraordinary
success at trading cattle futures. Her press secretary explained
that Hillary had made her own trading decisions after "reading
The Wall Street Journal." After noting the press frenzy triggered
by the revelation of her profits, I wrote:

> No claim was more pilloried than the insistence that Hillary
> had made the decisions herself after consulting friends and read-
> ing *The Wall Street Journal.* The *Journal* looked in its archives,
> and produced a compendium of commodities stories that had
> run in the paper during the period of Hillary's trading. It was
> obvious that they would have been of scant value to any trader.
> Ultimately, in an impromptu news conference nearly a month
> after the story appeared—a press conference from which
> [*Times* reporter Jeff] Gerth was banned—the first lady backed
> off the claim, acknowledging that it was [Tyson Foods's lawyer
> Jim] Blair who had guided her trading.

Then I introduced an entirely different though thematically
related anecdote:

> Some weeks later, Gerth asked a White House official in-
> volved why he'd been given such a preposterous explanation
> in the first place. The official paused. "The first instinct from
> everybody from Arkansas," he said, "is to lie."

Note that this anecdote takes place outside the main chronology, at an indeterminate time "some weeks later." The identity of the White House official isn't disclosed, though I knew who he was and had used the name in my original draft. When I questioned him about the remark, he confirmed it, but asked that I delete his name. I was under no obligation to do so; but I admired his candor in acknowledging the remark, and I readily recognized that the repercussions in a White House obsessed with loyalty and leaks would have been dire. I did delete his name. This official not only continued in his job but, so far as I can tell, has maintained his integrity through subsequent trying times.

The evolution of Hillary Clinton, a woman seemingly torn between the creaking Victorian tradition of the political wife and the postfeminist model of equality and independence, a woman who aspired to be a modern-day Eleanor Roosevelt but emerged instead as a humiliated figurehead, is one of the great tragic stories of our time. To my mind, the sequence of anecdotes about Hillary Clinton showed the transformation of a candid, principled young woman willing to defy convention into a political professional hardened by the quest for power. But I let the anecdotes speak for themselves. It was for readers to make up their own minds about what they revealed about Hillary Clinton. At one point I did ask a high-level official why the Clintons seemed to have lied about so many incidents, many of them trivial. I said I was baffled. He looked at me with a blank stare, as if wondering on what planet I lived. "They're the president. You're not," he replied, contempt for my naïveté evident in his voice.

11
HUMOR AND PATHOS

WHEN STORIES are well told, and readers absorb what they read as though they were experiencing the events themselves, the stories engage the emotions as well as the mind. I find there is only one achievement greater than making readers laugh, and that is making them cry.

Since succumbing at a tender age to the death of Blitz the Wonder Horse's mother, I have wept many times over stories I have read, though not so often that I cannot remember nearly every instance. While I was Page One editor at *The Wall Street Journal*, I worked at a desk in a low cubicle that was open to my editing staff and the newsroom, so when I was overcome by a story, it was embarrassingly obvious. When reporter Judy Valente turned in the story about the father whose son died of AIDS, and I read it for the first time, I put my head down and wept, prompting worried inquiries from my colleagues. I have my students read this story, and last semester I was reviewing it on the subway en route to my class. Though I have read it many times, I still had to brush away tears.

I have also laughed out loud even more often, occasionally so hard that I have had to wipe my eyes. One of the funniest reporters during my years at *The Wall Street Journal* was Lee Berton, who wrote about the accounting profession, of all things. He wrote a middle-column front-page story about a man who memorized the entire Iliad—in Greek—and would recite the four-hour epic at the slightest suggestion. I was doubled over at my desk. Such experiences always remind me how closely related to pathos is humor.

It goes without saying that comedy is popular, given the proliferation of comedy channels, comedy clubs, comedy stars, and comic talk shows, not to mention TV sitcoms. While sitting through a screening of *Titanic* recently, listening to the sobs emanating from all quarters around me, I was struck by how much people also like to cry. People seem hungry for emotion. Yet so much writing seems almost deliberately distancing; it drains material that is inherently funny or moving of any emotional content, substituting arid analysis and commentary.

In my view, any well-written nonfiction story can and should engage the emotions. In even the most serious of topics, there is usually room for a leavening touch of humor, and the contrast helps heighten the story's impact. Pathos, too, can emerge in the unlikeliest settings, and can be all the more effective for being unexpected. This doesn't mean that material has to be thigh-slapping hilarious, or tear-jerking sorrowful. More often, humor and pathos are subtle, growing naturally out of the events being described.

Recognizing humorous or moving material can be even more difficult than spotting an entertaining anecdote, since humor and pathos are highly subjective. Equally discouraging is the way most journalists are trained, which is to distrust their own feelings in the quest for objectivity. Sources themselves often indicate their emotions in interviews, especially when they find something funny. Yet the most important clue to the emotional content of a story or incident is the writer's own reaction and emotions, since it is difficult for even highly self-aware sources to recognize the humor and pathos in their own stories. These are easier to see in the experiences of others. My students seem to be startled when I say this, but one's own emotions need to be encouraged and cultivated, especially in a society which still seems to encourage emotional repression, especially in public. I will confess that I have laughed and wept at passages in my own work, and I consider that a good indication that someone else might be similarly moved.

I have wrestled over the years with whether humor and pathos are subjects that can be taught. They are unquestionably subjective, even idiosyncratic experiences. Events that some find uproarious often leave me scratching my head, wondering what was so funny. Yet what is funny or moving must have some common elements, and I have been encouraged by results in my class. That said, I can add with some confidence that it is almost impossible to predict who will prove to have the ability to convey humor or pathos, or in whom it seems possible to cultivate it. Some of the funniest writers I know first struck me as humorless, and I have also known engaging raconteurs who fall flat on the page. One reporter at *The Wall Street Journal* was actually an amateur stand-up comic who performed in comedy clubs. She was also a good writer, but not a funny one, perhaps because she tried too hard. Some of the funniest writers I have worked with seem so oblivious to the effect of their writing that I'm not even sure they themselves find it funny. What I find most funny and moving rarely feels forced or contrived.

Classic one-liners and jokes aside, humor and pathos are usually situational. While it is difficult to generalize, certain situations do seem generically rich in comic potential, and are staples of comedy. These include anything that is absurd; pratfalls of all kinds; and misunderstandings, such as confused identities. The humor in these situations often derives from the fact that the audience is omniscient, but the characters are not. (To cite just one of innumerable examples, the classic episode of *I Love Lucy* in which Lucy is employed at a candy factory where the conveyor belt speeds up depends on the viewer recognizing what is happening to the conveyor belt while Lucy remains hilariously unaware of it.) The reason the absurd lends itself to comedy is usually that the character doesn't recognize the absurdity; it requires superior knowledge on the part of the audience. In the story about the Iliad, it was plain to readers that the central figure was excruciatingly boring, yet he remained oblivious. So, too, the pratfall: we see the banana peel, but the victim does not.

Topical humor, the staple of one-liners and other jokes, derives from much the same principle: it usually requires the listener to add information that is common knowledge. The spate of jokes about Monica Lewinsky, for example, requires some knowledge of recent events in the White House. For this reason, topical humor, however funny at the moment, rarely has a long shelf life. Shakespeare's comedies remain funny because the knowledge they require isn't topical, but is rooted in enduring qualities of human nature.

The writer of such material must scrupulously maintain the character's point of view. The writer's superior knowledge must never be projected onto a character. This requires, in my view, a tone of empathy rather than ridicule, of kindness rather than cruelty. I stress this to my students, some of whom seem to have been raised to believe that a joke can only come at someone's expense. The current popularity of mean-spirited comics baffles me, but I suspect their appeal derives less from humor than from shock and resentment. I recall a *Journal* story by Claire Ansberry about a man's fixation on growing the world's largest hog. The lengths to which he went, not to mention the end in itself, were absurd. But what made the story so memorable to me was the man's obvious affection for his pig. Written from his point of view, in a tone that was itself affectionate, the story was funny and curiously touching.

I have considered but ultimately rejected the notion that some subjects are inherently funnier than others, but people—usually people other than ourselves—are what we find funny. That said, a disproportionate number of amusing stories seem to be about pets and their owners (the *Journal* received more letters about a humorous story on Dalmatians than about any other story while I was front-page editor); about petty feuds taken to absurd lengths; about misunderstandings between the sexes; about regional rivalries; about odd obsessions; about class divisions, especially if they involve minor aristocrats who take themselves too seriously.

In my experience, stories about the mentally ill and physically disabled are almost never funny. Such stories (which are attempted more often than one might suspect) usually seem cruel. They are also dull, because the explanation for seemingly bizarre behavior usually lies not in a quirk of human nature, but in a pathological condition, which quickly becomes evident and drains the story of any suspense.

As with any other kind of writing, people develop their own styles for comedy and pathos. I would describe my own as deadpan; I try to rely entirely on the reader to extract any comedy or other emotional potential. This was my approach to the story about Jim Wilcox. Jim himself is a comic writer, who uses a similar approach, and one of my goals in writing the story was to capture some of his style. Here is a passage in which I describe meeting Jim at a dinner party given by Amanda Urban, who is both Jim's literary agent and mine.

> "Sort of Rich" is one of my favorite books. I bought it after reading a Times review, found something to think about on almost every page ("The twenty-four chicks Mrs. Dambar had purchased last week had dwindled to three as a result of an unpleasant disease and six or so getting lost on a walk she had taken them on to strengthen their leg muscles"), and returned to the bookstore a week later to buy another copy, as a gift. It was no longer in stock and wasn't being reordered—a situation that may help explain why it ultimately sold just forty-seven hundred copies in hardcover. Jim himself, I must confess, made less of an impression on me at Urban's dinner. Besides being overshadowed that night by last year's playoff between the Knicks and the Bulls, he was characteristically shy. We barely spoke.

Jim is an example of the kind of writer I described earlier, someone who, on first meeting, I would never have guessed could be so funny. I introduced the brief excerpt from *Sort of Rich* by saying I found "something to think about on almost every page." I didn't say that I found something to *laugh* at on every page, preferring to let readers digest the import of the passage, even though I do find it funny. It is even more true of humorous passages than of anecdotes in general that if you have to explain them, they are pointless. But for our purposes, let's examine the passage I quoted from Jim's novel.

Why is it funny? Because it is absurd. That Mrs. Dambar, who has moved to the fictional Tula Springs, Louisiana, from New York, would be purchasing live chicks at all is a prescription for disaster, as is readily apparent to the reader but not, of course, to Mrs. Dambar herself. Disaster has predictably struck, in the forms of an "unpleasant" disease and Mrs. Dambar's hiking expedition. Mrs. Dambar plainly doesn't know what disease felled the chicks, only that it was "unpleasant." This suggests that not only is she no veterinarian, but that she is squeamish, a quality ill-suited to poultry farming. The unexpected and preposterous detail that she is also trying to strengthen the chickens' legs adds to the humor. Readers know this is ridiculous, but the well-intentioned Mrs. Dambar plainly does not. None of this, of course, needs to be made explicit, nor should it be.

The circumstances of my meeting Jim were not particularly funny, but I included the seemingly irrelevant detail that the Knicks and Bulls were in a playoff that same night. Why? It seemed peculiarly fitting that on the night of Jim's book party, when he should by all rights have been the center of attention and allowed to bask in his accomplishment, everyone was in fact more interested in a basketball game.

Later in my story, I describe Jim's success at getting his first story published in *The New Yorker.* "Mr. Ray" appeared in the January 26, 1981, issue.

> "The old woman had worked hard on the 'No Smoking' sign, embellishing the stark black letters with ivy and birds and a dog she forgot to put the tail on," it began. Being published in *The New Yorker* was a milestone for Wilcox—an affirmation of sorts —and he happily sent a copy of the magazine home to his parents. But the piece didn't exactly cause a stir in Hammond, Louisiana. "Jimmy sure has good punctuation" was one neighbor's only comment. Another, pointing to an unrelated cartoon on one page, asked, "Where did Jimmy learn to draw like that?"

Like many of the characters in Jim's works, the old woman in "Mr. Ray" has trouble confronting reality, in this case the unpleasantness of commanding someone not to smoke. So she "embellishes" the message with ivy and birds. This is absurd in itself, but the gentle humor is heightened by her absent-minded failure to put a tail on the dog. We are immediately brought into a world where appearances both distort daily life and assuage its harshness, where things are somewhat askew. These qualities are lost on the people in Jim's real hometown, who respond to publication of the story with devastating, if polite and well-intentioned, misunderstanding. Their reaction is funny, but it teeters on the verge of sadness. It also mirrors the reactions of the characters in Jim's books and stories, who are often polite but befuddled, and suggests how Jim might have come about his own comic yet semi-tragic sensibility.

These qualities surface again in an excerpt I included from Jim's first, and highly acclaimed, comic novel, *Modern Baptists*. The main characters in *Modern Baptists* are Bobby Pickens (always known as Mr. Pickens), a forty-one-year-old bachelor who works at the Sonny Boy Bargain Store, and F.X., his improbably handsome half-brother, who has just been released from Angola State Penitentiary after serving time for dealing cocaine at a nearby dinner-theater-in-the-round.

At one point, Mr. Pickens, who has fallen in love with a young employee at the Bargain Store named Toinette Quaid, aspires to the cloth:

> Mr. Pickens knew that once he got his preaching diplomas, he would open a church for modern Baptists, Baptists who were sick to death of hell and sin being stuffed down their gullets every Sunday. There wasn't going to be any of that old-fashioned ranting and raving in Mr. Pickens's church. *His* Baptist church would be guided by reason and logic. Everyone could drink in moderation. Everyone could dance and pet as long as they were fifteen—well, maybe sixteen or seventeen. At thirty, if you still weren't married, you could sleep with someone and it wouldn't be a sin—that is, as long as you loved that person. If you hit forty and were still single, you'd be eligible for adultery not being a sin, as long as no children's feelings got hurt and it was kept very discreet. But you still had to love and respect the person; you couldn't just do it for sex.

Humor doesn't have to be extended, even to the length of a short anecdote. Single word choices can be funny. I chuckled that Mr. Pickens works at the "Sonny Boy Bargain Store." Why is "Sonny Boy" funny? Because it is folksy and disarming, Sonny Boy being a Southern and rural generic nickname. You're not going to find a Sonny Boy on Park Avenue. Toinette is a funny name, too, both idiosyncratic and descriptive. That I wrote Mr. Pickens "aspires to the cloth," a deliberately archaic and mannered phrase, suggests this quest shouldn't be taken too seriously.

Let's consider for a moment the situation in *Modern Baptists:* F.X. has been arrested for dealing cocaine at a theater-in-the-round, and Mr. Pickens is pondering donning the cloth and re-forming the Baptist church. What's funny about this? To begin, a dinner-theater-in-the-round somewhere in Louisiana is pretty absurd in and of itself, conjuring up images of sedate theatergoers who need food, along with other gimmicks, to coax them into the theater. Yet in this highly improbable venue, F.X. has been caught dealing cocaine. Juxtaposed against this moral lapse is Mr. Pickens, who is trying to impose "reason and logic" on the Baptist church. The absurdity of this quest becomes almost immediately apparent, as Mr. Pickens modifies his own rules almost as fast as he imposes them. Yet there is a poignancy about Mr. Pickens, who is so obviously still searching for love at an advanced age.

This becomes more evident in the next passage I quoted. Upon being spurned by Toinette Mr. Pickens finds himself alone with Toinette's chunky friend Burma LaSteele.

> He stood before her in his new orange bikini briefs and his matching orange undershirt. His belly button was plainly visible; the underwear was two sizes too small.
>
> "Why pretend?" Mr. Pickens said, pulling the T-shirt over his head. His white hairless chest swelled out into a sizable belly, from which Burma averted her eyes. . . .
>
> "Mr. Pickens," Burma said, turning away. "Please, get dressed. You're drunk."
>
> "This is your chance, Burma. Why blow it? You're getting old—there's gray in your hair, gray in mine. We're going to die, all of us, we're going to die miserable, unloved. I can't stand it anymore. At least one of us can be happy. You, Burma. You be happy. You deserve it more than any of us. You're good, Burma. You're a good, good woman. I can see your heart. It's pure and unselfish and good." Tears ran down his cheeks and his nose began to run. "Take it. Grab life before it passes you by." He stepped out of the briefs, and she beheld him stark naked, except for his left sock, the one with the hole in it, which he had forgotten to take off.

This passage veers wildly between comedy and pathos. That Mr. Pickens would be wearing orange underwear is absurdly misguided, as is the fact that he forgot to take off a sock with a hole in it. We readily recognize that Mr. Pickens looks ridiculous. That he would persist in his attempted seduction when Burma is so plainly unattracted to him is something that we also readily recognize, but Mr. Pickens does not. But his admonition to "grab life" is heartfelt and poignant. We recognize, though he may not, that he is speaking not so much about Burma as about himself. He is the one who wants and deserves to be happy. He is so moved that he himself weeps and his nose runs, which underscores the emotion inherent in the scene and is itself a funny image, given the lengths to which he has gone to make himself alluring.

In keeping with my attempt to write the profile of Jim in a style consistent with his own writing, I included an incident that actually befell Jim and that also veers between comedy and pathos:

> Wilcox's world view may have been reinforced one evening soon after he put the finishing touches on [his second novel, "Miss Undine's Living Room"]. At a dinner party he attended, he bit into a piece of chicken and broke off a crown from a tooth. As he was walking home, castigating himself for going to a cut-rate dental clinic (his "dentist," actually a student, had received a failing grade for the crown installation), an attractive couple, walking arm in arm, approached him. They told him they had a weapon, then mugged him. In addition to his cash and credit cards, they stole his crown, which he'd carefully kept in his pocket. The new crown set him back eight hundred dollars.

I find Jim's books very funny, and galleys of his most recent, *Plain and Normal,* had me laughing so hard on a recent plane trip that I had to wipe my eyes. I attracted puzzled stares and amused glances from my fellow passengers. On visits to my class to discuss his writing, Jim demonstrates convincingly that he understands the purpose of every word he uses. Comedy and pathos do not simply emerge effortlessly from his pen because he is innately funny or emotional. He understands how closely related humor and pathos are, and how effectively even the weightiest themes can be explored within the genre of comedy. I hope my profile of him did his work justice. I was gratified that numerous readers wrote to me after the story was published to say not that the story was funny, as I might have expected, but that it had moved them to tears.

The Wilcox story, given that it was a profile of a comic novelist, contained more overt humor than do most of my stories.

But I try never to miss an opportunity to inject something that, if not out-and-out funny, at least lightens the tone and helps put more serious events in perspective. In theater, such passages are usually referred to as comic relief, and they not only provide welcome contrast but also help underscore the seriousness of other material.

The *New York Times* reporter Sara Rimer contributed some light moments to my otherwise serious story about the flood:

> The *Times* reporter Sara Rimer, thirty-nine years old, outgoing and vivacious, quickly became a popular figure around town. Though she had never been to a levee, people admired her eagerness to learn, her thoroughness, and her accuracy. "I wanted the reporters to go away feeling they'd done more than just report, and I think Sara Rimer did," Nall says. "I respect her a lot. She got behind the tragedy and went for the human interest." Rimer also created some merriment at the Sny levee, which she visited, asking House at one point, "That Mr. Crim, he looks so powerful. Does he lift weights?" For the rest of the week, levee workers, convulsed by the idea that a farmer would lift weights, were ribbing Crim, asking him, in a mincing voice, "Do you lift weights?"
>
> Rimer says she knew Crim's strength didn't come from the gym. "What I was struck by is that all the people in New York are pumping iron even though they push paper and answer phones. I don't want to put down New York men, but these were larger-than-life men. They were also such gentlemen. They'd carry you over a mudhole." Rimer, who is single, and the twice-divorced sheriff seemed to get along so well—he brought her a taste of some homemade deer sausages and met her at the Green Parrot—that some of the farmers on the levee speculated that they'd make a good match.

I must confess that I never found the weight-lifting anecdote as hilarious as did Crim and his friends, who were convulsed while telling it to me. And the story would have been funnier, in my view, if I didn't have to include Rimer's explanation—it comes perilously close to "explaining" the anecdote, which is forbidden, as I've said. Still, the incident provided a welcome diversion from the mounting tension of the story.

The Sheinberg insider-trading story, too, had its comic moments. Here is the scene where Jonathan; his estranged wife, Maria; their daughter, Thea; Maria's boyfriend, Barry Fogel; and Jonathan's girlfriend, Susan, gather to discuss trading MCA stock (I found the cast of characters itself both amusing and highly revealing of the prevailing mores in Hollywood):

> When Maria and Barry picked up Thea that evening, they joined Jonathan and Susan at his home, in Venice Beach, to refine their strategy. For obvious reasons, Jonathan and Fogel weren't close friends, but they knew each other reasonably well. As boys, they played on the same Little League team in Beverly Hills, and on Halloween, 1989, several months after Fogel started dating Maria, they had all had dinner together and had taken Thea trick-or-treating. En route to Jonathan's that evening, Fogel called his mother from his car phone to borrow money; he says he didn't tell her what the money was for. At about eight-thirty, he and Maria and their dog joined Jonathan, Susan, Thea, and their dog. The dogs promptly had a set-to, running around and barking. Maria and Susan came in and out of the conversation, sometimes leaving to play with Thea or, in Susan's case, to study for a test she had to take the next day in one of her fashion classes.

This is high-level insider trading? With dogs and lovers and spouses and children on the scene? With Fogel having to borrow money from his mother, over his car phone? None of these details is strictly relevant to whether anyone was guilty of insider trading. But they were useful, I thought, to convey the peculiar, almost surreal atmosphere in which this alleged crime took place.

Not many would associate the Whitewater scandal with anything amusing, but in *Blood Sport,* members of the press sometimes provided comic relief. Here, for example, is a passage describing the transformation of tiny Flippin, Arkansas, as the national press corps descended:

> Ever since Flippin, Arkansas, was founded in the late nineteenth century, a highlight of the year has been the annual Turkey Trot just before Thanksgiving. Originally, wild turkeys had been dropped from the courthouse roof as local citizens scrambled to catch one for their Thanksgiving dinner, but since World

War II the turkeys had been dropped from a low-flying plane. Accompanied by the crowning of Miss Drumstick—in those years when there are enough teenage girls to serve as contestants—the Turkey Trot was something of a homecoming, where Flippin natives could count on meeting just about everyone in the county. It was the town's main claim to fame, as people put it—at least until 1994, when the national press descended.

The media calls had started in November, but it was only in January, after the revelations of the files removed from Foster's office and the calls for the special counsel, that the town found itself inundated by representatives of the media. The media activity was so intense that news organizations sent reporters who had no idea what the story would be—they were simply under orders to send something back. *The New York Times* alone had sent three reporters to Flippin—Michael Kelly and Engelberg, now followed by Gerth. They and other reporters settled in at the Red Raven Inn, a large Victorian house with seven guest rooms, and other area motels and guest houses. Usually occupied only intermittently by smallmouth-bass fishermen headed for the White River, the Red Raven was now fully booked, two reporters per room. They made the trek between the inn and the local courthouse, returning with armloads of documents. One evening Gerth entertained everyone with a medley of Gershwin tunes on the piano.

Business boomed at the nearby Front Porch restaurant, where crews from as far away as Europe, China, and Japan, along with their translators, dined on the all-you-can-eat $4.95 Bar-B-Q buffet. Local entrepreneurs cashed in by offering guided tours of the hard-to-find Whitewater property for $50.

One morning Chris Wade walked into his modest real estate office and found reporters from CBS, CNN, *Time,* a St. Louis paper, and a Japanese network waiting for him. "Take a number," he told them, adding, "This isn't where the story is. This is just a bunch of land." But with all the media attention, he dreamed up a scheme to capitalize on the remaining lots he owned. He took one of the least desirable of the undeveloped Whitewater lots and began selling "dirt deeds"—ownership of one cubic foot—for $19.95. Little Rock radio station 103.7 K-ROCK launched a contest in which listeners could win the dirt deeds, complete with the signatures of Jim and Susan McDougal. Wade got over fifty requests for interviews and was suddenly featured on radio call-in shows and articles. McDougal himself appeared on *Larry King Live* and plugged the deeds, leading to hundreds of sales. Some deed buyers drove cross-country to Flippin to have Wade take their picture digging up their foot of dirt at the Whitewater property.

At the courthouse, county clerk Mary Jo Layton and her three assistants were swamped with reporters' requests, but they welcomed the diversion from looking up marriage records, which usually took up most of their time. All the real estate records, dating to 1887, when a fire had destroyed the old courthouse, were kept in a vault; a computer had only been recently introduced to coordinate driver's licenses with voter registrations. When she realized how much interest there was in Whitewater, Layton brought a rock from the Whitewater property, painted "Whitewater" on its side, and used it as a paperweight in the office. She thought she might sell a few, but found no takers.

Despite the media attention, Layton was at a loss to figure out what was so interesting in the Whitewater records, which she'd looked over many times herself. Finally she asked a reporter, "What are you all thinking you're going to find?"

"Well," the reporter replied, "if that Madison Bank up in Huntsville, if they were defrauding people and the government, then that's important."

"Oh well, whatever." Layton shrugged.

Flippin's population was solidly pro-Clinton, proud of a native son who owned land nearby, Layton, like many residents, had actually met Clinton, and she liked him. Still, local residents welcomed the media folk with open arms; they were slow to connect them with stories that were not only damaging to the president, but conveyed a distinctly negative impression of Flippin and Arkansas. The Red Raven's owner, Cam Semelsberger, was delighted by all the excitement. Cam's husband loved discussing national issues with the visiting Washington press corps. He was keenly interested in the proposed health care legislation, and had obtained copies of the competing plans, including the first lady's massive reform proposal. After a lively debate between Semelsberger and the local pharmacist, *Times* reporter Michael Kelly joked that people in Washington rarely talked about big policy issues. "We only talk about gossip," he told Semelsberger.

At the even more remote Whitewater development itself, John and Marilyn Lauramoore lived in the modest modular home now known nationwide as the Hillary house. He built log homes for a living, and she sewed sails at a nearby sailboat factory.

They'd moved to Whitewater to get away from the "stress" of Atlanta, and they liked the quiet, remote location. Still, they were initially flattered by reporters wanting to take pictures of them in front of their home. But more and more reporters and TV crews started appearing on the doorstep, often demanding answers to questions having to do with Whitewater's financing. The Lauramoores knew nothing about it, but they felt the reporters acted like they were hiding something. Worse, at least one helicopter a day was making a low pass over their house, whipping up a fierce wind and droning like something out of war movies like *Apocalypse Now.* (It was on the Lauramoores' lawn that Bossie and Silverman had been forced to land their helicopter.) Tourists, complete strangers, started pulling in to their driveway. The Lauramoores finally strung up a six-by-ten-foot canvas banner on which they painted the message "Go home, idiots!"

The press interest becomes so self-referential that Whitewater itself is all but forgotten, and the visiting press corps never seems to perceive the absurdity of the situation. And that aside, I never fail to be amused that the town nearest to land involved in an allegedly fraudulent deal is actually named Flippin.

In *Den of Thieves,* the character of Dennis Levine often seemed to provide comic relief. This isn't to say that Levine wasn't guilty of serious crimes—his arrest for insider trading triggered the scandal leading to the arrest of Ivan Boesky and the indictment of Michael Milken—but his behavior often bordered on the absurd, though he never seemed to be aware of that. I hadn't actually thought of him as a comic character, but I was struck and delighted by how many early readers of the manuscript found themselves laughing over passages such as this, in which Levine tells his co-conspirator Bob Wilkis about his arrest:

Pleading illness, Wilkis left Omaha and flew back to New York the next day. He immediately phoned Levine, who had been arraigned, pleaded not guilty, and posted $5 million in bail that morning. He had put up $100,000 in cash and pledged his apartment and shares of Drexel.

"You'd better come right over," Levine said.

Wilkis took a cab over to Levine's apartment. Laurie [Levine's wife] answered the door, looking as though she hadn't slept, her eyes red and swollen from crying. In contrast, Levine was casually dressed in athletic clothes and seemed cheerful, even excited.

"Jesus, Bob, can you imagine? They threw me in jail. Christ, I had notes and my phone book with Ivan Boesky's name all over it! I had nine hundred bucks in my pocket." But Levine was already hatching a plan.

"You'll get a lawyer in the Cayman Islands to claim he owns the account," Levine began, but Wilkis wasn't paying attention.

"It's too late, Dennis," he pleaded. "Don't you realize this? It's over."

Wilkis spent a tortured week, unable to sleep, unable to concentrate at work, not eating. He told his wife nothing about his own involvement, but she knew how close he was to Levine. She insisted he contact a lawyer, and Wilkis called a cousin at one of Baltimore's leading firms, Piper & Marbury. He didn't tell the whole truth, admitting only that he had had vague "dealings" with Levine that worried him. The cousin arranged for him to see a lawyer in New York on Tuesday.

Meanwhile, against his better judgment, Wilkis agreed to meet Levine again on Monday. To make sure they weren't bugged, they met at the garage on West 56th Street where Wilkis kept his car. They got in the car and drove aimlessly. Wilkis was so petrified that he'd be stopped by police that he barely drove 15 miles per hour.

"You look terrible," Levine began cheerfully. "Here I'm the one who's been in jail and you're the one who looks bad. None of this matters," he continued. "It doesn't matter as long as you're famous." He was impressed that *The Wall Street Journal* had run a front-page story on him, complete with an artist's drawing, the previous Thursday. He told Wilkis to pull over to the curb by a corner newstand, and hopped out of the car.

"I hear I'm on the cover of *Newsweek*," he said, and moments later returned brandishing the latest issue. But he was disappointed. He was featured in the cover story, headlined "Greed on Wall Street," but the illustration showed hands grabbing at a pile of money—not Levine. Levine's picture was deep inside the magazine.

"I'm ready to turn myself in," Wilkis said once Levine had finished with the magazine. "What do they know?"

"I don't know," Levine said.

"Has my name come up?"

Levine again said he had no idea, adding, "Don't get a lawyer. I've got the greatest lawyers in the world and we're going to fight it. I'm sealed up like a tomb." Levine continued, "If I talked, the Russian would put a bullet through my head. Now you, you couldn't handle this. You'd snap. But not me, I'm a stand-up kind of guy.

Then Levine unveiled a new plan. Levine would confess, and implicate Wilkis as a source of some of the information. But he'd conceal the fact that Wilkis traded on inside information in his own foreign bank account. "We'll go to jail. It will be one of those country-club prisons. We'll be roommates, we'll play tenniss, and get a tan. Then we'll retire to the Cayman Islands, and live off of your money," Levine said.

"Dennis, where does this lead?" Wilkis asked in despair.

That Levine, under arrest, would be worrying about whether his picture made the cover of *Newsweek* strikes most readers as absurd, as it did me. Like all good anecdotes, humorous anecdotes often convey a great deal of description. Levine's reaction to his own arrest spoke tellingly of his ability to self-dramatize, and to his ability to divorce himself from reality. Meanwhile, the inherent pathos in the situation quickly emerged as I shifted the point of view from Levine, who was oblivious to his plight, to Wilkis, who was only too self-aware:

The next day, Wilkis broke down with the lawyer recommended by his cousin, confessing his crimes. "I don't want to fight," Wilkis said. The lawyer promptly referred him to a criminal lawyer, Gary Naftalis, a former assistant U.S. attorney and a partner at the New York firm Kramer, Levin, Nessen, Kamin & Frankel. Wilkis told Naftalis the whole story, sobbing periodically, including details of his own account and his recruitment of Randall Cecola. Naftalis sternly ordered Wilkis never to talk to either Levine or Cecola again.

After so many years, however, Levine's hold couldn't be so easily broken. When Levine called soon after, Wilkis took the call, though he tried to resist.

"Dennis, it's not good to talk," he said, but Levine pressed on with more plans for their eventual escape to the Cayman Island. Wilkis cut him off.

"The newspapers are focusing on the cover-up. They're acting like that's worse than the trading. I won't get involved. I'm never going to talk to you again."

Levine seemed stunned and hurt by Wilkis's reaction. "Oh Bob," he said, "you mean after everything we've been through, this is it?"

Yet Wilkis called Levine on Memorial Day, and again the following Friday, telling him he just wanted to see how he was doing.

"I'm holding up," Levine said, but his spirits seemed to be waning. He seemed near despair, asking Wilkis to take care of his wife if he went to prison. He was especially emotional on Friday.

"I love you like a brother," he told Wilkis repeatedly. "I'll be ruined financially," he continued. "I don't give a fuck about the business. I've done all the big deals, fuck them. But I'm ruined. I won't see my son's bar mitzvah." For the first time in his contacts with Wilkis, Levine seemed near tears.

Wilkis told Naftalis nothing of his exchanges with Levine, nor of another phone call. Two days after Levine's arrest, Wilkis had heard from Cecola, the Lazard associate he'd recruited into the ring. "Do we have anything to worry about?" an anxious Cecola wanted to know.

"I do," Wilkis replied. "My life is probably over. But I'll protect you." Cecola said he was going to be in New York soon, since he'd be working that summer at Dillon, Read; Wilkis promised they'd get together.

Cecola arrived on June 4. Wilkis attended what was supposed to be a festive dinner for Hutton's M&A department, but couldn't eat. Already thin from jogging, he'd lost 15 pounds since Levine's arrest, and he looked emaciated. He'd begun seeing a therapist. As soon as he could get away, he left and took a cab to a restaurant at 77th Street and Broadway, where he met Cecola. The two walked east into Central Park, where they'd be shielded by the darkness.

"Do I have to worry?" Cecola asked anxiously.

"Dennis Levine knows who you are," Wilkis said ominously.

"But they can't prove anything, can they?" Cecola asked. "You'll cover for me, won't you?"

"Randy, my life is over," Wilkis said wearily. "I hope you don't get involved in this, but I won't lie. I can't commit perjury."

Cecola paused. "You could position the truth," he said.

"Randy, it wouldn't do any good. Levine knows all about you."

"Look," Cecola said, "if you deny what he says, and I do, it's two against one."

"I'm sorry, I won't lie," Wilkis insisted. The two trudged in despair out of the park.

The next day was the last day of classes at The Brearley

School, and Wilkis's daughter, Alexandra, an exceptionally talented young pianist, was being honored at an assembly. When he arrived at the auditorium, Wilkis realized suddenly that he couldn't take his place among the other parents. Instead, he stood at the back. As the program began, he began to cry. Through his tears he could see his daughter, glowing with excitement at the school year's end, a picture of innocence. Now he was going to ruin her young life. He fled from the room.

As in the passage from *Modern Baptists,* the pathos of the situation is signaled by the fact that a character involved in it is crying. While this can effectively indicate the emotional content of a scene, it alone can't be expected to induce tears in readers unless they identify with and share the character's concerns. Michael Milken sobbed during his guilty plea, as he apologized and said, "I have hurt those who are closest to me." While I assume that most readers would feel compassion for his plight, I doubt that many shed tears of their own.

Just as it is hard to generalize about what is funny, it is hard to do so about what is sad, or moving, or poignant. Relatively few events, even death, or loss, or something that induces tears in a character, are in and of themselves moving. Few people burst into tears over news reports of mass killings in Africa or Bosnia. But when those events are personalized, as when we see the faces of suffering children, our emotions may be engaged. Death in a noble cause often moves us; the loss of something beautiful and irreplaceable may; and viewers may readily weep along with a character experiencing such events. Great joy and beauty may as readily prompt tears as tragedy does.

Some have hypothesized that the ability to empathize is what makes us fully human. Certainly the capacity for such feelings is deeply rooted in human nature. The ability to experience such emotions must be elicited from readers, not manipulated. For that reason I find that pathos lends itself less well to the short anecdote; it often needs to be developed over the entire length of a story or book, sometimes emerging fully only at the end. If comedy often arises out of a character's lack of self-awareness, pathos often seems to come from self-awareness, which can be established by describing someone's thoughts and words. Establishing this awareness is necessary to present a character's behavior as noble or courageous or heroic.

Last summer I happened to visit the battlefield at Gettysburg, and was struck by how somber visitors became, with some weeping openly at the narration of the doomed charge by the Confederate forces. What rendered the Confederates' behavior almost unbearably poignant was their heroism in the face of what they knew would be almost certain death. People weep at the Vietnam Memorial in Washington, another monument to death in what proved a doomed cause, with just the names of the dead listed "in the order they were taken from us." I found the film *Schindler's List* incredibly powerful, and I don't think there was a dry eye in the audience. Schindler, the main character, knew the fate of those he was trying to save, and the risks he undertook to do so. Yet millions perished.

Fortunately we do not often face the need to write about war or mass tragedy. But I have discovered and tried to convey courage and integrity in the face of hardship and adversity in almost every story I've written, and many readers have written and told me that they were moved. In ways large and small, what is noble about the human spirit emerges frequently, and often in unlikely places: a factory floor in Detroit; an accounting office in Pennsylvania; a muddy levee on the Mississippi; a small town in Missouri, where a father grieves for his son. I weep in the story about the father whose son died of AIDS not because the son contracted AIDS and died, but because in the face of the son's illness the father was able to surmount prejudice and find love.

12
ENDINGS

AFTER THE LEAD, the ending is the most important part of a story. If the lead provides the first impression necessary to propel readers through a story, the ending provides the last. What is freshest in readers' minds is what they read most recently, which is the ending. The ending will often determine whether readers talk about a story or book and whether they recommend it to others. Good stories have the potential to enter the popular consciousness and become the subject of national conversations—if they have effective endings.

I spend more time on endings than on anything else but leads. This, of course, stands traditional journalism on its head: the pyramid style dispenses with endings, simply taking a cleaver to make a story fit the allotted space. This assumes that most readers will never reach the end anyway—and, given the conventions of the pyramid style, in which everything of interest has been crammed into the top of a story, that assumption is surely justified.

Many writers I know experience some fatigue as they approach the endings of their stories, which is understandable. I find it is sometimes helpful to pause, to take a night off, and then return to my draft with a fresher eye. Endings require concentration and imagination, and shouldn't be written in haste just because the finish line is in sight.

If it isn't fresh in your mind—and by this point, the ending probably isn't—you should review the opening of the story. For all the suspense and curiosity so painstakingly generated in the opening paragraphs must now be resolved and satisfied. What were the questions explicitly or implicitly posed in the lead? Which of them have already been answered in the course of the narrative? Which remain to be resolved? The answers to these questions should be firmly in your mind before you write the ending. If they can't be answered, this needs to be acknowledged and addressed. The reader must not leave a story feeling unsatisfied or betrayed by the writer. A story must deliver on its promises.

At the same time, a good ending should provide more than the satisfaction of intellectual curiosity. It should also be satisfying on an emotional level. As I mentioned in the previous chapter, it may take an entire story to coax the appropriate emotions from a reader, and they may be fully triggered only at the end. Since endings are the writer's last words to readers, they are also your last opportunity to inspire further reflection, often by the use of vivid imagery and symbol.

I find it helpful to divide endings into four categories: the climax and denouement; the summation; the anecdote; and the hybrid, which embraces elements of all these. The choice of which type of ending to use is usually indicated by the type of story.

The simplest ending is the climax. This is the scene that concludes a crisis, resolves a conflict, or marks a turning point in which the outcome becomes clear. An ending of this type should be considered in every narrative story. Obviously, it can be used only in a story that embraces some degree of narration, even if only a sequence of anecdotes. One approach to stories that consist of such a sequence is to break apart the principal anecdote, beginning with it, interrupting it at the point of greatest narrative suspense, then returning to it only at the end. More frequently, however, the climax is used as an ending in purely narrative stories, in which the overriding question from the outset is simply "What happened?"

The denouement is simply those scenes that follow the climax. Denouements are generally brief, because the narrative suspense has been resolved by the climax, and little curiosity remains to sustain readers' interest. Denouements often take the form of bringing readers up-to-date about what has happened to the various characters since the date of the climax; doing so is particularly important if, as in the Sheinberg story, the climax occurred some time in the past.

Whether the climax itself or the denouement should serve as the end of the story is usually evident from the narrative outline of scenes I discussed in chapter 8. Are any scenes included that follow the climax, and are they necessary to satisfy readers' curiosity? If so, then a denouement should follow the climax and serve as the ending of the story.

You may recall that the lead for the flood story ended with the simple question "Would the levee hold?" It was pretty obvious that, once that question was answered, the story would be over. As I said earlier, when I left the levee to return to New York, I didn't yet know the answer, but I suspected the levee would hold. The water had begun dropping; the volunteers had done all they could and were now simply patrolling their stretch of the dike. I didn't give it a great deal of thought when I began writing, but this seemed a satisfactory ending to me. This was a story about the impact of the river, and nature, on a community. The broader themes had been explored: the leveling of class barriers, the discovery of shared dependence, the awe at the power of nature, the helplessness of experts. This was a story of heroism, and it had succeeded, or so I thought. I quoted farmer Ken Crim: "Evidently, we've done something right, wouldn't you say? We're one of the few still standing." And there the story might have ended.

I was writing this very passage the following Sunday morning when the phone rang. Here is the ending to the flood story:

> That weekend, the rains resumed, and slowly the river began to rise again. On Sunday the twenty-fifth, at 11:20 A.M., the Sny levee gave way from its base at a point right next to House's farm and Crim's house. By the end of the day, an area three times the size of Manhattan was inundated to depths of up to fifteen feet. The instant House and Crim heard on the radio that the Sny was weakening and might give way, they rushed to Peanuts' house to save what they could of his remaining belongings. Then they hurried to Crim's house to save his refrigerator. Even as they unplugged it, they saw water rush-

ing toward them. They abandoned the effort, stranding the refrigerator in the middle of the kitchen, ran to the pickup, and
sped out with the flood close behind them. Within minutes, the
house and the farm were submerged. When they parted, on
higher ground, House shook Crim's hand. "We fought the good
fight," he said, for the board levee, their levee, never failed. Its
thin line of boards and white bags can still be seen snaking
across the surface of the vast, placid inland lake.

The failure of the levee, of course, resolves the suspense in
the story. When I heard the news, I was devastated, so caught up
was I in the struggle of my characters. I had to call my editor,
John Bennett, who consoled me and pointed out that however
grave the tragedy for these people, this development probably
enhanced the story. I think he was right, just as the Confederate
charge at Gettysburg is so much more moving because it failed.

Physically, the entire ending takes place in one geographical
place at the Sny levee, and constitutes a single scene. But it has
four significant components: the collapse of the levee (which
is the actual climax of the story); the attempt of the principal
characters to save some of their belongings; the characters' expression of their feelings at this turn of events; and the image of
the "thin line" of boards protruding above the water. Note that
the chronology is very slightly altered within this paragraph: the
levee breaks, then the story jumps back to just before this development to show the characters racing to save their belongings. I
had to make this interruption because the fact that the levee
might be giving way, which prompted their return, so plainly
foreshadowed what was about to happen that it would have
drained the actual climax of some of its impact. As much as
possible, I wanted the ending to be a surprise—even within the
last paragraph.

The story could have ended with the collapse of the levee.
The reactions of the characters, hardly startling or unpredictable,
could have been left to readers' imaginations. The "scene" of
Peanuts, Crim, and House racing out of the house and fleeing in
the truck just ahead of the floodwaters is a denouement, albeit
an extremely brief one. I felt the burst of action at the end was
necessary to illustrate the human dimension of the story, and
their parting words—stoic in the face of the levee's failure—
were an attempt to comfort each other that I thought readers

would find touching. Still, these are matters in which the advice of a good editor is crucial. In this case, John's contribution was to keep my account of the postcollapse events to an absolute minimum, recognizing that the suspense was over and no extended reprise of the story's themes was necessary or desirable. Nonetheless, I did want the final words to resonate and encourage readers to ponder the broader meanings of this story.

I labored at some length over the final image. The farmers were so proud that the boards had held, even though their strength proved futile. While I wasn't there to see this scene, one of the participants sent me a snapshot, and I found it such a haunting image: the tiny, meandering tip of the board levee lost in a vast expanse of water. The image triggered many reactions and feelings on my part: it was beautiful in a strange way, like a Richard Serra sculpture, only more delicate. The boards had taken so much human labor, yet they were dwarfed by the expanse of nature. To me, they symbolized the power of nature and the futility of human attempts to harness it. The watery expanse triggered biblical images of the flood, the timeless idea that whatever was will be. And it looked so calm, so peaceful despite the destruction and the tense drama that had preceded it. The only possible human reaction seemed to be a similarly calm and peaceful submission to forces beyond our control.

That's the best I can do at putting my feelings into words. But I had no doubt that it was a powerful and beautiful image, and I hoped it would resonate for other readers, functioning on both a literal and symbolic level to inspire emotion and contemplation.

As I mentioned in discussing transitions and nut grafs, sometimes the significance and implications of a story need to be made explicit for readers, and the passage that performs this task can often be most effective at the end of a story rather than near the beginning, where it's commonly placed. If the resolution of any narrative suspense is required to make clear the significance of a story, then this function must be reserved for the end so as not to prematurely reveal a story's resolution.

As I mentioned earlier, readers—or at least editors—seem increasingly to crave some kind of direction from writers and authors. But the advantage of providing such guidance at the end of a story rather than at the beginning is that doing so at least gives readers the opportunity to think for themselves as the story unfolds, rather than predisposing them to certain conclusions by revealing those at the outset. It's often very difficult for a writer to gauge whether any guidance is needed; this is another issue on which the opinion of a good editor can be invaluable. The import of some stories—the flood story being just one example—is so obvious that to insert editorial guidance would seem patronizing. Yet the implications of many stories are far more subtle and complex.

I wrestled with this question in coming up with an ending for the Sheinberg story, for the climax of the story—the resolution of the SEC's insider-trading charges—and even the denouement, which comprises what happened to Jonathan and his colleagues after they settled the charges, left me feeling unsatisfied. This is partly because the climax, while it resolves the conflict between the Sheinbergs and the SEC, has never been in doubt. It comes as no surprise to the reader and, given that the case was settled, it is almost anticlimactic. For guidance, I reread the lead. You may recall from chapter 6 that two principal questions were established in the lead and intended to generate curiosity: What really happened? And why would someone as privileged as Jonathan violate the law and ignore his father's warning?

This exercise is another reminder of how important the underlying questions are that give rise to a story, and how important it is that they be posed in the lead. If they are, it is always possible to return to the lead for guidance in writing an ending. In this instance, I recognized that the first question had already been answered in the text. The progress of the scheme—from Jonathan's overhearing his father, to the meeting in his apartment, to the spread of the information to his friends—was the substance of the narrative. But the other major question—about Jonathan's motive—remained unanswered. For that reason, I couldn't have ended the story with the denouement even had I felt it worked in purely dramatic terms. Given the importance of that unanswered question to the story, it had to be resolved, or at least addressed.

Before I finished the reporting, it had seemed plausible that Jonathan's motive might be explored within the narrative. Usually, for example, if someone confesses to breaking the law, either to law enforcement authorities or confidants, he offers some explanation of his motive. I thought it possible that such a discussion might figure in any conversations Jonathan might have had with his father. Certainly, if I were a novelist, there would have been such a scene. But it turned out there was not; or, if there had been, it remained undisclosed by any of the participants. As I mentioned earlier in the chapter on reporting, it is sometimes maddening that information relevant to a writer is irrelevant to prosecutors, investigators, and judges. Jonathan's motive wasn't explored by the SEC lawyers in their investigation. In settling the case without admitting or denying guilt, the Sheinbergs further ensured that motive wouldn't be a subject of investigation.

That meant that the overriding question in the narrative couldn't be answered with any certainty, unless Jonathan stated what his motives were, which he did not—and even that might have been suspect, given Jonathan's lack of candor and self-awareness. But that doesn't mean readers had to feel short-changed, or that the question wasn't an interesting and legitimate one. For Jonathan's motives could be inferred from what had already happened in the narrative.

There were several ways I might have approached this situation. I could have simply ended the story, leaving readers entirely on their own to draw any conclusions. At the other extreme, I could have stepped into the story and told readers what inferences I drew. I could also have reminded readers of the question, then recapitulated those elements of the narrative that seemed to bear on the question of motive. Or I could remove those passages from the narrative and withhold them until the ending.

I discarded the first option, partly because the story was a long one, and I didn't expect readers to remember all the questions posed in the lead. Much as I want readers to draw their own conclusions, here I felt guidance was needed.

The second option struck me as far too didactic. I must concede, however, that summations written entirely in the writer's voice are appearing in feature stories and even books with growing frequency, for all the reasons I discussed in the chapter on transitions and nut grafs. As a reader I find these summations jarring, but if they have to be used, they are far better at the end, where they serve a wrapping-up function.

The third option, recapitulating incidents from earlier in the story, risked boring readers by revisiting events they surely remembered. It reminds me of those mystery movies where the scenes are shown again as the detective unravels the mystery and explains what happened. So I opted for the fourth approach. Here is the ending I ultimately wrote:

Yet the known facts leave the most baffling mystery officially unresolved: What drove Jonathan to risk his career, his reputation, and his relationship with his father to enlist others in an insider-trading scheme? As in many other insider-trading cases, the answer is clearly not money; indeed, for such a quintessentially financial crime, it is striking how many insider traders have been wealthy men who, like Jonathan and the people he tipped, were in no rational need of their illicit gains.

In the portion of his deposition made public Jonathan was never directly asked to explain his motives. However interesting, they weren't legally relevant, so he didn't give any insight into his feelings about his own career, about his father, about his brother or Spielberg, or about any sense of loneliness or inadequacy he may have experienced. Perhaps Jonathan, who seems anything but a contemplative or self-aware person, has little sense of what drove his ultimately self-destructive behavior. But to some of the questions that were posed he and his father seem to have indirectly offered answers. The answers suggest that, despite all the high-profile law-enforcement efforts and numerous convictions, the forces driving insider trading are growing harder to curb as information becomes increasingly synonymous with power, and power with self-identity. Hollywood may be a small town where information moves with unusual speed and intensity, and Jonathan's relationship to his famous father may have fostered an unusually complicated situation. Nonetheless, these dynamics exist to varying degrees everywhere, from exclusive resorts in the Hamptons to Memphis golf courses, to name just two places where similar insider-trading schemes have recently been hatched.

Another witness in the MCA case, a man named Martin Katz, who wasn't charged with any wrongdoing, described the atmosphere in Hollywood. "You hear things in weird places, you know—the sports club, the sales clerks that wait on these people in stores that you know—and they all want subliminally, I suppose, to impress you with who they work with or who they know," he said. "There's a pulse, there's a sense of hearing things. If you go to lunch in Beverly Hills, or something, you'll see what I mean. You won't believe the things you'll hear."

Jonathan mentioned at several points in his testimony that conveying the news of the MCA takeover made him feel "spe-

280 FOLLOW THE STORY

cial," like "a big shot," to the point where telling other people
was "a compulsion." And Jonathan's father, with thirty-five years
in Hollywood under his belt, put it even more directly: "You
know, this is a town, and maybe other towns are like it, but this
is a town and this is an industry where information is perceived
as being a great power, and if you have information — well, information in the hands of a certain type of personality is a very—
You know, it's a very powerful thing. Makes you feel you're a
big man."

Note that this ending is really very simple and straightforward. The end of a story is no place to be coy. The first paragraph
simply restates the question, even more explicitly than did the
lead. In the second paragraph I step into the story to prepare
readers for what will follow. I do not say what inferences I have
drawn, only that Jonathan and his father "seem to have offered
answers." Then, without saying what those answers are, I characterize them as shedding light on the motives behind many insider-
trading cases that seem similarly baffling.

Martin Katz appears in the third paragraph, further preparing
readers for the import of what Jonathan and his father will say. It
is highly unorthodox to introduce a new character in the penulti-
mate paragraph, but in this case, Martin Katz's identity is irrelevant. What he has to say is important, because he addresses the
role of information in a place like Hollywood.

Finally we hear from Jonathan and, at the very end, from his
father. The answer to the overriding mystery is saved for the very
last line: "Makes you feel you're a big man." These quotations are
from the Sheinbergs' depositions, which actually took place
much earlier in the narrative, and could have been included in
the story at that point. But to avoid repetition and to avoid resolving the mystery prematurely, I removed those quotes from that
part of the story and placed them at the end. I wanted readers to
leave the story with Jonathan's and his father's words in their
minds. The Sheinbergs are, after all, the only firsthand sources.
While I may have subtly steered readers toward certain conclusions, I hoped they would reflect on these statements and draw
their own. And I hoped Sid's words about his son would resonate
on a deeper level. They make clear what has been implicit throughout the story: that far more than a story about insider trading and
the securities laws, this is a story about human nature.

■

As my movement of the Sheinberg quotations suggests, it is possible to extract scenes from a narrative chronology and move them to the end, just as it is possible to extract them and move them to the beginning. The last scene in a story need not be the last scene chronologically, and often it is not. Anecdotes are often used in the same way to end stories, whether they function as a scene or not. Just as certain scenes and anecdotes work effectively as leads, because they dramatize the questions that will be explored, other scenes and anecdotes function well as endings because they dramatize the questions' answers or the story's themes. Consequently, as an editor I have often steered writers to incidents they have already incorporated in their stories when they have trouble finding an ending.

As I mentioned in the chapter on leads, interruptions in chronology are easiest for readers to swallow early in a story. But readers will also accept them at the end, with one important caveat: the narrative suspense must have been resolved. In other words, any chronological break at the end must come after readers are satisfied that the chronological arc of the story is complete. But some question must remain. Breaks in chronology cannot be used when the overriding question is itself narrative, as in the flood story, since no mystery remains once the narrative arc is complete. Anecdotal endings are commonly used in most explanatory stories, where the narrative resolution may never have been in doubt, and in point-of-view stories. In the latter case, a scene or anecdote is chosen for the ending because it points readers toward desired conclusions, because it provides insight into the meaning of a story, and because it functions on a symbolic level.

I used an anecdotal ending for the profile of Jim Wilcox. It was not a scene in his biographical narrative, because it had nothing to do with Jim's success or failure as a novelist, either critically or financially. It was also taken out of chronological order, having happened years before the most recent events in the story. Here is the ending:

Wilcox now adheres as strictly as he can to a hundred-dollar-a-week budget. He almost never buys clothes. He owns one suit, which is five years old. His blue denim shirt he bought on the sidewalk for $5.99. A blue chambray shirt was bought at a bargain store on Third Avenue. ("It's amazing the bargains you can find in Manhattan," he says.) For a while, he had a queen-sized bed, but he tired of having to turn sideways to get into the bathroom. Now he sleeps on a worn brown velour sofa bed, a friend's castoff. He has just bought a used air-conditioner. He does his own laundry (a dollar-fifty a load) and ironing. He tries not to eat out, and he never takes cabs. When he's working on early drafts of his novels at his electric typewriter, he uses non-self-correcting ribbons; he switches to the more expensive self-correcting ribbons only for the final draft. Despite all these efforts, though, he has lately had to borrow money from his parents to pay his rent, now four hundred dollars a month—something he hates to do. He has lost all confidence that his future as a novelist is secure.

The most recent advance has left Wilcox no choice but to supplement his income. Last semester, he taught a fiction-writing seminar at the Camden campus of Rutgers University. That brought in $5,700. Unfortunately, the train fare to and from Philadelphia caused him to run-up fourteen hundred dollars in not yet reimbursed charges on his Visa card, which contributed to a recent cash crisis. He appeared as an extra in a Macy's television commercial for a hundred dollars. He has just completed a piece for *Allure* on the difficulties of being a handsome man. He sees it as research for a character in his new novel, and he's grateful for the assignment. The piece, if it runs, will bring in four thousand dollars, nearly half his last book advance.

There is no bitterness in Wilcox, no sense that life or the publishing industry has treated him unfairly. On the contrary, in many ways Wilcox seems to be living the life he always wanted —that of the artist. He grew up in a musical family, steeped in the lore of Mozart, the archetype of the struggling genius. "He is essentially romantic," the writer Gene Stone, a friend of Wilcox's told me. "This is how a serious novelist is supposed to live. He may be the last of his kind in America." Yet nearly all his closest friends say they have now detected in him a worrisome level of anxiety about his financial plight. "There are days when he's frustrated and nearly in tears," Stone said, and Polly King, another friend, observed, "He lives in his own private hell of worry."

Wilcox concedes as much, yet brushes aside such concerns. "Publishing is filled with ups and downs," he says. "I know that. I feel, frankly, very fortunate to be able to write, to have the time and the means. It's almost beyond my wildest dreams. Writing a novel was the be-all and end-all for me. When

I thought I could live on advances, after the Anne Tyler review, I was thrilled. Now it's going downhill, but I still feel lucky to be under contract. I'll do whatever I have to do to make money and keep writing."

Ultimately, he says, he's sustained by his readers, however small a group they may be. "Comedy is very mysterious. I'm thankful some people find what I'm doing amusing." He gets a small but steady stream of fan mail, from such improbable places as Montana and Indiana. He showed me one letter, from a reader in Canada, dated June 28, 1989:

Dear James,

It has been a day. And now I can't sleep. I am dying for a glass of lemonade but of course I have no lemons or fake stuff, even, to make it with. Instead, I have a cup of iced tea which is probably unhealthy to drink at this time of night. . . .

I was lying in bed trying to sleep—my husband's asleep, my coming little baby in my stomach (I'm five months pregnant) is asleep, my three cats are asleep, my old daddy, who lives in the apartment upstairs since my mom died four years ago, had another heart attack tonight—his second in two months, this one is worse, they say—and so I'm worried and thirsty and tired.

Which does bring me to why I'm telling you this. . . . I'm clutching to the things that I love. And I love your books. Tonight when I couldn't sleep I thought I would read a book —so I went to my bookshelves and started scanning titles— I came to your three books which I've read at least twice each (though I don't usually do that). Anyway—please write another novel fast because I can't sleep (and even if I could I wouldn't if I had one of your books to read afresh). Is that a lot to ask? I'd do the same for you. Is it very hot where you are? My air conditioner's coming Thursday,

Yours sincerely

Plainly, the story could have ended with the last quote from Wilcox: "I'll do whatever I have to do to make money and keep writing." At this late juncture, the principal questions in the story —how could an acclaimed novelist fare so poorly financially, and what does this say about the publishing industry?—have been answered. Yet his straits are so dire that they invite the question "Why?" Why would Wilcox subject himself to this kind of life? By this point in the story, I hoped readers' interest would have largely shifted from the facts of publishing in general to Jim in particular; if they had, it would be unnecessary for me to explicitly pose that question.

The letter answers it, in any case, far more eloquently than anything I or Jim could say. I thought its author could have been a character in one of Jim's novels. As Wilcox himself would say, she is like most people—coping with an ill relative, suffering from the heat, worrying about a new air conditioner. . . . She is not a heroine of genre fiction, about to launch a new high-fashion line of designer clothing, embarking on a whirlwind romance in Paris, or being stalked by a crazed psychopath whom she can see from the terrace of her Central Park West penthouse. In the midst of the kind of personal crisis that afflicts nearly everyone from time to time she writes, simply, "I am clutching to the things I love. And I love your books."

Surely no more need be said. As I mentioned in the last chapter, beauty and nobility of spirit, especially in the midst of hardship, which here unite the letter's author and a struggling writer, can be moving. I wasn't surprised that some readers wrote to say they had wept.

While it is useful to divide endings into analytical categories, many endings, especially of long articles and books, partake of all the elements I've described. The goal remains identical, however: to resolve unanswered questions, to sum up the significance of a story and suggest its ramifications, and to inspire further reflection and contemplation, perhaps through the use of symbol. I call these hybrid endings, and I used them in both *Den of Thieves* and *Blood Sport.*

In *Den of Thieves,* the ending moves briskly from the dramatic climax of the story, to a summation in my voice, to a short anecdote chosen for its symbolic significance.

Here is the story's dramatic climax, the sentencing of Michael Milken:

> By November 1990, despite all the efforts of the Milken team, public opinion had turned against Milken with a vengeance. It was as if all the negative publicity Robinson, Lake had managed to stave off had been unleashed at once. Milken was blamed, often unfairly, for all of America's failings. A recession had begun that summer, ending the economic boom of the

eighties. The savings and loan debacle, in which junk bonds had played a significant role, was growing worse by the week, costing taxpayers billions of dollars. Milken had now supplanted Boesky as the embodiment of a decade of greed.

On Wednesday morning, November 21, 1990, Milken returned to the same courtroom where he had entered his guilty plea. His wife, his mother, his brother Lowell, Ken Lerer, and Richard Sandler sat behind him in the first row. As Milken sat listening, occasionally brushing away tears, Liman read at length from letters favorable to Milken and asked the court for leniency. Fardella, representing the government, urged that Milken be sentenced to a prison term as a deterrent to other potential criminals. In their sentencing memo, the prosecutors excoriated Milken for "a pattern of calculated fraud, deceit and corruption of the highest magnitude" and argued that "Milken's crimes were crimes of greed, arrogance and betrayal," part of a "master scheme to acquire power and accumulate wealth."

Suspense mounted as Judge [Kimba] Wood began to speak in calm, measured tones. She emphasized the "extraordinary interest" in the proceeding and said she wanted to dispel several misconceptions, among them that Milken should be punished for the economy's and the savings and loan industry's ills. She also rejected leniency on the grounds of Milken's role in the economic boom. She noted the "legitimate" principle "that everyone, no matter how rich or powerful, obey the law," and "that our financial markets in which so many people who are not rich invest their savings be free of secret manipulation. This is a concern fairly to be considered by the court."

Judge Wood's gracious demeanor did not mask the fact that, as she spoke, she demolished one plank of the Milken platform after another. She stated unequivocally that overzealousness on behalf of clients was no excuse; that Milken's avoidance of more brazen crime might indicate "you were willing to commit only crimes that were unlikely to be detected." She said that she had found evidence that he had obstructed justice. On the other hand, evidence that, as Milken claimed, the vast majority of his business was honest, "is sparse and equivocal."

Milken seemed to be in a daze as he listened, even as Judge Wood's remarks became more pointedly judgmental. "When a man of your power in the financial world, at the head of the most important department of one of the most important investment banking houses in this country, repeatedly conspires to violate, and violates, securities and tax laws in order to achieve more power and wealth for himself and his wealthy clients, and commits financial crimes that are particularly hard to detect, a significant prison term is required in order to deter others," she continued. "This kind of misuse of your leadership position and enlisting employees who you supervised to assist you in violating the laws are serious crimes warranting serious punishment and the discomfort and opprobrium of being removed from society."

"Mr. Milken," Judge Wood commanded, "please rise."

Milken got to his feet, and Liman and Flumenbaum moved to his side, Liman taking Milken's elbow in support. "You are unquestionably a man of talent and industry and you have consistently shown a dedication to those less fortunate than you," Judge Wood began, looking directly at Milken. "It is my hope that the rest of your life will fulfill the promise shown early in your career. . . .

"However, for the reasons stated earlier, I sentence you to a total of ten years in prison"—a gasp rose from the courtroom—"consisting of two years each on counts two through six to be served consecutively. . . . You may be seated at this point."

As the judge rose and left the courtroom, Milken showed no reaction—but his family and friends looked grief-stricken. They rushed to his side, shielding him from curious reporters, and moved him quickly toward the door at the rear of the courtroom leading to the judge's antechamber.

When Milken and his entourage had gathered in the corridor outside, the heavy door to the courtroom was firmly closed, blocking access. Milken had still said nothing, and looked confused and disoriented. Then he tured to Liman. "How much did I get?" he asked, as if he hadn't heard Judge Wood. "Two years?"

There was a moment of stunned silence. His lawyers suddenly realized that Milken, hearing he was being sentenced to two years on each of the various counts, hadn't understood he'd been given *consecutive* sentences. Liman broke the news. "Ten years, Michael," he said gently. "The sentence is ten years."

The blood drained from Milken's face. He took Lori's arm and the two disappeared into a small witnesses' waiting room off the corridor, closing the door behind them.

Moments later, first Lori, and then Milken, emitted blood-curdling screams. Sandler burst into the room as Milken collapsed into a chair, hyperventilating, struggling for breath. "Oxygen!" someone yelled, as a federal marshal raced for help.

In purely dramatic terms, this was the end of the story. Milken's fate had now been resolved; the conflict with investigators was over. Discerning readers would surely have divined on their own the deeper moral themes of the story, but I felt they needed, and were entitled to, some guidance and context from me. After all, I had just asked them to read over 500 pages, I had withheld my voice, and while I trusted them to shape their own views, I felt they were entitled to mine. But I kept their expression to a minimum:

Michael Milken may be an extreme example, but every major participant in these crimes emerged from the experience as a wealthy man, at least by the standards of the average American. Such results have understandably led many to question whether justice was served, and whether future scandals will be deterred.

Since the end of the 1980s, profound changes have already taken place on Wall Street. Suffering from extensive layoffs and a recession as well as the aftermath of this scandal, Wall Street has given every sign of being severely chastened. Individuals may have survived the scandal, but their institutions have foundered, with Drexel in bankruptcy and a struggling Kidder, Peabody quietly put up for sale by General Electric. Salomon Brothers, caught in a Treasury-market scandal, was eventually fined $290 million, and it, too, had to struggle to survive. New instances of major securities prosecutions were few, and the takeovers that spawned so much crime nearly vanished from the financial landscape. The perception, at least, was that insider trading and more devious forms of securities fraud had become far less prevalent.

Yet history offers little comfort. The famed English jurist Sir Edward Coke wrote as early as 1602 that "fraud and deceit abound in these days more than in former times." Wall Street has shown itself peculiarly susceptible to the notion, refined by Milken and Boesky and their allies, that reward need not be accompanied by risk. Perhaps no one will ever again dominate the financial world like Milken with his junk bonds. But surely a pied piper will emerge in some other sector.

Over time, the financial markets have shown remarkable resilience and an ability to curb their own excesses. Yet they are surprisingly vulnerable to corruption from within. If nothing else, the scandals of the 1980s underscore the importance and wisdom of the securities laws and their vigorous enforcement. The Wall Street criminals were consummate evaluators of risk—

and the equation as they saw it suggested little likelihood of getting caught.

The government's record on appeal did little to change the sense on Wall Street that most securities crimes were beyond the reach of law enforcement. Part of the Princeton-Newport verdict, including the RICO convictions, was reversed on appeal, and John Mulheren's conviction was entirely reversed. Mulheren's securities-manipulation charges were dismissed in an opinion that concluded, "No rational trier of fact could have found the elements of the crimes charged here beyond a reasonable doubt." His year-and-a-day prison term and $1.5 million fine were set aside.

The Mulheren result wasn't surprising. It seems obvious from the events themselves that Boesky manipulated Mulheren, not that Mulheren manipulated the market. If Mulheren was guilty of anything, it was the parking charges on which the jury couldn't reach a verdict. The Princeton-Newport reversal and reversals in other securities cases were on largely technical grounds. Still, confronted with Wall Street crime on an unprecedented scale, prosecutors were desperate to convict on practically any grounds. In some cases, they overreached.

These results don't change the fact that there was massive wrongdoing on Wall Street. But they do call into question the wholesale criminalization of the securities laws. Congress should enact a tough but precise criminal securities code that targets the most serious violations of securities fraud while leaving enforcement of matters such as net capital requirements to the SEC.

At the very least, Congress should enact a statutory definition of insider trading, and should define a "group" as part of a criminal ban on fraudulent disclosure practices, so "arrangements" such as Icahn's and Boesky's would have to be made public. Securities firms should be barred from arbitrage; self-policing has clearly failed, as Kidder, Peabody recognized when it abandoned arbitrage. And courts should continue to define mail and wire fraud broadly; fraud has proven itself to be, as Lord MacNaghten predicted at the turn of the century, "infinite in variety."

Historians and philosophers will debate for years the question of whether, in the cases of Milken, Boesky, Siegel, Levine, and their allies, the punishments fit the crimes. With the benefit of perfect hindsight, it is easy to argue that prosecutors and the SEC should have extracted more draconian terms. The money forfeited, enormous though it is, will never make up for the losses caused to investors, to taxpayers, and to innocent workers whose jobs were sacrificed to make junk bond payments.

But no one had the benefit of such hindsight in 1986. All that was known was that a cancer was eating away at the moral fabric of Wall Street and the American economy. That cancer was stopped in its tracks. The principal wrongdoers were caught. All their vast money and power couldn't buy the outcome they craved. The markets survived and even flourished; the American economy was showing modest signs of recovery by mid-1992. Perhaps most important, integrity seemed to have regained a place among the values at the center of American life.

Fifty years passed between the scandals of the 1920s and their counterparts in the 1980s. If Wall Street escapes another major threat to its integrity for even half as long, the crackdown that culminated in Milken's conviction will have proven of historic value.

There, too, the story might have ended, but I believed that readers would be curious to know what had happened to the story's major characters in the few years since Milken's sentencing. I kept these updates very brief, trying to choose details that would shed further light on the personality and moral character of each, keeping my voice to a minimum. At the end, I turned to investment banker Martin Siegel. Why did I save Siegel for last? As one of the first of the accused to plead guilty, Siegel had largely disappeared from the story many pages ago. Milken was arguably the book's central character, and he was of greater historic importance. Yet as I mentioned earlier, an important consideration in the development of any character is whether he or she is changed by experiencing the events of the narrative. As even these brief updates suggest, most of the major characters in *Den of Thieves* had not changed fundamentally, despite the trauma of their arrests and guilty pleas. Milken, in particular, seemed largely to deny what had happened. If a character is unmoved by events, and that character's point of view is expressed, it invites readers to be unmoved as well. Because Siegel was the only major character who admitted his guilt, showed repentance, and was seeking to restore his good name, I wanted the last word in the story to be his.

Here are the final passages:

Martin Siegel entered the federal prison at Jesup, Georgia, on July 1, 1990, and was released on August 24. He painted lines on the prison parking lot and helped computerize the prison library.

Phil Donahue, once Siegel's next-door neighbor in Connecticut, bought Siegel's former home in Greens Farms for $4.75 million. Donahue leveled the house to expand his own grounds.

Siegel created a computer camp for underprivileged Jacksonville high school students, where he now works full-time as part of his two-year community service sentence. The program has grown from 8 to more than 150 participants, under the auspices of Florida Community College at Jacksonville and its Urban Resources Center, which aims to improve the training of the Jacksonville-area workforce.

Since his sentencing, Siegel has had a recurring dream. Dressed like an investment banker in a conservative suit, he walks into the law office of his former mentor, Martin Lipton. In the dream, Lipton gets up and walks toward Siegel. Lipton embraces him, and then says, "I forgive you."

The last paragraph is an anecdote. It describes a recurring dream, and thus isn't fixed at any particular point in time. Lipton's words, as dreamt by Siegel, provide the last sentence in the book: "I forgive you."

It doesn't take a Freudian to recognize that any dream is fraught with significance. Lipton is a father figure to Siegel. He is also a God-like figure. The final image is one of redemption. *Den of Thieves* is not only about insider trading and other securities crimes. It is a story of crime and punishment and touches on themes that have resonated in literature going back even further than the Bible, which is the source for the book's title.

The anecdote makes clear that Siegel, alone among the characters, craves forgiveness. Is he entitled to it? Do we sympathize with his quest? How should we feel, as opposed to think, about the events of this story?

Life doesn't always lend itself to tidy answers. These are questions for reflection and contemplation. A good story may raise new questions even as it answers the ones it originally posed.

The ending of *Blood Sport* followed a similar structure, with one significant difference. For the first time since the introduction, in which I explained how the Clintons themselves, through their emissary Susan Thomases, had enlisted me to write the book, I returned to the narrative in the first person, explaining what had happened to me since. In this I was like all the other characters, whose lives I brought up-to-date after the concluding scene in the narrative. My presence made it somewhat easier to provide a summation in my own voice, although, as in *Den of Thieves,* I tried to keep it brief and to avoid stating the obvious. The subject matter of the book had become politically charged, and I was strenuously trying to maintain a nonpartisan approach. So, before I provided my assessment of the events that had just unfolded in the book, I said, explicitly, "I hope readers will make up their own minds." I concluded with the words of independent counsel Kenneth Starr in an attempt to shift the emphasis away from whether the president or first lady was guilty of any crime, to the broader themes of the book:

> Whitewater is not solely about events and crimes in Little Rock. It is also about questions—and I stress that they are only questions, which we are very far along in examining—about the official processes of government in Washington. It is about whether participants in Washington deceived federal investigators trying to reconstruct those processes of government. It is about the White House travel office. . . . It is about contact between the Treasury Department and the White House concerning law enforcement matters. . . . It is, in short, about public trust.

That could have been the ending. But I turned once again to an anecdote to bring the book to a close:

> In November 1994, five months after he left Washington, Bernie Nussbaum was exercising on his treadmill when his wife called him to the phone, "It's Camp David."
>
> It was President Clinton. The Republicans had just swept Congress. Hubbell was about to plead guilty, and Lindsey was under investigation. Whitewater wasn't going away.
>
> "Hi, how are you?" the president asked.
>
> "Fine."

Clinton began a monologue, blaming himself for the congressional defeat. He sounded uncharacteristically down, discouraged.

"Are you okay?" Nussbaum asked.

"Yes."

"You have to stay strong."

"The special counsel legislation, the whole institution," Clinton said. "We should have thought about it more. Can it be fair?"

"As you recall, we discussed that," Nussbaum answered, remembering almost reluctantly the pitched battle in the Oval Office.

"I know. . . ." Clinton mused. "You're a good guy, Bernie. Your advice was good advice."

Clinton sounded as if he wanted to keep talking, but Nussbaum felt like an old romance had ended.

"It was nice of you to call," he said.

"Yeah, let's talk some more," Clinton said.

"Maybe another time."

Nussbaum hung up.

That was their last significant conversation.

The date of the anecdote, November 1994, places the scene much earlier in the narrative. Yet I extracted the scene from that point and moved it to the end. Why? Just as I did with Martin Siegel, I wanted a scene that would focus on a character who had learned something from the events in the book, and who had changed. In this case it was Bernie Nussbaum, the former counsel to the president. Nussbaum, who had consistently advocated a policy of honesty, was forced to resign and is now far from the center of power, exercising on his treadmill. The president, fresh from defeat in the congressional elections, calls from Camp David. The conversation is stilted, filled with unspoken thoughts. Nussbaum feels that a "romance" has ended. There are vague promises to talk again, which seem not to hold any promise of being fulfilled.

What is this scene meant to suggest? As with the other endings I have discussed, I hoped it would inspire contemplation and reflection. The scene is a sad one, especially given the enthusiasm with which Nussbaum had embarked on his government service just two years earlier, enthusiasm readers had witnessed several hundred pages earlier in the book. The demise of Nussbaum's high spirits, his sense that a romance had ended, mirrored the experience of many people who had voted for Clinton, shared the optimism of the new administration, and then watched it become mired in scandal, ethical lapses, and lies, with so many of the problems self-inflicted. Nussbaum's disillusionment seemed entirely understandable.

In this scene Clinton, too, seems wistful and uncharacteristically filled with self-doubt. He implies that mistakes may have been made, something he has never publicly acknowledged. His party has suffered a devastating defeat at the polls, despite his personal popularity. The scene and the president's mood foreshadow trouble rather than triumph.

I also hoped readers would reflect on Nussbaum's fate. He was someone eminently qualified, enthusiastic, dedicated to the public interest, loyal to the president—precisely the qualities we presumably seek in our political officeholders. Yet he and many like him were driven out of the Clinton inner circle, some forced to resign, others simply exiled. Why would this be the case? If politics has indeed become a "blood sport," as Vincent Foster suggested in his suicide note, why is that? Is it because of the right-wing conspiracy alleged by Hillary Clinton? Because politics has become so nasty and partisan that people of integrity are destroyed? Or because the Clintons themselves told so many lies in their climb to the top that others would have to sacrifice their own integrity trying to defend them, or be forced to leave?

These aren't questions that lend themselves to easy answers. But I hoped readers could see for themselves the consequences of a politics of deception that has become increasingly pervasive, pursued by Republicans and Democrats, liberals and conservatives. Different readers would no doubt have different answers. I hope I provided the factual material for informed contemplation, discussion, even argument that would continue long after readers had finished my book.

By all rights, completing a manuscript should be a joyous moment in any writer's career. Yet most writers I know suffer to varying extents from some form of postpartum depression. They may be suddenly racked by doubts that the story is any good.

They worry about whether their editor will like it. Everyone I know worries about this, including me, which is why good editors respond promptly, even if it's to say, "I'm not sure about this." (Though I tried hard, I wish I had responded more quickly myself while I was Page One editor.) Writers worry about where their next story or book will come from.

It has taken me years to overcome most of these doubts, but the principles I've described in this book have gradually brought me considerable peace of mind. If the idea was good, if the proposal was good, and if the story has delivered on what was promised, then the story is good, or will be when it is edited and polished. There are always more stories than there are journalists to do them. It doesn't matter whether any given story is the best one you will ever write—all that matters is that it be worth writing.

On a more practical level, the submission of a manuscript is not the end of work on a story. The editing and fact-checking can be very labor-intensive and time-consuming, especially when it is done under deadline pressure, which it almost always is. This isn't a book about the editing process, so I will make only a few broad points: editing can be grueling and frustrating, but if you know why you have written a story the way you have—which you should, if you've gotten this far in this book—you always have a principled basis from which to argue with an editor. More often, I have found that a good editor will apply the principles I've been discussing and advocating even when I have failed to do so. It never fails to amaze me how easily I can write a sequence in garbled chronological order, which an editor clarifies. Or how often I state the obvious when it would be far better to let the reader draw that conclusion. I recall a colleague once telling me after submitting a book manuscript that his editor had told him "it was so brilliant it didn't need editing." This was worrisome, for no manuscript is so brilliant it doesn't need editing. My colleague's book was about twice as long as it needed to be and eventually languished, mostly unsold, on bookstore shelves. Good editing is a godsend. However much additional work it entails, it will enhance a story and ultimately redound to the writer's credit.

The same can be said for fact-checking. Fact-checking is a luxury; it doesn't exist at most newspapers and book publishers.

I consider it sufficiently valuable that I paid for fact-checkers myself on both *Blood Sport* and *Den of Thieves,* and considered the money extremely well-spent. Errors creep into even the best reporter's work. Fact-checkers have spared me immense embarrassment and have saved the credibility of my stories on more occasions than I like to admit. At the same time, I have had bad experiences with fact-checkers, one of whom nearly drove me over the edge. A freelancer, determined to prove that she could find enough errors in my work to justify being hired for a full-time job, she challenged almost everything I had said, hectored sources to repudiate what they had told me, and manufactured crises that required constant intervention from the editor. All I can say is that I and the story survived; she found another career. By contrast, all the fact-checkers I have worked with at *The New Yorker* have been dedicated, professional, tireless, and, in my view, underpaid for the remarkable work they do.

Important elements of the published story are the layout, accompanying artwork, and most importantly, the headline and any subheads. In books, the jacket and the title are important. These elements are generally not the responsibility of the writer. But it is a mistake to ignore them, for no one, in all likelihood, cares more about how your work is presented than you do. When it comes to art, I have found it is generally best to stay out of the way. While *Den of Thieves* was in the editing process, a cover design was dummied but was rejected by Simon & Schuster's then-chairman, Dick Snyder. (This no doubt cost the publisher thousands of dollars, and I'm grateful he did, because the original design was dreadful.) As months passed with no new design surfacing, I took it upon myself to survey bookstores and came up with a list of book covers I thought were attractive and effective. I brought the list to my editor, Alice Mayhew, and said it might be nice to have something that looked like one of these. She perused the list, then put it down. "Those are all beautiful books," she said. "And none of them sold." That was the end of that conversation.

At *The New Yorker,* I'm usually shown the art for my stories at the last minute, and then only to see if there is any factual error. That's just as well, for I usually don't get the point of the art at all. I couldn't even recognize the characters in the flood story, the gay auto worker, or the people in a story I did about Susan McDougal. But readers have told me they liked the art, so who am I to judge? I'm not a professional artist. Just as I expect the art department to respect my work, I trust their judgment about the art.

Headlines and book titles are another matter, one in which the writer has to be involved. It's just as well to have someone else write the heads and titles, because someone more distant from the facts often has an easier time coming up with something that suggests the essence of the story. The editors who worked on Page One at the *Journal* were highly skilled and inspiring in this regard, capturing many headline-writing prizes over the years. I have only one hard-and-fast rule: the headline must not give away the ending of a story. While this may seem obvious, many headline writers, especially at newspapers, tend to do exactly that. What a headline should do, in shorthand form, is sell a story in the same way that the opening paragraphs do. Its sole function should be to make people want to read the story. In most magazines and newspapers, headlines are followed by subheads, which expand on the message of the headline.

Here are the headlines and subheads for some of the stories we've been discussing:

THE TIPSTER

Unusual trading in MCA stock options just before news leaked of the giant Matsushita buyout naturally caught the attention of the S.E.C. But even the S.E.C. was baffled when it learned that the insider source had never sought to profit himself—and that he was the producer son of a legendary Hollywood studio chief.

MOBY DICK IN MANHATTAN

Can an acclaimed writer devote himself purely to his work and still make money? James Wilcox tried, and he's paying a high price for the literary life.

Battle on the Sny

Coached by a farmer known as Peanuts, the people came out to fight the Mississippi as it threatened to breach a levee that had stood firm for more than a century.

In my view, these were brilliant headlines and subheads, and if you think they're easy to write, try one yourself. None was my idea, but I endorsed them all enthusiastically. I believe they were John Bennett's; he presented them to me. Some went through several permutations before they were finished, and John may well have received inspiration from others at *The New Yorker.* Headlines are collaborations. In each case the headline itself is extremely brief and evocative. "The Tipster" suggests a story about a person, someone slightly shady, secretive, possessing valuable information—a type we have all met. Note how a mystery is created but not solved in the subhead—"even the S.E.C. was baffled." Sheinberg's name isn't even used. Curiosity is further heightened by describing him as the son of a "legendary Hollywood studio chief."

"Moby Dick in Manhattan" is deliberately baffling. What does it mean? Clearly it is a literary allusion—every reader can be expected to know the novel *Moby-Dick,* and clearly the story is set in the corridors of literary power of New York. But the imagery is deliberately provocative, even ridiculous—is this story about a beached whale flopping around in the big city? Of course not. Readers will understand the allusion only when they reach the end of the story, since Wilcox himself uses the phrase. This may seem daring by today's standards, but it is actually a time-honored convention of book and headline writing that was far more popular years ago than it is now. Any possible confusion is quickly obviated by the subhead, in any event.

"Battle on the Sny" promises conflict, but gives no hint whatever as to its outcome. The subhead makes clear this will be a story of people, like someone named "Peanuts," who "came out" to the levee. It sounds like jacket copy for a Steinbeck novel.

All of these headlines reflect the story proposals, emphasizing the same strengths while minimizing the weaknesses. "The Tipster" sells the identity of the main character, not mentioning the phrase "insider trading." Wilcox is described as an "acclaimed writer" before he is named, and the paradox is plainly stated in a question. He's paying a "high price," but what that price might be is unspoken. "Battle on the Sny" promises a narrative drama without revealing the resolution. In other words, the goal of a good headline is to instill curiosity while simultaneously providing some description of what a story is about. This is an art form unto itself.

If anything, book titles are even more difficult. I find it very hard even to consider titles until I am finished or almost finished with a manuscript. Unlike headlines, book titles may be the final responsibility of the author, but I find an editor's assistance to be indispensable. Alice Mayhew and I have always discussed possibilities and chosen one on which we agree. I know some writers prefer to abdicate responsibility for their book titles, but the title is so important to a book's identity that I can't imagine not being involved. For *Den of Thieves,* I owe my inspiration to Steve Swartz, currently editor in chief and chief executive of *SmartMoney* magazine, then a member of my staff at Page One. We were tossing ideas around one day when he referred to Boesky, Levine, and Milken as a "merry band of thieves." This triggered an immediate association with the biblical phrase "den of thieves," though I had no recollection where it appeared or how it was used. Alice had once mentioned that many good book titles come from the Bible, and I immediately checked *Bartlett's Familiar Quotations,* where I learned that the phrase appeared in the context of Jesus' evicting the moneylenders from the Temple. It seemed entirely appropriate to me, and I immediately called Alice. "That's it," she said, without hesitation.

Even more than headlines, book titles rely on imagery, symbolism, and association to hint at broader themes. *Den of Thieves* described a place and a setting—in this case, the financial community; it suggested the book was about people; and it conveyed a strong point of view that was warranted by the book's content. It was short and to the point, easy to remember. I thought the cover design was brilliant: four shadowy figures silhouetted on an escalator or stairway, an image that suggested intrigue and mystery. The book's title and cover lured readers by hinting at the content, but gave nothing of substance away.

Blood Sport was a much easier title to come up with. The phrase had stuck in my mind ever since I first read the text of

Vince Foster's suicide note: "I was not meant for the job or the spotlight of life in Washington. Here, ruining people is consid- ered sport." This suggested that "sport" had symbolic resonance even though I wasn't conscious of what it was. The more I pon- dered the phrase, the better suited I thought it was to describe the conflict under way between the Clintons and their adversar- ies, with both sides locked in a high-stakes quest for power in which the Fosters of the world were mere cannon fodder. As with "Moby Dick in Manhattan," readers won't understand the title's full significance at once—they encounter the reference when Foster drafts his note—but the phrase "blood sport" also stands alone as an appropriate metaphor for the political climate in Washington.

It was important to me that neither book's title refer obvi- ously to the narrow subject of insider trading or Whitewater. (I believe "The Insiders" was briefly under consideration for *Den of Thieves,* but I never liked it.) You may recall from the chapter on ideas that I assume most potential readers aren't interested in any given subject. Those who are will probably read the book or article whether or not they like the title or headline. A good title reassures readers who aren't that interested in the immediate subject that this work includes broad themes transcending any narrow category. Like all aspects of engaging readers' curiosity and encouraging them to read, the books and articles the titles and headlines described must deliver on that promise.

If there is a high point in writing, it is publication. There is nothing to compare to the experience of seeing one's words, which not so long ago resided in the recesses of one's mind, on the printed page, available forever to anyone who chooses to read them. The publication of *Den of Thieves* was particularly emotional for me, since in the preceding weeks I had undergone a barrage of threatening letters from lawyers and thought there was a distinct possibility the Milkens would sue to halt or delay publication of the book. When I saw the first copy, and knew that trucks were delivering books to stores, I was nearly over- whelmed with relief that the truth, told as well as I could tell it, had been published.

13
CONCLUSION

And so we near the end of our journey. This is a book about writing, not about marketing and publicity, so I will not dwell on the events that usually follow publication of a major article or a book—press releases, appearances on TV and radio talk shows, reviews by critics, and an outpouring of reaction from subjects, from sources, and, if you're lucky, from readers. Much of my work has been highly controversial. It has held up a mirror to the wealthy and powerful, and it has in turn been subjected to intense scrutiny and criticism. I have even been sued, for $34 million, by a lawyer for Michael Milken's brother Lowell.

There is only one way to ensure peace of mind during the usually gratifying but inevitably stressful period that follows publication: the knowledge that you did the best you could, that you were as accurate as humanly possible, and that your writing did justice to the information with which you were fortunate enough to be entrusted. I try to talk to everyone who calls after a story is published. I make a point of always taking calls or responding to letters from anyone who contributed to a story or participated in any way in the reporting process, and I will always speak to someone named in a story. This isn't always pleasant. I have spoken to angry subjects and sources. I have been the subject of a few blistering reviews (the *New York Times* review I discussed earlier being only a mild example).

Still, I have always slept peacefully, confident that I can defend myself and that I did my best. I don't expect everyone to agree with me, or to admire my work—it would be a dull and homogeneous world if that were the case. I know I am not infallible. Sometimes I have made mistakes; I have tried to acknowledge and correct them. A few critics have faulted my word choice or sentence structure, and when their criticisms made sense, I have vowed to do better. I have also been gratified by much positive reaction and many laudatory reviews. But no reviewers, positive or negative, know my work as well as I do, nor do they know the effort I have expended.

Good writing should be the exclusive province of neither fiction nor nonfiction, yet "literature"—writing of artistic merit—is generally associated with fiction. I see no reason why techniques that have been honed over centuries of storytelling shouldn't be embraced by writers of nonfiction as well. These techniques have proven themselves because they work: they clarify stories, they enrich them, they make them more immediate and accessible. In short, they help readers incorporate stories into the events of their own lives, inspiring contemplation and reaction.

In my view, the uneasiness with which some nonfiction writers view literary techniques arises largely from a myth prevalent in journalism: that journalists are always present as a filter between events and readers, yet are always objective, with no views of their own. This approach has been at least tacitly embraced by most major newspapers and journalism schools in America.

The convention that a writer is always present to witness what is reported has given rise to many of the controversies surrounding literary nonfiction. Does describing a place imply that the writer was there at the moment described? Does dialogue imply that the writer overheard the remarks at the time they were made? Some advocates of traditional nonfiction writing would argue in both cases that it does; in that case, the result is false, and it crosses an inviolable line between fiction and nonfiction.

In the quest for objectivity, the convention has also arisen that the journalist must be invisible, present as a filter only by implication. Thus, it has traditionally been acceptable to quote almost anyone, but not to mention the writer's own observations.

This helps explain the traditional aversion to the first-person pronoun, an aversion that persists in newspapers today. And it extends to simple descriptions, in which it is acceptable to see events through the eyes of someone the journalist interviews—but not through the eyes of the journalist.

These conventions are giving way; journalists are more likely to provide direct description when they were not firsthand witnesses, to appear in their stories when they are, and to disclose their own biases or any facts that might bear on their objectivity. They use narrative dialogue; and, when appropriate, they use the first-person pronoun. Truth, accuracy, and objectivity have not been impaired. On the contrary, the argument can be made that they have been enhanced. Whether a table is round or square is not a fact that turns on whether the writer observed the table, saw it in a photograph, or heard it described accurately by another. To my mind, that a table is square is a fact. If the table is square, quoting someone to the effect that it is round is as inaccurate—as fictional—as saying directly that it is round.

Writers do not write in a vacuum, or only for other journalists, writers, and editors. Readers, often voting with their hard-earned money, have also resoundingly expressed their preference for direct, immediate, and accessible writing. Simply look at the writing that dominates nonfiction best-seller lists, successful magazines, like *Vanity Fair* and *The New Yorker,* and newspapers, like *The Wall Street Journal* and *The New York Times.* These publications not only print engaging, readable narrative stories, but they are pillars of journalistic integrity and accuracy in reporting.

What must be guarded against in nonfiction writing is any erosion of the truth. In my experience, more falsehoods have been perpetrated in the form of manufactured quotations and bogus "sources," all of which conform to the style of traditional journalistic writing, than in the far more publicized instances of outright fabrication of narrative events. But the point I am trying to emphasize is that the truth, integrity, or fairness of a story doesn't turn on the techniques used to tell it.

Thus, whether a writer uses a direct narrative style or the old-fashioned pyramid, it is not acceptable to create "composite" characters who do not exist, to use false names to protect someone's identity without disclosing this, to change scenes and settings or reorder chronology to "streamline" a story, or to state inferences as facts—all of which I have seen done in work that's supposedly nonfiction. Docudramas, "faction," and historical fiction all have their place, but they are fiction, and should be clearly labeled as such.

It should go without saying that outright fabrication, even of the smallest details, is the journalistic equivalent of a felony. Under no circumstances should it be indulged in or condoned. Yet fabrication remains a common occurrence, as recent egregious episodes at *The New Republic* and the *Boston Globe* attest. I have often pondered why such incidents persist. They remind me of insider trading, a crime that often seems rationally inexplicable. Like inside traders, nonfiction writers who fabricate have presumably weighed the risks and rewards, concluding that they are unlikely to get caught and that professional advancement and public acclaim, not to mention journalism prizes, require sensational "facts" that can't be discovered by reporting. I am sorry to say that I have known editors who willingly conspired in such schemes, and while at least one was fired, it was done quietly and the real cause was never made public, no doubt for fear of lawsuits. Like crime, fabrication must be deterred by public exposure and penalties, so that the risk side of the equation looms much larger. What I find saddest is that fabrication is so unnecessary. The best nonfiction stories are so startling and unexpected that they defy imagination. No one would dare make them up and expect to be believed.

In my experience, dedication to the truth, a state of mind that should permeate every step of the nonfiction writing process, will obviate most controversies. It guarantees a commitment to accuracy. It means that whatever preconceptions a writer might have will have been put aside. It means the writer will tolerate no conflicts of interest or appearance of conflicts, knowing that these might undermine the integrity of the story. And it guarantees that one's work will withstand whatever scrutiny and criticism may be brought to bear on it. For I remain convinced that in a free society, the truth ultimately prevails.

My parents worked hard to put me through college and then law school, so it was with some trepidation that I flew home to Quincy for Christmas at the end of 1978 to announce that I was quitting my well-paid and secure job as a lawyer to join an as yet unpublished new magazine as a staff reporter. I delivered this news in the car as we left the airport. My parents weren't exactly thrilled, but to my relief they made no attempt to influence my decision or change my mind. They said it was my life and my decision, and that if I ran out of money, I could always reclaim my boyhood room.

I have always been grateful for their support, and I'm glad that I had the courage to make that leap into the unknown. I've often been asked why I changed careers. I was guided more by my heart than my head. I vividly recall sitting with my friend and colleague Ed Flanagan on a balcony at the Watergate Hotel in Washington when I made the decision. I was an associate lawyer at Cravath at the time, and had watched the winnowing-out process as a class of about twenty-five lawyers moved toward possibly becoming partners seven or eight years after they began at the firm. Of the twenty-five, perhaps one would be chosen. Who prevailed? Not necessarily the brightest, the most personable, the hardest-working. The common denominator I perceived was that those few who succeeded loved their work more than any of the rest of us. I liked my work, and I liked the paycheck. But I didn't *love* it. Discussing this on the hotel balcony, Ed and I began musing about what we might love as much as our colleagues loved the practice of law. I thought back to my tenure as editor of *The DePauw*, my college newspaper. I loved journalism, and I loved to read and write. It had never seemed like work—but since moving to New York, I had met people who actually made a living at it. (Ed, by the way, went into politics, and is now the state auditor of Vermont.)

I have never regretted choosing to do something that I loved rather than something that I thought would be financially rewarding. And I have been doubly blessed. Not only have I loved my work, but I have made a decent living. There were times, I must confess, when I doubted that would happen. My first book advance was $20,000, only $10,000 of which was paid up front, and my adjusted gross income for 1981, $16,000, was the lowest in my Harvard Law School class, according to the five-year class report. At the time I fantasized about how I would spend the $10,000 I would get upon completion of the book, contemplating a trip to Europe, extravagant gifts for my parents and siblings . . . When it finally arrived, I used all of it to pay off the balance on my MasterCard.

That book, *The Partners,* made it onto the *New York Times* nonfiction best-seller list for a few weeks, something that at the time was beyond my wildest dreams. Since then I have continued to develop the principles I've described in this book and tried to apply them in my own work, and readers have responded in gratifying numbers. Sales figures are certainly no measure of literary merit, but they do suggest that readers want and are willing to pay for writing that not only informs them but also engages their curiosity, holds their interest, and trusts their judgment.

Gratified as I have been by sales of my books, I learned long ago that what's important in writing isn't how many people read what you write. Millions of people read major newspapers and magazines each day and promptly forget what has passed before their eyes. Much has been written about the power of the press, the power of the written word. I have often wondered what, in these aphorisms, was meant by "power." As a writer, I have never felt particularly powerful. I carry no weapon, I cannot coerce, I lack the force of a subpoena, I cannot invoke the law and the authority of the state to make anyone do my bidding. If by "power" is meant the ability to inform, then it must be the most benign power imaginable. Information precipitates action solely at the discretion of the reader. Sometimes the impact of a story is predictable, but more often it is not. I often warn my students that if they seek to be writers because they are at heart polemicists and activists seeking social or political change, they are destined for disappointment.

What matters is whether a story makes an impression, prompts further thought and reflection, and is remembered. Our physical existence is bound by the reality that we lead only one life. Yet the mind is not. Through reading we can lead many lives. If events are depicted vividly and memorably, we incorporate them into our own lives, as if they had happened to us. We remember, we may be moved, we ponder and react. That has been my experience when I read the work of other writers I admire, and the desire to convey that experience to others motivates my work. Over the years many readers have written and spoken to me about how what I have written has changed their lives. It is always a gratifying but humbling experience, and a reminder of what great responsibility and trust are bestowed upon us by our readers.

There is ultimately only one reader who matters, and that person is you. Unless you destroy the only copy, what you write will last forever, certainly for the duration of your life. You know whether you were accurate, fair, thorough, honest, and whether you worked to the best of your ability. You know whether you are proud of your work, or embarrassed because your motives were impure or because you betrayed your own standards. You can return to your writing time and again to assess whether it expanded your universe, your horizons, your life, in a way that informed you, moved you, or prompted you to reflect and take action. If so, you can be sure it will have the same effect on others. You will then be able to experience within yourself the greatest rewards that writing, or surely any endeavor, can offer. For through your work, you will have helped create a better world.

Acknowledgments

THIS BOOK had its genesis in a conversation with my agent, Amanda Urban, after which she and my editor, Alice Mayhew, sat in on one of my classes at Columbia. They provided continuing encouragement, guidance, and confidence in this project.

The Columbia School of Journalism has generously provided a forum for my sometimes unorthodox ideas, and the faculty and administration have been both encouraging and stimulating, especially Michael Shapiro, Sam Friedman, Steve Isaacs, and Sandy Padue. Several editors and writers have regularly contributed to and enriched my class, including John Brecher, Ron Suskind, Jane Berentson, Jim Wilcox, Monica Langley, and especially Bryan Burrough, who has assisted in teaching the class for several years.

Steve Swartz, editor and president of *SmartMoney*, provided a journalistic home for this project as well as invaluable editorial counsel and friendship. My assistant, Julie Allen, rendered immeasurable assistance, both in helping me finish this manuscript and in preparing my class materials.

My parents made my writing career possible, and hence this book. As always, they have my love and gratitude, as do Jane Holden, my sister, and her family, and my brother Michael and his.

My friends remain some of my most enthusiastic supporters and critics, and have shaped my writing more than they realize.

Benjamin Weil provided daily inspiration and support during the writing of this book, even at a distance, and read and commented on the manuscript. I will be forever grateful.

APPENDIXES

Battle on the Sny

*Coached by a farmer known as Peanuts, the people
came out to fight the Mississippi as it threatened
to breach a levee that had stood firm for more
than a century.*

by JAMES B. STEWART

ON WEDNESDAY, JUNE 30TH, at about 10 P.M., as Alexander J. House turned
in early for the night, he heard the first drops of rain on the metal roof
of his house, in Payson, Illinois—a farmhouse that was built by his
great-grandfather in the nineteenth century. Just before going to bed,
House had gazed out over his pond and the rolling fields to the west,
where the land descends toward the Mississippi. There, in a basin
formed by the old Sny Channel, which runs parallel to the east bank of
the Mississippi, lies some of the richest farmland in the world, fourteen
hundred acres of which belong to House and his family. Over the fields
that night he'd seen an ominous bank of black clouds, confirming local
forecasts of potentially heavy rains and thunderstorms.

House was hoping to fall asleep quickly, since in only a few hours
he had to be up to help load trucks with calcium carbonate, a white
mineral that his company extracts from the high bluffs defining the
floodplain of the Mississippi. Like many farmers in the area, House is
also a businessman: he helped found and co-owns Quincy Carbonates.
After graduating from Kenyon College and the Loyola University business
school, he could have moved to Chicago, St. Louis, or some other big
city. (At thirty-five, he is tall and handsome, with dark-blond hair. The
Times Magazine once ran a full-page photograph of him in an article on
bachelors. He has since married.) But, he says, "I grew up in Payson and
always knew I'd come back." Though he does a fair amount of farming
himself, he rents out his Sny acreage to Kenneth Crim, a powerfully built
forty-six-year-old, who farms not only House's land but also nearby land
belonging to his own mother-in-law.

That night, as the thunder crashed and the rain beat more heavily
on the roof, House couldn't sleep. Finally, around midnight, he got up
to look outside. Worried about getting the trucks in for loading, he
dressed, jumped into his own truck, a Dodge Ram four-wheel-drive

pickup, and headed west toward his plant. Along the way, he noticed that power failures had plunged the area into darkness. By eerie, sudden flashes of lightning, he could see that ditches and creeks were overflowing. When he got to Illinois Route 57, which runs from Quincy—the commercial hub of the area, fifteen miles to the north—along the old Sny Basin, it had turned into a rushing waterway. At 1 A.M., House got into a front-end loader and started digging a drainage ditch to protect his plant. "Basically, there was a wall of water coming at us," he says. Farther south, on House's farmland, Ken Crim got up to watch the deluge, and thought, Holy shit.

About eleven o'clock, in Quincy, Robert Nall, the sheriff of Adams County, seeing the torrential rains, got into his unmarked squad car and drove out along some of the country roads north of town. Gazing upward periodically through the windshield, the sheriff, who is fifty-one, saw what he describes as the "most spectacular show of lightning I've ever seen." It lasted not the usual minutes but hour after hour. As the severity of the storm became obvious, he headed down to his office, on the first floor of the Adams County Courthouse, and began calling his deputies, sending them out on the roads to look for dangerous conditions and for any cars that might have been swept off in the deluge. From around the county came reports that creeks had burst their banks, flooding roads to the point where the roads had all but formed small rivers themselves. When Nall went home, at about 2 A.M., rain was still falling, and he had the ominous feeling that worse news was to come.

Around seven the next morning, Leo Henning, the operations manager for Quincy's WGEM TV and Radio, got up and checked for damage in his basement. He found that several inches of water had collected overnight. Henning, a native of Chicago, may have been one of the few people in Quincy who slept through the storm. Like many people there, he didn't ordinarily give much thought to heavy rains. Quincy's founders, back in 1822, had the foresight to establish their river port on some of the highest bluffs on the east bank of the Mississippi. From the old dock areas along the riverfront, where stern-wheelers once called regularly, the streets rise steeply to the east. From the buildings surrounding the old town square, high above the river, and from WGEM's offices, in the Hotel Quincy, which is just around the corner, one has sweeping views across the river of miles of the fertile lowlands of Missouri. Those lands, and also vast tracts both north and south of Quincy, with their farms and with the towns and hamlets that dot the landscape, are protected by an elaborate system of levees and drainage districts. Seeing the water in his basement, Henning recognized a story. Two years ago, WGEM Radio had shifted to a twenty-four-hour news-and-talk format, and this was more than a routine weather bulletin.

Overnight, Quincy had received a record six inches of rain. Some areas to the north had been drenched even more heavily. The Mississippi, which typically rises or falls an inch or so in a twenty-four-hour period, had risen two feet. The downpour, coming after what had been an unusually wet spring, left Henning, Nall, Crim, House, and just about everybody else in and around Quincy wondering the same thing: Would the levees hold?

■

From my apartment, on the Upper West Side of New York, I was wondering that, too. Quincy is my home town. I was born there, in Blessing Hospital, in 1951, and spent nearly all my life there until I graduated from Quincy High School and went on to college. My father is the national sales manager of WGEM, where he has worked for most of his life, and he and my mother still live in a comfortable subdivision on the south edge of town, which looks out over a white farmhouse and a red barn across the street. That's about as close to a farm as I came, growing up in Quincy. At Quincy High, the largest club in school was the Future Farmers of America, whose members headed home right after the last bell to help with chores, leaving sports and other extracurricular activities to the city kids. My first job was as a reporter at the Quincy *Herald-Whig,* where I worked during summers. One of my first assignments was covering the Adams County Fair, and I can still discuss the fine points of Duroc and Poland China hogs. I also learned something about floods: I especially remember one in the late sixties, when my high-school friends and I helped throw sandbags. I returned to Quincy to see the flood of 1973, which damaged large areas of Missouri across from the city. Now, twenty years later, I knew my immediate family in Quincy would be safe, since they were on high ground. But in May I'd seen the high river level lapping over a just completed riverside park in Quincy, and I'd heard from my parents about all the rain since. I knew they were worried, and I decided to go out there. As I flew up the Mississippi in a commuter plane from St. Louis, I saw that the familiar landscape had been transformed. Small streams were swollen to the usual size of the Mississippi, and in places the Mississippi itself sprawled all the way to the horizon, its old channel barely discernible from the pattern of trees and, beyond those, half-submerged roofs of barns, houses, towns. Already, it was obvious that this was a flood like none I had ever experienced.

Even before Sheriff Nall left home on Thursday morning after the downpour, his phone was ringing with calls from people living in the low-lying farmlands around Quincy. They had little doubt about what the night's deluge meant. They'd been keeping an uneasy eye on the river since April, when the Mississippi first rose above the technical flood level at Quincy's lock and dam. That in itself wasn't unusual or worrisome; the river frequently rises above flood level following the spring melting, and the extensive system of locks and dams and flood-control levees established during the past century to contain the unruly river had led to a certain complacency. But this year, as the planting season came to an end and spring turned to summer, the river barely budged, and then, slowly but ominously, it began to rise. On June 25th, it had to be closed to barge traffic, and at the same time many of the locks and dams of the upper Mississippi, no longer able to contain the flow, were simply thrown open. Memorial Bridge, the older of Quincy's two bridges, was closed, its Missouri terminus, in an area unprotected by levees, having been submerged. No one in the area could remember when the spring floods had persisted into what is usually the dry season —a time when farmers customarily pray for rain to hasten the tasselling of the corn crop. This year, though, an unusually cool air mass had settled around a low-pressure system in the Pacific Northwest, drawing more cool air into the upper Midwest from Canada. At the same time, a high-pressure system over the Southeast had sucked hot, moist air from the Gulf of Mexico northward over the plains. Persistent storms had broken out where the two air masses met, along a broad band stretching northeastward from Kansas into Missouri, Iowa, and western Illinois. Because the jet stream remained further south than usual, these pressure systems, instead of breaking up and moving on to the east, had stayed put.

The most important of the calls to Sheriff Nall that Thursday morning came from some of the area's most influential citizens—the local levee commissioners, who preside over the drainage districts that line the Mississippi. Quincy sits at the center of a string of districts running from north to south along the east bank of the river: Hunt, Lima Lake, Indian Grave, South Quincy, and Sny Island. Just across the river from Quincy, in West Quincy, Missouri, is the Fabius River drainage district: it surrounds the western ends of the Quincy bridges. Of these six districts, the Sny Island, with a fifty-four-mile-long earth-and-sand levee, is by far the largest, covering about a hundred and ten thousand acres; in fact, its levee is the largest in Illinois, and one of the oldest in the country. Construction began, using mules and horses, shovels and manual labor, in 1872, and was completed three years later.

The area protected by the Sny Island levee includes some of the most fertile acreage on earth. The entire district lies in the floodplain of the Mississippi, and before the levee was constructed it was flooded routinely, collecting a fresh layer of silt each time. The rich, black, moist soil typically produces yields that are from twenty to forty per cent greater than the fertile upland soil of central Illinois, and those high yields are reflected in the prices Sny Basin acreage commands today— about twenty-five hundred dollars an acre.

When the levee was completed, the enhanced value of the newly protected farmland wasn't lost on neighboring landowners, some of whose farms were being flooded with the waters diverted by the Sny levee-and-drainage system, and litigation broke out almost immediately. No less a personage than former President Benjamin Harrison represented the Sny landowners, who ultimately prevailed before the United States Supreme Court. To administer the vast project, local farmers got a court order approving the creation of the state's first drainage-district-and-levee commission, which financed the project by issuing bonds. To retire the bonds, local farmers and landowners paid an assessment, spawning a system that has been copied throughout the region, and that led to the formation of numerous levee commissions, with commissioners elected by the local landowners. Alex House's grandfather Lowell House served as a Sny commissioner for many years. The Sny proved a model in other ways, too. Not since 1888 had the levee been seriously breached—a source of enormous local pride but also, perhaps, of some hubris. In recent times, most farmers in the area have carried hail insurance, but virtually no one farming in the Sny district carries flood insurance.

■

When Nall talked to the commissioners Thursday morning, they were getting worried but weren't panicking. They were beginning to organize preservation efforts in their districts, and already they could see that they would need more manpower. Sheriff Nall was someone they called not just to keep him posted about road conditions and the need for sheriffs' patrols but as a source of manpower, for Nall was their link to a relatively recent program in Illinois that provides prison inmates for local labor. The problem was that everybody, not just in the Adams County levee districts but all the way upstream, was clamoring for help. Nall said he'd see what he could do. If anyone could deliver, the commissioners thought, it was Nall, for he has been something of a legend in the area ever since he was first elected sheriff, in 1974. Nall had been a farmer himself, and one day, returning from the fields, he discovered that his house had been burglarized—practically everything was gone. As he tells the story, he called the man who was the sheriff at the time, and was told that everybody on the force was too busy to come out just then. A furious Nall grabbed his gun and, after some intrepid detective work, managed to round up a four-man burglary ring within a week and deliver them to the sheriff. "We could use somebody like you around here," the sheriff acknowledged, and Nall's career in law enforcement was launched.

Just after lunch on Thursday, Alex House, having managed to get his trucks loaded with calcium carbonate, got a call from Rebecca Jean Cox, at the Sny, as the Sny levee commission is generally referred to. House keeps a large bulldozer at his limestone quarry, and is on a list that the Sny keeps of people who are willing to volunteer their equipment in case of emergency. Could he get his bulldozer and bring it down to the levee to help reinforce it? House said he'd be right down, but when he reached Marblehead, a hamlet just north of the levee, a stream had overflowed its banks, flooding the bridge east of town leading to the quarry. The bulldozer was stuck.

When House arrived at the levee, without his bulldozer, about twenty farmers and their relatives had gathered at Norman Brockmeyer's farm there, including Ken Crim; his aunt, Betty; his son, Eric; and his uncle, Harold Robbins. For House, looking out from the simple two-story white farmhouse that was being transformed into the levee headquarters, it was hard to believe that danger lurked just to the west. The season's heavy rains had left the vast fields of corn and soybeans luxuriant and vividly green, and a field of sunflowers blazed yellow in the distance. But the farmers' faces betrayed their anxiety. Ordinarily, the depth of the river at the Sny is about eleven feet; seventeen feet is considered the technical flood level. The Sny levee rises twenty-eight feet above the channel. Nobody knew the precise level of the river at that moment, but it looked to be about a foot below the top of the levee, or about twenty-seven feet. And it was rising at an alarming rate—about an inch an hour. Water was already seeping through the base of the levee into the fields, and the dirt road leading from the farmhouse to the levee had already turned into a quagmire. Worse, the National Weather Service had just issued a revised forecast, predicting a thirty-foot crest —a record—on Saturday, which was only forty-eight hours away. The evacuation of the entire Sny district had begun that morning, and was proceeding with amazing speed. People packed up their belongings for the trip to friends' or relatives' houses on higher ground. Animals, including those on some major hog farms in the immediate vicinity, were herded into trucks and driven to other farms for boarding. Some farmers, like Crim and House, simply took their livestock to market prematurely. In the background was the constant roar of trucks, laden with livestock, rumbling over gravel access roads.

In their years of farming, the group at the Brockmeyer farm had assembled an astonishing array of skills, from carpentry and veterinary medicine to the running and the repairing of heavy machinery. But most of them had never lived through a serious flood threat. They didn't really know much about levees. Because House had still been in high school during the last big flood, in 1973, he had to admit that he knew next to nothing. Crim had been a senior in high school back in the flood of 1965, and had done some sandbagging on this same stretch of levee, but then he'd gone on to Western Illinois University and subsequently farmed farther upstate, returning to the Sny area only in 1976, so he, too, missed the flood of 1973.

Fortunately, one of the early volunteers, whose farmhouse lay just beyond a row of trees, even closer to the river, was a man who had lived through every flood since 1947. His name is John Guenseth, but he's known to everyone in the area by his nickname, Peanuts, and some of his close friends have abbreviated that to Nuts. Peanuts is ordinarily a man of few words. He's thin, his angular face tanned and lined from decades of farming the Sny Basin. When he is asked a question, he tends to pause interminably, then answer in a deep, barely audible voice. Peanuts knew the river better than just about anybody. This was the first time he'd evacuated his family and animals. He himself stayed on in the farmhouse, but he recognized that it was perhaps just as well that his neighbors and fellow-volunteers didn't know much about what it takes to raise a levee. If they did, they'd be staggered by the magnitude of the task.

Farmers like Peanuts and Crim stood to lose not just their entire investment in this year's crop but perhaps their future livelihood as well. One of the reasons they didn't have flood insurance was that it would have added to their costs, and their profit margins were already razor thin. House had the resources to come back if the land flooded, but the others doubted whether they could. In any event, their farms and all the work they'd poured into them were here, and the river was here, too, threatening them.

Peanuts knew that a one-mile stretch of the levee lying just to the west of the Brockmeyer farm was a particularly weak link in the fifty-four miles of the Sny. Most of the Sny had been rebuilt in the late sixties to incorporate more sand into the levee, sand now being the preferred material for levee construction. Sand allows a certain amount of controlled seepage, and it is easily bulldozed from the base of the levee, even when wet, to increase the levee's height; indeed, by Friday morning about twenty-five bulldozers would be at work pushing sand from the bottom of the levee to the top along the length of the Sny. But, for some reason—none of the Sny's farmers seemed to know why—sand had never been added to this particular stretch. It remained an old-fashioned earthen levee, and Thursday morning's bulldozing had already proved futile there. The water-logged muck just slid back to the base of the levee. The one-mile stretch also inclined toward the river in a long convex curve, which is particularly vulnerable to the forces of a current. Peanuts explained that to raise this stretch of levee would require a wall made of wooden boards, two boards high (that is, two and a half feet), supported by wooden reinforcing beams and backed by sandbags, with the entire structure draped in plastic.

"What if it doesn't hold?" House asked.

No one answered, since the answer seemed self-evident. Finally, Harold Robbins, who is about five feet ten and weighs about two hundred and ninety pounds, said, "You're gonna see a blue flame this long" —he held his hands about four feet apart—"shoot out of this fat man's ass." That brought roars of laughter, which broke the tension. Robbins added, "You know, people think fat people can't run; but that's not true. They can run damn fast. They just can't run very far."

There wasn't any formal hierarchy to the levee-reinforcement operation; on the contrary, the volunteers got sensitive at any reference to anyone's being "in charge." But Crim seemed to possess a natural authority: he became the de-facto commander of this battle. On technical questions, everybody deferred to Peanuts. And House, mostly because he owned a cellular telephone, became the communications center, often working from the roof of his pickup. He got on the phone to various construction companies in the area, and soon trucks of lumber and gravel were arriving at the farm. Just restoring the road to the levee, so that the trucks could get to where they were needed, was a major engineering feat; tons of gravel had to be laid over the mud. Much of it sank and was soon covered with water, but in time a route was stabilized that could be traversed by four-wheel-drive vehicles.

As morning chores were finished and word spread through the area that help was needed, more and more farmers showed up, some from high ground many miles away. By evening, sections of boards were rising along the top of the levee as some seventy volunteers hauled the wood and sawed and hammered it. Somebody began calling this part of the Sny "the board levee," and the name stuck. Work continued through the night, though many of the original volunteers, who had been up since the storm broke the night before, were nearly dropping from fatigue. House finally quit at about ten to get some sleep and returned near dawn. Crim stayed the night. By 3 A.M., the first stretch of boards was in place. Still, as everybody knew, the boards were the easy part. The entire section now had to be buttressed with thousands of sandbags, each one of which had to be filled, moved along the levee, and put in place by hand. With the river now lapping just inches below the base of the boards, there was no way that even seventy farmers could outpace the river.

Early Saturday morning, Dean Paben, the levee superintendent, again got on the phone to Sheriff Nall, and this time told him that the situation was getting desperate—the Sny needed bodies, as fast as possible. Nall hadn't had much luck rounding up inmates. A new experimental program had gone into effect up in Greene County, in which first offenders facing up to five-year sentences got drastic reductions in return for entering a highly disciplined, boot-camp-like program. The program had been overwhelmed with applicants from Illinois's prison population, and had become quite selective: inmates chosen had to be no more than twenty-nine years old, physically fit, and highly motivated. Reflecting the demographics of the state's inmate population, most of them were from inner-city Chicago, were black, and knew nothing about farming or the river. Still, Nall thought they'd make ideal levee workers. But when he reached the warden he learned that the prisoners available were already in Niota, Illinois, a small town to the north. Nall's nearly twenty-year tenure as Adams County sheriff gives him a certain clout, which other sheriffs can't match. Nall won't say exactly what happened but just says he "called in his chips." By midmorning, thirty of the boot-camp inmates, along with fifteen prisoners from the county jail, were en route to the Sny. Nall called on the Quincy Salvation Army and the Red Cross to supply them with food and water, and both groups swung into action.

With the inmates on their way, Nall jumped into his car and headed for the levee. When he arrived, at about 8:30 A.M., sandbags were being filled and distributed, both by boat, along the outer edge of the levee, and by a human chain, inside it. "It looked like something out of 'Bridge on the River Kwai,' " the sheriff recalls. "The fear was there, all over their faces. I know most of these people. They had a look of tragedy." Nall himself grew up in Camp Point, a small farming community northwest of Quincy, but he didn't know much about the river—"I'm an upland guy," he explains—and to his eyes the situation already looked pretty bad. "There was heavy seepage all along the bend—I thought it was done, busted," he says. But then Peanuts came by. "He said it looked great," Nall recalls. "I didn't understand that."

Crim approached him, and asked, "Was you able to do anything for us?"

"I pulled strings," Nall said. "They're on their way."

Meanwhile, caught up in the spirit of emergency, Nall himself began hurling sandbags.

Crim, House, and the others on the levee heard the new arrivals before they saw them. As the prison van pulled up, the inmates jumped out, chanting and singing a rhythmic military cadence, and marched toward the levee. To the tired workers, the drug dealers and thieves were a welcome sight. They were smartly attired in white T-shirts and dark-blue trousers with orange stripes. More to the point, their biceps and chest muscles bulged. They formed a human chain and began heaving sandbags at twice the volunteers' rate, all the while continuing their singing and chanting. Their work was closely monitored by black-uniformed guards wearing dark glasses. All the other watchers were simply awed by the new workers, who showed no signs of tiring in ninety-five-degree heat. House was so impressed by them that late in the day he asked their supervisor if he might thank them on behalf of the other workers. As House recalls it, the supervisor snapped, "You certainly may not. I'm not satisfied with them. They were slacking. They ate like pigs—they didn't wait for everyone to be served." Indeed, he singled out one of the inmates and marched him down from the levee. "Drop," he commanded. The inmate fell into a half-raised pushup position over what House says was poison ivy. "Now freeze." The supervisor turned away and resumed his conversation with House. As time passed, House could see the inmate's arms begin to quiver, and finally he collapsed.

He wasn't the only one suffering from heat and exhaustion. In the best of circumstances, a levee in midsummer is a place to avoid. The moist bottomland breeds mosquitoes said to be the size of horseflies. There's no shade, and the sun, reflecting off the river water, is doubly oppressive. Humidity builds, and the levee deflects any river breezes. A few workers sought relief by plunging into the water, but most of them shunned the river, unwilling to risk floating debris and ever-present water moccasins. Nightfall brought some relief, but work continued by flashlight and moonlight. Then, around midnight, someone noticed that the river's rise seemed to have slowed, and was holding steady at just under twenty-eight feet. Soon, they learned that a levee upstream had given way, easing the pressure farther south as water was siphoned off from the river onto thousands of acres in Lewis County, Missouri. It is a fact of flood life that someone else's disaster is good news downstream (a fact that has given rise, in the past, to some treacherous episodes of sabotage). At about 2 A.M., work was halted, and everybody except the prisoners and their guards retired to the Green Parrot tavern, in nearby Fall Creek. House started running an open tab, and pledged to keep it open for the duration of the flood. Forty-two thousand bags had been put in place in the last thirty-six hours.

The reprieve was brief. On Sunday, the Fourth of July, with fireworks displays and picnics cancelled throughout the area, there was heavy rain across the region. On Tuesday morning, the National Weather Service issued a forecast that had the Mississippi cresting at Quincy the following Sunday at 31.5 feet—three feet above the record. That meant that the entire stretch of board levee had to be raised, by the addition of more boards. Peanuts had never raised a levee more than two boards high. Now he called for a raise of three boards, but he didn't know whether such a levee could actually hold. The workers desperately needed more help, and House got on his cellular phone to WGEM.

The day after the heavy downpour, Leo Henning, upon learning how much the river had risen, went in to see Ralph Oakley, the station's general manager. "This is gonna be big," Henning said, and he asked that the radio station move to twenty-four-hour coverage of the flood. Oakley, whose family owns a controlling interest in the station, readily agreed, saying that it didn't matter how much it might cost. Henning rushed to beef up his small staff, securing the services of a disgruntled ex-employee of a competing station in town, and also those of someone who'd recently left WGEM in a huff. Reporters blanketed the area, and Henning threw open the line to callers. Over a period of twenty days, the station took thirty-four thousand calls, all answered on the air with no screening. Only two callers used any profanity. One ordered pizza—the only prank the station received.

News of the revised forecast had brought calls for help from all the levee districts. None of the levees along this stretch of the river, from Lima Lake to West Quincy and below, had been built to withstand a thirty-one-and-a-half-foot wall of water. Governor James Edgar called in the National Guard, but that move initially bred ill will. Local workers say they were furious when Guard contingents reported that they were there only to "monitor" work on the levees, standing by as others did the heavy labor. Nall, among others, got through to the Governor to complain, and the Guard contingent was soon ordered into full activity. Quincy took on the appearance of a war zone, with choppers ferrying troops from the airport to their barracks, in the high-school gym, and to the levees. Heavy-transport vehicles rumbled through ordinarily quiet city streets.

Now everybody wanted the inmates. Nall got a call from Harold Knapheide, who owns Knapheide Manufacturing, a truck-bed and heavy-equipment manufacturer that is one of the area's biggest employers. Knapheide had a plant in West Quincy, Missouri, threatened by the rising water. "Bob, we're in trouble," Knapheide said. "We desperately need people. Can we get the inmates?"

Oh my God, Nall thought. It was hard enough shuttling the inmates around the Illinois side of the river, but West Quincy was in another state. Go to Missouri and abandon the Illinois taxpayers? Nall shuddered at the possible political fallout. He did make some calls, but, as he expected, the idea was scotched. So he called WGEM and issued a plea for volunteers to go to West Quincy. And that evening, when his own inmates—inmates from the county jail—returned from a twelve-hour day on the Illinois levees, he asked if any of them would volunteer to work in Missouri. To his amazement, ten of the men did. After getting them to sign hastily drafted forms stating that their participation was strictly voluntary, Nall and the inmates piled back into the sheriff's van and crossed the river, where they bagged until midnight.

The plea on WGEM had brought scores of volunteers to West Quincy, and the success of the radio appeal wasn't lost on workers at the other levees. By now, everyone in town was listening, and the radio gave city dwellers a sense that this was their fight, too—probably the first flood in recent memory of which that could be said. Many Quincians had never been to a levee, and were only dimly aware of the city's dependence on the surrounding farm areas. Because of its proximity to the river, Quincy prospered first as an agricultural center and then, after the Civil War, as an industrial base. As the city's industry grew, Quincians came to think of themselves less and less as dependent on their agricultural hinterland. Yet their demeanor—friendly, easygoing, slow-talking, genteel—betrays their river heritage and their links to the South, to cities like St. Louis and Memphis. They tend to look askance at places like Chicago, where people seem too hard-edged and aggressive. At the same time, they sometimes dismiss the local farmers, especially those from Missouri, as rednecks.

This time, however, Quincians from all walks of life responded to House's radio appeal, including two lawyer friends of House's, Mark Drummond and Jon Barnard, who worked at one of Quincy's leading law firms. Drummond, in fact, had once represented Peanuts in a legal matter, but Peanuts didn't recognize him now, dressed in work clothes for sand-bagging. The lawyers found themselves alongside the prisoners, hurling sandbags. At the behest of Quincy's mayor, Chuck Scholz, a center to make sandbags was opened at Quincy University, and an appeal for labor there went out over WGEM. Thousands of volunteers showed up to shovel and bag—so many that some had to be turned away. Quincians also descended on the Salvation Army and Red Cross centers to make sandwiches. At the Sny, more than a hundred people from the city turned out, which caused some of the farmers to look at their urban neighbors in a new light. "People in Quincy, well, they'd always acted like they were above us," Crim says. "They thought they were cosmopolitan, like it was Paris or something." He admits that he came away with new respect for the city people. "They just pitched in, working real hard, like everybody else."

Almost without noticing, WGEM became a part of the story, serving as the central means of communication throughout the area. House became the unofficial correspondent reporting on the board levee: he made regular calls to update listeners, ask for help when it was needed, and also ask for supplies such as shoelaces, drill bits, and fresh water. He was given a special phone number that could put him right on the air. Other people called the station to offer services. "We've got fifteen- and sixteen-year-old girls willing to babysit down at Fifth and Cedar," Debbie from Quincy reported. A woman called to complain that the Red Cross wouldn't accept her homemade brownies, on the ground that it took only packaged food. "Ma'am, I'd just take those brownies and stand down by the levee, and I bet you won't have any trouble getting rid of them," Henning responded. He was now spending eighteen- and twenty-hour days patrolling the levees, keeping listeners updated, and coördinating the coverage. In a red tie and blue suspenders, he was easy to spot on the muddy slopes.

A constant problem at the Sny was figuring out just how high the river was at any given moment. "That's been a big fiasco," Crim says. "No one can give you any absolute river stages or elevations. You can get men on the moon, but you can't get an accurate river stage." So after the Corps of Engineers reported a nearby measure of twenty-nine feet House took a piece of lumber, sharpened one end, calibrated its length in feet and inches, and plunged it into the submerged slope of the levee, marking the level at 29. Now they had a ready measure they could rely on. It confirmed that the river was still steadily rising.

Bad as the situation looked at the Sny, it was even worse upstream, where the river would crest sooner. That day, Nall got a call asking for more inmates from a levee commissioner named Kent Deter, at the Indian Grave drainage district. "He screamed at me," Nall says. "It was barely holding. They were desperate." Nall already had his contingent of inmates at the Meyer levee, farther north, which protects the Lima Lake district. All he had left in the county jail was suspects awaiting trial who had been denied bail—some of the most dangerous criminals in the county. Nall was afraid they would escape, but he'd heard the desperation in Deter's voice. He put them in leg chains and personally escorted them up to Indian Grave to dig sand. There and at Meyer, the inmates and other workers continued to work furiously, in continuing rain, with the river rising.

Then, on Friday, July 9th, at about 5:30 P.M., a fifteen-foot-long stretch of fence backed by sandbags on the top of the Meyer levee, similar to the board levee on the Sny, keeled over from the force of two feet of water that had risen along its side. The breach quickly sucked the underlying levee into the adjoining fields, and widened to a hundred feet within two hours. Many of the workers near the site wept, including some of Nall's inmates. Others simply dropped their tools and left in silence.

At the Sny, the river suddenly started dropping. It went down more than six inches on House's stick, easing the pressure on the workers' still uncompleted stretch. They knew that there could be only one explanation: a levee break upstream. "You really feel bad," Crim said later. "You bought some time, and maybe this will put you over the hump. But they've battled just as hard as you have, and worked just as long, and done everything they could possibly do, and they've lost. You know how you'd be if you were in that situation." But what Crim said when he heard the news confirmed was "Great. I'm going home to catch some sleep." He had been up for thirty-six hours.

In past floods, a levee break the size of Meyer's, flooding more than ten thousand acres, might well have been enough to end the crisis, sending the river level on a steady downward course, but this time it brought only a brief respite at the Sny. Because of continuing heavy rains in Iowa, the National Weather Service actually raised its crest forecast to 32.5 feet at Quincy, though it did postpone the crest date to the following Wednesday. The forecast eliminated any margin for error at the Sny, where the top board had been intended merely to provide a backsplash for waves. At thirty-two feet, that board would now have to help contain the river itself, complete with waves. Worse, after examining the height of the water and comparing it with the distance from the top of the levee, someone dared to ask whether the existing sand levee really was at the twenty-eight-foot level it was supposed to be. Careful measurement showed it to be almost a foot shy—information that nearly caused panic along its length. Crim had to issue orders for an unprecedented fourth board to be added.

The new prediction prompted an even more intensive period of work at the Sny. WGEM broadcast another plea for help, and the National Guard brought in more troops and shifted some others. Hundreds of volunteers poured in from Quincy. They worked around the clock, under searchlights at night, and through pouring rain, which only made the heat feel worse. Most workers donned rain gear consisting of black plastic garbage bags with slits cut for their heads.

By Tuesday morning, they had just about completed the fourth board on the top of the levee. Sandbagging was well under way—about

half a million bags had been put in place since the July 4th weekend—
and they were working frantically to beat the crest. But then a dark bank
of clouds loomed in the west, and a wind kicked in, adding to the
destructive force of wave action and causing some waves to splash over
the top of the new boards. "I thought we were going to lose it right
there," Peanuts recalls. They'd worked through heavy rains, but now
large lightning bolts began hitting the area. Some of the workers flat-
tened themselves in the mud for protection. "I thought, If we lose even
one life, it's not worth it," Crim says. Crim got on a radio to House, who
was up at the north end of the levee, about two miles away. "We've
got a severe storm warning, with fifty-five-mile-an-hour winds," Crim
reported. "You have to get off the levee. We're getting off." After Crim
gave the order, all along the levee workers abandoned their bags and
shovels and started trudging back to the Brockmeyer farmhouse. National Guard troops withdrew in a convoy of military transports that
clogged the narrow, submerged road back to the farm. As House plodded
back along the levee, with the river looming at his ear level, only inches
from the top of the boards, he faced the possibility that nothing could
stop the river this time.

Later, when almost all the workers had dispersed and the rain,
thunder, and lightning continued, House stood alone with Crim on the
porch of the farmhouse, gazing across the waterlogged fields at the
distant levee. He recognized that the river had become an obsession—
that his fervent need to hold it back was something that went beyond
any rational calculation of his own interests. Now he thought that he'd
lost, that his work and all the thousands of man-hours of heavy labor
would become meaningless in minutes. "So this is how it all ends,"
House said to Crim, unable to conceal the bitterness in his voice. Crim
looked at him, and said nothing. He just shrugged and turned back
toward the levee.

The Meyer break on Friday had brought the national media to
Quincy. When they arrived, many were pleasantly surprised. Not only
was Quincy dry but it offered amenities not often found in Midwestern
communities of its size. (Its population is thirty-nine thousand.) Many
residents boast that Quincy was a city when Chicago was just a frontier
outpost. As an old river port, it had its heyday in the mid-nineteenth
century, when it was the site of one of the Lincoln-Douglas debates and
served as an important stop on the Underground Railroad. Much of its
architecture dates from the antebellum period. A large section of the
central city is now a national historic district. Quincy has an active
community theatre—Arthur Kopit's version of "The Phantom of the
Opera" was on that weekend—and a symphony orchestra, in which Leo
Henning played oboe for many years.

Most Quincians were of two minds about visitors from the national
media. On the one hand, they were flattered by the reporters' interest
and attention, and were eager to make a good impression, to show them
a good time, and to be helpful. On the other hand, many of the reporters
were rude, inclined to spend as little time as possible on the story, and,
worst of all, error-prone. "I have to admit I was almost angry at some of

them," Nall says. "We were there to work, and they were getting in the way. I said, 'Put those pencils down and start throwing some bags.' Most did, some didn't. Finally, I said to everybody, 'Look, they're just doing a job. Let's help them, let's get them to the key spots. Let's get them out of our way.' "

Exasperation may have peaked with a report by the CNN correspondent Don Knapp, who did a live broadcast from Front Street, which had flooded. Pointing to a facility surrounded by water, he warned that Quincy's water-treatment plant and drinking water were under imminent threat. In fact, he was pointing at the sewage-treatment plant; the water-treatment plant was on much higher ground, on the other side of the street, and was under no immediate threat of flooding. But worried viewers immediately began phoning WGEM, so WGEM issued its own report, assuring listeners that the water supply was safe. It was the first of many occasions on which local reporters found themselves correcting errors by others, with the result that many in Quincy came to question the accuracy of the national media on other matters, too.

In contrast, the *Times* reporter Sara Rimer, thirty-nine years old, outgoing and vivacious, quickly became a popular figure around town. Though she had never been to a levee, people admired her eagerness to learn, her thoroughness, and her accuracy. "I wanted the reporters to go away feeling they'd done more than just report, and I think Sara Rimer did," Nall says. "I respect her a lot. She got behind the tragedy and went for the human interest." Rimer also created some merriment at the Sny levee, which she visited, asking House at one point, "That Mr. Crim, he looks so powerful. Does he lift weights?" For the rest of the week, levee workers, convulsed by the idea that a farmer would lift weights, were ribbing Crim, asking him, in a mincing voice, "Do you lift weights?"

Rimer says she knew Crim's strength didn't come from the gym. "What I was struck by is that all the people in New York are pumping iron even though they push paper and answer phones. I don't want to put down New York men, but these were larger-than-life men. They were also such gentlemen. They'd carry you over a mudhole." Rimer, who is single, and the twice-divorced sheriff seemed to get along so well —he brought her a taste of some homemade deer sausages and met her at the Green Parrot—that some of the farmers on the levee speculated that they'd make a good match.

That Tuesday evening, thinking that the battle for the Sny was lost, Crim and House went home for some sleep. Before nightfall, however, Peanuts ventured back to the levee. Someone called out excitedly, "Hey, Nuts, I think it's falling." Peanuts quickly confirmed that it was. It dropped about six inches in twenty minutes. Overnight, it dropped two feet. Of course, that could only mean another levee break upstream. This time, it was the Indian Grave South levee that had given way, just above Quincy, flooding about nine thousand additional acres. Work crews rushed to a second levee at Indian Grave North, but that, too, soon gave way, submerging eight thousand acres more. House's stick indicated that the river had actually brushed up against the thirty-two-foot mark during Tuesday's storm, and, against all odds, the Sny had held. Despite the breaks and the immediate reprieve, the National Weather Service renewed its prediction for a 32.5-foot crest, but put it back another day, to Thursday. "It just kept coming at us like a bouncing ball," House says.

The day after the Sny levee survived the storm and the first thirty-two-foot crest, representatives of the Army Corps of Engineers descended on the levee. According to House, a Corps of Engineers captain had been there briefly the previous Friday, and had got off to a bad start by criticizing House for the way he was building the access road. "Are you putting down mats to keep the gravel from mixing with the mud?" the captain had asked.

"No," House replied.

"That's what the Corps recommends," the captain rejoined, in what House deemed an officious tone. "We have a supply at Rock Island."

"I bet we'll have this road done before you find the matting," House countered.

On this second visit, the captain had some new suggestions. Gazing along the length of the levee, which had taken such prodigious effort to build, he said, "We need to raise that board levee."

Crim and House were stunned, but shrugged and said, "O.K., what's your suggestion?"

"Well, we've got this giant dragline, and we'll just put it down there" —he pointed to the field adjacent to the base of the levee—"and get some dirt and make a new levee." Crim rolled his eyes in disbelief. There was no dry dirt within ten miles. And, even if there had been, anyone who tried to dig at the base of the levee would have just caused water to rush up, weakening the whole structure.

Crim says, with some exasperation, "He stands there telling us this, and about that time in came a National Guard pickup and tried to pull up. He buried it. Then this character says, 'Mr. So-and-So, getting out of this truck, is an excellent dragline operator. Excellent.' Now this numb-nuts just buried his pickup in the mud. And *he's* going to run the dragline for us? I said, 'Whoa! This is a very dumb idea.' "

Shortly afterward, House says, he came upon two Corps engineers bickering about the height of the river. "I can tell you pretty close," House said. "Thirty point five."

"How do you know?" they asked skeptically. "My stick," he said, pointing into the river's flow. "I marked it." One of the engineers waded into the water. After examining the rudimentary measure, he infuriated House by pulling it out. He later replaced it with a stick of his own, using the same principle as House's, and said that it was a Corps device.

From then on, the farmers and volunteers on the levee listened politely to the Corps's suggestions and then ignored them. For what they all thought, and Peanuts actually said, was that practically all the levees upstream to which the Corps had lent its expertise had met the same fate: they broke.

The new thirty-two-foot crest rolled through on Thursday evening, and the river stayed at just about that level all day Friday. Amazingly, the Sny, though increasingly saturated from the prolonged pressure, held.

House, Crim, and the others at the levee couldn't help feeling a little euphoric. The fourth board had held. Work at the Sny now slowed somewhat, focussing on maintenance and twenty-four-hour patrol. Occasional "boils" popped up inside the levee—sudden geysers, triggered by the river's immense pressure—but Peanuts had assured everyone that as long as they ran clear they weren't undermining the structural strength of the levee. Still, they had to be contained behind rings of sandbags. And the vigilance couldn't let up, for the longer the river remained above flood level the weaker the levee became. House found that, for the first time in two weeks, he had some time to himself. Given the group's dependence on the expertise of Peanuts, he worried about the day in the future when Peanuts wouldn't be around. He thought that it would be a good idea to film their work on a video camera, in order to leave to future generations a record of how they had fought—and, God willing, defeated—the great flood of 1993.

Friday evening, House managed to get a seat on a National Guard helicopter that was patrolling the flood region from Lima Lake down to the south end of the Sny. From the air, the scope of the river's conquest was awesome. Nearly all the major levees, including several on the Missouri side of the river, had now broken. The Mississippi, normally contained in a channel less than a mile wide, was now nine miles wide in places. House trained his camera on the Sny levee as the helicopter passed it—a thin, suddenly frail-seeming bulwark, dotted with a chain of white sandbags, where workers were crawling like ants in places. The chopper crossed to the Missouri side near Hannibal, then turned north, toward West Quincy.

After Knapheide's call for emergency help, the West Quincy levee had made as much progress as the Sny, and it, too, had withstood the successive thirty-two-foot crests. Apart from a few boils, it looked strong. But House knew that the hours just after a crest are often the most dangerous ones, as the levee tries to adjust to the sudden shift in pressure. As House leaned out the open door of the chopper to get a better shot, he saw what looked like a trickle of water going over the top of the West Quincy levee. He couldn't believe his eyes. Suddenly, the trickle leaped into a torrent. He grabbed the pilot's shoulder and pointed frantically. The pilot radioed the authorities, then banked the helicopter over the levee so House could capture the break on video. Soon the grim news was on WGEM Radio, and later that night House's video was featured on television. Leo Henning, who was having a rare night off, was pulled out of the audience at the theatre's production of "Phantom," and went straight back to the station to coördinate coverage. "I ran up to the roof of the Hotel Quincy and started doing 'The War of the Worlds,' " he says. At intermission, the audience, many of whose members lived in or near West Quincy, was told of the break. Many burst into tears. As the news of the break spread, Quincians drove to vantage points along the river. Water quickly gushed west. Idle barges tethered along that side of the river were sucked into the breach, and one hit a fuel-storage tank. Oil spread over the surface of the rushing water and soon erupted in a spectacular fire. When the flames subsided, the usual lights of West Quincy had disappeared: there was only darkness. "In the end," Henning says, "it was like West Quincy wasn't even there. It was like a black pit. You could see the lights of Hannibal, the lights of Quincy, the lights of Canton, but over there it was just jet black."

The Bayview Bridge, the last link between Quincy and Missouri, was closed immediately. Now there was no bridge crossing open between Burlington, Iowa, and St. Louis, a stretch of over two hundred miles. Greater Quincy was suddenly isolated from about forty per cent of its population, many of whom worked in, shopped in, and used the services of Quincy. The economic disruption was immediate and painful. More than any of the other levee breaks, the West Quincy disaster hit hard. Not just among the levee workers but throughout Quincy, a collective sense of despair seemed to replace the near-euphoric mood of coöperative enterprise. "It's devastating," Nall says. "You've done everything, and then you lose. You're let down, depressed. I talk to people, and they ask, 'Could we have worked harder? Was it our fault?' They felt so bad."

Nall himself was in his patrol car, coming home from the grocery store, when he heard the news on WGEM. Then the city police radioed him. As soon as he got home, he flipped the television on and saw House's footage of the break. "I felt like packing it in," Nall says. "Shit, it's over now." But he went back to his car and headed for the Sny, the last major levee still standing. West Quincy, of course, had brought the Sny another reprieve—the river dropped two feet almost immediately —but anxious workers, including Crim and Peanuts, had gathered there to discuss the implications of this latest break upstream. They were soon joined by Nall, and they vowed not to let up, and to keep fighting to hold off the river. Nall says that the people there gave him renewed inspiration. "We still had the Sny," he says, "and as long as we had the Sny we hadn't lost."

Quincians were also bolstered the next day by a phone call to WGEM. Steve Cramblit, a sales manager turned reporter, answered the phone at about 8:30 A.M., and an operator said, "This is Air Force One calling. Will you take the call?" Cramblit was so astonished that at first he thought the operator was asking him to pay for the call—would Air Force One call collect? Then an aide got on the phone, and said, "The President would like to be on your radio station." Henning was connected via his car phone but opted to let his reporters in the studio handle the interview. Cramblit and three of his colleagues gathered in the studio, and at about nine-fifteen President Clinton, speaking from his plane en route to a governors' conference in St. Louis, came on the air. "I wanted to call you," the President said, "because your radio station has done such a remarkable job of coördinating the information, keeping people in touch, and keeping them up in the middle of this. I really respect your effort and appreciate it very much." One reporter, Rich Cain, mentioned how exhausted the National Guard troops and volunteers were, and asked if Clinton had considered bringing in federal troops—an idea that Clinton later broached in St. Louis. When the interview was over, the veteran reporter Bob Turek told Henning it had been the proudest moment of his career. "I've done City Council meetings and zoning meetings and lost dogs for forty years," he said. "Finally, I got to say, 'Thank you, Mr. President.' "

■

As Nall watched WGEM's coverage of the West Quincy break, he had a nagging feeling that something wasn't right. One of the first people interviewed by Michelle McCormack, the WGEM reporter in West Quincy, was a slight young man who claimed to have been near the site of the break and to have warned unnamed "brass" that dangerous boils were present. No one had taken him seriously, he said.

Minutes later, Nall got a call from a county probation officer. The person he'd seen on TV, the officer said, had been released from prison after serving three and a half years of a seven-year term for arson. His plea had been guilty by reason of mental illness; in other words, he was some kind of disaster freak. Nall put his force and the city police on alert, saying that he wanted the man held for questioning. "I said, 'Grab this S.O.B.,' " Nall recalls.

When Nall reached the suspect at his home the next night, he said he was on his way to board a shuttle bus to the Sny. "I told him, 'I don't want to catch you anywhere near the Sny,' " Nall says.

Rumors immediately coursing throughout Quincy accurately reported the suspicion of sabotage and the identity of the suspect. There seemed to be a collective eagerness to abandon the presumption of innocence—a sense that somehow, if it could be shown that the workers had been betrayed by one of their own, they had not been defeated by the river itself.

At the Sny, news of the investigation led to increased patrols and a heightened sense of vigilance. House, Crim, and the others there recognized how easy it would be for one person with a shovel to undo their efforts; on the other hand, the force of the river was a constant presence just over their shoulders, and perhaps made them a little less willing to jump to conclusions. Nor did these developments, exciting though they were, interrupt the routine of holding off the river. Day after day, night after night, a band of farmers kept watch, sitting under a makeshift canopy of boards and plastic sheets, measuring the river's progress.

"A lot of people think the trouble's over, because we withstood the thirty-two feet, and there's nothing to do but monitor around the clock," Crim told me. "But you're still dealing with a thirty-foot river. If you'd ever told me I'd be sitting here hoping for a twenty-eight-foot river, I'd have said you were crazy. But now here I am. We're a long way from being out of the woods."

Sheriff Nall, too, warned that no one should get complacent; tears welled in his eyes as he described the destruction he had already witnessed, from Meyer to West Quincy. He said the experience had helped change the way he viewed his job. "My focus used to be, How many can we arrest and how many can we put away?" he said. "After twenty years, I'm thinking more, How can I help the community? What can I do?"

Late that week, an unsettling calm settled over the Sny Basin. The river began to creep lower, but, a week after the West Quincy break, it still held at something over thirty feet. Virtually all the farmhouses were now deserted, their usually neat lawns overgrown from the heavy rains, an occasional lawn ornament rising from them into the still, humid air. In place of the usual lively farmyard cacophony were empty barns and feeders. Magnificent stands of corn and soybeans stretched in waves toward the high ground in the distance. Gazing over the fertile expanse, Crim mused on the struggle. "Even if, God forbid, this thing breaks and floods, there will come a time when the water will all disappear," he said. "Some of the people will be back. I don't know if I'll be back, but the time will come, somewhere down the road, when everybody can move back. You'll pick things up and try to put them back together." Then he shrugged, and said he tries to stay philosophical. "We've done everything we know how to do. Evidently, we've done something right, wouldn't you say? We're one of the few still standing."

That weekend, the rains resumed, and slowly the river began to rise again. On Sunday the twenty-fifth, at 11:20 A.M., the Sny levee gave way from its base at a point right next to House's farm and Crim's house. By the end of the day, an area three times the size of Manhattan was inundated to depths of up to fifteen feet. The instant House and Crim heard on the radio that the Sny was weakening and might give way, they rushed to Peanuts' house to save what they could of his remaining belongings. Then they hurried to Crim's house to save his refrigerator. Even as they unplugged it, they saw water rushing toward them. They abandoned the effort, stranding the refrigerator in the middle of the kitchen, ran to the pickup, and sped out with the flood close behind them. Within minutes, the house and the farm were submerged. When they parted, on higher ground, House shook Crim's hand. "We fought the good fight," he said, for the board levee, their levee, never failed. Its thin line of boards and white bags can still be seen snaking across the surface of the vast, placid inland lake.

Moby Dick in Manhattan

Can an acclaimed writer devote himself purely to his work and still make money? James Wilcox tried, and he's paying a high price for the literary life.

by JAMES B. STEWART

WHEN James Wilcox is working at the St. Francis Xavier Welcome Table, as the church's Sixteenth Street soup kitchen is called, on the first and second Sunday of every month, it's hard to tell he's an acclaimed novelist. It took some of his fellow-volunteers years to figure it out. None of them had read "Modern Baptists," his first novel, published in 1983, which was hailed in a *Times Book Review* front-page piece by Anne Tyler as "startlingly alive, exuberantly overcrowded." Nor were they familiar with its five siblings, three of them set in the fictional Tula Springs, Louisiana, which has been compared by more than one critic to William Faulkner's Yoknapatawpha County.

Wilcox himself was much too shy to tell them about any of this. He looks younger than his age, which is forty-five, and has a slightly ruddy complexion, medium build, and sandy hair. Though he's nice-looking, he agonizes over his author photographs and didn't want one on his last book. Yale-educated, he speaks with no trace of a regional accent. His Southern roots are evident only in the elaborate courtesy with which he waits on the soup kitchen's "guests," as he unfailingly calls them when he is dispensing juice and coffee. He betrays little reaction even when something really grabs his attention, like the saga of a woman who was plagued by the stench from a neighbor who kept twenty-two cats in her Murray Hill one-bedroom apartment.

"For years, I never knew what Jim did," I was told by George Deshensky, a lawyer who is one of the directors of the soup kitchen. "Then, one day, someone said, 'He's a published author.' So we'd introduce him that way. We didn't know what he published or where." Deshensky began relying on Wilcox as a "calming influence" when altercations threatened to break out in the line—something that happened with some regularity. Since then, during the eight years that Wilcox has been working at the soup kitchen, he and Deshensky have become close friends and Deshensky has read his books. Still, Deshensky was surprised when, after he complimented Wilcox on the empathy he shows for the soup kitchen's impoverished patrons, Wilcox replied, "I'm only a check or two from being in the line myself."

There have always been struggling novelists, of course, as well as a handful of best-selling, highly publicized multi-millionaires. But in the past twelve years James Wilcox has published six novels to rave reviews. While his books are classified as "literary fiction" by the publishing industry, they aren't inaccessible or highbrow. He has been described as a "comic genius" *(Vogue)*, "a master" *(Kirkus Reviews)*, "a natural. . . . One of the most promising fiction writers on the national scene" (Los Angeles *Times*), "among the classic American humorists" *(Newsday)*, and "Dickensian in [his] wealth of eccentric characters" (New York *Times*). He has a high-powered agent, Amanda (Binky) Urban, of International Creative Management, who has consistently got him advances that were larger than could be justified strictly on the basis of the number of his books sold. In other words, among novelists Wilcox counts himself one of the lucky ones. Even so, the current state of publishing has consigned him to a life of near-poverty.

At my insistence, Wilcox, who is single and lives alone, showed me his tax returns for the past ten years. His best year was 1988, when he had a gross income of $48,600 before agent commissions (of ten percent) and expenses. He now remembers that year as an aberration—a time when he could eat out occasionally, and even take a cab. And since that time, as the market for trade-paperback fiction has shrunk and authors' advances have declined, his income has dropped accordingly. In 1992, he earned twenty-five thousand dollars. Last year, it was fourteen thousand dollars. The advance for his current novel was ten thousand dollars; in a concession, his publisher gave him two-thirds up front, rather than the customary half. When I visited him recently, he had just finished the last of three meals he'd extracted from eighteen pieces of chicken he bought at Key Food for three dollars and forty cents.

Nor is Wilcox's plight confined to making ends meet. HarperCollins, which published his last five books, didn't exercise its option for his current project. Only Hyperion, the Disney publishing subsidiary, showed any interest in the manuscript, and then mostly because Rick Kot, the editor who championed Wilcox at Harper, had recently moved to Hyperion. Hyperion is a smaller house, less able than HarperCollins to indulge a distinguished but unprofitable author. In Wilcox, commerce and art are now at a standoff, with Wilcox's future as a novelist at stake. At a time when some unpublished first novelists are igniting bidding wars and hauling down advances of half a million dollars, "we were lucky to get ten thousand dollars," Urban says of Wilcox's current contract. "This book is absolutely critical. Something has to happen."

Like Deshensky, I'm a friend of Jim's, who, before I began this story, had no idea of his dire financial plight. I met him a little more than a year ago, at a dinner party given by Urban to celebrate his latest novel, "Guest of a Sinner." Urban is my agent, too, but I hadn't realized that she represented Jim until I spotted a copy of "Sort of Rich," his fourth book, one day on her bookshelf and, because I was already a Wilcox fan, asked her to introduce me.

"Sort of Rich" is one of my favorite books. I bought it after reading a *Times* review, found something to think about on almost every page ("The twenty-four chicks Mrs. Dambar had purchased last week had dwindled to three as a result of an unpleasant disease and six or so getting lost on a walk she had taken them on to strengthen their leg muscles"), and returned to the bookstore a week later to buy another copy, as a gift. It was no longer in stock and wasn't being reordered—a situation that may help explain why it ultimately sold just forty-seven hundred copies in hardcover. Jim himself, I must confess, made less of an impression on me at Urban's dinner. Besides being overshadowed that night by last year's playoff between the Knicks and the Bulls, he was characteristically shy. We barely spoke. Afterward, though, he phoned and reminded me that we had actually met at a party five years before. He even remembered what we had discussed—piano playing.

Since then, we've met from time to time to play piano duets. Jim could have been a professional musician, and almost was, on both the cello and the piano. In our duets, he generally plays the more difficult "primo" parts, and, although he always maintains that he doesn't want to perform, we've given three small recitals this year. We've even joked about taking our act to the American Booksellers Association annual meeting: anything to ingratiate ourselves with—or, at least, make an impression on—booksellers. In the course of our practice sessions, I began to suspect that Jim wasn't exactly flush. He mentioned that he couldn't afford to have his piano tuned, and that, in any event, it was on loan to a friend, since he couldn't fit it into his studio apartment. Otherwise, I didn't think much about his finances; and, given Jim's nature, they are not a topic he'd ever mention. We'd sometimes eat out after our sessions, usually in modest restaurants, but once at a place that must have run forty dollars a person. Only now do I realize how that must have shattered his budget, or that he would often walk the sixty-six blocks between his apartment and mine to save the fare.

Wilcox's first break as a writer came at Yale, when he submitted a short story to Robert Penn Warren, then on the Yale faculty, and was one of twelve students admitted to his fiction seminar. Like Warren, Wilcox hails from the South. He grew up in Hammond, Louisiana, a town of fifteen thousand, not far from Baton Rouge, where his father, James H. Wilcox, plays the French horn and headed the Music Department of Southeastern Louisiana University before he retired. At Yale, Wilcox had dabbled in theatre, at one point dancing in the aisle clad only in a fur loincloth, in an avant-garde production of Ionesco's "Rhinoceros." But Warren's book "Understanding Fiction" has been an enduring influence on Wilcox's work. He wrote several short stories for Warren's seminar and a novel as a senior thesis. Though he was awarded honors for his effort, he was disappointed that Warren showed none of his work to his agent. But Warren did recommend Wilcox to Albert Erskine, a legendary editor at Random House, who was looking for a new assistant.

Wilcox arrived for his job interview neatly dressed and well groomed—an anomaly in 1971, when shoulder-length hair and T-shirts were the norm at Yale. Erskine, a Southerner, who had also lived in

Baton Rouge, later told Wilcox he had got the job because he was the only applicant with the manners to remain standing until he was invited to sit. Erskine had worked with William Faulkner and John O'Hara. He was credited with discovering Malcolm Lowry and Eudora Welty. He edited James Michener. "It made me tremble that he'd known Faulkner," Wilcox says. He was hired, at a yearly salary of seventy-five hundred dollars.

Wilcox was plunged into the world of high-end trade publishing, writing flap copy and doing line editing, and he was gradually allowed to offer more substantive criticism. James Michener, after receiving editorial comments from Wilcox on the manuscript of his best-selling novel "Centennial," sent Wilcox a letter telling him to call his travel agent. He invited Wilcox to go anywhere in Europe at Michener's expense; Wilcox chose Paris, and spent ten days there in 1974. At the other end of the publishing-income scale, Wilcox worked on novels by Cormac McCarthy, which sold only modestly. Even Erskine, Wilcox learned, could be taken to task for literary fiction that didn't sell. But Erskine stubbornly backed writers he believed in, and his stature enabled him to get away with it.

The job gave Wilcox plenty of insight into what worked and what didn't, in both the literary and the commercial sense. Much of his effort, like his editing of "The Save Your Life Diet," which became a best-seller, was hardly destined for literary seminars. He advanced from editorial assistant to associate editor at Random House, and in 1977 he moved to Doubleday as an associate editor. That meant being caught up in the swirl of agent lunches, book parties, and deal-making, and also meant rising at five-thirty to read manuscripts. "It was incredibly demanding. I had no time to write," he says. His life was at least superficially glamorous. Through Random House, he had become friends with the dashing photographer, author, and Africa enthusiast Peter Beard and was invited for a pair of weekends at Beard's house in Montauk, where he and Beard discussed Conrad and Faulkner, and he found himself mingling with celebrities. He met Catherine Deneuve, Terry Southern, Margaux Hemingway; he had dinner at Mick Jagger's; he came to know Andy Warhol, and Warhol's agent, Roz Cole, agreed to represent Wilcox.

In 1978, at the age of twenty-nine, Wilcox felt that time was running out. At Random House, Toni Morrison had had the office across the hall. She'd already written two novels, and she'd encouraged Wilcox to write. At Doubleday, he was further bolstered by Jacqueline Kennedy Onassis, who also encouraged him to try writing. Though he was now making eighteen thousand dollars a year, he had no savings. He had published none of his own writing. But he knew he had to devote himself to writing full time; his efforts during nights and weekends had been both draining and unsuccessful. It took him a year to muster the courage to leave Doubleday. The first time he approached the office of the editor-in-chief, he was too nervous to go in. He circled in the hallway, mustered his courage one more time, and came back. "I couldn't go through life, wondering if I could write something," he says.

In the disciplined and methodical way that is characteristic of him, Wilcox addressed himself to reducing his living expenses. He had found

a twelve-by-twenty-foot studio apartment on East Twenty-fourth Street
for a hundred and ninety dollars a month. It was a fourth-floor walkup
and was lighted only with a bare fluorescent fixture, but the building
was clean and comparatively quiet. Just then, too, he was lucky enough
to sell a treatment for a screenplay he'd collaborated on with a friend
from Yale. That brought in ten thousand dollars, less commissions, when
it was optioned by Columbia Pictures. (It was never produced.) The
money sustained him for a year.

Wilcox wrote one short story after another. He sent his manuscripts
to *The New Yorker, Harper's, The Atlantic, Redbook,* and they were
rejected everywhere. He began submitting them to smaller, less well-
known outlets. "All I got was rejections," he says. When one story had
made the rounds and come back, he sent off another. His money was
running out. In 1980, he started typing address labels for a lawyer. He'd
spread them out on his apartment floor, then organize them by Zip
Code. He could tell that that upset his mother—the thought of her
Yale-educated son on hands and knees fiddling with address labels.

He sent seven stories to *The New Yorker,* and all of them were
rejected, but he was heartened by correspondence with one of its editors. His first letter from the editor, which accompanied the first rejection, was "an encouraging rejection," Wilcox says. "It was a thrill to get
a real, typewritten letter from *The New Yorker.*" In response to the
second story, the editor wrote at greater length, offering criticism of the
work. He also commented on each of the five ensuing submissions.
Finally, after a year, the editor called Wilcox to say he was accepting a
story, and the magazine would pay twenty-two hundred dollars. It
seemed a fortune to Wilcox.

"Mr. Ray" appeared in the January 26, 1981, issue. "The old woman
had worked hard on the 'No Smoking' sign, embellishing the stark black
letters with ivy and birds and a dog she forgot to put the tail on," it
began. Being published in *The New Yorker* was a milestone for Wilcox
—an affirmation, of sorts—and he happily sent a copy of the magazine
home to his parents. But the piece didn't exactly cause a stir in Hammond, Louisiana. "Jimmy sure has good punctuation" was one neighbor's only comment. Another, pointing to an unrelated cartoon on one
page, asked, "Where did Jimmy learn to draw like that?"

"Mr. Ray" is set in the fictional town of Tula Springs, Louisiana, and
that aspect of the story had drawn approving comment from the editor.
After the story was accepted, but before it was published, Wilcox began
a novel set in Tula Springs. He wrote the first half in six months, while
living on the money from "Mr. Ray." Since Cole was no longer representing him, he offered the unfinished manuscript to another agent; after
reading it, the agent said he couldn't sell it. Wilcox was discouraged,
but a little later a friend read it and said it was funny. Wilcox persevered
for another year, and in June of 1982 he finished the book, which he
had entitled "Modern Baptists." He offered it to two more agents, and
both rejected it as unsalable. Then Harriet Wasserman, an independent
agent, agreed to handle it. Knopf, Simon & Schuster, and Viking all
turned it down.

Rick Kot, then a young editor at the Dial Press, heard about "Modern Baptists" from another editor, who said he had read it and had hated to turn it down, but it was a comic first novel—a tough sell. Kot called Wasserman and asked for the manuscript. Though he liked it, he was cautious about publishing it. "It's always a gamble publishing a first novel," Kot says. "With a comic novel, it's an even bigger gamble. It's a marketing truism that the sense of humor is very subjective. Comedy is a very tough category. 'Modern Baptists' fitted the convention of Southern humor, but it was more serious, more ambitious." The *New Yorker* story offered confirmation that Wilcox had talent. Though Kot had concentrated on nonfiction, he offered sixty-five hundred dollars for the book, and, not surprisingly, since that was the only offer, it was accepted.

The main characters in "Modern Baptists" are Bobby Pickens (always known as Mr. Pickens), a forty-one-year-old bachelor who works at the Sonny Boy Bargain Store, and F.X., his improbably handsome half brother, who has just been released from Angola State Penitentiary after serving time for dealing cocaine at a nearby dinner-theatre-in-the-round.

At one point, Mr. Pickens, who has fallen in love with a young employee at the Bargain Store named Toinette Quaid, aspires to the cloth:

> Mr. Pickens knew that once he got his preaching diploma, he would open a church for modern Baptists, Baptists who were sick to death of hell and sin being stuffed down their gullets every Sunday. There wasn't going to be any of that old-fashioned ranting and raving in Mr. Pickens's church. *His* Baptist church would be guided by reason and logic. Everyone could drink in moderation. Everyone could dance and pet as long as they were fifteen—well, maybe sixteen or seventeen. At thirty, if you still weren't married, you could sleep with someone and it wouldn't be a sin—that is, as long as you loved that person. If you hit forty and were still single, you'd be eligible for adultery not being a sin, as long as no children's feelings got hurt and it was kept very discreet. But you still had to love and respect the person; you couldn't just do it for sex.

However, upon being spurned by Toinette Mr. Pickens finds himself alone with Toinette's chunky friend Burma LaSteele:

> He stood before her in his new orange bikini briefs and his matching orange undershirt. His belly button was plainly visible; the underwear was two sizes too small.
>
> "Why pretend?" Mr. Pickens said, pulling the T-shirt over his head. His white hairless chest swelled out into a sizable belly, from which Burma averted her eyes. . . .
>
> "Mr. Pickens," Burma said, turning away. "Please, get dressed. You're drunk."
>
> "This is your chance, Burma. Why blow it? You're getting old —there's gray in your hair, gray in mine. We're going to die, all of us, we're going to die miserable, unloved. I can't stand it anymore. At least one of us can be happy. You, Burma. You be happy. You deserve it more than any of us. You're good, Burma. You're a good,

good woman. I can see your heart. It's pure and unselfish and good."
Tears ran down his cheeks and his nose began to run. "Take it. Grab
life before it passes you by." He stepped out of the briefs, and she
beheld him stark naked, except for his left sock, the one with the
hole in it, which he had forgotten to take off.

Kot says that "Modern Baptists" needed little editing—given Wilcox's own editing background, his manuscripts are meticulously written
—but he insisted that Wilcox rewrite the ending. "He had Mr. Pickens
die in a train wreck, which violates every convention of comedy," he
explains. So Mr. Pickens' car runs out of gas as he tries to commit suicide
by crashing into a telephone pole.

Shortly after Kot finished the editing, early in 1983, he was fired—
not for signing up books like "Modern Baptists" but as part of a sweeping
cost-cutting campaign that accompanied the consolidation of Dial into
its owner, Doubleday. Fortunately, a surviving editor at Dial, Allen Pea-
cock, liked "Modern Baptists" and kept it alive. The publicist for Dial
was also enthusiastic about the book, and she had a good track record
with reviewers. Positive blurbs were rounded up from prominent writers, including Robert Penn Warren and Brendan Gill. The book soon
developed the momentum of a modest hit. In its Forecasts section,
Publishers Weekly, the trade bible, gave "Modern Baptists" a "boxed"
review—one that not only was favorable but put booksellers on notice
that "Modern Baptists" could be a hit. The book was published in June,
1983. Then, in mid-July, rumor had it that Anne Tyler, a "hot" novelist
on the heels of the huge success of "Dinner at the Homesick Restaurant,"
was reviewing the book for the *Times.* Many books are review-proof,
and their publishers can afford to be indifferent to the *Times,* but literary
fiction like Wilcox's lives or dies on the strength of its Sunday *Times*
review.

On July 31st, on the *Book Review's* front page—the most coveted
position in the book industry, one that Kot says many writers would
"give their right arm for"—Tyler wrote, "Every reviewer, no doubt, has
methods for marking choice passages in a book. Mine is a system of
colored paper clips; yellow means funny. 'Modern Baptists' should be
thick with yellow paper clips on every page, but it does even better
than that. While I was reading it, I laughed so hard I kept forgetting my
paper clips. Mr. Wilcox has real comic genius. He is a writer to make us
all feel hopeful."

The review was a godsend, triggering a wave of favorable reviews,
from nearly every major paper. Wilcox had a brush with celebrity when
a producer for Barbara Feldon (Agent 99 of "Get Smart") called to say
that Ms. Feldon might be interested in having Wilcox as a guest on her
cable-TV talk show. Hollywood was said to be interested in the screen
rights. It was, of course, dizzying to be the subject of so much acclaim
so soon—especially for someone as modest as Wilcox. "He was thrilled,
or what passes for thrilled with Jim," Kot says. "He said something like
'Oh, gosh.' " Wilcox never inquired about the size of the first printing
("I didn't want to know; I assume it was low," he says), which was five
thousand copies. The book went back to press four times, and ultimately

sold eleven thousand copies in hardcover. The Literary Guild optioned it. Penguin bought the paperback rights, for ten thousand dollars. It was published in the United Kingdom. For his next novel, Wasserman was able to negotiate an advance of $27,500. Dial bid on it, but Harper & Row, which had meanwhile hired Kot as an editor, outbid Dial. Wilcox dared to believe that his future as a novelist was secure. He stopped writing short stories.

Having read the first hundred pages of the new manuscript, Kot had high hopes for it. "It was a coup to get him," he says. "I saw a writer with a promising career, someone we wanted to develop. I loved his work and liked him personally. Harper wanted to do more literary fiction." As it happened, literary fiction was driving what was then the hottest category in publishing—trade paperbacks. The runaway success of Jay McInerney's "Bright Lights, Big City," which was originally published in trade paperback rather than hardback, had publishers scrambling to develop their own lists of hot novels in that large-type, softcover format, which typically sold at about half the hardcover price, rather than the one-fifth to one-fourth charged for mass-market paperbacks. In the past, trade publishers had typically auctioned reprint rights to paperback publishers and split the ensuing royalties with the author; that was what had been done with "Modern Baptists." But because costs for trade paperbacks were only slightly higher than those for mass-market paperbacks they could be profitable with even relatively modest sales. The Harper deal for Wilcox's new book included both hardcover and softcover royalties, a so-called hard-soft deal, which has now become commonplace.

Wilcox's second novel, "North Gladiola," was published in 1985. Its heroine, Ethyl Mae Coco, is the prime suspect in the murder of Tee-Tee, a chihuahua belonging to the Tula Springs beauty college—and Mrs. Coco had, in fact, once thrown a pan of luke-warm bacon grease on Tee-Tee. Kot's main concern was to build on Wilcox's audience for "Modern Baptists" and avoid the notorious "sophomore slump" that has felled numerous promising first novelists. He was quickly reassured. The novelist Bobbie Ann Mason hailed "North Gladiola" as "a scream." Reviews were again enthusiastic, though the *Times Book Review* didn't again give it the front page. There were no author tours, however, and no bookstore readings. Not every review was positive. After Harper's publicity department sent Wilcox a copy of a negative review, he asked that only positive reviews be sent him. Harper complied, but one negative review slipped through, leaving Wilcox much upset.

Ominously, sales of "North Gladiola" fell well below those for "Modern Baptists." It never came close to "earning out" the advance, as the publishers' phrase has it. Wilcox could barely bring himself to look at the royalty statement. "I'd open it and sort of squint at it," he says. "All I saw was a minus. Then I filed it away." He was concerned. "The momentum of 'Modern Baptists' was being rapidly lost," he says. Like many authors, he began to wonder if his agent—Wasserman—was the best agent for him. "A movie deal fizzled out, even though there seemed to be a lot of interest," he says. "I like and respect Harriet, but I wanted more to happen." Though it was painful, Wilcox severed his ties to Wasserman. Then he called Urban, who had been recommended by colleagues, and who had had great success with literary fiction, representing, among others, Jay McInerney and Bret Easton Ellis. Urban loved "Modern Baptists" and "North Gladiola," and agreed to represent him.

Despite the weak sales of "North Gladiola," Urban negotiated Wilcox's best deal yet—a two-book contract for seventy thousand dollars. That advance largely accounts for Wilcox's peak earnings of $48,600 in 1988. In 1987, when the first of the two manuscripts came in, "Miss Undine's Living Room," in which Olive Mackie runs for superintendent of Tula Springs' Department of Streets, Parks, and Garbage, Kot had the first serious problems he'd encountered in Wilcox's work. An ensemble of characters, none of them particularly sympathetic, flew in the face of literary convention. Kot invited Wilcox to dinner to discuss possible solutions.

"With 'Miss Undine,' Rick was very clear," Wilcox says. "After I turn in a manuscript, Rick takes me out to a nice dinner. We've been to Union Square Cafe, Bouley. It's a shame, really—the only time I get to go to these places, I'm too nervous to eat. He didn't like any of the 'Miss Undine' characters. He said there was no center."

Wilcox considered Kot's criticism. But his mild demeanor conceals a strong will. "Maybe I've read too many positive novels with wonderful characters," Wilcox says. "I've read genre fiction. I read Judith Krantz when I was at Doubleday. The main characters are always rugged and handsome if they're men and gorgeous and buxom if they're women. They have a drive to succeed, and they do succeed. They forge ahead in life. Why can't I write about more heroic characters?" He answers his own question. "I'm not a positive thinker. Southerners tend not to be. Faulkner, Welty, O'Connor—they're in the tradition of Hawthorne or Melville. There is depravity. We're not good people unless we really try. Popular fiction is Emersonian. He transcends the dark side of human nature. Self-reliance. We can become better people. I don't subscribe to this. The sense of reconciliation readers want is not that easily won. Unearned idealism usually does more harm than good. I absorbed this from Robert Penn Warren. He wrote a poem about a night flight to New York in which he thought about Emerson at thirty-eight thousand feet, the point being that at that distance from life you can indulge in Emerson's view of human perfectibility. I don't see Olive as positive or negative. We're all pretty mixed bags. Our faults are very much tied in to our virtues. Most of our lives are not weddings, funerals, and crises. We're not in a plane that's about to crash, and we're not about to launch a new line of high-fashion clothing. We mostly have routine days. We can't see where we're going. I've heard the most interesting things standing in the checkout line at Wal-Mart." Wilcox declined to make any significant changes in "Miss Undine."

Wilcox's world view may have been reinforced one evening soon after he put the finishing touches on that book. At a dinner party he attended, he bit into a piece of chicken and broke off a crown from a tooth. As he was walking home, castigating himself for having gone to a cut-rate dental clinic (his "dentist," actually a student, had received a failing grade for the crown installation), an attractive couple, walking arm in arm, approached him. They told him they had a weapon, then mugged him. In addition to his cash and credit cards, they stole his crown, which he'd carefully kept in his pocket. The new crown set him back eight hundred dollars.

Then he received a letter from the Internal Revenue Service announcing that he was being audited for his 1985 income, of $11,800. In addition to examining all of Wilcox's banking records, the auditor, obviously suspecting that Wilcox was hiding income, insisted on visiting his apartment. Wilcox deducted a third of his annual rent, because he had divided his small studio space into three areas—a sleeping area, a sitting area, and a work space. The auditor examined the table where Wilcox worked—which, given the size of the apartment, was close to the refrigerator—and accused Wilcox of eating there. Wilcox said he didn't ("It's much too depressing to eat next to the typewriter"), but the auditor argued that he *could* eat there, so the area wouldn't count as an office. It also lacked a solid wall, which would have cut off his view of both windows. The auditor found no undeclared income, but did disallow Wilcox's home-office deduction, which came to four hundred dollars. "He seemed very respectful," Wilcox says of the auditor, who had admitted that this audit was his first assignment for the I.R.S. "He didn't make me feel creepy, like a tax cheat, which I guess he could have."

"Miss Undine" was published three weeks later. (A dental college figures prominently in the plot.) Some readers and reviewers have said it's their favorite among his works. The reviews were almost uniformly positive. But the influential Michiko Kakutani, in the daily *Times*, sided with Kot, noting the lack of positive characters. Sales slipped to five thousand copies.

"Sort of Rich," Wilcox's next novel, which came out in 1989, brought a New Yorker, the newly married Gretchen Dambar, to Tula Springs, which somehow reminded her of both Baroness Blixen's African farm and Parsippany, New Jersey. Kot thought it Wilcox's best work —"a close to perfect novel." In an effort to boost sales, Wilcox attended the American Booksellers Association annual meeting, in Washington, D.C., and he was featured at a Harper luncheon for literary novelists. He was also sent to bookstores for readings and did a brief tour of the South. He got a television booking on a 6 A.M. show in New Orleans. A painfully small crowd showed up for autographs in Jackson, Mississippi. The reviews were very positive. But sales slipped again.

By now, Wilcox couldn't bring himself even to open his royalty statements. "They're very depressing," he says. None of the advances had earned out since "Modern Baptists." "I'd really been hoping to earn out with 'Sort of Rich,' " he says. "I knew that the publishers were paying out more than they were making. I was doing the best I could. This isn't a good situation. I'd love them to see some benefit from all they'd done for me. This was hard on me. I felt they were all hoping something would happen."

Kot and Urban talked, and agreed that something had to change in order for Wilcox to "break out" from sales of fewer than five thousand hardcover copies. On the strength of the manuscript for "Sort of Rich,"

Urban had negotiated a new, forty-five-thousand-dollar, one-book deal. But Wilcox had now done four novels set in Tula Springs. No momentum was building. No one told Wilcox this in so many words, but when he himself suggested a change of pace from Tula Springs both Kot and Urban were enthusiastic. He decided to bring some of his characters to New York.

"I hate to be so marketing-driven," Kot says. "But we had to get a handle for Jim. The big-selling novelists, like McInerney, were tapping very specific markets. Young. Urban. David Leavitt had the first gay short story in *The New Yorker.* They were generating extra-book publicity. What could we put Jim forward as?"

Without such publicity, the once promising market for literary fiction was faltering. Nan A. Talese, who publishes literary fiction as the president of her own imprint at Doubleday, says, "There are four thousand serious book buyers in this country that you can count on for literary fiction. That's your basic number, including libraries, if there isn't a bell or a whistle, like having a very beautiful author do a tour across the country without any clothes on. That's how we're selling books these days." At the same time, the trade-paperback fiction market had become saturated. Even as hardcover sales were fading, so was the Wilcox backlist. As computers proliferated in bookstores, the Harper sales force was growing more discouraged about Wilcox's prospects. "They'd look on their computers and see that his last book only sold three, so they'd say, 'We'll only take two this time,' " Kot says. "The sales force was grumbling mildly, saying it was getting harder and harder to get his books out in stores."

Kot was enthusiastic about the new book. It had a great title, something much more contemporary—"Polite Sex." F.X., the handsome miscreant from "Modern Baptists," made a reappearance. Kot pitched the book to the sales force as "Wilcox comes to New York." For the book, he hoped for a bigger urban sale. He commissioned distinctive new cover art, which won an award for graphic design. Harper managed to get seventy-five hundred copies into stores. *Time* asked for a photograph of Wilcox in anticipation of a major review.

But publication day came and went, and no major review appeared. The "news" that Wilcox had moved his setting to New York made no waves. Not only did "Polite Sex" fail to attract the urban readers Kot and Urban had hoped for but it seemed to alienate his core group of Southerners. Despite consistently favorable reviews, Wilcox's fifth book sold worse than any of the previous ones.

Kot called Urban. "I said, 'Binky, we only sold three thousand. I can't afford to pay any more. We have to be realistic.'" He reminded her that Harper (now HarperCollins, as a result of a merger) had kept all Wilcox's books in print, even buying backlist rights to "Modern Baptists." Kot offered twenty thousand dollars for Wilcox's next book—half his prior advance. Urban knew she couldn't sell Wilcox on the open market after the numbers on "Polite Sex," and, besides, she was not thrilled with the new book, which Wilcox was already writing. She worried—even as she remained convinced that Wilcox had the potential to produce a huge success—that his writing was becoming too serious, too inward, increasingly esoteric. Wilcox took the twenty thousand dollars, happy to be able to keep writing.

There was a quiet sense of dread about Wilcox's sixth novel, "Guest of a Sinner," which was published last year. Inspired in part by the woman with twenty-two cats he'd heard about at the soup kitchen, it is darker, more complex, than the earlier books. "After his father had swerved into a tree to avoid hitting a squirrel," one passage goes, "Eric had never once, in the fifteen years since, questioned if the squirrel's life was worth his mother's. Not out loud, at least. Mrs. Thorsen had been killed, while Lamar, properly buckled up, had survived without a scratch. Eric's mother always refused on principle to wear a seat belt, mainly because she thought it was the liberals who made its use a law, but also because it wrinkled her clothes." Kot was concerned because Eric, the main character, is less likable at the end of the story than at the beginning. And, though nothing seems forced or didactic, the book does have weighty themes of religion and faith. Worse, it proved impossible to describe the plot to the sales force, let alone give the book a marketing "handle."

"Guest" sold four thousand copies. For his latest book, Kot has offered Wilcox ten thousand dollars. "What was I going to do?" Kot asks. "I'd given it our best shot. We had to get a lower advance."

The economics of literary fiction are stark. Consider the cost to HarperCollins of publishing "Guest." While specific numbers are closely guarded, several people with access to HarperCollins' results provided this summary. Every book has a fixed "plant cost," which covers copy editing, setting type, proofs and proofreading—about ten thousand dollars for "Guest." Added to that is the "PPB" (printing, paper, and binding), a variable cost, depending on the number printed; a press run of six thousand for "Guest" added about nine thousand dollars. Marketing expenses, which in the case of "Guest" included advertising (a one-fifth-page ad in the *Times Book Review* cost five thousand dollars), author touring, and posters, came to just over ten thousand dollars. The advance added twenty thousand dollars. And before any of these costs are covered, twenty-five per cent of gross sales goes to general overhead. Six thousand copies of "Guest," retailing at twenty dollars, would yield $57,600 in gross sales to HarperCollins (retailers and middlemen keep just over half the cover price), so a charge for general overhead would be $14,400. Thus, total costs were approximately $63,000. "Guest" yielded no subsidiary-rights revenues. (In a hard-soft deal, the paperback edition is accounted for separately.) At four thousand hardcover copies sold, "Guest" produced about $38,000 in revenue to HarperCollins, leaving a deficit of $25,000. HarperCollins aims for a fifteen-per-cent return on investment, which means that "Guest" would have had to sell more than seven thousand copies to generate the roughly $73,000 necessary to meet that standard.

Given the way that the publishing industry allocates costs—particularly the practice of assigning an arbitrary percentage of gross sales to cover general overhead—it's easy to see the appeal of the blockbuster. A novel that sells a hundred thousand copies may never pay back its advance yet can be solidly profitable. Those are the books that generate the large revenues for general overhead, which includes, among other things, the editors' salaries.

But what about the speculative first novels that, with no author track record whatsoever, can command astronomical advances? Lately, people in the publishing industry have been buzzing about "The Day After Tomorrow," a first novel by Allan Folsom published this spring by Little, Brown, which brought a two-million-dollar advance. That money could more than sustain Wilcox for the rest of his natural life. Nan Talese explains, "The first novel that is sexy or promotable, or has just been sold to the movies, can get a huge advance, because it's something new," and she points out that "The Day After Tomorrow," the work of a Hollywood scriptwriter, had been pre-sold to the movies. "You know how Americans are about 'new.' There's no track record for the book-stores to pull up and say, 'That author only sold five thousand copies.' They see that the publisher has a lot at stake and is really going to get behind this, touring the writer, making special galleys, and so on. That's the plan." This strategy has been fuelled by the success of novels like "Damage," by Josephine Hart, and "The Secret History," by Donna Tartt, both sexy first novels with attractive authors which were enormously profitable despite large advances. "It's a very odd atmosphere," Talese says. "Publishers are willing to gamble lots of money on something that might hit big, but more hesitant to invest smaller sums and stay with an author as he or she builds an audience."

Who knows whether "The Day After Tomorrow" will change that thinking. A *Times* critic dismissed it, noting that "the author has a great deal to learn." The book's jacket copy claims that it "reinvents the thriller." It does not say what the book is actually about: an international conspiracy to clone Hitler from his frozen head. Although ads have touted it as a "No. 1 National Best-Seller," the book recently dropped off the *Times* best-seller list after eight weeks, never having reached the top spot.

Brand-name fiction writers remain the safest commercial bets, even though they, too, can command huge advances. Bill Shinker, who until recently was the publisher of HarperCollins, says, "You know that on a Sidney Sheldon or a Barbara Taylor Bradford there's no way in hell the advance will ever pay out. You can still make money. Those authors will sell at such a predictably high level that it will cover a lot of overhead. Wilcox is a labor of love. He's never going to pay your overhead."

But even a labor of love—and Shinker says he loves Wilcox's fiction—can't go on indefinitely. "After one or two books, we saw a pattern emerging. He wasn't alone in this. Trade paperbacks that once sold in multiples of what the book sold in hardcover were now selling half the hardcover sales. A very sad development, but we were up against it."

Even though Kot moved to Hyperion in 1993, HarperCollins did make a bid under its contract option for Wilcox's next work. It was low—seventy-five hundred dollars. "We felt we'd got into a rut with Jim," Shinker says. "I had no explanation for why the books weren't performing. He had fabulous reviews but never the sales to live up to them. The kind of fiction he was writing, there might have been a time in the sixties or seventies when he would have sold in mass-market paperback. But taste has changed. Today, multicultural, black, Hispanic, Japanese — that's the trend. The books that Jim did, as good as they are, fell through the cracks."

Shinker felt that HarperCollins had to make a bid that stood a chance of earning out. "God bless him if he goes someplace else" is what Shinker says he felt. "Maybe they'll bring a fresh eye and can do something. It's frustrating when you like somebody's work and you can't make it happen for them."

Wilcox has struggled with his current novel, in part because of the mounting pressure he feels from his publisher and his agent. After "Guest," Urban took him to lunch for a serious talk. (He can't bring himself to discuss money with Kot.) She said he had to consider his audience. "A problem with selling his books is who will buy them," she says. "That's what a bookseller asks. Literary fiction is not selling well. You need a target market. Women buy books, but his aren't women's books. It's pathetic. Why can't you just write good books? But there's too much competition for people's attention. I told him, 'We have to have something.' "

Urban's message got through. Wilcox is a great fan of the English novelist Barbara Pym, a brilliant writer of small-scale social comedy, and he is haunted by the knowledge that Pym wrote six published novels and the seventh was turned down. She spent the next sixteen years writing unpublished novels, and was rediscovered only at the end of her life, when the London *Times Literary Supplement* hailed her as one of the most underappreciated novelists of the twentieth century. Wilcox's first instinct was to go back to "Modern Baptists"; after all, it had sold reasonably well. He thought he might do a more comic, slapstick story of a New Yorker who returns to his Southern roots. He tried a short story in that vein, written in the first person, and sent it to *The New Yorker.* It was rejected. He tried about sixty pages of a novel, and sent them to Urban and Kot. He could tell they were cool. Urban told him it seemed forced; it wasn't funny. "I've never worked so hard starting a book," he says. "My advance was going down. It was a difficult time for me. I was very aware of the need for an audience. I don't want to be like Barbara Pym — I want to sell this to someone."

Then something new came to him. In "Guest of a Sinner," a minor character had come to terms with being gay and had begun having an affair with a garbageman. Wilcox found himself pondering the possibility of a relationship between a gay man and a straight man — not a sexual affair but a coming together on common ground of two people who didn't share the same sexuality. He mentioned this idea to Kot, who remembers Wilcox describing it as "a comic 'Death in Venice.' "

Kot was excited. "I could play this, run with this," he says. "It sounded like fun." A comic "Death in Venice" might not exactly fly off shelves, but the phrase was *something* — it was a "handle" for the sales force. Mann's classic novella had a beautiful young male character that might appeal to a gay audience, yet the novella as a whole appealed to mainstream readers and it inspired both a movie and an opera. With the

Pulitzer Prize-winning "A Thousand Acres," the novelist Jane Smiley had just scored with a "King Lear" in Iowa. Was a comic "Death in Venice" any less probable? Hyperion's publicity people loved it. Urban, too, liked the idea. Kot could sell his new publisher, Hyperion, a fresh approach to Wilcox. It gave him the ammunition to outbid HarperCollins and continue editing Wilcox. Even without a finished manuscript or an out-line, Hyperion committed itself to publishing it, albeit with a small ad-vance and little money at risk. The initial contract explicitly referred to the work as "a comic updating of "Death in Venice.' " The marketing idea was to graft a gay audience onto Wilcox's existing readers.

No one knows how large the gay book-buying audience is. Kot says that a successful nonfiction book on a gay theme can sell twenty-five thousand copies; Randy Shilts sold many more. "It's well defined," Urban says. "Publishers can market, sell, advertise to this audience. This is an audience that could support Jim's books. It has developed in the last few years. It's strong. We have to have *something.*"

But Wilcox's shrinking advance has, somewhat perversely, dimin-ished rather than heightened his commercial sensibility. "It's so little money that I'm going to write this exactly the way I want," he says now of his new book. "I feel a burden has been lifted. When I was getting the pages together, I was worried. Can Binky sell this? Now I know it's never going to be a big commercial book. In a way, I'm much happier."

The first sign that Wilcox might not play along with the new "gay" marketing scenario came when he crossed out the reference to "a comic updating of 'Death in Venice' " before signing his new contract. "This thing just got out of hand," he says. "I never said it was a comic 'Death in Venice.' I said it was a comic *reversal* of 'Death in Venice,' and even that's inappropriate. All Hollywood wants is high concept. That means you can describe it in one sentence. 'Twins' is what you get. That whole mentality has become a part of publishing. It's sold before you write it. Reviewers review the concept, not the book. That's why first novelists are getting five hundred thousand dollars. I worry about these marketing categories, trying to define things. Can't people just be people? I don't want it marketed as a gay novel. People hear 'gay' and they think 'sex.' If this were commercial, there'd be Big Sex. Well, there's no sex. None. The gay man is unattractive, a little overweight. He can't get a date. He's a Catholic." Worse, from a commercial perspective, the beautiful young man, the Tadzio of "Death in Venice," has vanished. The main characters are now aged seventy and forty-one. "Tell the sales force it's going to be 'Moby Dick' in Manhattan," he says of his new novel. "Maybe they can sell that."

Wilcox now adheres as strictly as he can to a hundred-dollar-a-week budget. He almost never buys clothes. He owns one suit, which is five years old. His blue denim shirt he bought on the sidewalk for five-ninety-nine. A blue chambray shirt was bought at a bargain store on Third Avenue. ("It's amazing the bargains you can find in Manhattan," he says.) For a while, he had a queen-sized bed, but he tired of having to turn sideways to get into the bathroom. Now he sleeps on a worn brown velour sofa bed, a friend's castoff. He has just bought a used

air-conditioner. He does his own laundry (a dollar-fifty a load) and iron-
ing. He tries not to eat out, and he never takes cabs. When he's working
on early drafts of his novels at his electric typewriter, he uses non-self-
correcting ribbons; he switches to the more expensive self-correcting
ribbons only for the final draft. Despite all these efforts, though, he has
lately had to borrow money from his parents to pay his rent, now four
hundred dollars a month—something he hates to do. He has lost all
confidence that his future as a novelist is secure.

The most recent advance has left Wilcox no choice but to supplement his income. Last semester, he taught a fiction-writing seminar at
the Camden campus of Rutgers University. That brought in $5,700. Un-
fortunately, the train fare to and from Philadelphia caused him to run up
fourteen hundred dollars in not yet reimbursed charges on his Visa card,
which contributed to a recent cash crisis. He appeared as an extra in a
Macy's television commercial for a hundred dollars. He has just completed a piece for *Allure* on the difficulties of being a handsome man.
He sees it as rescarch for a character in his new novel, and he's grateful
for the assignment. The piece, if it runs, will bring in four thousand
dollars, nearly half his last book advance.

There is no bitterness in Wilcox, no sense that life or the publishing
industry has treated him unfairly. On the contrary, in many ways Wilcox
seems to be living the life he always wanted—that of the artist. He grew
up in a musical family, steeped in the lore of Mozart, the archetype of the
struggling genius. "He is essentially romantic," the writer Gene Stone, a
friend of Wilcox's, told me. "This is how a serious novelist is supposed
to live. He may be the last of his kind in America." Yet nearly all his
closest friends say they have now detected in him a worrisome level of
anxiety about his financial plight. "There are days when he's frustrated
and nearly in tears," Stone said, and Polly King, another friend, observed,
"He lives in his own private hell of worry."

Wilcox concedes as much, yet brushes aside such concerns. "Publishing is filled with ups and down," he says. "I know that. I feel, frankly,
very fortunate to be able to write, to have the time and the means. It's
almost beyond my wildest dreams. Writing a novel was the be-all and
end-all for me. When I thought I could live on advances, after the Anne
Tyler review, I was thrilled. Now it's going downhill, but I still feel lucky
to be under contract. I'll do whatever I have to do to make money and
keep writing."

Ultimately, he says, he's sustained by his readers, however small a
group they may be. "Comedy is very mysterious. I'm thankful some
people find what I'm doing amusing." He gets a small but steady stream
of fan mail, from such improbable places as Montana and Indiana. He
showed me one letter, from a reader in Canada, dated June 28, 1989:

> Dear James,
>   It has been a day, And now I can't sleep. I am dying for a glass
> of lemonade but of course I have no lemons or fake stuff, even, to
> make it with. Instead I have a cup of iced tca which is probably
> unhealthy to drink at this time of night. . . .
>   I was lying in bed trying to sleep—my husband's asleep, my

coming little baby in my stomach (I'm five months pregnant) is asleep, my three cats are asleep, my old daddy, who lives in the apartment upstairs since my mom died four years ago, had another heart attack tonight—his second in two months, this one is worse, they say—and so I'm worried and thirsty and tired.

Which does bring me to why I'm telling you this. . . . I'm clutching to the things that I love. And I love your books. Tonight when I couldn't sleep I thought I would read a book—so I went to my bookshelves and started scanning titles. I came to your three books which I've read at least twice each (though I don't usually do that). Anyway—please write another novel fast because I can't sleep (and even if I could I wouldn't if I had one of your books to read afresh). Is that a lot to ask? I'd do the same for you. Is it very hot where you are? My air conditioner's coming Thursday.

Yours sincerely. . . .

The Tipster

*Unusual trading in MCA stock options just before
news leaked of the giant Matsushita buyout
naturally caught the attention of the S.E.C. But even
the S.E.C. was baffled when it learned that the
insider source had never sought to profit himself—
and that he was the producer son of a legendary
Hollywood studio chief.*

by JAMES B. STEWART

ON FRIDAY, September 21, 1990, Jonathan Sheinberg, then the president
of Lee Rich Productions, in Hollywood, arrived with his daughter, Thea,
for a weekend at the Malibu beach house of his parents—Sidney Sheinberg, the president and chief operating officer of MCA, and his wife,
the actress Lorraine Gary. Sid Sheinberg and Lew Wasserman, MCA's
chairman, rank as two of Hollywood's most eminent figures, having
transformed MCA from a small music-publishing and talent agency into
the owner of Universal Studios and one of the nation's leading entertainment companies. The Sheinbergs, given their prominence, are besieged
with invitations, and had bought the Malibu house as a retreat from their
Beverly Hills mansion—as a place where they and their two grown sons
and the sons' wives and children could gather for quiet family weekends.

The Sheinbergs had long prided themselves on their dedication to
family. In a town and an industry where conventional values fare better
on the screen than in real life, their reputations had never been sullied
by affairs, separations, divorce, or even rumors. Lorraine, in particular,
had devoted herself to family-oriented causes, serving as vice-president
of the Westside Children's Center, in Los Angeles, and, together with
Sid, helping launch the Children's Action Network, which has made
promotional films devoted to such issues as childhood vaccinations.

When Jonathan, the Sheinbergs' older son, who was then thirty-
three, arrived that Friday afternoon, entering through the back door, Sid
was on the phone in the next room. Like many of the multimillion-dollar
houses that crowd the hillside above Malibu's Broad Beach, the Sheinberg house is relatively narrow—about thirty feet wide—and Jonathan

couldn't help hearing his father on the phone. Though Sid Sheinberg can be charming, he has long been notorious for yelling at executives, even when he isn't angry. On this occasion, he was shouting excitedly into the phone about the prospect of selling MCA to the Japanese in a $6.6-billion transaction that would, among other things, transform the already wealthy Sheinberg into one of the richest men in the country. His MCA stock alone would be worth $92 million. In addition, he was due to receive a "bonus" of $21 million, $9.6 million to replace various "incentives," and an annual salary of $8.6 million. Jonathan not only stood to inherit a large part of that fortune but he also owned MCA stock. Some had been given to him as a child, and some he'd bought on his own over the years.

Though MCA stock had appreciated handsomely since its beginnings, it had recently proved a disappointing investment. Despite such hits as "Jaws" and "E.T.," MCA had had its share of bombs, like the ill-fated "Howard the Duck," and for years its stock had languished. The superagent Michael Ovitz (who was a Sheinberg neighbor at Broad Beach and had been the matchmaker for Sony's purchase of Columbia Pictures from Coca-Cola for five billion dollars the year before) had initiated secret talks between Matsushita and MCA just a month before Jonathan's visit, having approached Felix Rohatyn, of Lazard Frères, who was a member of MCA's board and the company's principal financial adviser. Ovitz had met with Wasserman and Sheinberg in early September, and only two days earlier they and Rohatyn had been told that Matsushita was definitely contemplating a bid for MCA. Meanwhile, investors not privy to this top-secret development had grown impatient at the lack of any concrete developments, and the stock was sliding to new yearly lows.

As Jonathan passed through the house, he ran into his mother. She looked alarmed at his untimely arrival, for she knew what her husband was discussing and she assumed that Jonathan had overheard the conversation. Those discussions are obviously secret, she said, or words to that effect, warning Jonathan not to mention the information to anyone. Then she rushed into the study, and as soon as Sid hung up the phone she told him that she thought Jonathan had overheard, and that Sid had better talk to him.

Sid agreed. He subsequently testified, in a deposition that I obtained through the Freedom of Information Act, that he had learned not to trust Jonathan with "this type of information." Sid has described Jonathan as "vocal" and "gregarious"—someone who might, at the least, be indiscreet. Jonathan is highly excitable and almost compulsively talkative, and is given to bursts of enthusiasm, but he has a short attention span. ("I always thought it was hereditary," one former colleague observes.) Sid knew that what he'd been discussing on the phone was classic inside information, and that he had a legal duty to keep it confidential. He himself is a lawyer; early in his career, he was a law professor, at U.C.L.A., before moving to MCA as a young inhouse lawyer. Moreover, public awareness of the insider-trading scandal that had rocked Wall Street was then at its height. Michael Milken, whose infamous trading desk was in Beverly Hills, had pleaded guilty to six felonies that spring, and Ivan

Boesky, whose wife's family owned the Beverly Hills Hotel, had been fined a hundred million dollars and incarcerated in a federal prison at Lompoc, California, not all that far from Malibu. Discussions with Matsushita had been cloaked in extreme secrecy to preclude any taint of scandal in what could have been a politically controversial deal, since it involved the purchase of an American studio by the Japanese.

Sid was about to set out for a walk along the beach. (He walks every day he is in Malibu — to "amortize" the high cost of the house, he has said.) Now he asked Jonathan to come along, so they could talk without being overheard.

On the walk, Sid, mentioning that Lorraine had told him Jonathan had overheard the conversation, took his son into his confidence. He filled in some details, identifying the likely buyer of MCA as Matsushita. Jonathan had never heard of the Japanese company, and Sid told him that it was best known in the United States for its consumer-electronics brands, which included Technics, Panasonic, Quasar, and JVC. While Sid was trying to confine his disclosures to what he thought Jonathan already knew, Jonathan managed to take away both a sense of the anticipated price per share of the deal (approaching eighty dollars, though it ultimately sold for less) and its timing (imminent). Then Sid got to the real point of the conversation: he warned Jonathan that he must not trade in MCA stock; he must not do anything with the information, and must keep it secret. "Keep that to yourself," he said. "For God's sake, don't trade on the stock."

Months after this walk along the beach, Sid was asked whether he had believed that his son would obey these admonitions. "I would have bet anything on it," Sid replied.

The following Tuesday morning, September 25th, as Andrew J. Geist, a twenty-seven-year-old lawyer with the Securities and Exchange Commission's regional office in New York, was heading into the shower in his modest Manhattan apartment, he caught a snatch of an item on WCBS all-news radio. "Today's *Wall Street Journal* is reporting that MCA is in talks . . ." Geist missed the rest of the item, but he hung around for the business-news update a half hour later, and learned that MCA was in negotiations concerning acquisition by a Japanese company — big news both in Hollywood and on Wall Street. That day's *Journal* reported that Matsushita "is in talks with MCA, Inc., regarding a possible acquisition of the U.S. entertainment giant for eighty to ninety dollars a share, or a range of about $6.7 billion to $7.5 billion, people familiar with the talks said." It was the first leak in the closely guarded talks, and while no one involved was willing to confirm the existence of talks, no one denied it. Geist immediately recognized the development as an opportunity to make money — especially for anyone armed with inside information. The day the *Journal* article appeared, MCA stock leaped from about thirty-five dollars a share to nearly sixty.

Geist had joined the S.E.C.'s enforcement division in 1988, soon after graduating from Fordham Law School. He grew up in suburban Westchester County, where his father was a lawyer and certified public accountant, and he attended the University of Virginia. An uncle had worked at the S.E.C. in the late fifties, and Geist had become interested in white-collar crime, especially securities fraud. Geist is pleasant-looking, dresses conservatively, and is somewhat reserved, and he quickly established himself at the office as hardworking and quietly ambitious. In the short time he'd been there, he had gravitated toward insider-trading cases, working on several matters that grew out of the so-called *Business Week* case, in which printers for the magazine leaked the contents of articles before publication to a ring of traders who profited from the advance information.

That Tuesday morning, as soon as Geist arrived at the S.E.C.'s offices, in downtown Manhattan, he asked for a summary of trading in MCA stock and options for the days preceding the *Wall Street Journal* story. The stock trading itself offered few clues: MCA shares had actually dropped fifty cents, suggesting that there weren't any widespread rumors fuelling purchases. The options trading looked more interesting. Because of greater leverage, insider traders often prefer to speculate in options. Geist talked to officials at the Philadelphia Stock Exchange, where MCA options are traded. On Monday, a significant number of MCA call options had been purchased which were as much as twenty dollars "out of the money"—that is, they would require a significant run-up in the stock price before any profit would be realized—and were due to expire in a relatively short time. Such buying often signals an unusual level of confidence on the part of the buyer. When Geist got a breakdown of the options traders for that day (information that is routinely supplied to the S.E.C. by the New York Stock Exchange and other stock exchanges), he saw the usual institutions, money managers, and hedge funds, and also a handful of individuals. Most of the individuals lived in Southern California, a geographical concentration that caught his attention.

Otherwise, the names meant nothing to Geist: Richard E. Shephard, Richard Ursitti, Barry C. Fogel. Was there a common link among them? Whom might they know? Why had they bought MCA options that day, with such exquisite timing?

Armed with this cluster of names and the trading data, Geist's office wrote a short memo outlining the facts as he knew them, and suggesting possible violations, and sent it to the S.E.C. commissioners, in Washington, seeking a formal order of investigation into the MCA trading. It seemed a routine request. Had prominent investment bankers or lawyers been involved, or had the trading been linked to a large brokerage firm or other institution. the enforcement division in Washington might have referred the investigation to the Justice Department for a parallel criminal investigation. (Insider trading is both a civil violation of the securities laws and a crime.) But nothing in Geist's memo suggested anything beyond a small, garden-variety matter. The S.E.C. granted the order in late March of 1991, formally designating the case as "In the Matter of Trading in Securities of MCA, Inc.": it gave Geist and his colleagues the authority to issue subpoenas and compel testimony.

In the meantime, the office's investigators had further scrutinized the suspicious trading. Richard Shephard and Barry Fogel had both signed brokerage forms authorizing the trading in options *after* the trades had actually been executed. Apparently, neither had traded in options before; the MCA purchase had been Fogel's only transaction. Richard Ursitti, though he had a brokerage account, had opened a new account expressly for the MCA trading.

The trading itself had also been highly suspicious. Records showed that Fogel, who owned four pizza restaurants in Beverly Hills, had begun calling his broker about 6:30 A.M. Pacific Time on Monday, September 24th, the day before the *Wall Street Journal* article appeared. That morning, he bought a thousand shares of MCA common stock at $34.50 per share, five November 35 MCA call options, and forty November 40 MCA call options. He'd borrowed twenty-five thousand dollars from his mother to help finance the purchases. Shephard had bought thirty October 35 MCA call options the same day. Ursitti had bought ten thousand shares of MCA at thirty-five dollars a share. To trained investigators, such a pattern is a red flag.

Geist wasted little time; subpoenas for Shephard, Fogel, and Ursitti were prepared, executed, and sent by certified mail. While the subpoenas were en route, other enforcement lawyers in the office, Teri Brotbacker and Stanley Skubina, who had helped analyze the trading patterns, placed cold calls to the three men. In such calls, the S.E.C. lawyers are required to identify themselves, and to tell the subjects that they aren't obligated to answer questions and that they have a right to counsel. They identify the purpose of their inquiry and remind the subjects that if they do talk they are obligated to tell the truth and could face criminal penalties if they don't. Despite such a daunting prologue, the recipients of such calls, in their eagerness to appear to have nothing to hide, often do volunteer valuable information before it has been filtered through their lawyers. The S.E.C. lawyers knew nothing about any of the men they called beyond their names and their trading activity; they had got their home phone numbers from directory assistance. Neither Fogel nor Ursitti answered, but on March 25th Brotbacker did reach Shephard. After the required preliminaries, he agreed to answer questions.

Brotbacker could tell immediately that Shephard was apprehensive, though collected. By his own subsequent admission, he was evasive, if not dishonest. On being asked why he bought the shares, he referred vaguely to having followed MCA stock all summer, and to a long-standing interest in entertainment stocks. He denied knowing anyone connected to MCA. "It was, you know, a surprise call," he later explained. "I hadn't received any . . . written notification of any sort and—and she asked me a number of questions about the trading of MCA. I don't believe I mentioned any significant information in that conversation. I hadn't spoken to an attorney and I figured the least said the better. At this point in time, I didn't know the nature of the investigation or what questions were really being asked."

To Geist and Brotbacker, his answers were hardly satisfying.

Later that same day, Shephard called Brotbacker back. He had found the subpoena, served by certified mail, waiting for him when he arrived at his office. He told her he would be complying with the subpoena but offered no new information. By that time, he'd decided to hire a lawyer.

Several days later, Brotbacker also heard from Fogel, through his lawyer, Roger J. Rosen. Like Shephard, Fogel had received a subpoena. When Rosen spoke to Brotbacker, he argued that Fogel shouldn't have to testify, that turning over his trading records should suffice. Brotbacker said that that wouldn't do. She and Geist were eager to get his testimony as soon as possible, so they agreed that Fogel wouldn't have to come to New York: they would interview him over the telephone, even though they would have preferred to observe Fogel's demeanor during questioning. "After you talk to him, you'll see there's nothing there," Rosen told them, sounding blasé.

On April 24th, Rosen and Fogel arrived at the S.E.C.'s offices in downtown Los Angeles; Geist and Brotbacker used a speakerphone in Geist's New York office. Fogel was sworn in and began testifying. After some preliminaries, in which he said he had graduated from Beverly Hills High School, class of 1976, and had attended one quarter at Los Angeles Valley College, Brotbacker got to the point, asking, "Why did you buy MCA? What were your reasons for it?"

"I had been following it for some time in the L.A. *Times,* and it seemed like a very good investment," Fogel replied. "It was at one of its all-time lows, as far as I could tell."

"How long had you been following it?"

"Well, I believe I started sometime in 1990, probably first part of the year."

"How did you follow it?"

"L.A. *Times.* . . . I followed the L.A. *Times* business section and occasionally I would see articles on it in periodical magazines."

"What article can you recall seeing?"

"I don't recall any. I don't recall a specific article."

Shifting tack, Brotbacker asked him if there was any other reason he had bought MCA options, other than the vague sense that he'd read about the company somewhere.

"I've been raised in Los Angeles, familiar with MCA/Universal Studios. I know they have amusement parks and they make movies. And I've known from what I've heard and what I've read . . . that entertainment stocks traditionally do best in recessionary times."

"Where did you hear that entertainment stocks do best in recessionary times?"

"*Wall Street Journal,* L.A. *Times,* magazines."

"What magazines?"

"*Time, Newsweek,* I don't really recall."

Geist, who was listening in in New York, couldn't resist interrupting. "Do you recall reading about that in *Time* magazine?" he asked, barely keeping the disbelief out of his voice.

"Not specifically."

"You were guessing when you said *Time* and *Newsweek?*"

"I have a recollection, I don't know if it would be called a guess."

"Do you have a recollection of reading about it in a newsweekly magazine?"

"I believe so."

"You don't recall which one it was?"

"That's correct."

"Do you know when, roughly, in time it was?"

"No, I don't remember."

There had been no articles on MCA in any of the news magazines just prior to Fogel's trading. In conducting an insider-trading investigation, S.E.C. lawyers routinely examine any published reports referring to the company in order to anticipate possible defenses and to be able to put further questions to a witness who mentions them.

By this time, Fogel's lawyer, Rosen, also asked whether there were any other reasons that Fogel had purchased the stock.

"No," Fogel replied, unconvincing and barely audible.

"Is that a 'No'?" Brotbacker asked.

This prompted a whispered conference between Fogel and Rosen. Then Fogel answered. "I guess to some, I was following it. I was familiar with it. It was at an all-time low, and that's all I can remember right now. If there is something else I remember, I'll bring it up again, but that's it. I was following it and it seemed like a good deal."

Yet again, Brotbacker asked if there was anything else that had influenced his decision. "Not that I can recall," he said.

Later, she asked if he'd had any conversations with anyone about MCA, and Fogel said he had. With whom, she asked. "I don't remember who. There have been times I was looking at the stock and I had talked to people in my restaurant. I don't recall who, but, I mean, I was interested. I was following stock, and I must have had conversations about it. I don't recall with who or any particular place or time."

"Then your testimony is that you can't recall anyone that you specifically discussed MCA with at any time during the summer of 1990?"

This question prompted another whispered conference between Fogel and Rosen. Finally, Fogel replied, "No, my testimony now is that there may have been specific conversations that I don't recall. And if I do recall them I will bring them up."

"As you sit here today, do you recall anyone mentioning MCA to you during July, August, or September of 1990? Do you remember any specific person doing that?"

Fogel did not answer.

Here the deposition ended, convincing Geist and Brotbacker of only one thing: Fogel was lying. To keep the pressure on, they immediately issued subpoenas for all of Fogel's phone records. They sensed that they were onto something. But they were far from the breakthrough they'd hoped for. They still had no idea how a Beverly Hills pizza restaurateur would have gained access to one of the most closely guarded secrets in corporate America.

Just about everyone in Hollywood talks about how hard it is to be the son or the daughter or the spouse of somebody famous. Jonathan's mother, Lorraine Gary, for example, is said to have complained to friends that marriage to one of the most important men in Hollywood has handicapped her own career as an actress. (True, it didn't prevent her from being cast as the mother in Universal's "Jaws" and two of its progeny, including "Jaws IV—The Revenge," for which she was paid five hundred and ninety-four thousand dollars.) Yet surely there are few industries as riddled with nepotism as the movie business. The Los Angeles *Times* magazine noted in a cover story last year, "Affirmative action for family members is an accepted practice in a town where everyone seems to be related to everyone else. . . . A solid education and good grades are not necessarily relevant or even desirable and are considered much less valuable than the kind of insider's knowledge acquired at the dinner table night after night."

That description might seem to fit Jonathan Sheinberg, whose academic career could charitably be characterized as lackluster. As Jonathan has described his academic record, he attended Franklyn College, in Switzerland, "although I left before the end of the second year." He never graduated from any college, but he did study at the College of the Immaculate Heart, in Los Angeles, and "I maybe took classes before that at U.C.L.A. and some other schools around town." During his adolescence, he and some of his surfing buddies were once arrested for camping in a Volkswagen van on Nixon's beach at San Clemente, in what was deemed to be threatening proximity to the Presidential compound.

Universal itself had once been so riddled with relatives of the studio's founder, Carl Laemmle, that it eventually became the only studio to institute an anti-nepotism policy, and Jonathan once told the Los Angeles *Times,* "I had to make it on my own." Yet, though he lacked a college degree, he had no trouble landing a job at Columbia Pictures, and he worked there for three years in marketing and promotion. "I was able to pick up the telephone," he boasted. "I could call Frank Price"— then the chairman of Columbia Pictures—"and he knew who I was. It's either sink or swim after that." Even Sid Sheinberg, who grew up in Corpus Christi, Texas, far from the film industry, and by Hollywood standards is the quintessential self-made man, got his first job at Universal, in 1959, through his father-in-law, then a business manager for several MCA executives.

Once Jonathan had got his own toehold in the industry, his career proceeded in a steady if unspectacular rise. He moved from Columbia to Lorimar, and there served as director of production for television movies and miniseries; moved on to Twentieth Century Fox, in feature films; went from there to Orion Pictures, as head of production; and then went to Lee Rich Productions (an independent producer under Warner Brothers), as president. None of those jobs lasted longer than three years —a situation that is not unusual among peripatetic Hollywood executives, though a far cry from his father's legendary thirty-five-year career at MCA.

Jonathan's colleagues offer decidedly mixed reviews of his performance. He is almost uniformly described as likable—a "puppy dog," several said, meaning someone who goes out of his way to earn the affection of others. He is capable of enormous enthusiasm and energy when he throws himself into a project. Robert Fried, who worked closely with Jonathan both at Twentieth Century Fox and at Orion and is now an independent producer, says, "Jonathan accomplished more— I've observed many executives; he was one of the most productive. I've always thought he has a style of operating, he appears to be less impressive or effective than he is. He's not recognized. I find him impressive but misunderstood."

Among the projects for which Jonathan deserves at least some credit, various colleagues say, are "Dirty Rotten Scoundrels," "Married to the Mob," "Great Balls of Fire!," "Navy SEALS," and "Throw Momma from the Train." He is credited as executive producer of three Lee Rich films, "Innocent Blood," "Hard to Kill," and "Passenger 57." How much credit remains a subject of some dispute. "I can tell you that 'Dirty Rotten Scoundrels' would never have been made without Jonathan," one friend says; and the former head of one of the studios that hired him says, "He's not a bad kid. He has a good heart. It's tough being the son of someone that famous." But, this man adds, Jonathan was a disappointment. "He's impulsive and not very bright. I thought of him as a fetcher"—someone who sniffs out promising movie projects.

Did he fetch anything that turned into a movie?

"I can't think of any real projects," he says.

Another producer, who worked with Jonathan at Fox, describes him as "a steamroller, a bulldozer," and explains, "You're only allowed to give a full-court press to two or three projects a month, and that's a lot. More than that, you're looked at askance. Jon would get excited about three scripts a week. He'd say, 'This is "Gone with the Wind." This is "Porky's." ' That's how he acted." Others describe him as a caricature of a Hollywood "player." "He tries to walk the walk and talk the talk," a lawyer who got to know him well says. "He was always on his cellular phone. 'Gotta run, gotta deal.' "

To his credit, Jonathan seems to have rarely, if ever, invoked his father's famous name to advance his own career. Yet "people tried to get close to Jon to get close to the family," one friend of his says. "People sucked up to him because of his name. He's eager, positive, 'up.' People tried to take advantage of this." Sometimes Jonathan would oblige such people by taking ideas to his father, sometimes with them in tow. Sid tended to listen patiently, but he invariably rebuffed them. People who had business dealings with MCA often tried to curry favor with Jonathan, evidently hoping for a kind word at the family dinner table. (In some ways, some executives say, Sid exacerbated this problem, however unwittingly, by "testing" ideas submitted to him at Universal on his sons. He also took Jonathan and his brother, Billy, to numerous Universal screenings, and solicited their opinions. "He'd listen, good or bad," a former top Universal executive recalls. "You'd have to talk your way around the children's opinions.")

However dutiful Sid and Lorraine were as parents, Jonathan's personal life often seemed troubled. He loved to gamble and stay out late, playing in poker games with colleagues in the industry. Though Jonathan himself often boasted that he'd beaten "Harvard and Princeton" lawyers in a poker tournament he won, others described him as a relatively easy mark, and said that often in the many times he had lost he had wanted to gamble more. His mood swings, high energy level, and short attention span were attributed by some to drug use; several years ago, he entered an outpatient drug-treatment program similar to Alcoholics Anonymous at a local hospital. Friends say that he deserves credit for confronting and surmounting those problems but that it wasn't easy on his family.

By the time of Jonathan's September visit to his parents' beach house, his wife, Maria, a beautiful young actress and model, had moved out of their home, taking their daughter, Thea, with her. Mother and daughter spent much of their time at the residence of Maria's new boyfriend—Barry Fogel, the president of Jacopo's, a chain of pizza restaurants in Beverly Hills. Maria told friends she was estranged from her own father and had run away from her home in the Midwest, and she complained that her prominent Sheinberg in-laws never really embraced her as part of the family. As for Jonathan, he was already living with another actress and model, Susan Ursitti, the star of "Teen Wolf," who at the time was studying to become a fashion designer. The strain of all this on Jonathan seemed evident. He had once been a trim, easygoing surfer—he was known to leave work early to surf, on one occasion with Sean Penn—but now his weight ballooned. He was seeing a therapist in Beverly Hills.

At Lee Rich Productions, it became increasingly apparent that Jonathan's career had reached a plateau. Some friends say they warned Jonathan not to take the job at Rich, even though he was getting a substantial raise. Lee Rich, as a wealthy and powerful Hollywood legend in his own right (he is a co-founder of Lorimar), was similar to Jonathan's father, some felt, and had the reputation of being difficult to work with. Both Jonathan and Rich are often described as headstrong and impulsive, and they proved a mismatch almost from the outset.

An executive from another company recalls a meeting with Jonathan and Rich. As Jonathan was making one of his typically animated presentations, Rich interrupted, told him, "Shut up, you're an idiot," and took over the presentation, while Jonathan obviously simmered. When Jonathan's contract at Lee Rich Productions expired, in the fall of 1991, "I told him that he wouldn't be in my plans," Rich told the Washington *Post*. "Jonathan is tough to live with," he added. Friends of Jonathan's attribute the rift to jealousy on the part of Rich, because Jonathan was getting too much credit in the Hollywood trade papers.

Several people who have worked with Jonathan recall that there was a saying among agents that Jonathan had "diarrhea of the mouth." One says, "He had zero discretion about giving out information. He'd tell you anything. He'd talk candidly about what an idiot his boss is. He'd talk about people you worked with—they could have been your best friend. He was incredibly indiscreet." After leaving troubled Orion Pictures, in 1988, Jonathan talked openly of alleged accounting irregularities at the studio—to the *Wall Street Journal* reporter Jane Mayer, among others—and that talk prompted Michael Medavoy, then the head of production at Orion, to remark to the Washington *Post* that Jonathan "wouldn't know a balance sheet if it hit him over the head."

Still, friends of the family say, Sid would sometimes wonder aloud why others didn't seem to see more in Jonathan. He often spoke proudly of Jonathan as "a hustler." And yet it was obvious that Sid had more praise for Billy, his younger son. William Sheinberg, who is now thirty-three, was an academic success, having graduated from the respected

Claremont College, and followed in his father's footsteps at law school. Billy has been working in the entertainment industry—currently at Spelling Television. Jonathan apparently never complained about his father's favoritism, but he has said in testimony that he isn't close to his brother. What may have been more distressing to Jonathan (and perhaps to Billy, too) was his father's relationship to Steven Spielberg, who is widely described as Sid's "surrogate son." (It was Sheinberg who insisted that the young Spielberg be given "Jaws." And it was Sheinberg who bought "E.T." from Columbia, where it was going nowhere, and gave it to Spielberg to direct for Universal. Sheinberg's friends say that without his total support and encouragement over a period of more than ten years, "Schindler's List" might never have made it to the screen.)

Like many wealthy young people in Hollywood, Jonathan showed little patience for the routine details of personal finance that occupy most people. A business manager is as much a status symbol there as a personal trainer is, and in 1987 Jonathan was referred to Richard Shephard, a Beverly Hills C.P.A. Shephard did just about everything for Jonathan that concerned finances, not only preparing his taxes and overseeing his investments but receiving all his income and paying all his bills. Occasionally, Jonathan would drop by Shephard's office, on Sunset Boulevard, to sign a document. Typically, he didn't even get out of his car; Shephard would bring the papers to the curb. Shephard and his wife often used to get together with Jonathan and Maria, going to movies and screenings, once to the San Diego Zoo, and to various Hollywood functions. He made no bones about the relationship's being a mixture of business and pleasure.

It was Shephard who got the first of the S.E.C.'s subpoenas, and one of his first thoughts that day was to speak to Jonathan, who happened to call in on his cellular phone as he was driving to work. Shephard told him he'd got a subpoena about the MCA trading and wanted to talk to him about it in person. "O.K.," Jonathan replied. "When?"

"Well, why don't we meet in front of your doctor's office?" Jonathan had a standing appointment with his psychotherapist on Monday afternoons, just across the street from Shephard's office. "Give me a call when you arrive," he said.

Even more alarming was another phone call that morning, from Maria. She was crying, and said that Jonathan had to come over; it had something to do with his daughter, she told him.

Trying to control a mounting sense of what he later described as "panic," Jonathan headed for Barry Fogel's house. When he arrived, Maria insisted that they talk in the garage. She wouldn't let him see their daughter; she thought it would upset her to see her father on a weekday, in Fogel's house, when Jonathan's visits were usually confined to weekends. Maria was obviously upset, but only indirectly about anything having to do with Thea. She told Jonathan that Barry had received a subpoena from the S.E.C. about his MCA trades. Jonathan told her that Rick Shephard had, too. She added that Fogel was going to have to get an attorney. The normally ebullient Jonathan seemed sad, anxious, quiet, Maria thought. According to their subsequent depositions, he seems to have said little. Then Maria touched a raw nerve. "I asked him to tell his dad," she later recalled. He didn't respond, and later testified that he was "in a state of shock."

That afternoon, when Jonathan arrived for his appointment with his psychotherapist, Shephard hurried out to the car and got into the passenger seat. He handed Jonathan the subpoena, emblazoned with the reference to trading in MCA securities.

Jonathan read it and asked, "What are you going to do?"

Shephard said he would try to keep Jonathan's name out of the investigation. As Shephard subsequently described the conversation, "I said that I would attempt to keep him out of it if I possibly could but that I would have to be truthful in any response if I were questioned, and if I could do so without involving him, that's my goal." Jonathan seemed stricken by the possibility that he would be identified, and Shephard tried to reassure him. "If I didn't have to bring up his name as part of the investigation, I wouldn't." Shephard later said. "If I weren't asked, you know, a question that I could not answer, answer in a truthful manner without giving his name and I—That's my point." Of course, Shephard knew he would be asked; he'd already been asked by Teri Brotbacker on the phone whether he knew anyone connected to MCA, and he had been evasive. Jonathan was Shephard's client and friend, but Shephard also met with him that afternoon to obtain information for his own defense. He'd already spoken to a lawyer, and the lawyer had warned him against discussing the case with Jonathan but had encouraged him to find out as much as he could about the S.E.C.'s probe. That turned out to be virtually nothing; all that Jonathan knew was that Barry Fogel had also received a subpoena. Jonathan, for his part, did his best to encourage Shephard not to say anything more than necessary. "He indicated to me that if he were asked about it, he would deny having given me any information relative to MCA," Shephard subsequently testified, and said he had replied, "I just wanted to, you know, have as much information as I can to know what's going on with this." And he warned Jonathan that "we wouldn't be able to talk" about the investigation anymore. Shephard got out of the car, leaving Jonathan with plenty to discuss with his psychotherapist. The whole thing "was a big shock to me," Jonathan later said. "I was really scared and panicked."

Shephard's reaction, in particular, had been ominous for Jonathan. In any conspiracy, the primary line of defense is silence. But the most that Shephard, having consulted his lawyer, was offering was to "try" to keep Jonathan's name out of the investigation. Worse, he had made it clear that he would agree to be deposed by S.E.C. lawyers and would "tell the truth." Meanwhile, his telling Jonathan that he wouldn't discuss the case with him further was another indication that Shephard's lawyer was, in effect, advising him to think of himself rather than of Jonathan. As time went on, Jonathan found that Fogel's reaction wasn't much better. One day when he was at Fogel's house to pick up his daughter, he met with Fogel in his weight room and tried to find out what was going on, but Fogel told him that he had a lawyer and was under instructions not to discuss the matter.

After his initial panic, Jonathan's reaction became one of denial.

After all, he himself hadn't been subpoenaed and he hadn't heard a word from the S.E.C. His name hadn't shown up on any trading records. The S.E.C. didn't even know of his existence, as far as he could tell. On April 8th, Jonathan attended a party at Fogel and Maria's house, and Fogel drew Jonathan aside to say that he was worried about the investigation and that he had a deposition due. Jonathan's reaction was "that he'd very much like to be left out of it," Fogel recalled. "He, you know, didn't trade. He didn't do anything wrong. He'd like to be left out of it."

Fogel and Maria and their lawyer, Rosen, weren't so sure. The S.E.C. lawyers had obviously targeted Fogel for their opening thrust (Shephard had managed to delay his deposition by pleading that it was the tax season, his busiest period), and they all needed to know where they stood before Fogel could be allowed to testify under oath. Rosen could stall only so long. Maria called Jonathan several times to set up a meeting, but Jonathan rebuffed her. She called again on April 23rd, the day before Fogel was scheduled to be questioned at the S.E.C. offices. Still, Jonathan refused to make any move. "I was operating out of fear," Jonathan later said. "I wasn't—I did not accept the fact of what had occurred. I was denying it. Not denying it like it didn't happen but denying it like not dealing with it."

Fogel's deposition of April 24th, which only inflamed Geist's and Brotbacker's suspicions, was a disaster for the defense. It isn't clear what Maria said to Jonathan about the deposition, but it finally moved him to act. He agreed to meet with Fogel and Maria at Rosen's office, in Century City. "I had kind of started to grasp the fact that in fact I was integrally involved, and the problem wasn't going away," Jonathan recalled. "And I wasn't going to act like an ostrich, you know, with my head in the sand, and pretend that it was going to go away. . . . So I talked to Maria finally. That was like the third time regarding this matter, and, in fact, I agreed to go have a meeting with them. I had no advice. I had no lawyers."

Jonathan later described the meeting at Rosen's office as "a turning point." Several things must have been clear: The pressure on Fogel was only going to get worse, and he couldn't continue to risk perjury charges. Maria's name hadn't yet surfaced in the investigation, but it surely would. She, too, risked perjury charges if she protected Jonathan. And Maria's exposure, even more than Fogel's, had a direct impact on Thea's continued welfare. In addition, it must have been clear that Rosen could not advise Jonathan, since he was already representing both Fogel and Maria. The Fogel deposition had by then shown that their interests and Jonathan's were sharply at odds.

Jonathan's panic returned. Except for discussions with his therapist and his girlfriend, Susan Ursitti, he had had no guidance on how to handle the growing problem. All his life, he had turned to his father. Now that option seemed unthinkable. "I was terrified, because I didn't know who to turn to," he said. "My father I couldn't talk to. At that point, like, the biggest fear that I had was not the S.E.C. . . . It was my father finding out about it and what his reaction might be, and how the hell was I going to deal with this."

Increasingly desperate, Jonathan called Rick Shephard, even though Shephard had said he wouldn't talk to him about the case. After all, in a sense it was Shephard and Fogel who had got him into this mess, by trading in MCA stock. "Hey, you have got to get me somebody," Jonathan told him. "You have got to tell me somebody I can talk to. You have got to get me a lawyer." Shephard suggested that he talk to Jim Mercer, a lawyer downtown.

Jonathan also called Richard Ursitti, Susan's father, a Pasadena businessman. He didn't know exactly what Ursitti had done, but he knew from Susan that Ursitti had got a subpoena. "Isn't this a terrible situation?" Jonathan recalled saying. "I can't believe this is happening. I really regret it. I can't believe it." In another conversation, he told Ursitti that "it was getting close to the time that I was going to have to tell my father," but he assured Ursitti that when he did he wouldn't mention Ursitti as being in any way involved. "I wanted to give him the opportunity to figure out how to tell him," Jonathan later explained. It's hard to know just how Ursitti felt about these disclosures from his daughter's boyfriend, Ursitti having invoked the Fifth Amendment privilege against self-incrimination in response to all questions about the affair. Jonathan's sense was that Ursitti "was really embarrassed and humiliated about the whole thing."

Jonathan couldn't put off the encounter with his own father much longer. He planned to break the news that weekend, at the beach house, but he couldn't muster the courage. Later in the week, he finally called his father and said he needed to see him. But Sid and Lorraine were going out to dinner that evening with other people; they were too busy to see Jonathan, even though he showed obvious signs of stress. "I really wanted to see him in person, but I couldn't," Jonathan later said. He now kept mumbling that he had to tell him something, and that he'd wanted to that weekend, and that he wanted to tell him now. "What?" Sid finally demanded, interrupting. In what soon proved to be an understatement, Jonathan revealed to his father that he'd been "indiscreet," and there was an "investigation" in progress. Despite his father's admonition on the beach that weekend in September, Jonathan said, he had blabbed about the Matsushita-MCA deal. As Sid later recounted, Jonathan told him that "he had told two people about this"—his wife, Maria, and his business manager, Rick Shephard—"and that these two people had . . . betrayed his trust and/or stupidly involved themselves in trading in MCA stock, and that the commission had made some inquiries of these people, that he had not been involved with this. Nobody had connected him to this yet." Jonathan told his father that he had hired a lawyer. He "felt terrible about it," he said—so terrible that he'd contemplated suicide.

However alarmed Sid may have been by this—both by Jonathan's revelations and by his state of mind—his immediate response was coolly professional. "Who are these lawyers?" Sid asked, and Jonathan told him. "Where did you get them?" Sid said practically nothing else. "I had a duty to help him and I did not want to make him feel worse than I knew he did," he later explained.

Felix Rohatyn has described Sid as "terribly distraught" over the news, coming, as it did, during the delicate period when he was trying to build relationships with MCA's new Japanese owners. "Sid is one of the brightest, most honest, and most ethical people I know," Rohatyn says. "I was on the audit committee as long as I was on the board, and we went over everything of any magnitude. He and Lew would go bonkers if anything was wrong."

One reason for Jonathan's sketchy account to his father was that his lawyer had told him to tell his father as little as possible. In the event that Sid became a witness, the less he knew the better. Sid had never heard of Jim Mercer, Jonathan's lawyer, and he immediately called his own counsel, Martin Lipton, at Wachtell, Lipton, Rosen & Katz, a prominent firm in New York that is best known for its corporate-takeover work. While Wachtell, Lipton would represent Sid, Lipton recommended that a major Washington firm, Wilmer, Cutler & Pickering, be hired to represent Jonathan. A Sheinberg was not about to be represented by a little-known lawyer in Los Angeles. Within twenty-four hours, Jonathan's belated efforts to deal with the problem himself were supplanted by a high-powered legal team from New York and Washington. From then on, the family cut off any further attempts to discuss the case among themselves.

In New York, the S.E.C.'s Andrew Geist, unaware of the anguish inflicted on the Sheinbergs, had been pressing to schedule a second deposition of Fogel and one of Shephard as well. Geist and Brotbacker agreed to fly to Los Angeles to accommodate the witnesses, and dates were finally set—June 25th for Fogel, Part II, and the following day for Shephard. Both Fogel's and Shephard's phone records had been subpoenaed, and in the critical period of September, 1990, both records contained several calls to and from Jonathan Sheinberg. Though the S.E.C. lawyers hadn't yet made the connection, Sheinberg's new lawyers at Wilmer, Cutler must have known that they inevitably would make it and that time was running out. (Sheinberg's lawyers eventually brought the lawyers for Fogel and Shephard into a joint-defense agreement with them, in which they all agreed to share information about the case.)

The Wilmer, Cutler lawyers called Carmen Lawrence, Geist's superior in the New York office, and told her they wanted to meet with her in person about a case. They wouldn't say which one until they met. In mid-June, two Wilmer, Cutler partners, Theodore Levine and Robert McCaw, arrived at the S.E.C.'s offices. As soon as they mentioned MCA, Lawrence had Geist join the meeting, along with other lawyers in the office who were involved in the investigation. Geist knew immediately that someone important had to be involved. He knew Levine and McCaw as two of the most prominent lawyers in the securities bar. Levine was a former associate director of enforcement at the S.E.C., and McCaw was one of the firm's most senior partners. They had helped defend Ivan Boesky. The two partners identified themselves as lawyers for Jonathan Sheinberg—a name that initially meant nothing to Geist. Once Sid Sheinberg was mentioned, of course, Geist knew he was dealing with someone who had intimate ties to MCA.

Jonathan Sheinberg, the Wilmer, Cutler lawyers revealed, was the missing link in the MCA investigation. They appear to have been eager to break the news to Geist before he and his colleagues found out on their own, thereby gaining a measure of good will and a reputation for candor. This is much the same strategy that Boesky followed in negotiating what most people believe to have been a highly favorable settlement: Boesky confessed his relationship to Milken long before investigators could have stumbled upon it themselves. Securities lawyers note another advantage to the strategy as well: satisfying the S.E.C.'s curiosity as soon as possible might prevent a wide-ranging fishing expedition into Jonathan Sheinberg's business affairs.

Levine and McCaw sketched in the relationships in the case: that Barry Fogel was Jonathan's wife's lover; that Shephard was his business manager; that Ursitti was Jonathan's lover's father; and so on. The S.E.C. lawyers were amazed. Despite the famously loose mores of Los Angeles, they thought it most unusual for an estranged husband and wife and their lovers to be so intimately involved in an insider-trading conspiracy. Levine and McCaw described the fateful phone call that Jonathan had happened to overhear. More important, they announced that all those involved, with the exception of Ursitti, had agreed to coöperate and answer fully the S.E.C.'s questions in the upcoming depositions. In those sessions, beginning in late June and continuing into September, Geist and Brotbacker finally learned just what had happened.

As long as Jonathan was at his parents' house that September weekend of 1990, he had managed to keep quiet about the news of the impending Matsushita-MCA deal. But, despite his father's admonition, he had apparently been bursting to tell someone. Jonathan later described his excitement about the news: "My relationship to that company, as a result of my father being there for over thirty years, was such that I guess I knew that ultimately one day something big was going to happen. And I had a distinct feeling, just over the little bit that I heard . . . that something was really happening now, and that maybe this was the real thing, or something. And it was all something that, in my own mind, got me very excited. . . . I had some MCA stock that was given to me when I was a little boy that—I mean, obviously, that excited me also. . . . It was just building inside me, the excitement."

On Sunday afternoon, Jonathan left the beach house to take his daughter to the amusement park on the Santa Monica pier. First, he called Maria on his cellular phone, and then, while Thea was on the merry-go-round, he called her again, from a pay phone on the pier. Fogel described the events, at his second deposition, as follows: "I was at home with Maria Sheinberg. . . . At about 4 P.M., Jon Sheinberg called my home and spoke with Maria. He said something exciting was going on with the company. I don't think he said MCA—or he may have and he couldn't talk about it on that phone—and he was going to call back in a few minutes from another telephone. I believe about ten minutes later Jon called back and spoke to Maria and told her—and I think I was on the phone also; I don't remember. . . . MCA was going to be bought by a Japanese company in the next two days and he was very excited and he was just excited and nervous and that we should talk about it some more and then I should buy some stock. It would be a good thing for me to go buy some stock."

When Maria and Barry picked up Thea that evening, they joined Jonathan and Susan at his home, in Venice Beach, to refine their strategy. For obvious reasons, Jonathan and Fogel weren't close friends, but they knew each other reasonably well. As boys, they had played on the same Little League team in Beverly Hills, and on Halloween, 1989, several months after Fogel started dating Maria, they had all had dinner together and had taken Thea trick-or-treating. En route to Jonathan's that evening, Fogel called his mother from his car phone to borrow money; he says he didn't tell her what the money was for. At about eight-thirty, he and Maria and their dog joined Jonathan, Susan, Thea, and their dog. The dogs promptly had a set-to, running around and barking. Maria and Susan came in and out of the conversation, sometimes leaving to play with Thea or, in Susan's case, to study for a test she had to take the next day in one of her fashion classes. If any of the participants felt that there was anything incongruous about a husband and wife and their lovers sitting down to plot insider trading, no one mentioned it, nor have any of them mentioned it since. While Susan has tried to place the onus on Maria ("I remember her being the instigator," she testified later), all the participants' accounts of the evening pretty much agree with Fogel's.

"I sat in the living room . . . and we talked about the MCA deal," Fogel recalled. "And Jon told me that it was going to get bought by, I think it's Matsushita, and it was going to happen in the next couple of days and it could go as—the purchase price could go as high as a hundred and fifteen dollars a share. I didn't really know much about trading stocks. I haven't done it for quite a while. . . . I asked Jon about what to buy and he told me about, he explained basically what options were. I knew, kind of, but he explained them to me, and Susan was there. Susan was excited also. It was a very excited kind of feeling." Jonathan never explained why he chose to share the news with his estranged wife and her lover, of all people, but others suggest that he may have felt rejected by Maria and supplanted by Fogel, and that passing on the information was a way to impress Maria and demonstrate his superiority over Fogel. Jonathan himself later explained the situation by saying, "I believe I was very excited at the time. . . . I think that I started to act in a way like kind of a big man with this information. I made it very special. . . . I felt that I was telling Barry and Maria something very special."

Insider traders have rarely described the sensation so candidly, but a factor that makes it such a difficult crime to deter is its inherent thrill —something akin to hitting the jackpot at a slot machine. Fogel said he still felt the excitement the next day, when he started calling his broker at 6:30 A.M., so eager was he to execute the purchases before any news broke.

Jonathan, too, was still excited the next day, more "psyched up" than usual on a Monday morning, as he put it. ("I go in to work and I make a lot of phone calls. I am very active.") Jonathan called Rick Shephard before Shephard arrived at his office. When he did arrive, he returned the call. "He said to me that he thought there might be an announcement in the next few days concerning a potential takeover of MCA," Shephard testified in his deposition, on June 26th. "He said, 'I can't purchase MCA shares, but you should.' " Jonathan himself was buying Paramount options—on the theory, he explained to Shephard, that after the announcement of the MCA deal "all the entertainment stocks would move together." After hanging up, Shephard called his broker and began trading in MCA.

That wasn't the end of Jonathan's indiscretions. That same morning, he burst into the office of his boss, Lee Rich, and swore him to secrecy. ("It made it more important," Jonathan later said of the secrecy. "It made it seem a little more special.") As Rich recalled the scene, Jonathan "came in and raised his arms and said, 'Buy, buy, buy! Matsushita is going to buy MCA!' " Rich says he cut him off. "Jon, you're crazy. There's no way I can buy any stock. It would be traced back immediately. I have no desire to buy any." Alone among the recipients of Jonathan's information, Rich didn't trade.

Like an L.A. brushfire, the information was spreading. Susan Ursitti was so excited that she called her mother. Friends say that Susan is much like Maria in that she is good-looking but seems something of a lost soul. In her deposition, she comes across as a caricature of a bubbleheaded actress, testifying that she was only vaguely aware of what was going on at Jonathan's apartment that night. ("I'm an actress and I model and do commercials. I'm not sounding stupid but I don't really get involved with business," she testified.) She nonetheless told her mother that "there's something going on with MCA." Mrs. Ursitti immediately passed the word on to her husband, and he called his broker that Sunday evening. "I hear something's going on," Ursitti told his broker before placing a large order for MCA. The broker replied, "I hope you don't know anything."

Meanwhile, Ursitti had called a senior vice-president at his company. The vice-president bought MCA and, in turn, urged one of his employees to buy. At that rate, it's anybody's guess how far the leaks would have spread if the *Wall Street Journal* article the next day had not brought the news out into the open, driving up the stock's price.

It seems noteworthy that in all the excitement over Jonathan's disclosures only Lee Rich seems to have given the slightest consideration to whether any of this trading might be illegal. Jonathan, despite his father's warnings, not only leaked the information but urged the recipients to trade, going as far as to explain options trading to Fogel. Much later, Fogel admitted that he did recognize at the time that Jonathan's behavior was improper. "I didn't think he should be giving me that type of information. Because it was wrong. Looking back on it, I see how wrong it was."

If the Sheinbergs' lawyers believed that full disclosure was likely to dampen the S.E.C.'s interest in pursuing the case, their strategy failed. Not only did Jonathan Sheinberg's presence at the center of the scheme guarantee high visibility but the facts that emerged in the depositions that summer and early fall played right into a matter that was of growing concern to law enforcement: insider trading among family members.

Insider trading is outlawed by the securities laws' generic prohibition of fraud in the purchase or sale of securities, but exactly what constitutes insider trading has been left to the courts to decide. Over the years, judges have generally broadened the concept, extending it from obvious insiders, like a corporation's officers or directors, such as Sid Sheinberg at MCA, to people who are not insiders themselves but are entrusted with inside information and assume a duty to keep it secret, such as lawyers and investment bankers.

That much has been well settled for some time. But an ongoing subject of litigation and controversy is whether to apply insider-trading sanctions to people further down the chain of information—people who hear potentially valuable corporate secrets but aren't themselves insiders and have no obligation to keep the information secret. These cases have generally turned on whether someone knew or should have known that the information was received in a breach of someone else's obligation to keep it secret. Thus, Ivan Boesky, a stock speculator rather than a corporate officer or an investment banker, could be guilty of insider trading after he bribed an investment banker to reveal corporate secrets. He obviously knew that he was inducing someone else to breach an obligation of confidentiality—a move that has become known as "misappropriation" of inside information. At the other extreme, however, courts have ruled that merely overhearing a conversation in the bleachers at a football game, as happened in one case, doesn't give rise to liability. There the person overhearing the secret information may not know the identity of the source, let alone know that the source had a duty to maintain confidentiality.

This kind of problem has been particularly acute among family members, since it is a common practice for corporate executives and even lawyers and bankers to discuss their work at home. The leading case in the area involved a director of the Amax Corporation, a large mining-and-metals concern, who allegedly confided to his son that Amax was going to get a tender offer from Standard Oil of California. The son was accused of trading on the information and was subsequently charged in a criminal case with insider trading. He was acquitted, but the case established the precedent that a son who routinely receives information from his father implicitly assumes his father's duty to keep the information secret. Recently, there seems to have been a proliferation of such cases. In one of the most talked-about instances, the wife of Sanford Weill, the chairman of Primerica, which owns Smith Barney Shearson, told her psychiatrist of secret takeover deals that she had heard about from her husband, and the psychiatrist traded in the stock. (He pleaded guilty.)

As Geist looked at the evidence that had emerged in MCA, he found some obvious differences from the leading family cases. Jonathan Sheinberg hadn't actually traded in MCA himself, yet he was the most important potential target: he was the one who, by leaking the information, set all the trading in motion. ("I can't trade, but you should," Shephard said Jon had told him.) In that one regard, he had heeded his father's admonitions. He was not an insider in the usual sense; he was the son of one. And, like the man in the bleachers, he'd overheard the secret information inadvertently. On the other hand, Jonathan had subsequently been taken into his father's confidence and specifically warned to keep the information to himself. His mother had also warned him. Nevertheless, he had actively encouraged other people to trade. His daughter and his girlfriend could be expected to reap the benefits of some of that trading, and in other cases he could expect to gain from the good will his tips generated. His behavior—his admonitions to Lee Rich to keep the information secret and his initial plan to deny that he'd been involved—indicated that he knew that what he was doing was wrong. It all would have made a good exam question in a law-school class in securities fraud.

In September of 1991, when Geist and his colleagues were finishing their analysis of these facts, a new regional head of the S.E.C.'s New York office was named. He was Richard Walker, a friend and former classmate of the S.E.C. enforcement chief, William McLucas, who had presided over the later stages of the Milken case, and he immediately recognized MCA as a means of further clarifying the law within the family context. Both he and Geist saw it as a strong case for broadening the S.E.C.'s power to curb abuses in this area. But just as they were finishing drafting an enforcement recommendation to be submitted to the S.E.C. in Washington, their legal position was dealt a blow by the federal court of appeals of the Second Circuit, the district that includes New York, which issued an opinion in another insider-trading family saga, this one involving the Waldbaum-supermarket-chain family. There, the company chairman, Ira Waldbaum, told his sister Shirley that the chain was going to be sold to A.&P. She immediately told her daughter, and the daughter told her husband, adding that he shouldn't tell anyone else. Nonetheless, the son-in-law told his broker, Robert Chestman, and the broker traded in the stock. The S.E.C. charged Chestman with insider trading, arguing that he should have known his client had misappropriated the information. Reversing the district court, however, the court of appeals ruled that the son-in-law had not taken on the obligation to keep the information secret. The act of "entrusting confidential information to another does not, without more, create the necessary relationship and its correlative duty to maintain the confidence," the court wrote. The S.E.C. lawyers read the opinion with dismay.

The Sheinberg lawyers at once argued strenuously that their case fell under the rubric of S.E.C. v. Chestman. Because the events occurred in California, the S.E.C. wasn't technically bound by the Second Circuit court's opinion. Still, since the S.E.C. is the leading interpreter of the nation's securities laws, and since the nation's financial center, New York, is where the preponderance of such cases arise, the commission traditionally accords great deference to Second Circuit opinions. The ruling sent Geist and his colleagues back to the drawing board. Could a meaningful distinction be drawn between the Waldbaum family and what had happened in Sheinberg?

On the face of it, the cases looked similar. The key question was whether Jonathan had assumed his father's duty to keep the information secret, either expressly or by implication. Though both father and son recalled that Sidney had instructed Jonathan to keep the information secret—thereby discharging his legal duty of confidentiality—neither could recall that Jonathan had actually agreed to his father's orders.

Jonathan seemed to barely remember the conversation; he didn't even mention the walk on the beach in his testimony. To the extent that he did recall it, he said, he thought his father meant that he shouldn't trade —not that he couldn't tell anyone else. Nor could his father say for certain that Jonathan had actually agreed to maintain the secret, though that was his impression.

Paradoxically, the more the facts resembled Chestman, the more the S.E.C. lawyers felt they had to bring a case, in the hope of eventually getting a clearer definition of the Chestman precedent. It was an opportunity to reaffirm the willingness of the S.E.C. to bring family cases despite Chestman. They had two facts in their favor: Jonathan had heard the news directly from his father, not at the end of a long chain of hearsay. And it could be argued that Jonathan was more than just a family member. He had a "family relationship plus," as the S.E.C. lawyers put it; that is, he was someone who could be expected to know that such information should be kept in strict confidence.

The Sheinberg lawyers also made another argument. Jonathan, they said, had been driven more by the peculiar psychology of his relationship with his famous father than by any intent to break the law. Despite appearances in the Sheinberg family, they said, the relationship between Jonathan and his father had long been a troubled one. Jonathan had been rebellious, foolish, but not criminal, they argued. Sid didn't trust his elder son, and that meant that Jonathan's commitment to keeping secrets couldn't be inferred simply from the fact that they were father and son.

This argument carried little weight with the S.E.C. enforcement staff. The staff notified the Sheinberg lawyers that they intended to seek the commission's approval to file a complaint, and, as is customary, offered them the opportunity to submit a written argument—a so-called Wells submission. Wilmer, Cutler not only submitted a voluminous document but asked to present the case orally to the enforcement staff before it took the case to the full commission. In September, Levine met with McLucas, in Washington, where he and the S.E.C. attorneys from New York both presented their arguments. (Curiously, the lawyers for the other potential defendants, Fogel, Shephard, and Ursitti, didn't make Wells submissions. Nonetheless, they assert that they maintained vigorous defenses of their own, uninfluenced by the Sheinberg position.)

The S.E.C.'s decision was not without political overtones. MCA lobbies constantly on matters of concern to the entertainment industry. Sid Sheinberg has numerous contacts in Washington, and Lew Wasserman was a close friend of Ronald Reagan, who, as a movie star, had worked under contract to Universal Studios. Yet there is no evidence that any political pressure was brought to bear. McLucas says he was only dimly aware of Sheinberg's stature, and says flatly that no member of the commission ever indicated that there had been any contact with the Sheinbergs, MCA, or any of their representatives other than through enforcement channels. McLucas threw his support behind Geist. In the end, the commission voted to authorize the enforcement staff to draw up a complaint and pursue settlement negotiations. In practical terms, the defense lawyers had lost their most crucial battle with the commission.

After the meeting with McLucas in Washington, Geist and Brot-backer notified the defendants' lawyers of the enforcement action, and then the staff waited with more than the usual curiosity to see how they would react. They suspected that Jonathan—or, more to the point, his father—would choose not to fight the charges. The hearing, if it should go that far, might well be a messy affair for the Sheinbergs, with both Sid and Lorraine likely to be called as witnesses against their son. The family laundry was sure to be aired in public, and all Hollywood would follow every development with rapt attention. The prospects for such intra-family cases had been clouded by the spectacle of Sukhreet Gabel, who, in 1988, testified against her mother, Hortense. Hortense Gabel was a judge on New York's Supreme Court and was alleged to have favored Bess Myerson's lover in a divorce action after the former Miss America gave Sukhreet a job. The press had had a field day, and Sukhreet had achieved short-lived celebrity status. Already, the Sheinbergs' atten-tion to secrecy was intense; their lawyers were furious when, in October of 1991, an item on the existence of an S.E.C. investigation into MCA trading surfaced in the Washington *Post*. (The S.E.C. lawyers said they were confident that no one connected to the government was the source.) And the *Post* story was nothing compared with the publicity that a full-blown trial would attract.

Of even greater concern to the Sheinbergs must have been the possibility of related criminal charges. The S.E.C. lawyers in the case did discuss the investigation from time to time with lawyers in the United States Attorney's office in the Southern District of New York. A former Justice Department lawyer involved in the matter says that serious con-sideration was given to launching a criminal investigation, but that the family issues gave them pause. "You'd have to immunize mother and father against the son," this lawyer says, adding that Justice Department policy discourages such cases.

The S.E.C. staff's speculation proved accurate: after the meeting in Washington, the Sheinberg lawyers quickly turned the discussion to what a settlement of the case might look like. While the negotiating process dragged on for months, it was soon clear that someone in the Sheinbergs' camp—presumably Sid—had given their lawyers orders to end the affair. People involved in the case say that Jonathan was willing to testify and fight the charges; indeed, one of the lawyers says, once Jonathan had recovered from his initial shock and depression he seemed to enjoy being the center of attention of a flock of high-priced lawyers. ("This is a common syndrome," that lawyer says of his insider-trading clients. "First, they want to know if they're going to jail. Then they're asking if it will be a country-club prison.")

However that may be, Jonathan was one of the first to agree in principle to a settlement, and the others fell in line—even Ursitti, who had never answered any of the staff's questions. Without admitting or denying guilt, Jonathan agreed to pay the government a penalty equal to all the profits earned by the people who had traded on his information —a total of four hundred and eighteen thousand dollars. The traders themselves agreed to pay back their profits and some additional penal-ties, which amounted to a total of five hundred and seventy-three thou-sand dollars for Ursitti, two hundred and twenty-three thousand dollars for Fogel, and a hundred and twelve thousand dollars for Shephard. The executed settlements were approved and filed with the commission on December 10, 1992. The penalties have been paid in full.

The Sheinbergs' lawyers argued strenuously that the S.E.C. should announce the settlement on a Friday, so that news accounts would be buried in the weekend papers. The staff refused, and the announcement was made on a Thursday, the same day the S.E.C. approved the arrangement. The text of the press release was the subject of extensive negotiations (Ursitti at one point threatened to withdraw from the settlement if the name of his company was mentioned in the complaint or the settlement), and the final text was terse, providing few details about what had actually happened. Despite the prominence of the Sheinberg family, the settlement received only minor press coverage, and no one connected with the case made any comment.

In Hollywood, there was more concern over that year's Christmas releases, including Universal's "Scent of a Woman." In conversations with friends, Jonathan made light of the affair, maintaining that he hadn't really done anything wrong, and attributing the charges to his famous name. He indicated that he'd settled simply to avoid the "hassle" and costs of litigation. Friends and business colleagues, among them Felix Rohatyn, called Sid to commiserate, many of them declaring that there's no accounting for the behavior of children. At MCA itself, where both Sid and Lew Wasserman had from the outset turned glacial at any mention of the case, virtually nothing was said. After another disappointing year, everyone was preoccupied with the studio's big-budget summer offering, "Jurassic Park." The dinosaur epic proved to be another Spielberg hit, and MCA now finds itself in a good position to be sold again, in whole or part. John Malone, the cable magnate recently involved in the skirmishing for Paramount Pictures, has looked into buying MCA. Officially, the company isn't for sale, but it's an open secret on Wall Street and in Hollywood that the Japanese, often bewildered by the mores and spending habits of Hollywood, would be happy to cash in on their investment now that entertainment companies are again hot properties.

Jonathan's career hasn't been nearly so successful as MCA's. After Lee Rich declined to renew Jonathan's contract, in September of 1991, Jonathan said that he would become an independent producer. Instead, he landed a job as a literary agent at Triad Artists, which was acquired last year by William Morris. Starting without any clients, Jonathan has been slowly building a list, though it includes "no one whose name you'd recognize," one of his colleagues says. According to his colleagues, he raised eyebrows at Triad when he signed up a grade-school child as a director on the strength of the child's home movie. (That relationship lasted just three months.) Colleagues say they don't believe that the S.E.C. settlement has had any impact on Jonathan's career; Hollywood has forgiven far worse sins. Nonetheless, they say that Jonathan has lost whatever career momentum he had before he joined Lee Rich, and that in Hollywood such perceptions can prove more difficult to overcome than breaking the law. At William Morris, Jonathan is described as popular and energetic. "He's taking scripts on spec and trying to get them into development," a fellow-agent says of his work. He also "covers" Warner Brothers and M-G-M for the agency, communicating studio needs to fellow-agents.

Jonathan's marriage to Maria ended in divorce last year, and colleagues say that the two continue to quarrel over their daughter and over support payments. Maria recently married Barry Fogel, who is still running his pizza chain. This fall, Jonathan and Susan Ursitti were married, and Susan recently had a baby. Jonathan's bachelor party featured a filmed mock-tribute to Jonathan, with Sid assuming a leading role.

Jonathan has told friends that he "learned a lot" from the whole affair, but he also seems to be more firmly under his father's thumb than ever. Sid ordered Jonathan to say nothing about this story—a command that, under the circumstances, Jonathan felt doubly obliged to honor, friends say. Sid also maintained his policy of silence. Although everyone notes that Sid himself did nothing wrong, and that parents can't fully control their grown children, Sid is said to fear that people do blame him for his son's failings, and is described as "beside himself" that attention to the case might overshadow years of good works just as his own reputation should be at its pinnacle.

Many of the details in this story come from deposition transcripts that I obtained after a Freedom of Information Act request. I was allowed to read all the testimony taken in the case, with the exception of some minor redactions that, for the most part, appear to contain references to psychological problems of various participants. After reading the transcripts, I called Jonathan at his office at William Morris.

In a brief conversation, Jonathan displayed many of the characteristics I had heard described by others. He seemed immediately excited, saying that the MCA affair was "my story"; that "this isn't a magazine article, it's a book"; and that "if anybody's going to tell this story, it's going to be me." I offered him that opportunity, but he changed his tack. "Don't you realize how painful this is for me and my family?" he asked, adding, "You wouldn't be writing this except for my name." While his voice was still rising, he hung up.

At the New York office of the S.E.C., Geist has been promoted to assistant regional director. Though he is limited in what he can say about the investigation, he says he feels little sympathy for Jonathan and the other defendants. "My own personal opinion is that everyone is surprised when people in Hollywood do things that seem weird and strange, but they're just like everybody else, if not more so." He is confident that "the right result was reached," he says. "It always struck me that what happened was improper conduct, and that this was the type of situation that was contemplated by the anti-fraud provisions. It would have been a great trial to do, and I'm confident that even in the Second Circuit we would have prevailed. Still, it's always good to have a case over with, with a good result." Though criminal charges could still be filed, it seems unlikely that the Justice Department will take any further interest in the case, and there is no indication that any criminal investigation continues. As far as law enforcement is concerned, the case is evidently over.

Yet the known facts leave the most baffling mystery officially unresolved: What drove Jonathan to risk his career, his reputation, and his relationship with his father to enlist others in an insider-trading scheme? As in many other insider-trading cases, the answer is clearly not money; indeed, for such a quintessentially financial crime, it is striking how many insider traders have been wealthy men who, like Jonathan and the people he tipped, were in no rational need of their illicit gains.

In the portion of his deposition made public Jonathan was never directly asked to explain his motives. However interesting, they weren't legally relevant, so he didn't give any insight into his feelings about his own career, about his father, about his brother or Spielberg, or about any sense of loneliness or inadequacy he may have experienced. Perhaps Jonathan, who seems anything but a contemplative or self-aware person, has little sense of what drove his ultimately self-destructive behavior. But to some of the questions that were posed he and his father seem to have indirectly offered answers. The answers suggest that, despite all the high-profile law-enforcement efforts and numerous convictions, the forces driving insider trading are growing harder to curb as information becomes increasingly synonymous with power, and power with self-identity. Hollywood may be a small town where information moves with unusual speed and intensity, and Jonathan's relationship to his famous father may have fostered an unusually complicated situation. Nonetheless, these dynamics exist to varying degrees everywhere, from exclusive resorts in the Hamptons to Memphis golf courses, to name just two places where similar insider-trading schemes have recently been hatched.

Another witness in the MCA case, a man named Martin Katz, who wasn't charged with any wrongdoing, described the atmosphere in Hollywood. "You hear things in weird places, you know—the sports club, the sales clerks that wait on these people in stores that you know—and they all want subliminally, I suppose, to impress you with who they work with or who they know," he said. "There's a pulse, there's a sense of hearing things. If you go to lunch in Beverly Hills, or something, you'll see what I mean. You won't believe the things you'll hear."

Jonathan mentioned at several points in his testimony that conveying the news of the MCA takeover made him feel "special," like "a big shot," to the point where telling other people was "a compulsion." And Jonathan's father, with thirty-five years in Hollywood under his belt, put it even more directly: "You know, this is a town, and maybe other towns are like it, but this is a town and this is an industry where information is perceived as being a great power, and if you have information— well, information in the hands of a certain type of personality is a very —You know, it's a very powerful thing. Makes you feel you're a big man."

INDEX